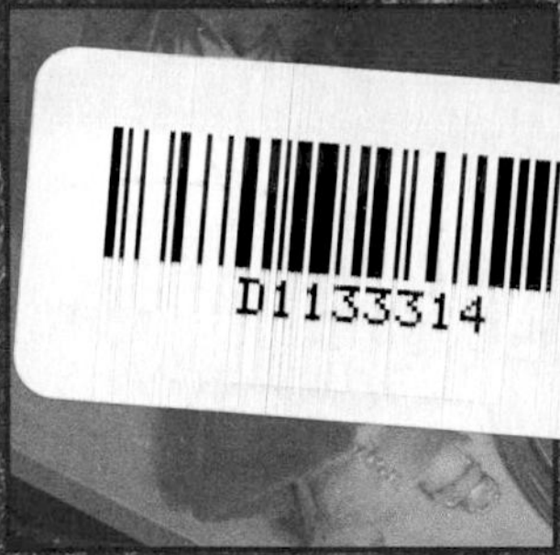

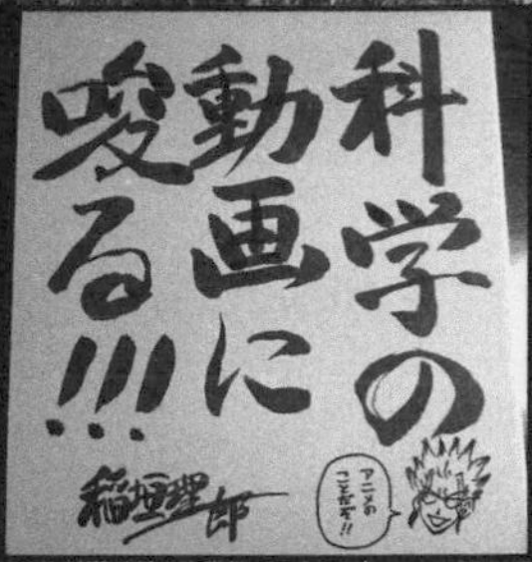

科学の
動画に
唆る!!!
稲垣理一郎

*Board: Get excited for science in motion!!!
*Senku: That means an anime!!

BOICHI

From the bottom of my heart, I'd like to thank all the fans who send in letters and gifts. I'm sorry that I can't send individual responses back.

I spend my days drawing *Dr. Stone* and thinking about Senku's inventions and the future world he lives in.

Sometimes I go on research trips and sometimes I discuss the science, the world building and Senku's feelings with my supervising editor. I do all that so I can pour my heart into every single drawing so that I can create more color pages, etc.

I want every line of every drawing to communicate just how much love I have for the fans.

There's a tale told by these drawings—a tale of gratitude and thanks.

RIICHIRO INAGAKI

The Jump staff had the creators write some calligraphy about their upcoming plans for the new year. Like aspirations, ambitions and so on.

For this meaningless, embarrassing exercise, I gripped the brush with a trembling hand that's never really written calligraphy before, and thought, "Why not shill for the anime adaptation while I'm at it?"

On that note, the *Dr. Stone* anime starts in July 2019. I hope you watch!!

Boichi is a Korean-born artist currently living and working in Japan. His previous works include Sun-Ken Rock and Terra Formars Asimov.

Riichiro Inagaki is a Japanese manga writer from Tokyo. He is the writer for the sports manga series Eyeshield 21, which was serialized in Weekly Shonen Jump.

Dr.STONE

9

SHONEN JUMP Manga Edition

Story **RIICHIRO INAGAKI**
Art **BOICHI**

Science Consultant/**KURARE**
Translation/**CALEB COOK**
Touch-Up Art & Lettering/**STEPHEN DUTRO**
Design/**JULIAN [JR] ROBINSON**
Editor/**JOHN BAE**

Consulted Works:

• Asari, Yoshito, *Uchu e Ikitakute Ekitainenryo Rocket wo DIY Shite Mita (Gakken Rigaku Sensho)*, *Gakken Plus*, 2013
• Dartnell, Lewis, *The Knowledge: How to Rebuild Civilization in the Aftermath of a Cataclysm*, translated by Erika Togo, Kawade Shobo Shinsha, 2015
• Davies, Barry, *The Complete SAS Survival Manual*, translated by Yoshito Takigawa, Toyo Shorin, 2001
• Kazama, Rinpei, *Shinboken Techo (Definitive Edition)*, Shufu to Seikatsu Sha, 2016
• McNab, Chris, *Special Forces Survival Guide*, translated by Atsuko Sumi, Hara Shobo, 2016
• Olsen, Larry Dean, *Outdoor Survival Skills*, translated by Katsuji Tani, A&F, 2014
• Weisman, Alan, *The World Without Us*, translated by Shinobu Onizawa, Hayakawa Publishing, 2009
• Wiseman, John, *SAS Survival Handbook, Revised Edition*, translated by Kazuhiro Takahashi and Hitoshi Tomokiyo, Namiki Shobo, 2009

First published in Japan in 2017 by SHUEISHA Inc., Tokyo.
English translation rights arranged by SHUEISHA Inc.

Printed in the U.S.A.

Published by VIZ Media, LLC
P.O. Box 77010
San Francisco, CA 94107

10 9 8 7 6 5 4 3 2 1
First printing, January 2020

VIZ MEDIA
viz.com

SHONEN JUMP
shonenjump.com

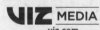

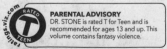

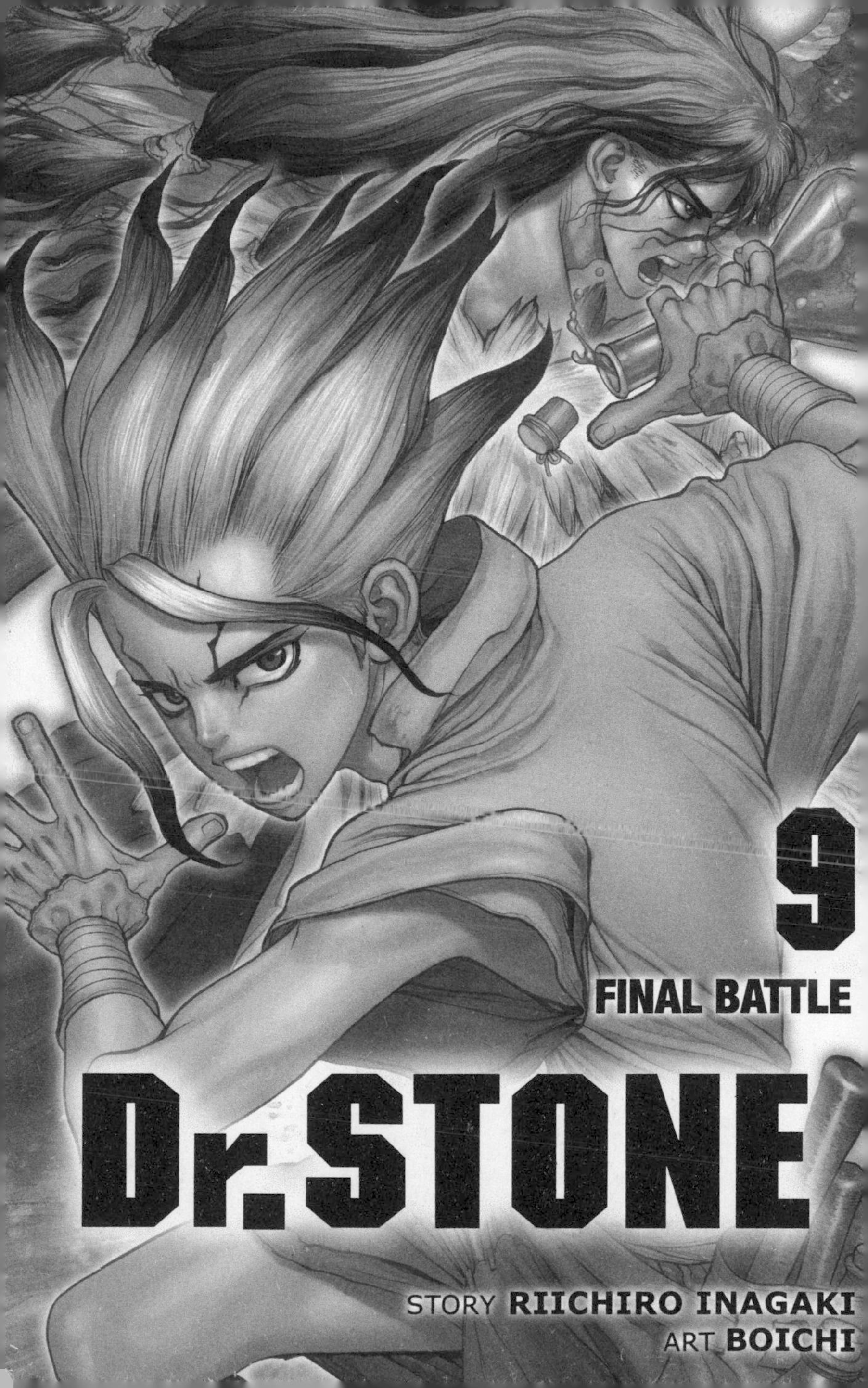
9
FINAL BATTLE
Dr.STONE
STORY RIICHIRO INAGAKI
ART BOICHI

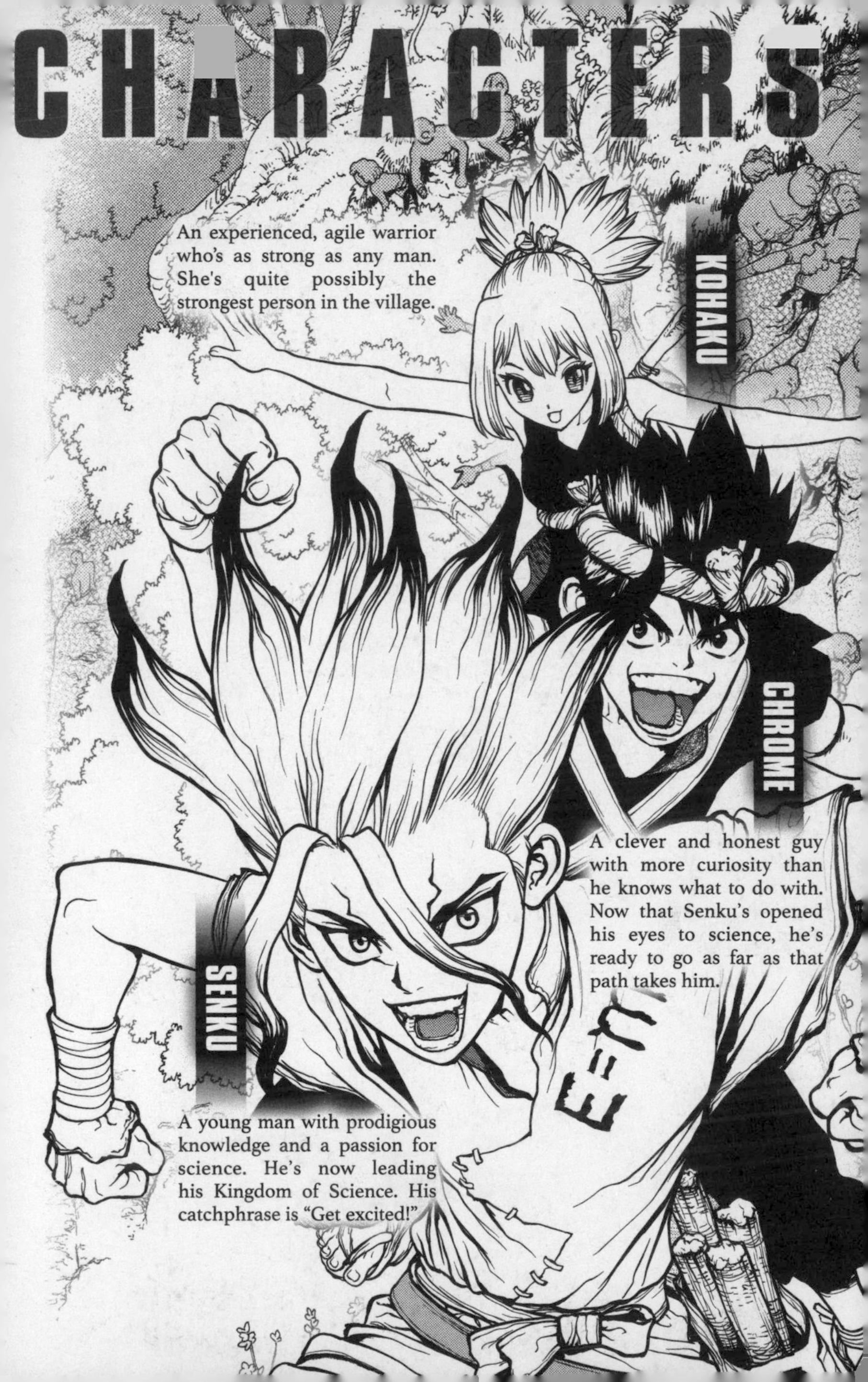
CHARACTERS
KOHAKU
An experienced, agile warrior who's as strong as any man. She's quite possibly the strongest person in the village.
CHROME
A clever and honest guy with more curiosity than he knows what to do with. Now that Senku's opened his eyes to science, he's ready to go as far as that path takes him.
SENKU
A young man with prodigious knowledge and a passion for science. He's now leading his Kingdom of Science. His catchphrase is "Get excited!"

Dr.STONE

STORY

Every human on earth is turned to stone by a mysterious phenomenon, including high school student Taiju. Nearly 3,700 years later, Taiju awakens and finds his friend Senku, who revived a bit earlier. Together, they vow to restore civilization, but Tsukasa, once considered the strongest high schooler alive, nearly kills Senku in order to put a stop to his scientific plans.

After being revived by his friends, Senku arrives at a village and wins the villagers' trust thanks to his scientific knowledge. When word of Senku's survival gets back to Tsukasa, the war between the two forces begins!

Senku and Gen have made contact with Taiju via their new cell phone, and now they've even won over Nikki—one of the Empire's guards. Meanwhile, the Kingdom of Science is hard at work on a steam-powered tank that could be just what they need to rescue Chrome!

YUZURIHA

HYOGA

TSUKASA

NIKKI

UKYO

TAIJU

GEN ASAGIRI

CONTENTS

Z=71: PRISON BREAK   7

Z=72: EXPERIENCE POINTS   29

Z=73: TOP SECRET MISSION   49

Z=74: FATEFUL 20 SECONDS   71

Z=75: 20-SECOND COUNTDOWN   91

Z=76: FINAL BATTLE   111

Z=77: THE POWER OF SCIENCE   130

Z=78: THAT WHICH DESTROYS OR SAVES   153

Z=79: FOR THIS VERY MOMENT   173

9

FINAL BATTLE

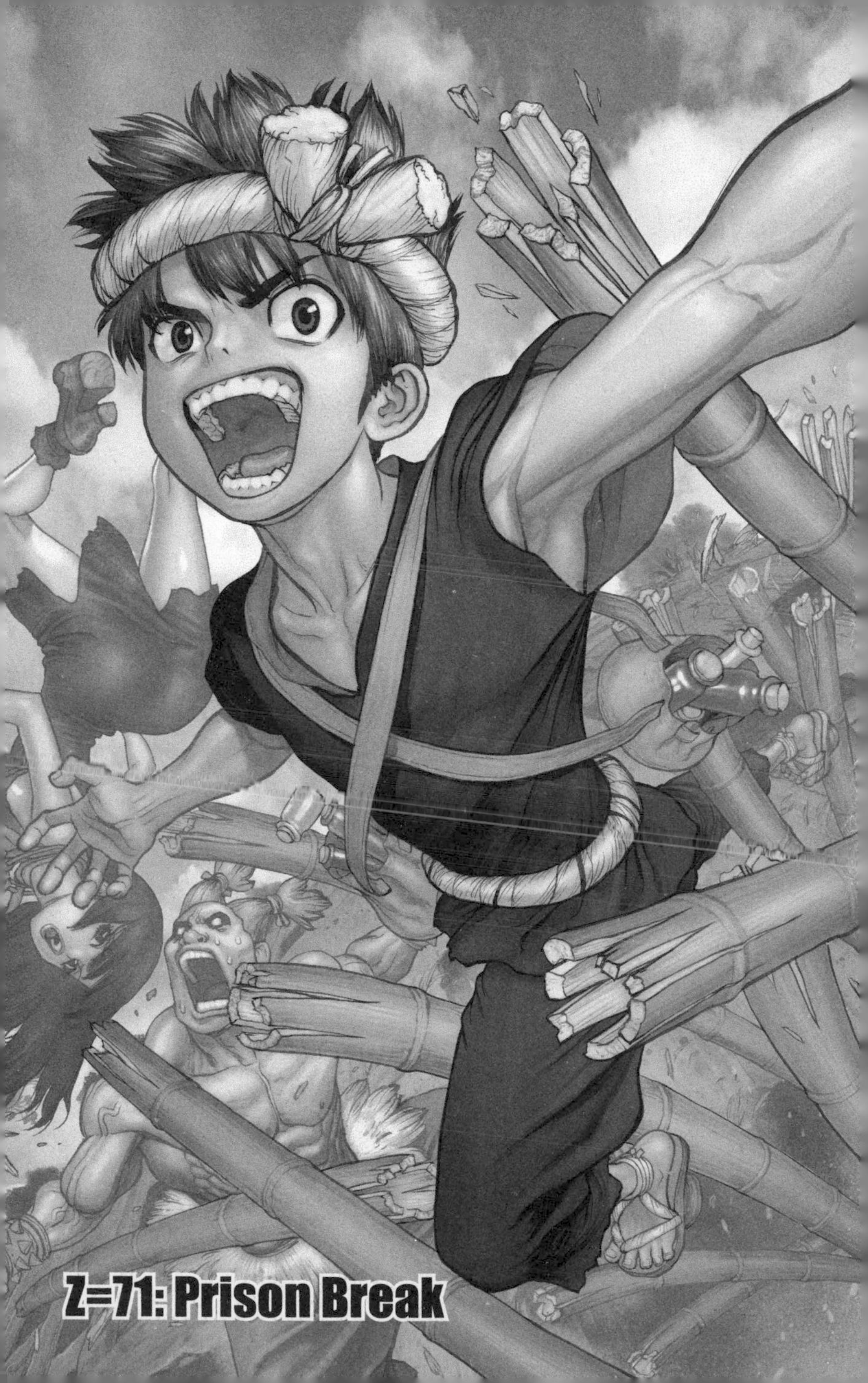
Z=71: Prison Break

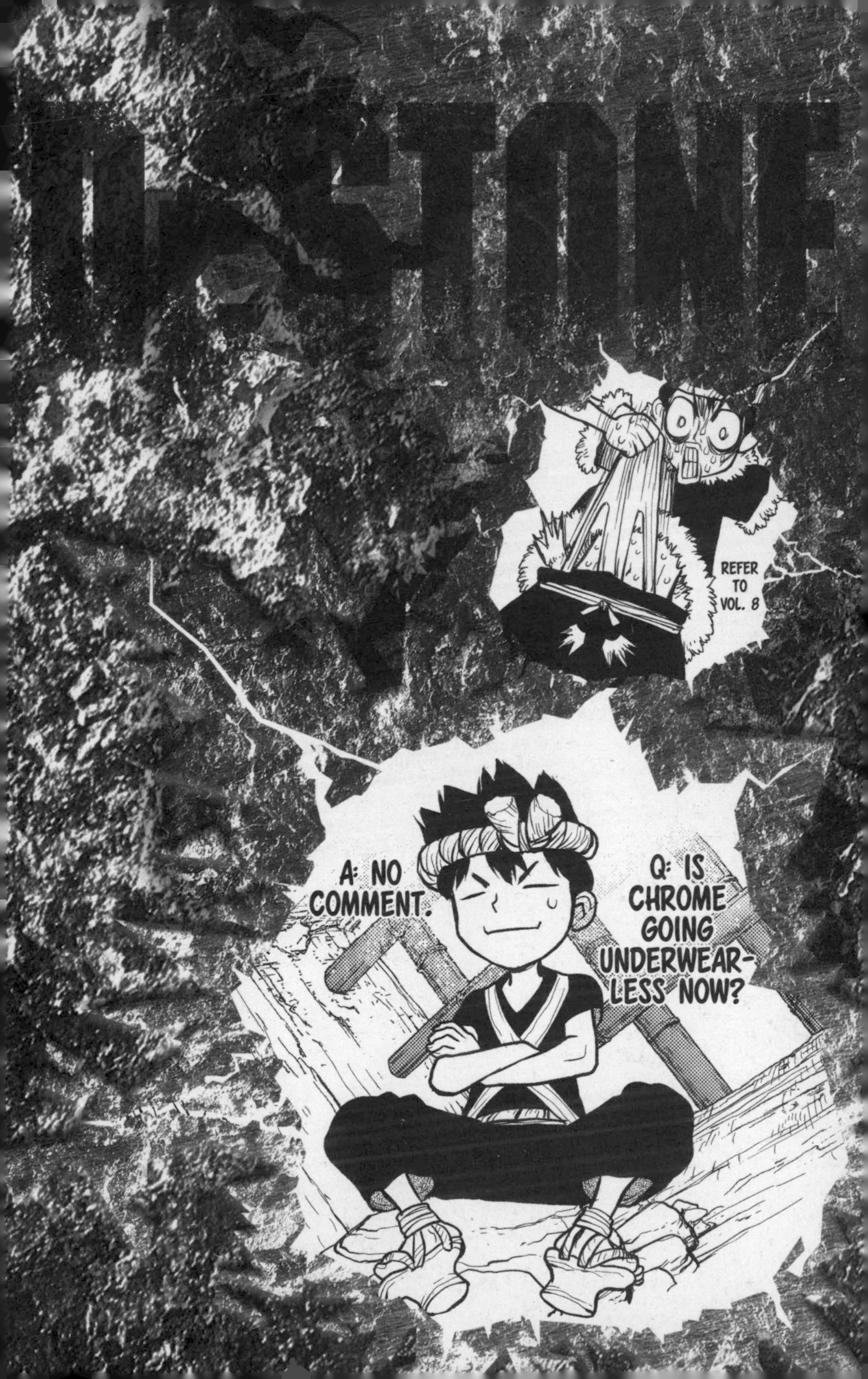
REFER TO VOL. 8
Q: IS CHROME GOING UNDERWEAR-LESS NOW?
A: NO COMMENT.

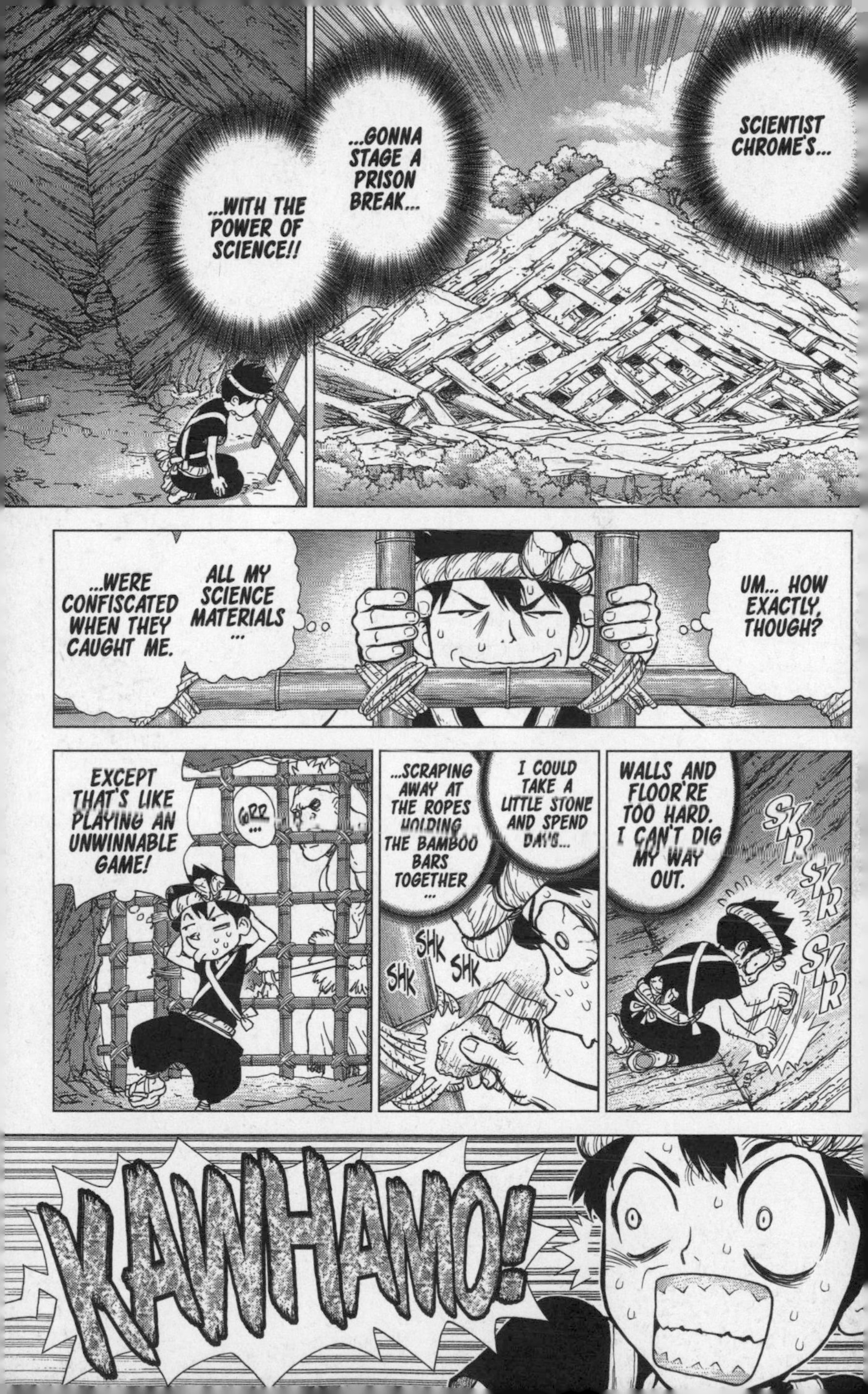
SCIENTIST CHROME'S...
...GONNA STAGE A PRISON BREAK...
...WITH THE POWER OF SCIENCE!!
UM... HOW EXACTLY, THOUGH?
ALL MY SCIENCE MATERIALS...
...WERE CONFISCATED WHEN THEY CAUGHT ME.
WALLS AND FLOOR'RE TOO HARD. I CAN'T DIG MY WAY OUT.
SKR SKR SKR
I COULD TAKE A LITTLE STONE AND SPEND DAYS...
...SCRAPING AWAY AT THE ROPES HOLDING THE BAMBOO BARS TOGETHER...
SHK SHK SHK
EXCEPT THAT'S LIKE PLAYING AN UNWINNABLE GAME!
GRRR...
KAWHAMO!

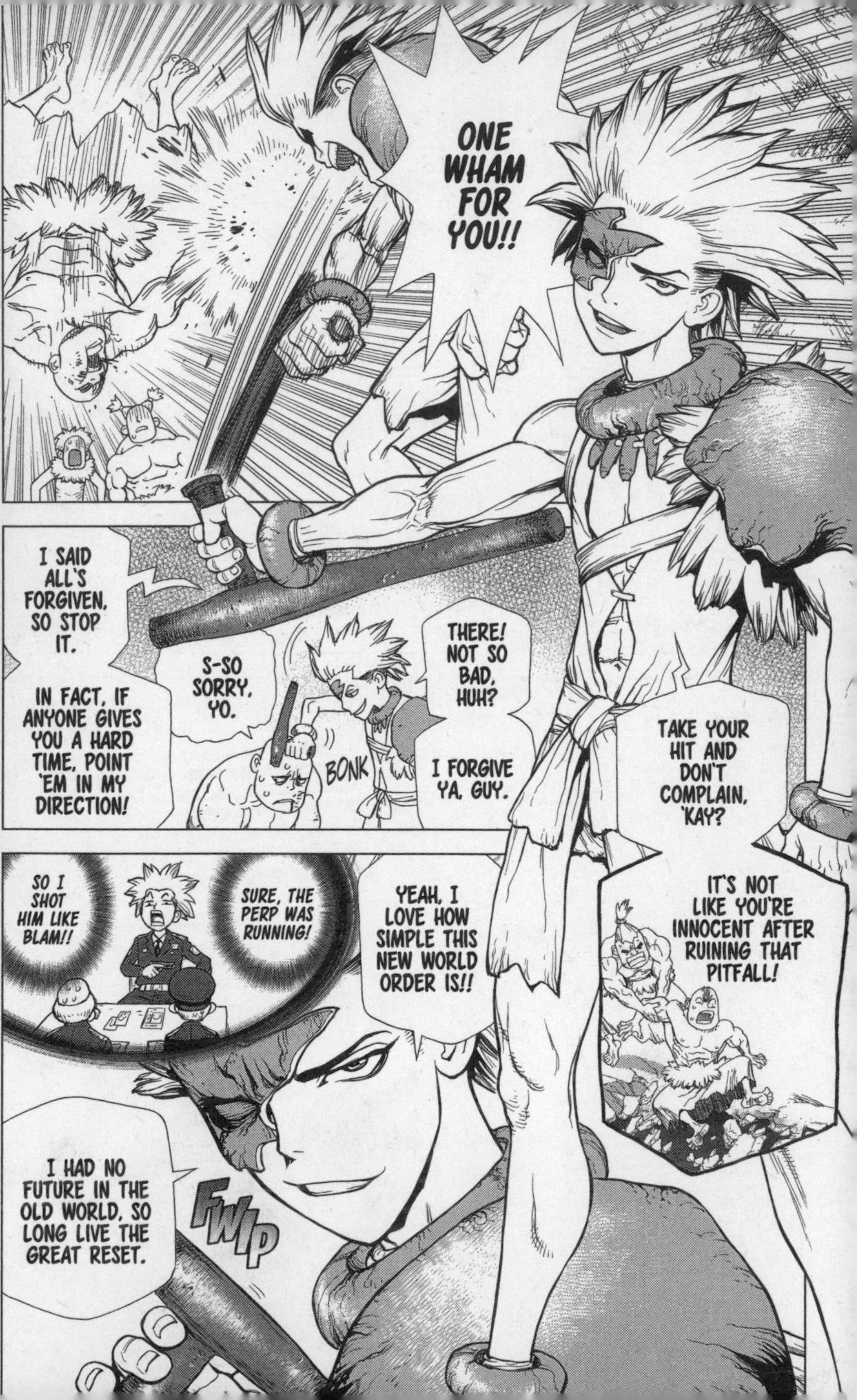
ONE WHAM FOR YOU!!
TAKE YOUR HIT AND DON'T COMPLAIN, 'KAY?
IT'S NOT LIKE YOU'RE INNOCENT AFTER RUINING THAT PITFALL!
THERE! NOT SO BAD, HUH?
I FORGIVE YA, GUY.
BONK
S-SO SORRY, YO.
I SAID ALL'S FORGIVEN, SO STOP IT.
IN FACT, IF ANYONE GIVES YOU A HARD TIME, POINT 'EM IN MY DIRECTION!
YEAH, I LOVE HOW SIMPLE THIS NEW WORLD ORDER IS!!
SURE, THE PERP WAS RUNNING!
SO I SHOT HIM LIKE BLAM!!
FWIP
I HAD NO FUTURE IN THE OLD WORLD, SO LONG LIVE THE GREAT RESET.

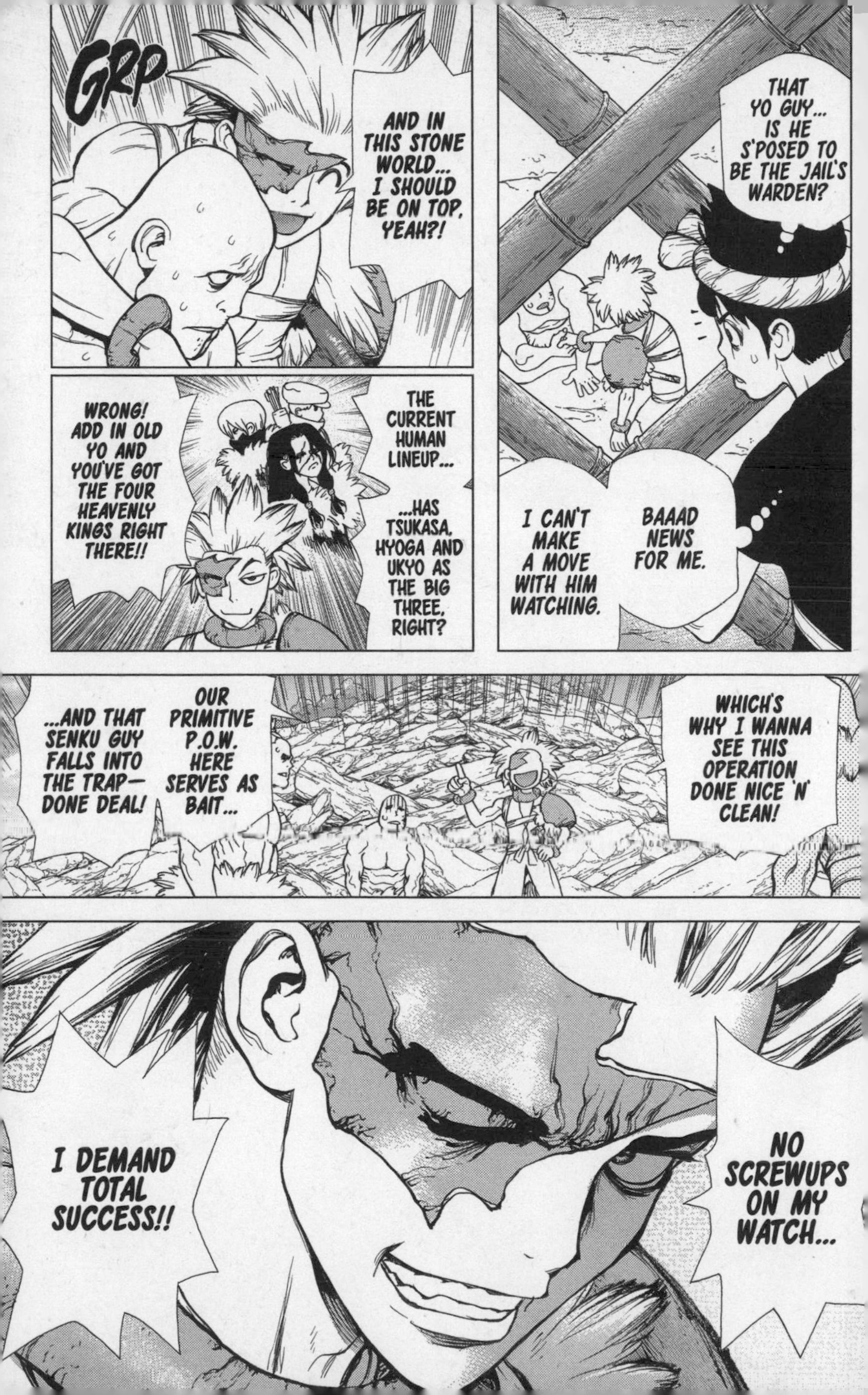
THAT YO GUY... IS HE S'POSED TO BE THE JAIL'S WARDEN?
BAAAD NEWS FOR ME.
I CAN'T MAKE A MOVE WITH HIM WATCHING.
AND IN THIS STONE WORLD... I SHOULD BE ON TOP, YEAH?!
GRP
THE CURRENT HUMAN LINEUP...
...HAS TSUKASA, HYOGA AND UKYO AS THE BIG THREE, RIGHT?
WRONG! ADD IN OLD YO AND YOU'VE GOT THE FOUR HEAVENLY KINGS RIGHT THERE!!
WHICH'S WHY I WANNA SEE THIS OPERATION DONE NICE 'N' CLEAN!
OUR PRIMITIVE P.O.W. HERE SERVES AS BAIT...
...AND THAT SENKU GUY FALLS INTO THE TRAP—DONE DEAL!
NO SCREWUPS ON MY WATCH...
I DEMAND TOTAL SUCCESS!!

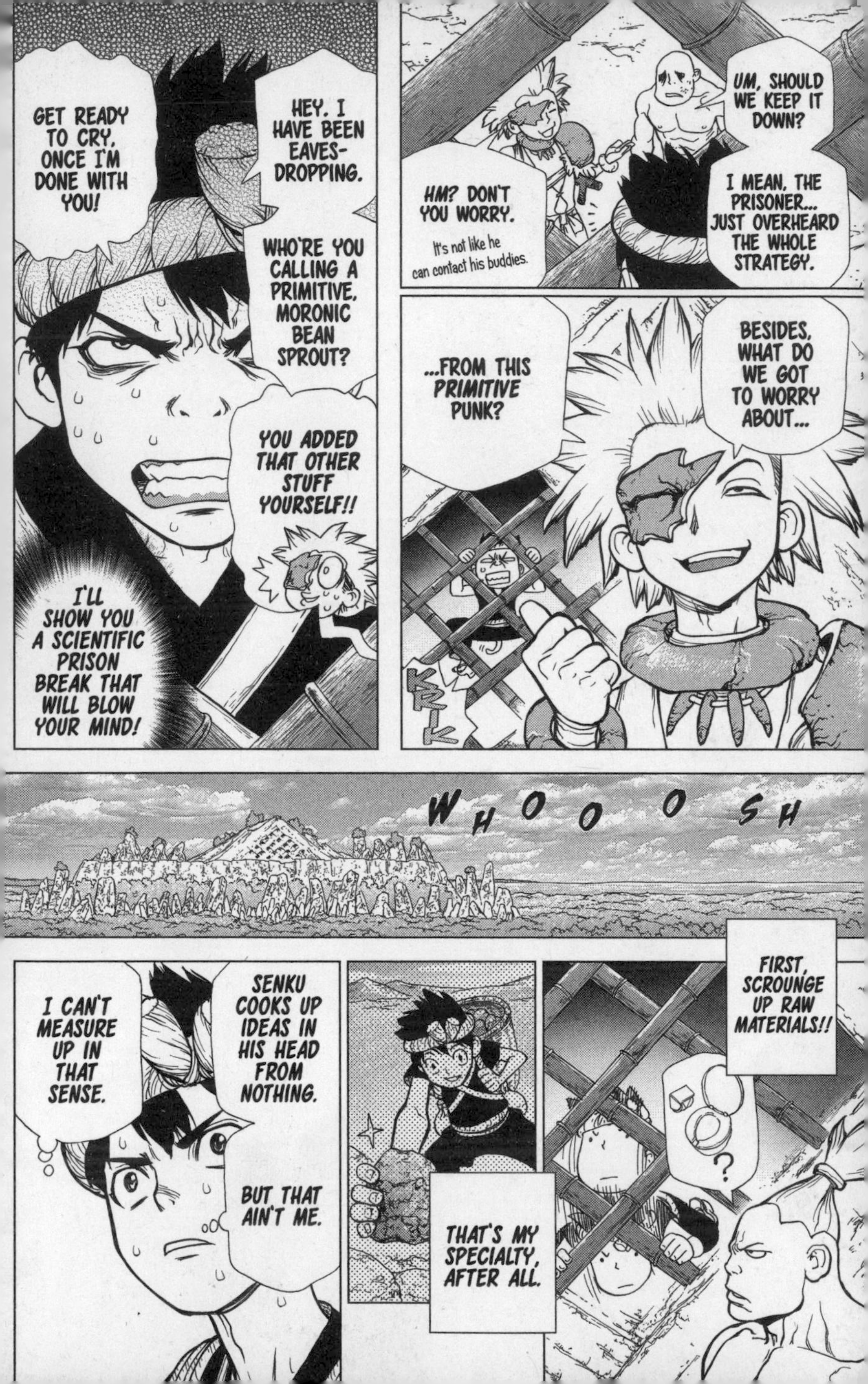
UM, SHOULD WE KEEP IT DOWN?
I MEAN, THE PRISONER... JUST OVERHEARD THE WHOLE STRATEGY.
HM? DON'T YOU WORRY.
It's not like he can contact his buddies.
BESIDES, WHAT DO WE GOT TO WORRY ABOUT...
...FROM THIS PRIMITIVE PUNK?
KRIK
HEY. I HAVE BEEN EAVES-DROPPING.
GET READY TO CRY, ONCE I'M DONE WITH YOU!
WHO'RE YOU CALLING A PRIMITIVE, MORONIC BEAN SPROUT?
YOU ADDED THAT OTHER STUFF YOURSELF!!
I'LL SHOW YOU A SCIENTIFIC PRISON BREAK THAT WILL BLOW YOUR MIND!
WHOOOSH
FIRST, SCROUNGE UP RAW MATERIALS!!
THAT'S MY SPECIALTY, AFTER ALL.
SENKU COOKS UP IDEAS IN HIS HEAD FROM NOTHING.
I CAN'T MEASURE UP IN THAT SENSE.
BUT THAT AIN'T ME.

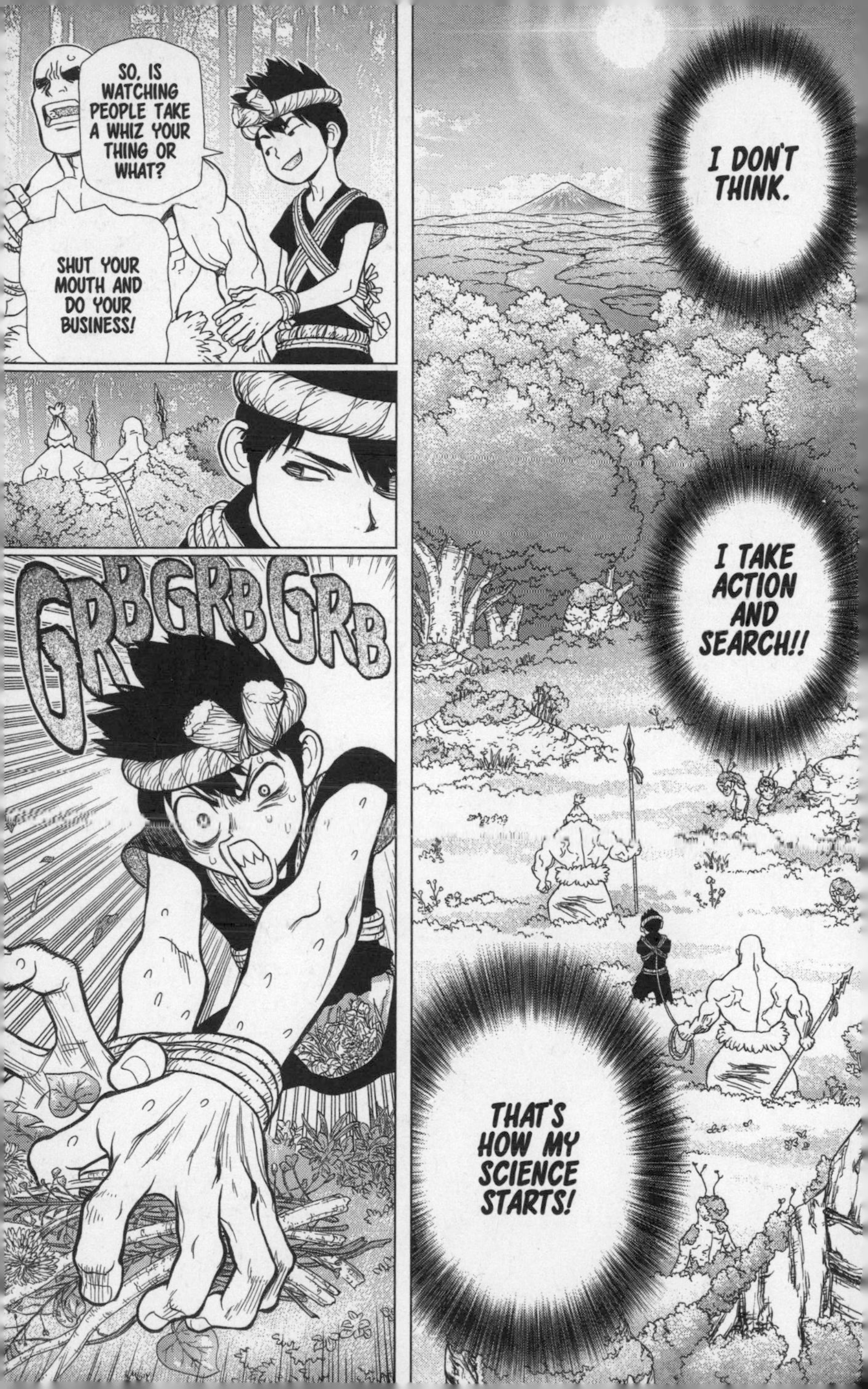
I DON'T THINK.
I TAKE ACTION AND SEARCH!!
THAT'S HOW MY SCIENCE STARTS!
SO, IS WATCHING PEOPLE TAKE A WHIZ YOUR THING OR WHAT?
SHUT YOUR MOUTH AND DO YOUR BUSINESS!
GRBGRBGRB

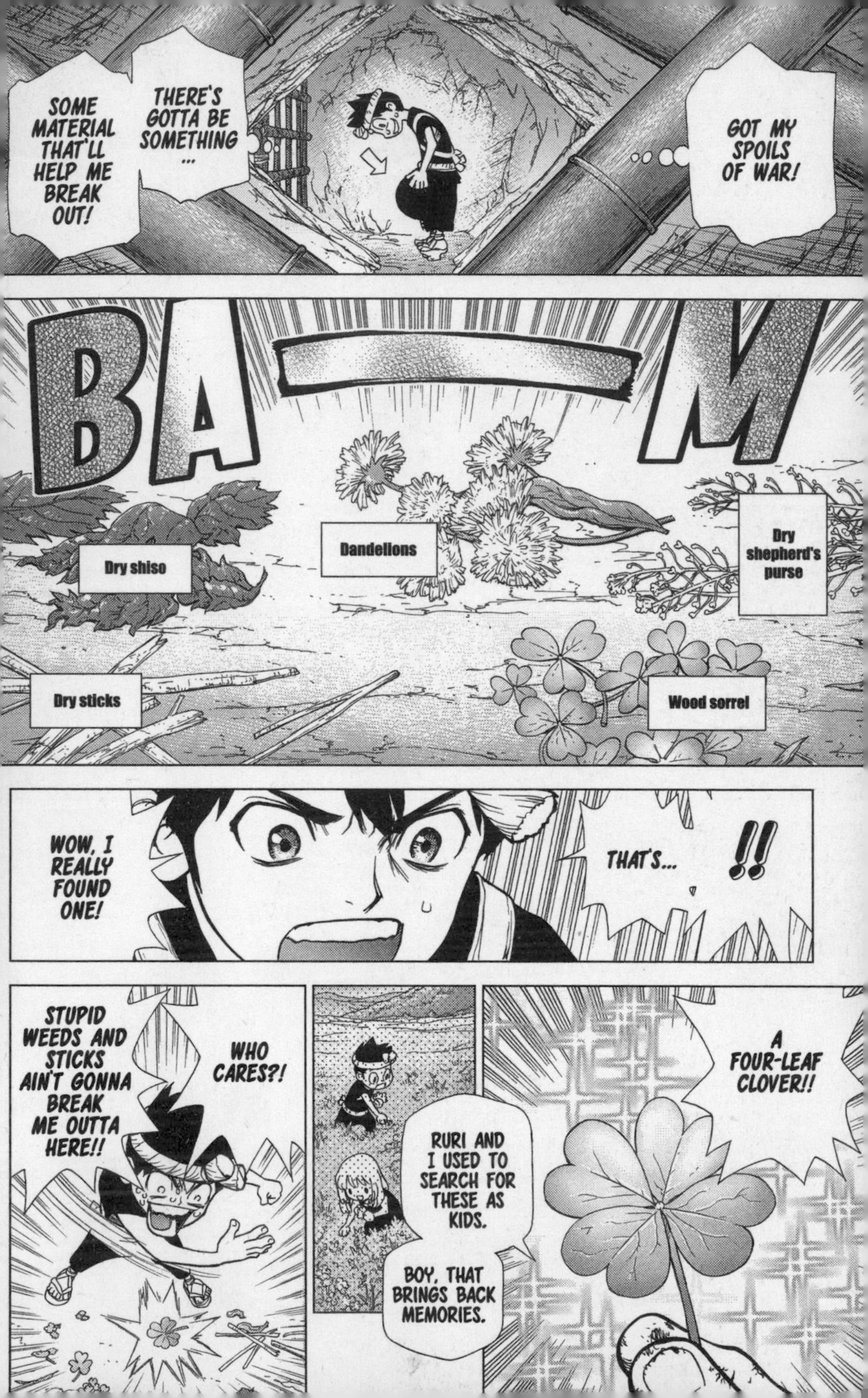
GOT MY SPOILS OF WAR!
THERE'S GOTTA BE SOMETHING...
SOME MATERIAL THAT'LL HELP ME BREAK OUT!
BA—M
Dry shepherd's purse
Dandelions
Dry shiso
Wood sorrel
Dry sticks
THAT'S...!!
WOW, I REALLY FOUND ONE!
A FOUR-LEAF CLOVER!!
RURI AND I USED TO SEARCH FOR THESE AS KIDS.
BOY, THAT BRINGS BACK MEMORIES.
WHO CARES?!
STUPID WEEDS AND STICKS AIN'T GONNA BREAK ME OUTTA HERE!!

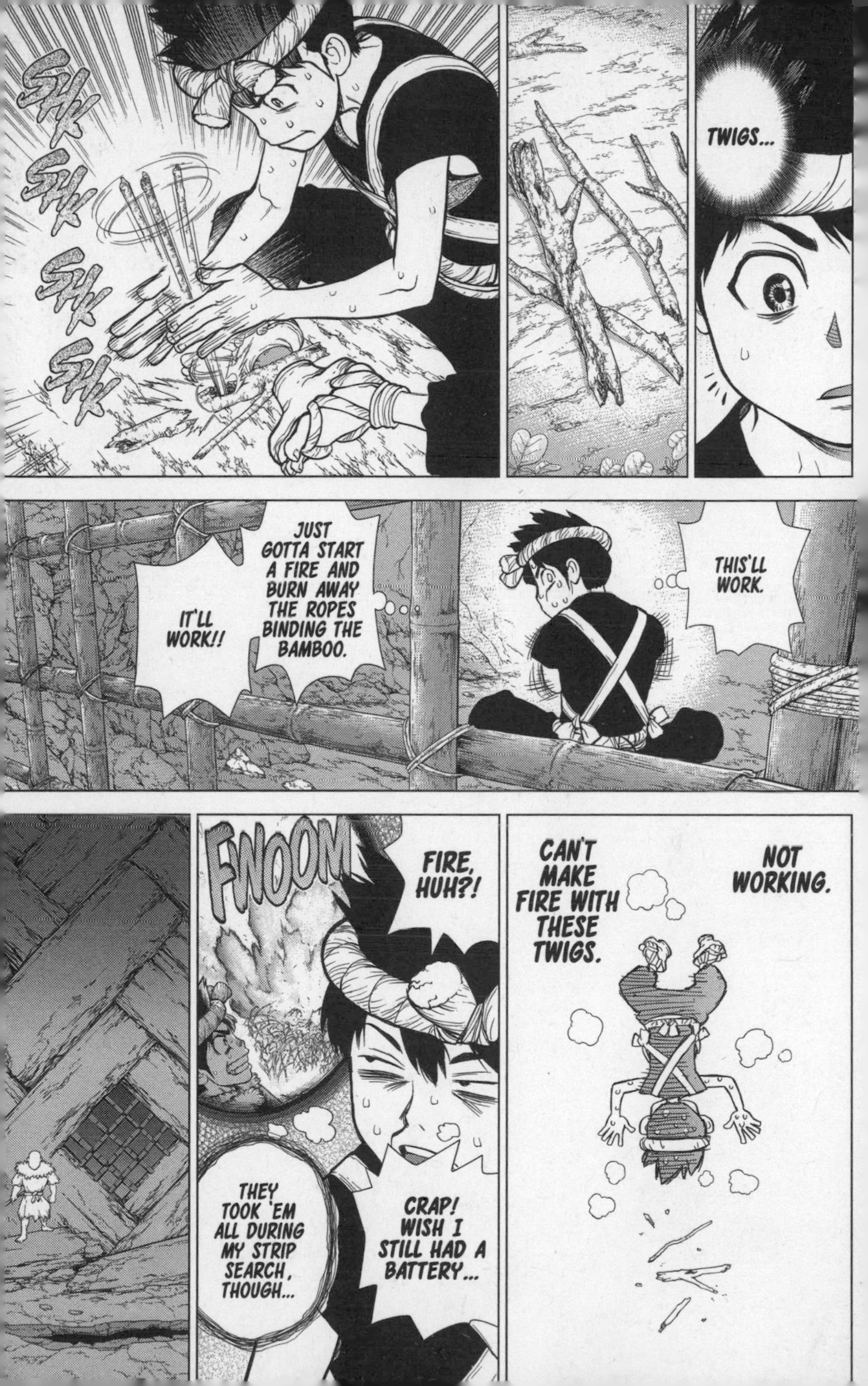
TWIGS...
SHK
SHK
SHK
SHK
THIS'LL WORK.
JUST GOTTA START A FIRE AND BURN AWAY THE ROPES BINDING THE BAMBOO.
IT'LL WORK!!
NOT WORKING.
CAN'T MAKE FIRE WITH THESE TWIGS.
FNOOM
FIRE, HUH?!
CRAP! WISH I STILL HAD A BATTERY...
THEY TOOK 'EM ALL DURING MY STRIP SEARCH, THOUGH...

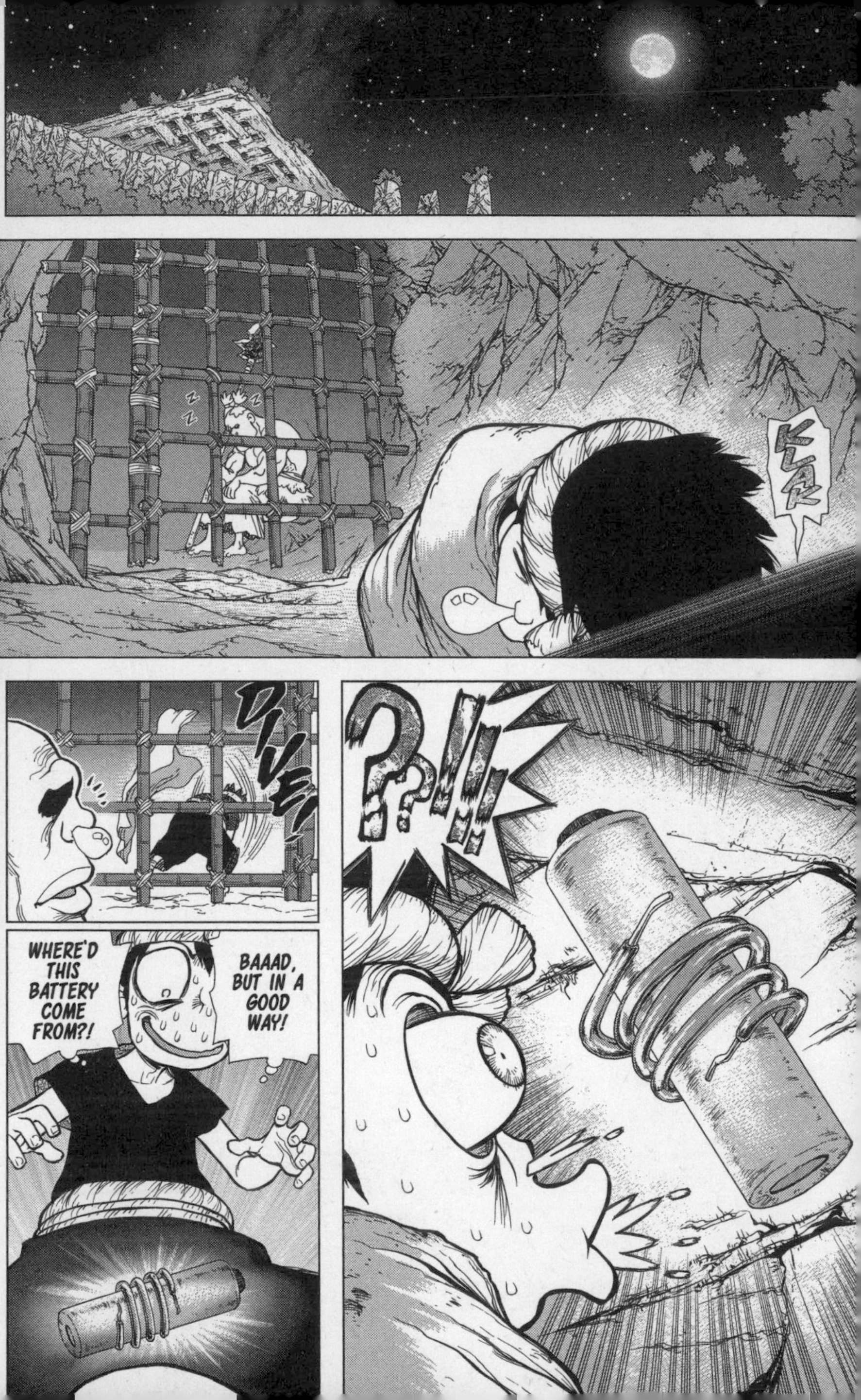
KLAK
DIVE!
BAAAD, BUT IN A GOOD WAY!
WHERE'D THIS BATTERY COME FROM?!

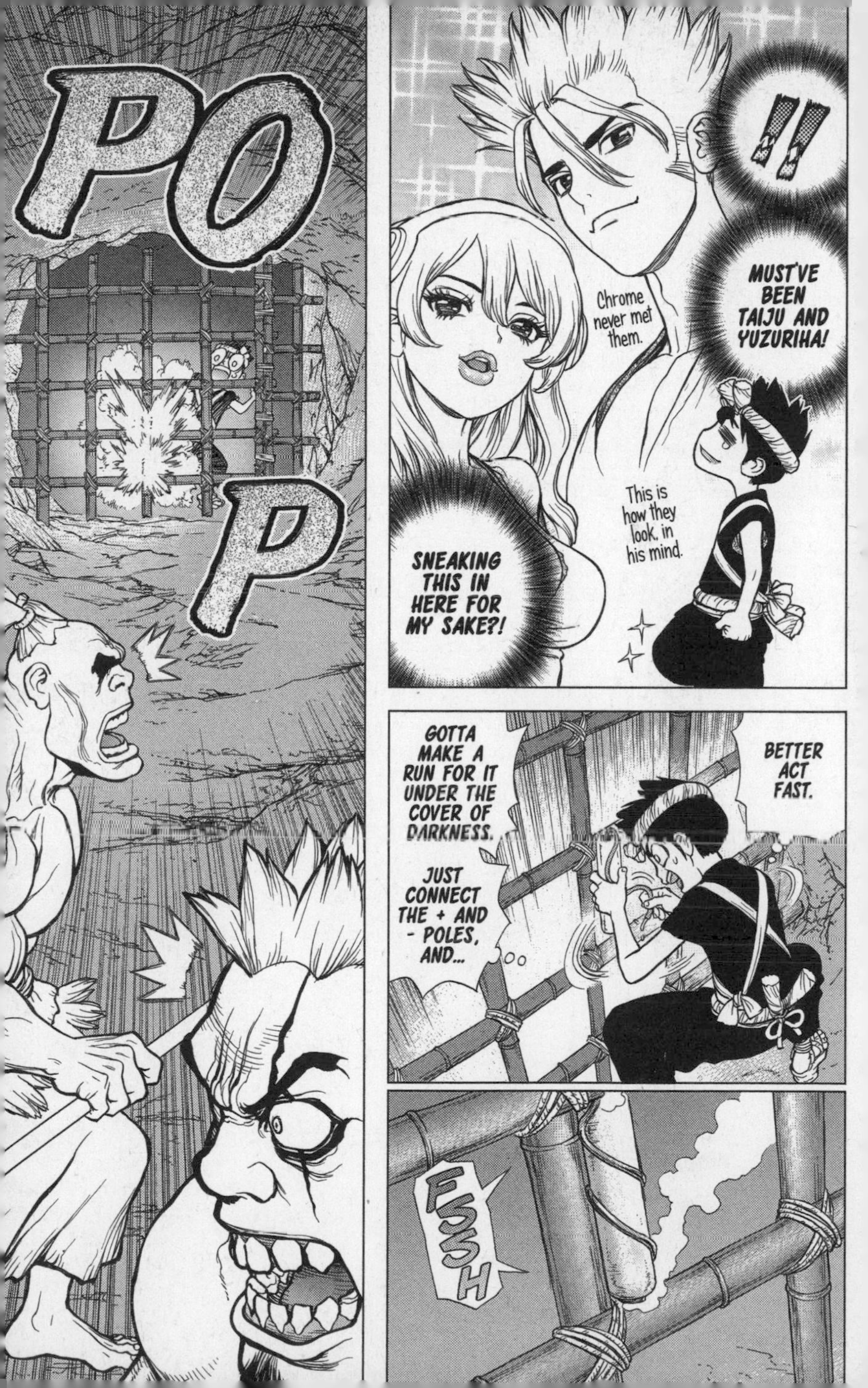
!!
MUST'VE BEEN TAIJU AND YUZURIHA!
Chrome never met them.
SNEAKING THIS IN HERE FOR MY SAKE?!
This is how they look, in his mind.
BETTER ACT FAST.
GOTTA MAKE A RUN FOR IT UNDER THE COVER OF DARKNESS.
JUST CONNECT THE + AND - POLES, AND...
FSSH
POP

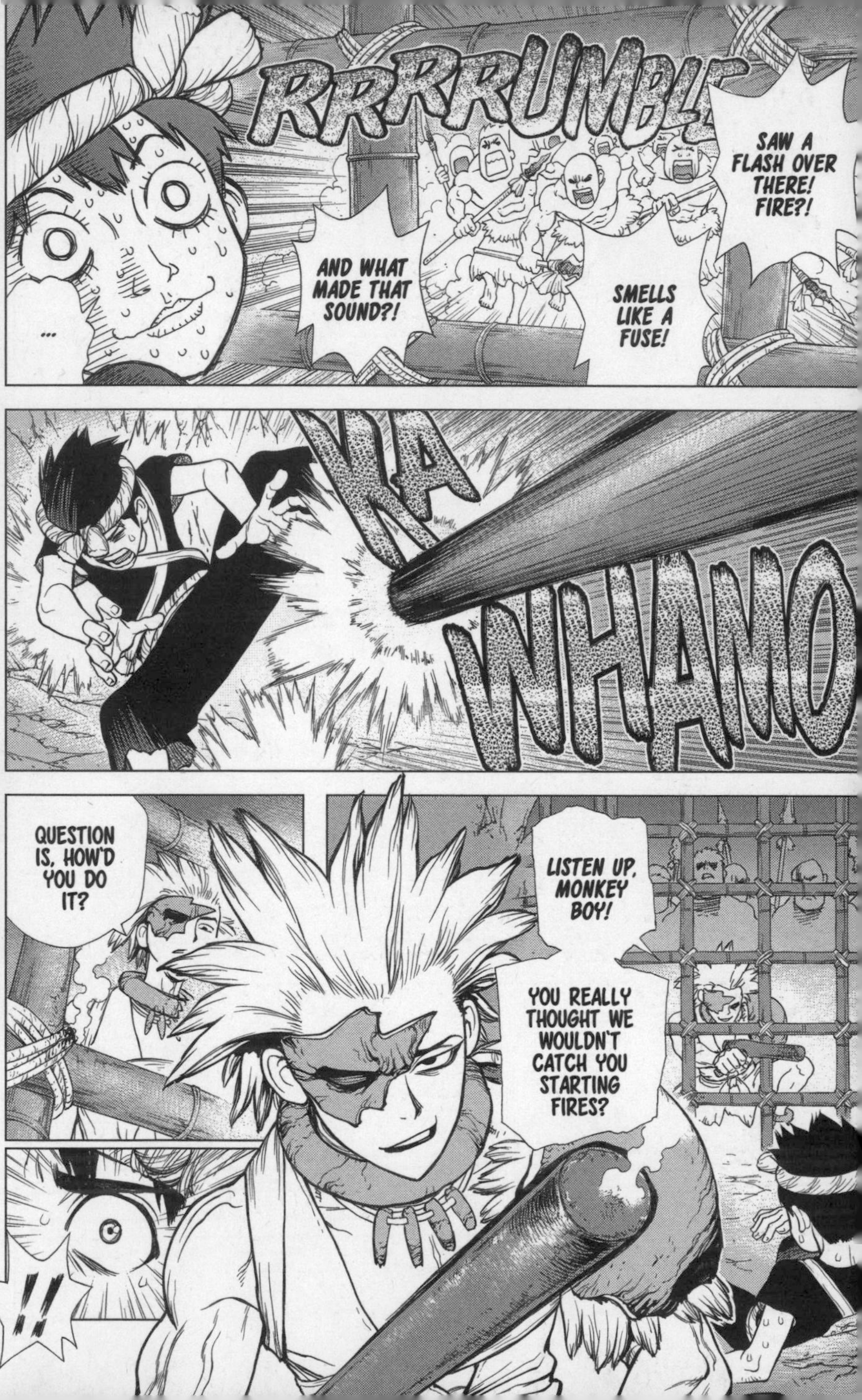
RRRRUMBL
SAW A FLASH OVER THERE! FIRE?!
SMELLS LIKE A FUSE!
AND WHAT MADE THAT SOUND?!
...
KA
WHAMO
LISTEN UP, MONKEY BOY!
YOU REALLY THOUGHT WE WOULDN'T CATCH YOU STARTING FIRES?
QUESTION IS, HOW'D YOU DO IT?
!!

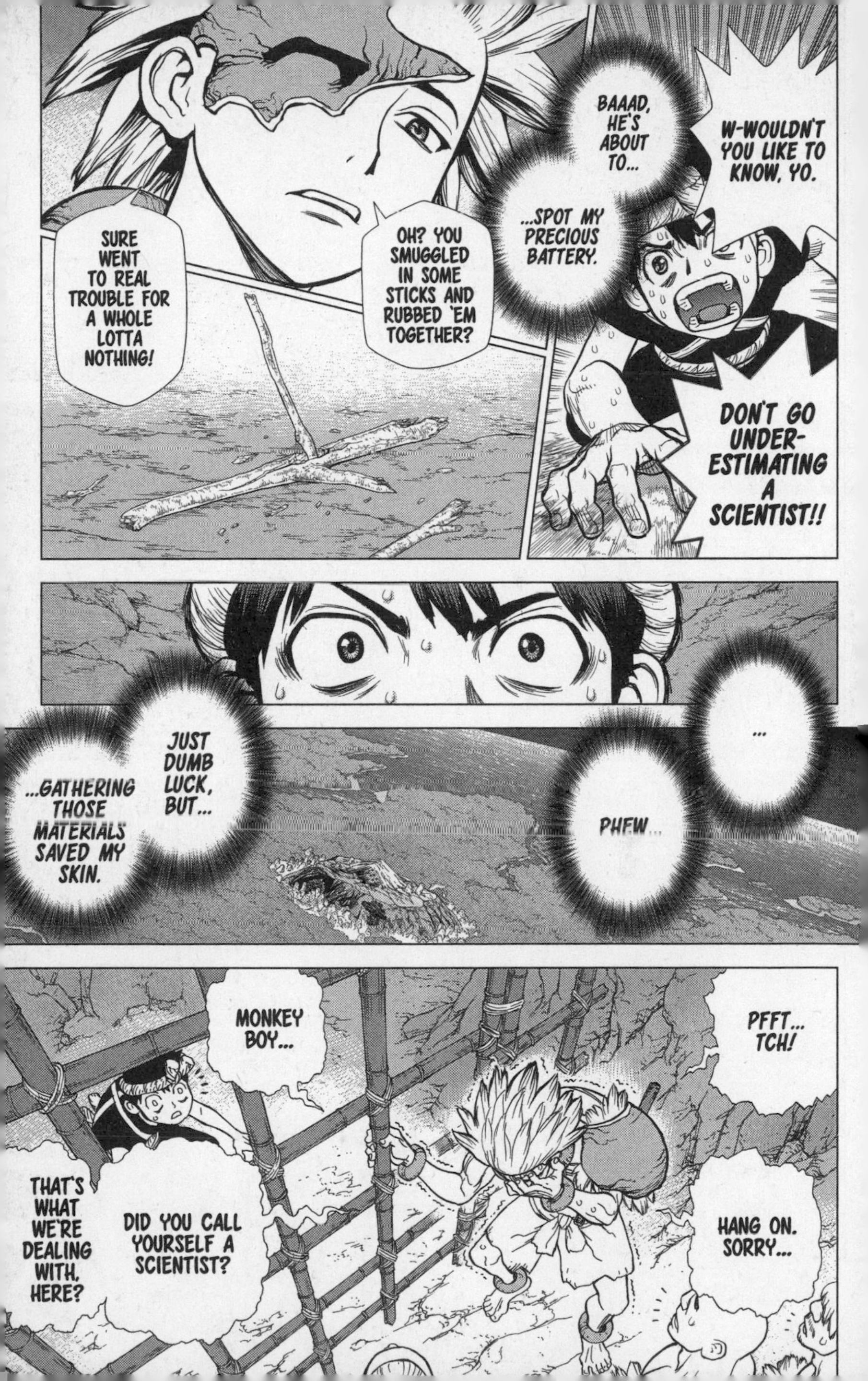
OH? YOU SMUGGLED IN SOME STICKS AND RUBBED 'EM TOGETHER?
SURE WENT TO REAL TROUBLE FOR A WHOLE LOTTA NOTHING!
W-WOULDN'T YOU LIKE TO KNOW, YO.
BAAAD, HE'S ABOUT TO...
...SPOT MY PRECIOUS BATTERY.
DON'T GO UNDER-ESTIMATING A SCIENTIST!!
...
PHEW...
JUST DUMB LUCK, BUT...
...GATHERING THOSE MATERIALS SAVED MY SKIN.
PFFT... TCH!
HANG ON. SORRY...
MONKEY BOY...
DID YOU CALL YOURSELF A SCIENTIST?
THAT'S WHAT WE'RE DEALING WITH, HERE?

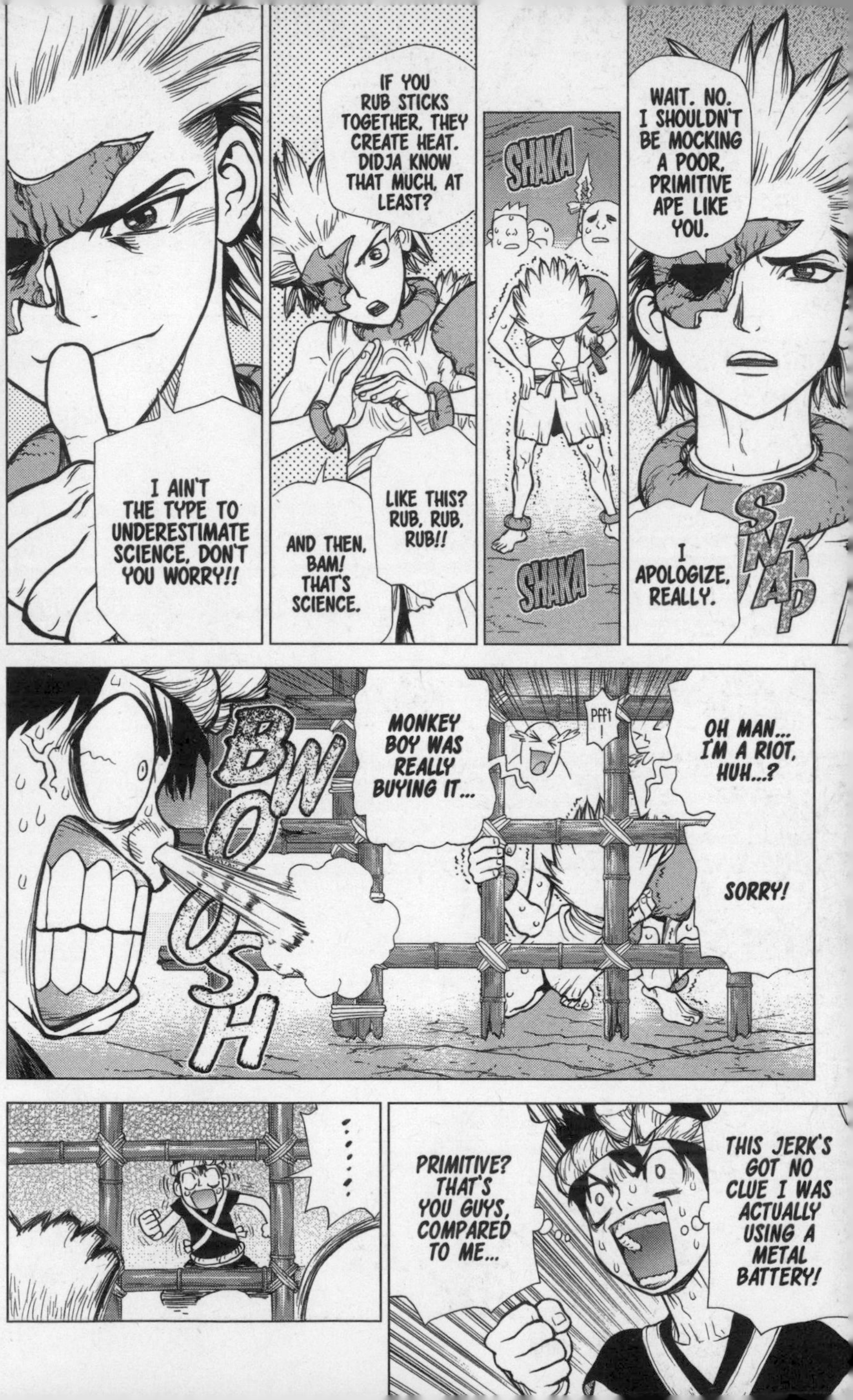
WAIT. NO. I SHOULDN'T BE MOCKING A POOR, PRIMITIVE APE LIKE YOU.
I APOLOGIZE, REALLY.
SNAP
SHAKA
SHAKA
IF YOU RUB STICKS TOGETHER, THEY CREATE HEAT. DIDJA KNOW THAT MUCH, AT LEAST?
LIKE THIS? RUB, RUB, RUB!!
AND THEN, BAM! THAT'S SCIENCE.
I AIN'T THE TYPE TO UNDERESTIMATE SCIENCE, DON'T YOU WORRY!!
OH MAN... I'M A RIOT, HUH...?
Pfft!
MONKEY BOY WAS REALLY BUYING IT...
SORRY!
BWOOSH
THIS JERK'S GOT NO CLUE I WAS ACTUALLY USING A METAL BATTERY!
PRIMITIVE? THAT'S YOU GUYS, COMPARED TO ME...
......

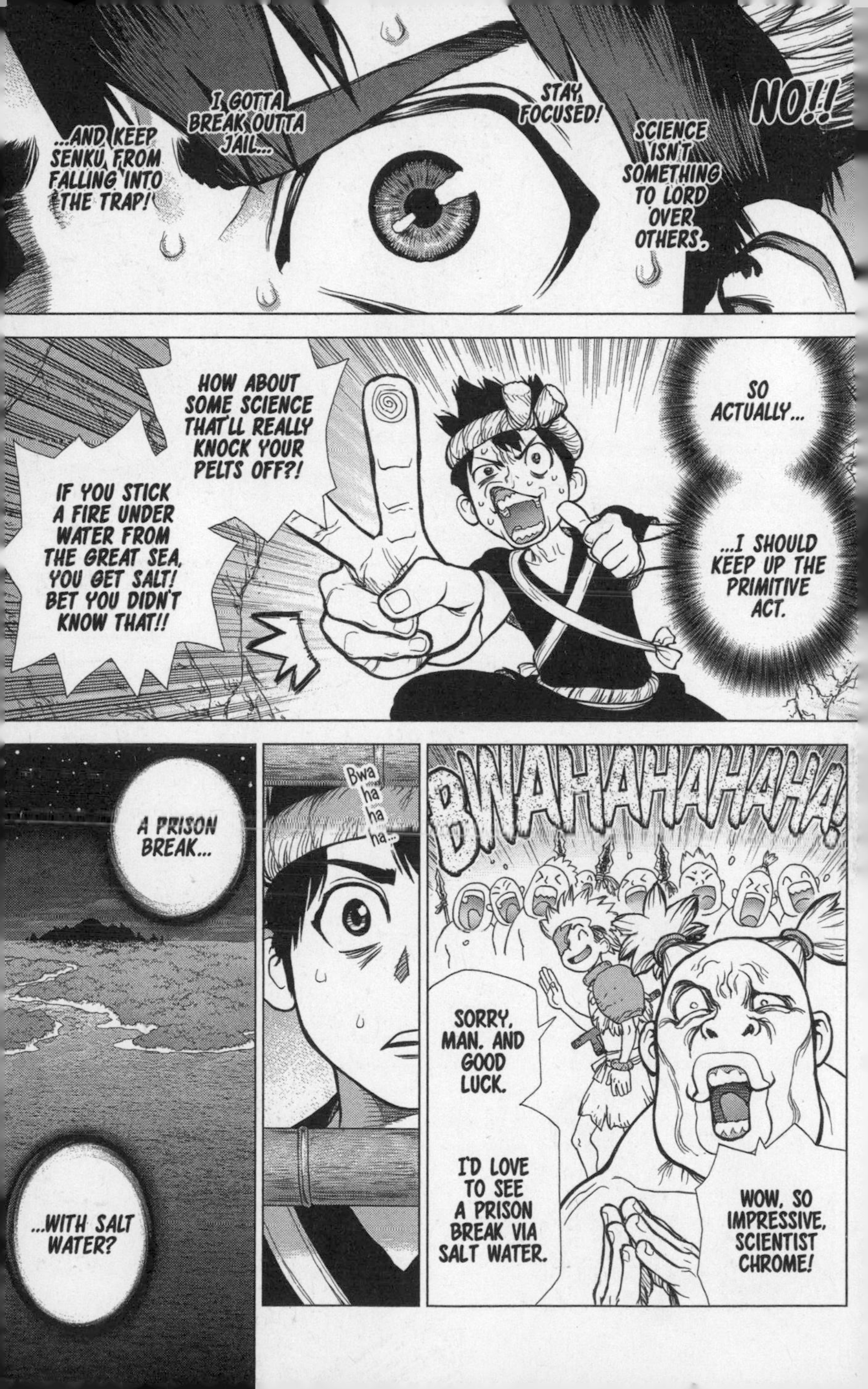
NO!!
SCIENCE ISN'T SOMETHING TO LORD OVER OTHERS.
STAY FOCUSED!
I GOTTA BREAK OUTTA JAIL...
...AND KEEP SENKU FROM FALLING INTO THE TRAP!
SO ACTUALLY...
...I SHOULD KEEP UP THE PRIMITIVE ACT.
HOW ABOUT SOME SCIENCE THAT'LL REALLY KNOCK YOUR PELTS OFF?!
IF YOU STICK A FIRE UNDER WATER FROM THE GREAT SEA, YOU GET SALT! BET YOU DIDN'T KNOW THAT!!
BWAHAHAHAHAHA!
SORRY, MAN. AND GOOD LUCK.
WOW, SO IMPRESSIVE, SCIENTIST CHROME!
I'D LOVE TO SEE A PRISON BREAK VIA SALT WATER.
Bwa ha ha ha ha...
A PRISON BREAK...
...WITH SALT WATER?

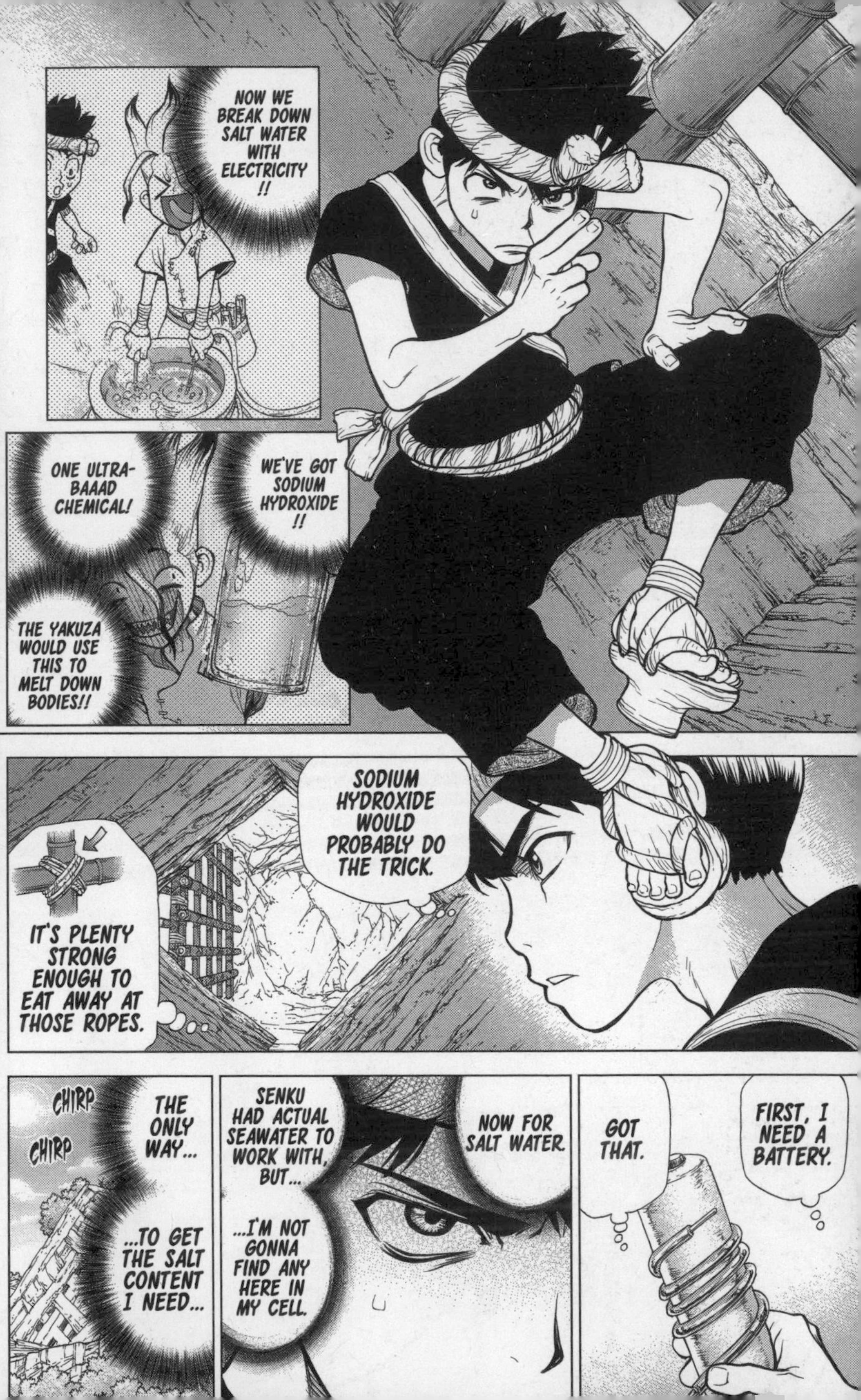
NOW WE BREAK DOWN SALT WATER WITH ELECTRICITY!!
WE'VE GOT SODIUM HYDROXIDE!!
ONE ULTRA-BAAAD CHEMICAL!
THE YAKUZA WOULD USE THIS TO MELT DOWN BODIES!!
SODIUM HYDROXIDE WOULD PROBABLY DO THE TRICK.
IT'S PLENTY STRONG ENOUGH TO EAT AWAY AT THOSE ROPES.
FIRST, I NEED A BATTERY.
GOT THAT.
NOW FOR SALT WATER.
SENKU HAD ACTUAL SEAWATER TO WORK WITH, BUT...
...I'M NOT GONNA FIND ANY HERE IN MY CELL.
THE ONLY WAY...
...TO GET THE SALT CONTENT I NEED...
CHIRP
CHIRP

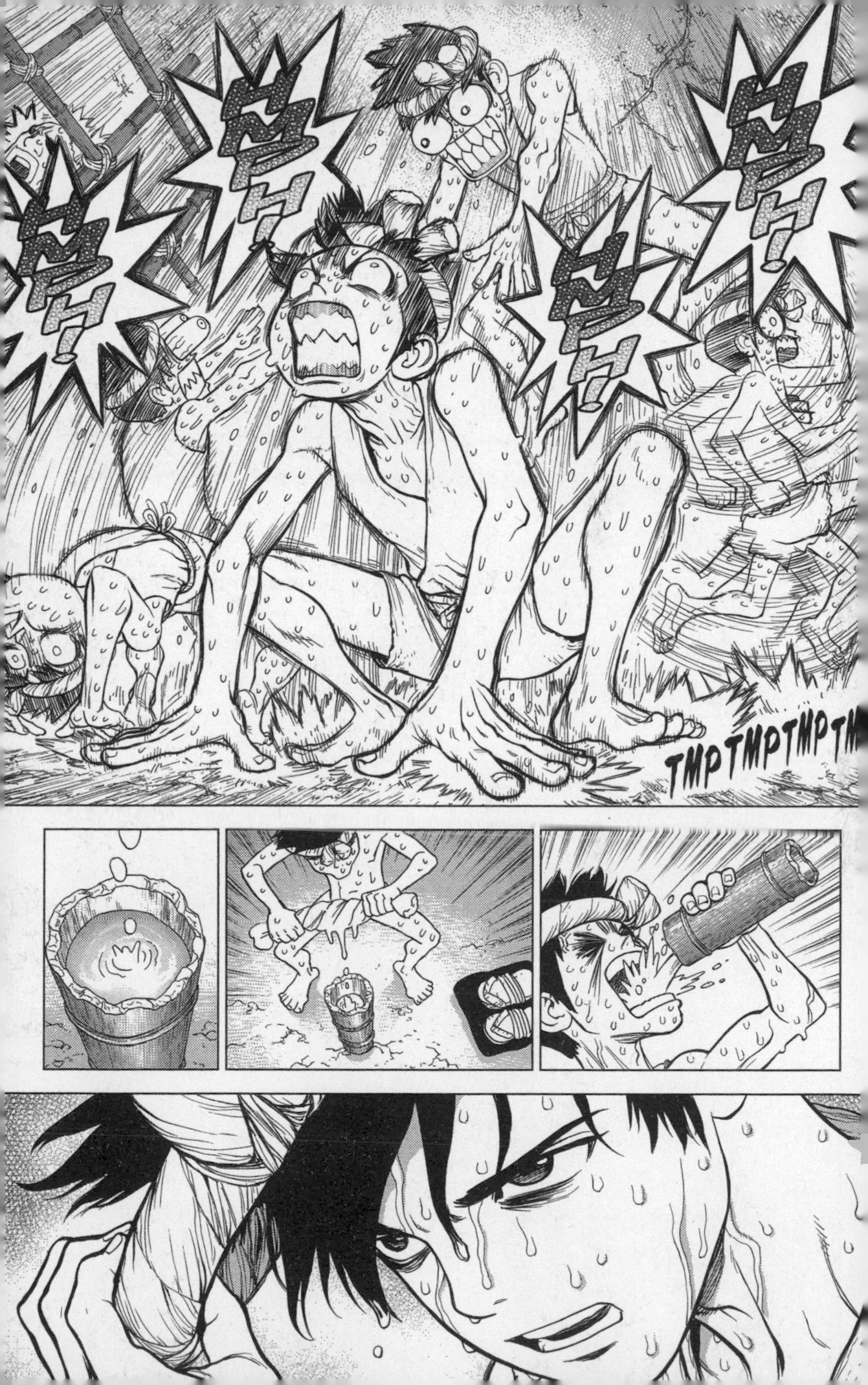
HMPH!
HMPH!
HMPH!
HMPH!
TMPTMPTMPTM

FSSSSSH

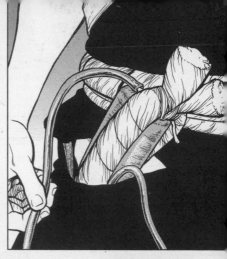

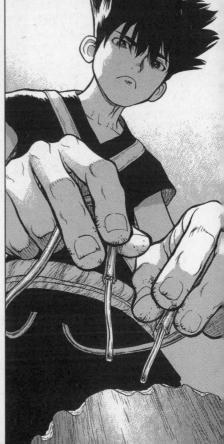

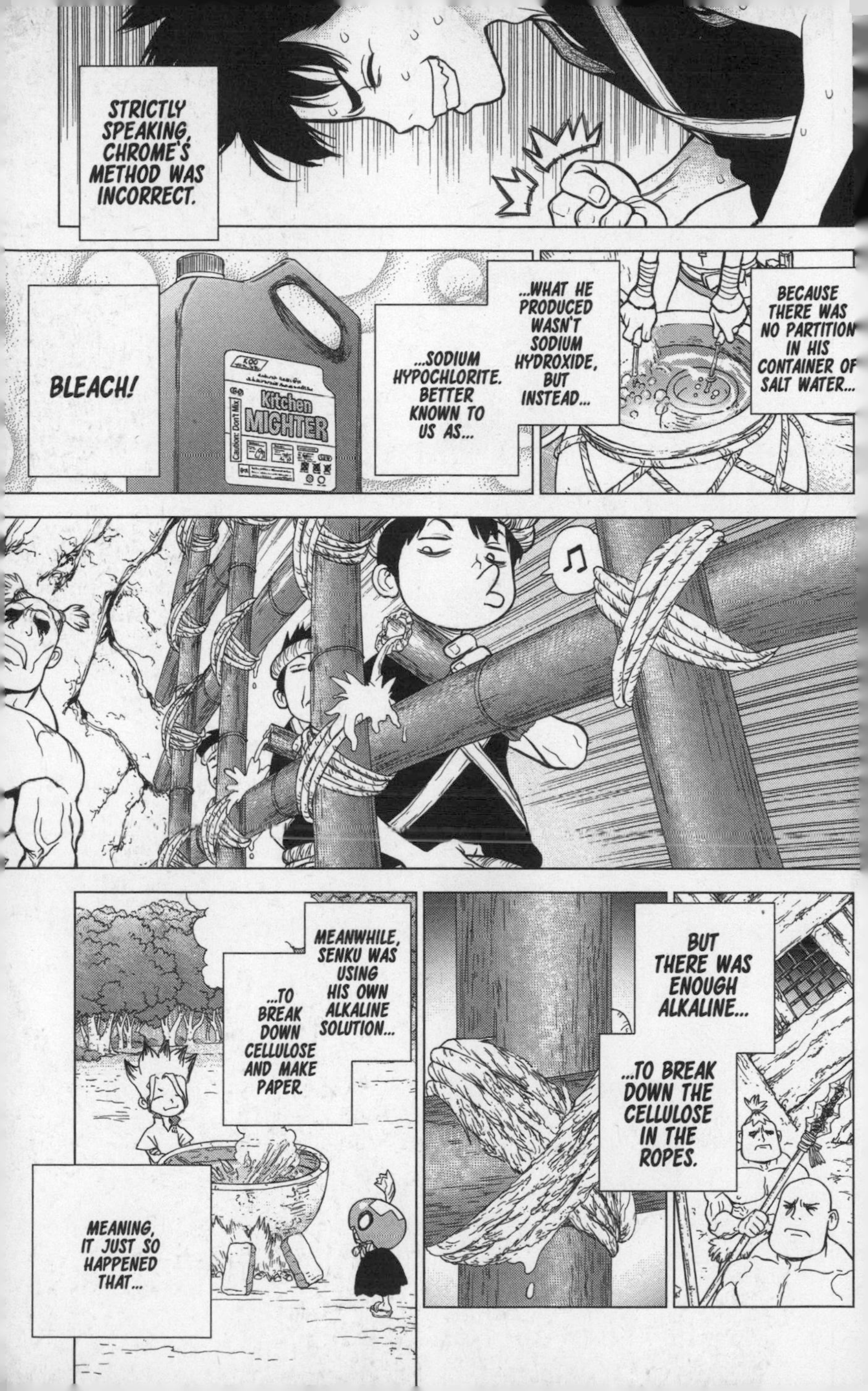
STRICTLY SPEAKING, CHROME'S METHOD WAS INCORRECT.
BECAUSE THERE WAS NO PARTITION IN HIS CONTAINER OF SALT WATER...
...WHAT HE PRODUCED WASN'T SODIUM HYDROXIDE, BUT INSTEAD...
...SODIUM HYPOCHLORITE. BETTER KNOWN TO US AS...
Kitchen MIGHTER
Caution: Don't Mix
BLEACH!
♫
BUT THERE WAS ENOUGH ALKALINE...
...TO BREAK DOWN THE CELLULOSE IN THE ROPES.
MEANWHILE, SENKU WAS USING HIS OWN ALKALINE SOLUTION...
...TO BREAK DOWN CELLULOSE AND MAKE PAPER.
MEANING, IT JUST SO HAPPENED THAT...

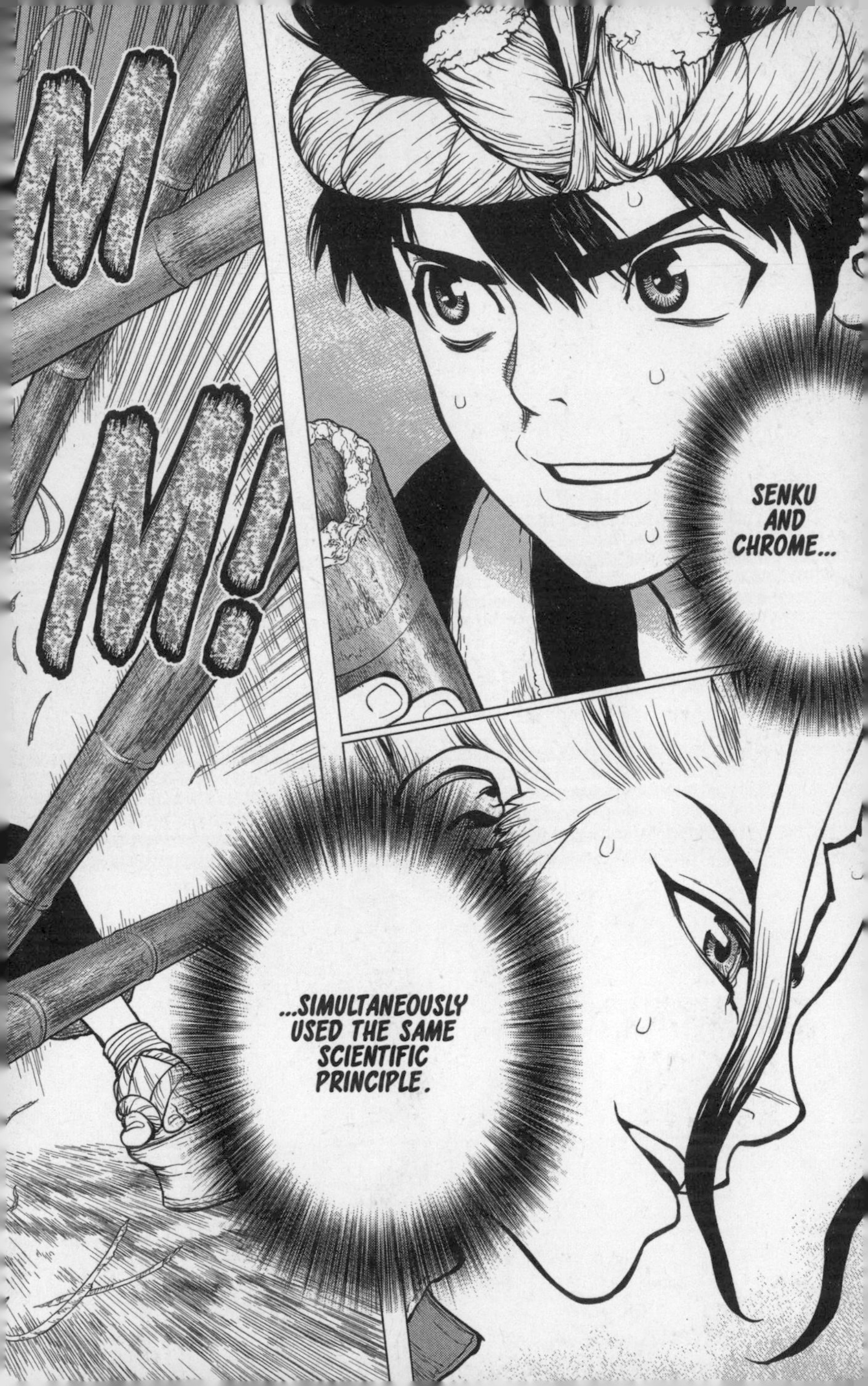
SENKU AND CHROME...
...SIMULTANEOUSLY USED THE SAME SCIENTIFIC PRINCIPLE.
MM!

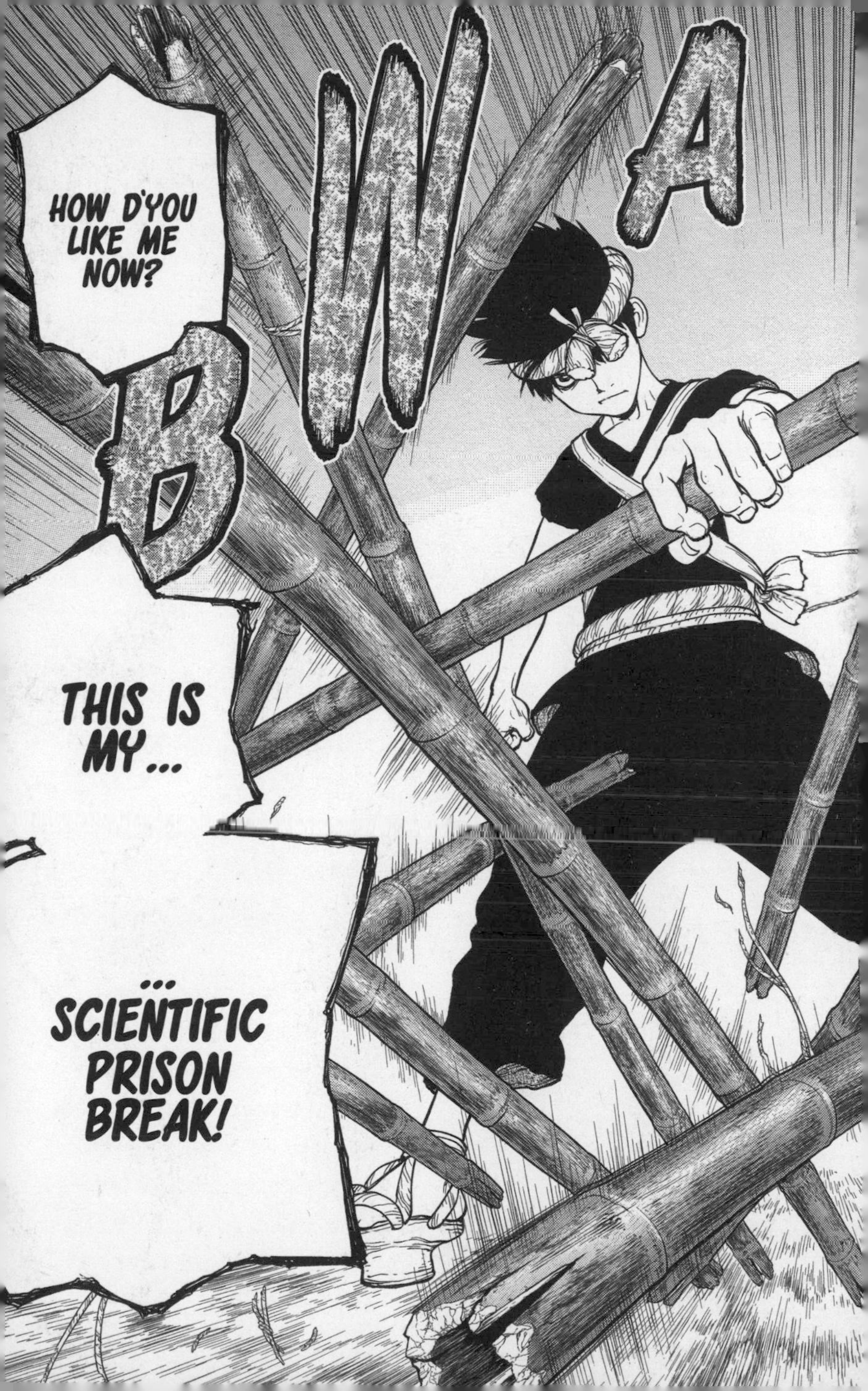
BWA
HOW D'YOU LIKE ME NOW?
THIS IS MY...
... SCIENTIFIC PRISON BREAK!

Tsukasa Empire

FIGHTER FILE 4

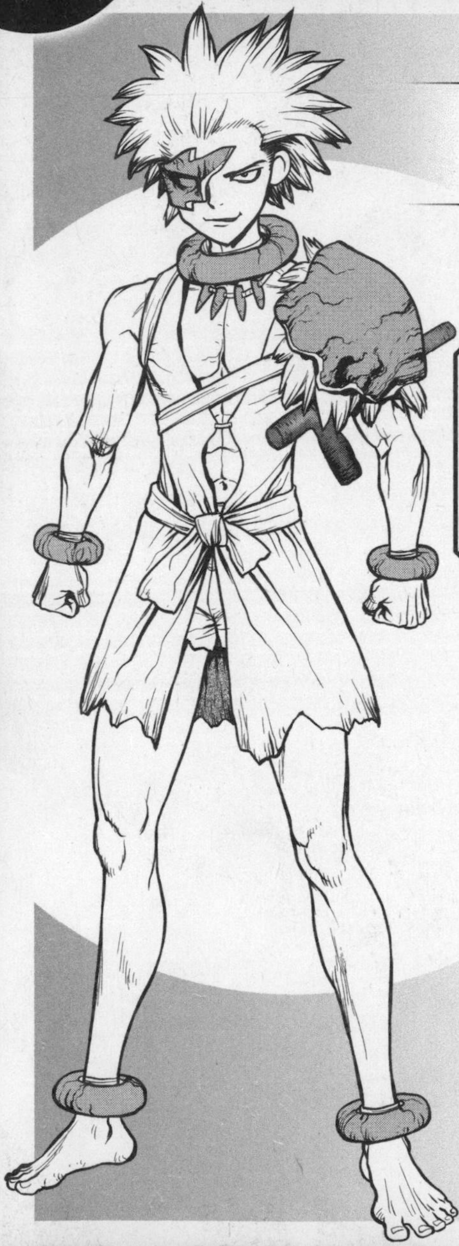

Yo

Power	☆☆☆
Speed	☆☆☆☆
Technique	☆☆☆☆☆
Range	☆

Full Name: Yo Uei

Height: 177 cm

A former police officer trained in martial arts and submission techniques. Master of the nightstick. Yo doesn't know the meaning of the word "compromise." He prefers to play judge, jury and executioner all by himself, crushing those he deems guilty without second thought.

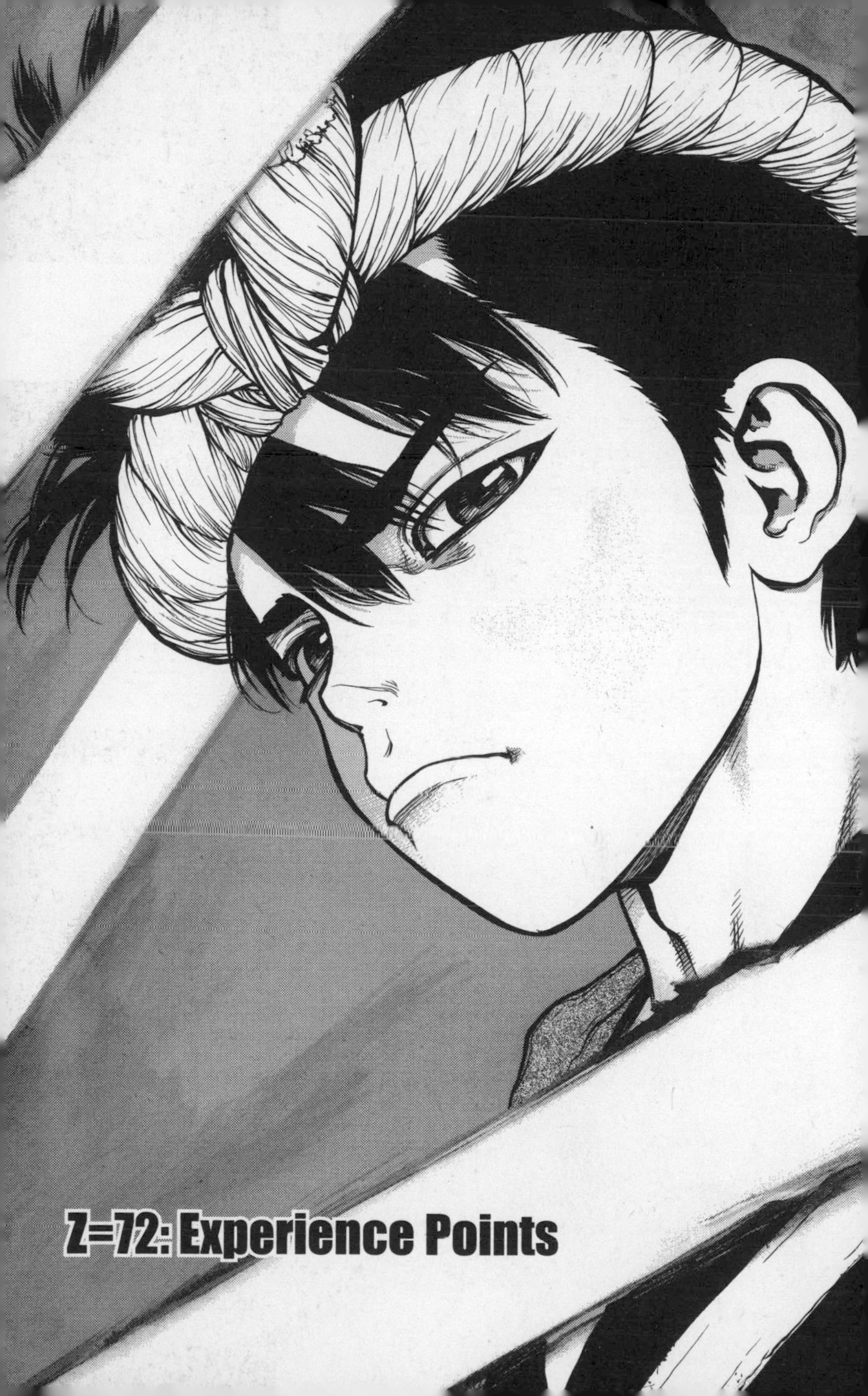
Z=72: Experience Points

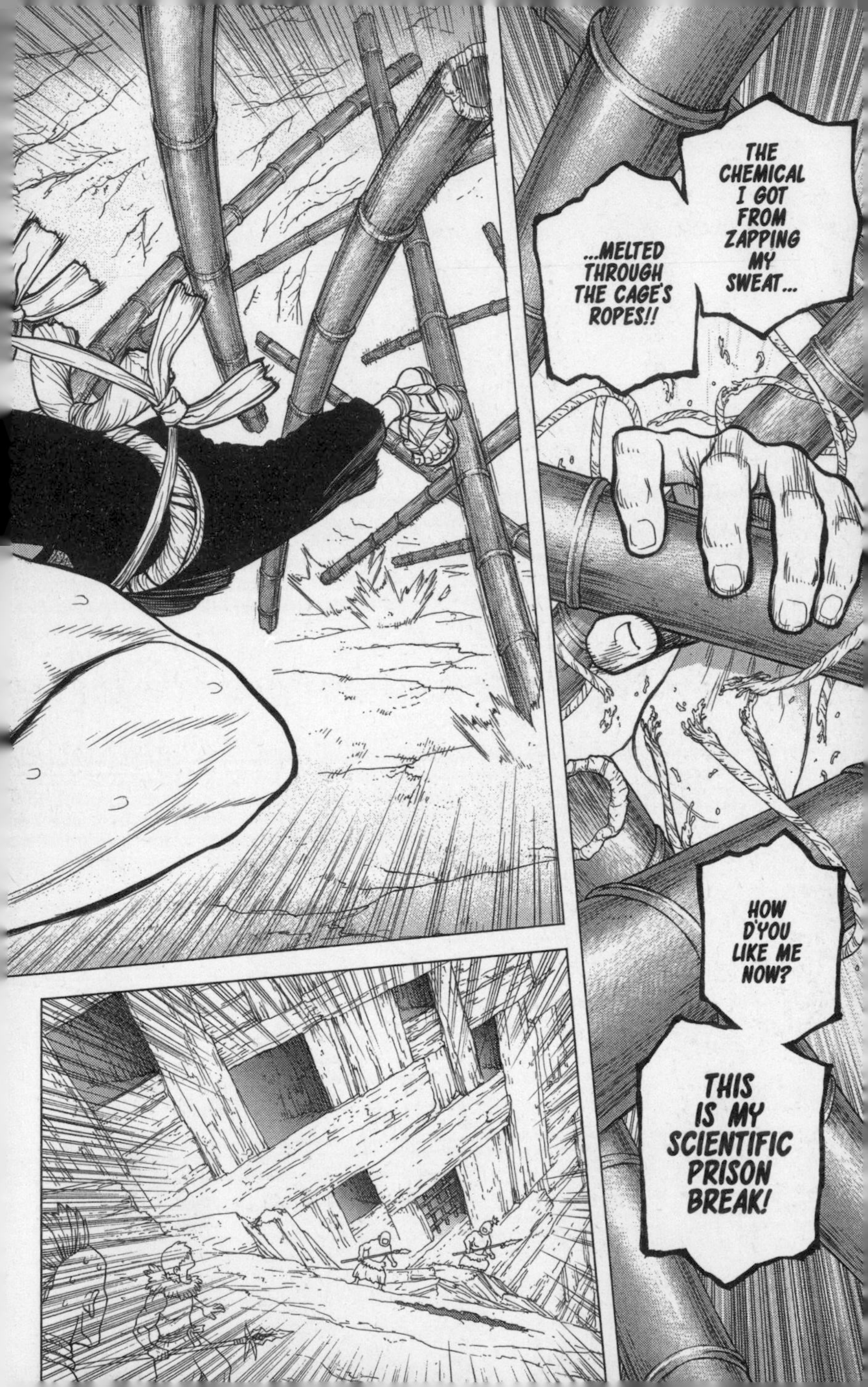
THE CHEMICAL I GOT FROM ZAPPING MY SWEAT...
...MELTED THROUGH THE CAGE'S ROPES!!
HOW D'YOU LIKE ME NOW?
THIS IS MY SCIENTIFIC PRISON BREAK!

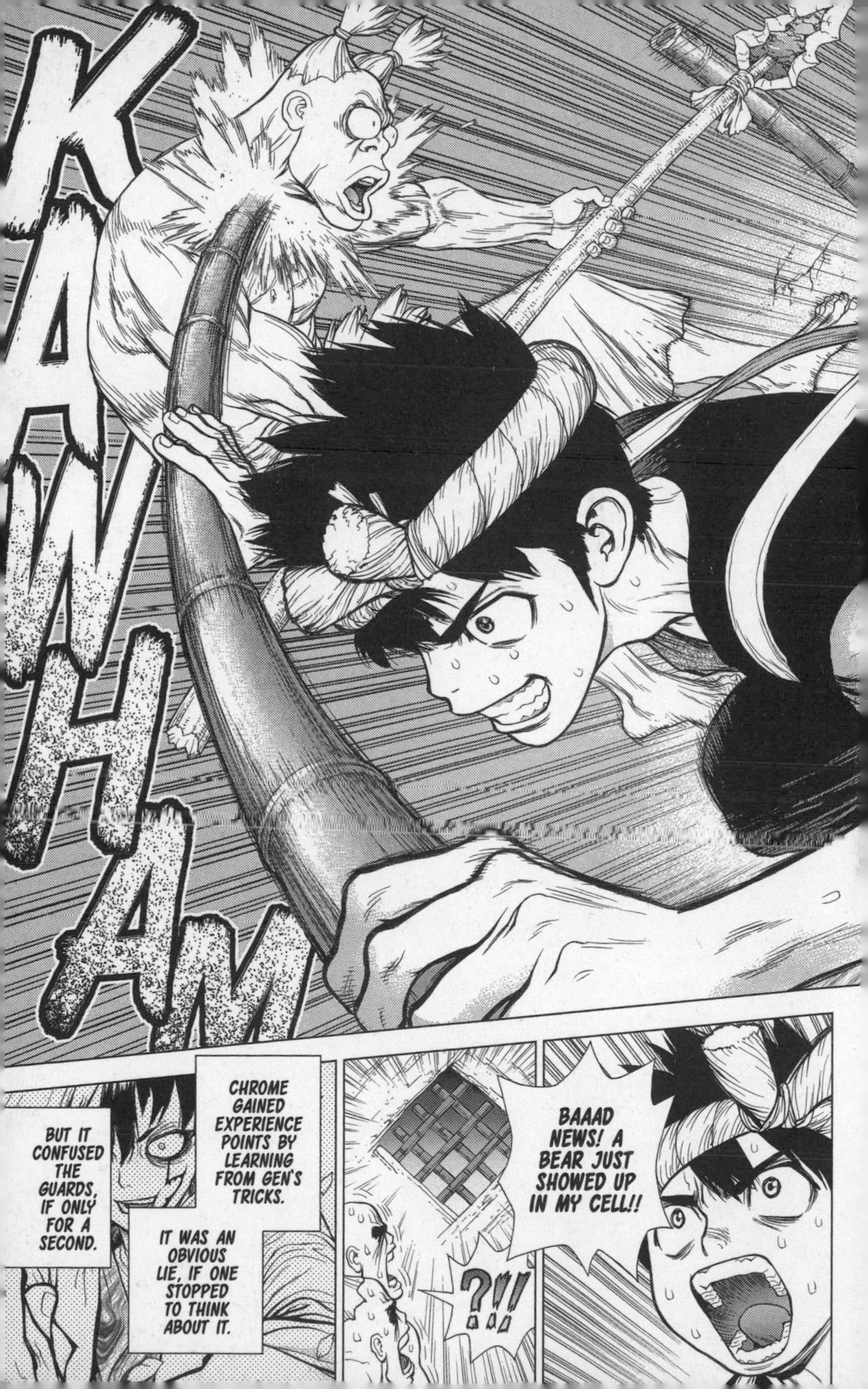
KAWHAM
BAAAD NEWS! A BEAR JUST SHOWED UP IN MY CELL!!
?!!
CHROME GAINED EXPERIENCE POINTS BY LEARNING FROM GEN'S TRICKS.
BUT IT CONFUSED THE GUARDS, IF ONLY FOR A SECOND.
IT WAS AN OBVIOUS LIE, IF ONE STOPPED TO THINK ABOUT IT.

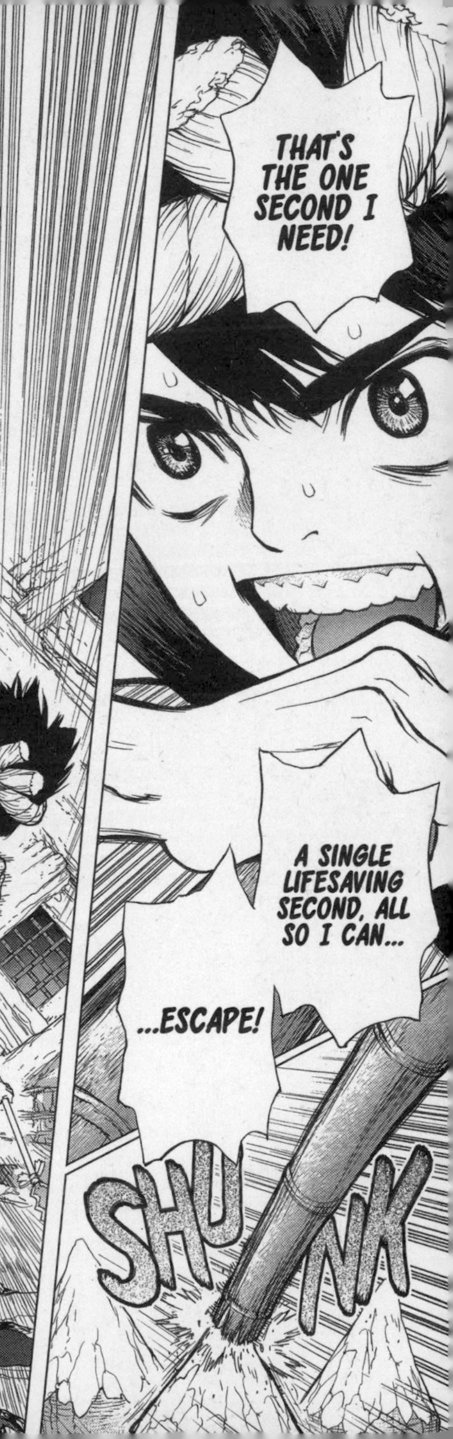
THAT'S THE ONE SECOND I NEED!
A SINGLE LIFESAVING SECOND, ALL SO I CAN...
...ESCAPE!
SHUNK
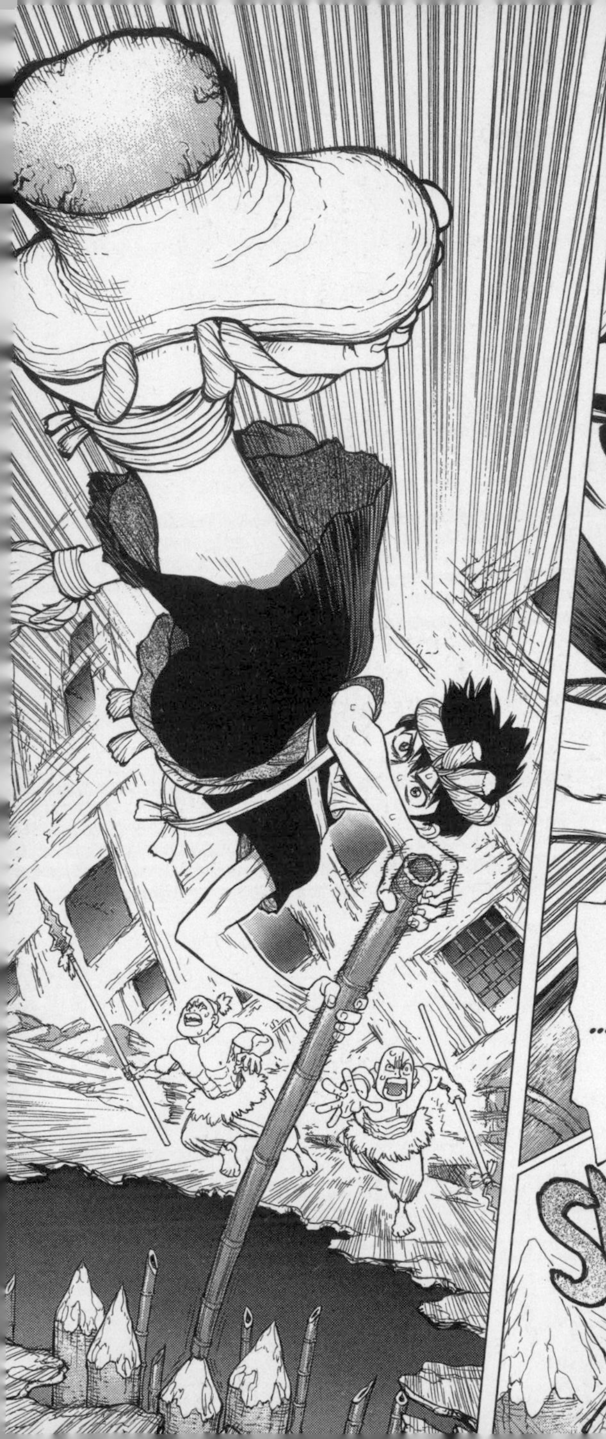

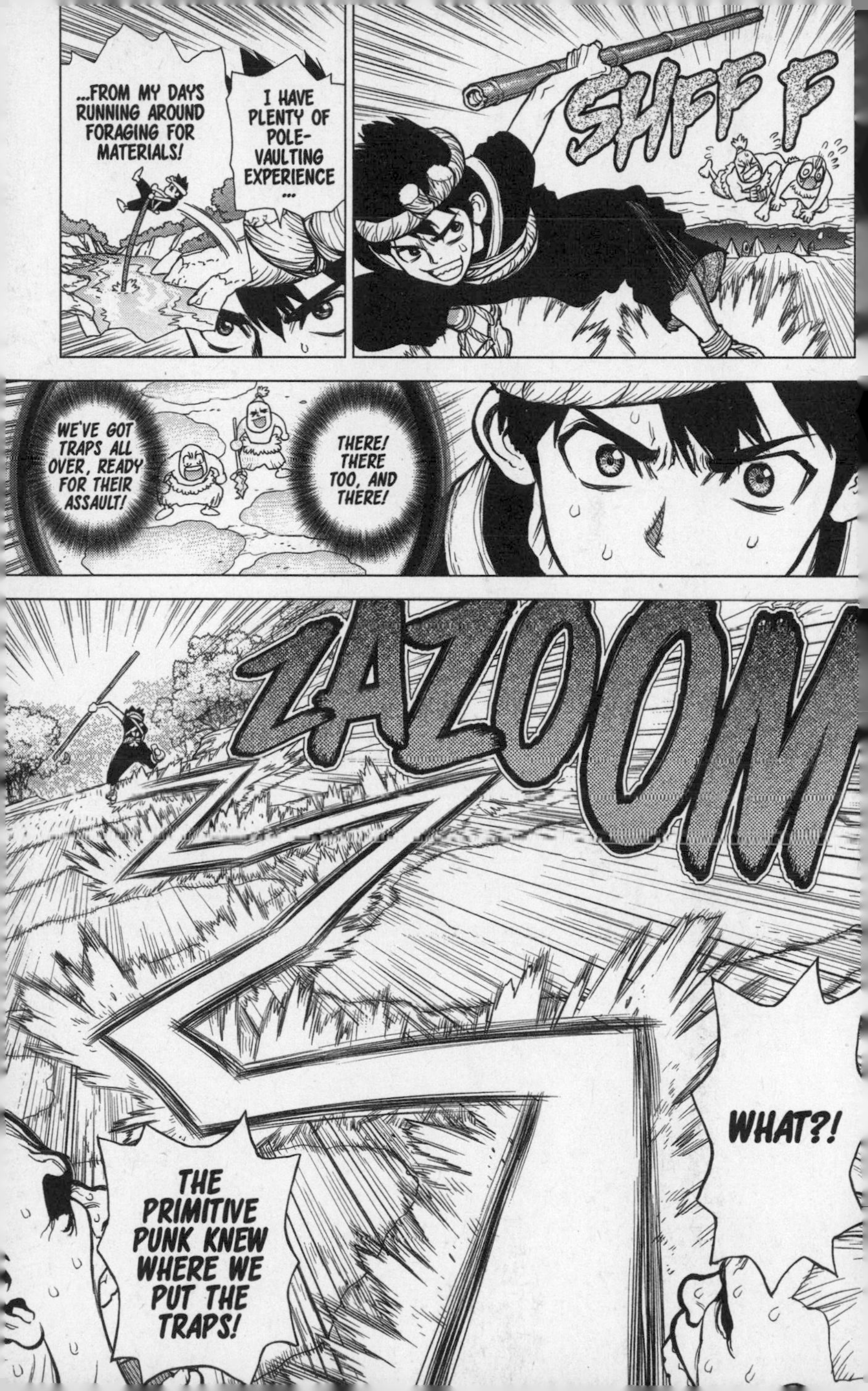
SHFFF
I HAVE PLENTY OF POLE-VAULTING EXPERIENCE...
...FROM MY DAYS RUNNING AROUND FORAGING FOR MATERIALS!
THERE! THERE TOO, AND THERE!
WE'VE GOT TRAPS ALL OVER, READY FOR THEIR ASSAULT!
ZAZOOM
WHAT?!
THE PRIMITIVE PUNK KNEW WHERE WE PUT THE TRAPS!

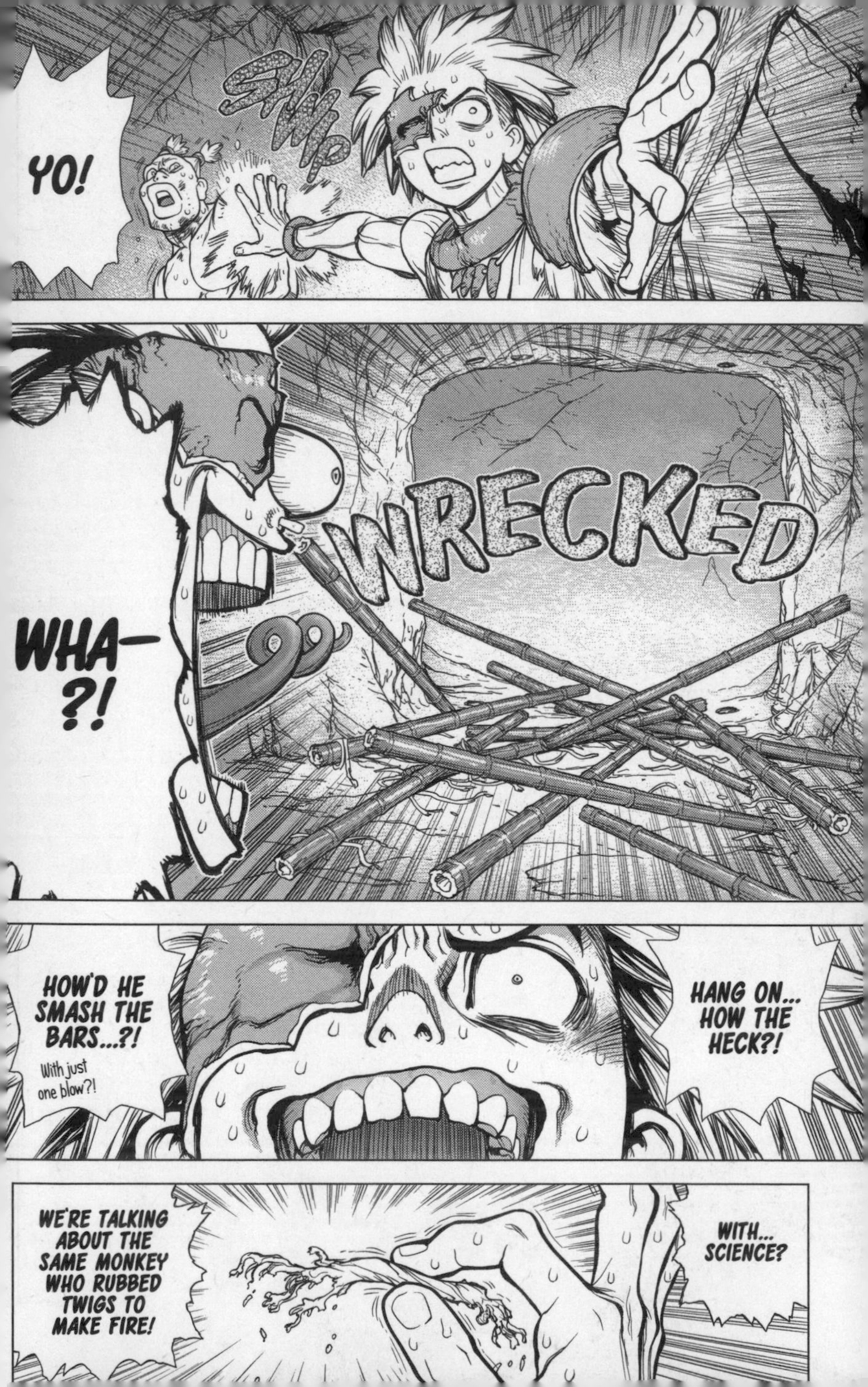
SWIP
YO!
WRECKED
WHA-?!
HANG ON... HOW THE HECK?!
HOW'D HE SMASH THE BARS...?!
With just one blow?!
WITH... SCIENCE?
WE'RE TALKING ABOUT THE SAME MONKEY WHO RUBBED TWIGS TO MAKE FIRE!

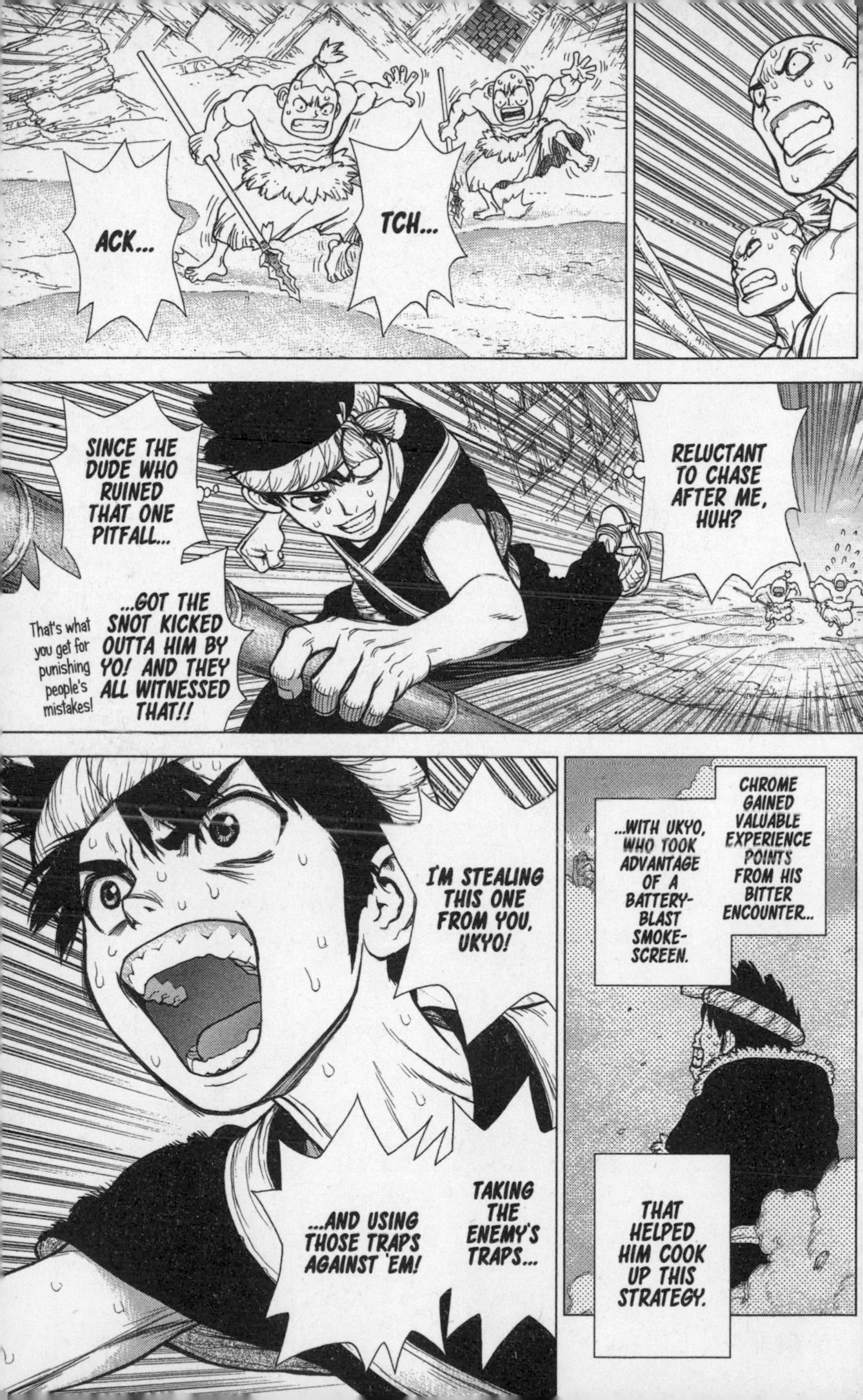
TCH...
ACK...
RELUCTANT TO CHASE AFTER ME, HUH?
SINCE THE DUDE WHO RUINED THAT ONE PITFALL...
...GOT THE SNOT KICKED OUTTA HIM BY YO! AND THEY ALL WITNESSED THAT!!
That's what you get for punishing people's mistakes!
CHROME GAINED VALUABLE EXPERIENCE POINTS FROM HIS BITTER ENCOUNTER...
...WITH UKYO, WHO TOOK ADVANTAGE OF A BATTERY-BLAST SMOKE-SCREEN.
THAT HELPED HIM COOK UP THIS STRATEGY.
I'M STEALING THIS ONE FROM YOU, UKYO!
TAKING THE ENEMY'S TRAPS...
...AND USING THOSE TRAPS AGAINST 'EM!

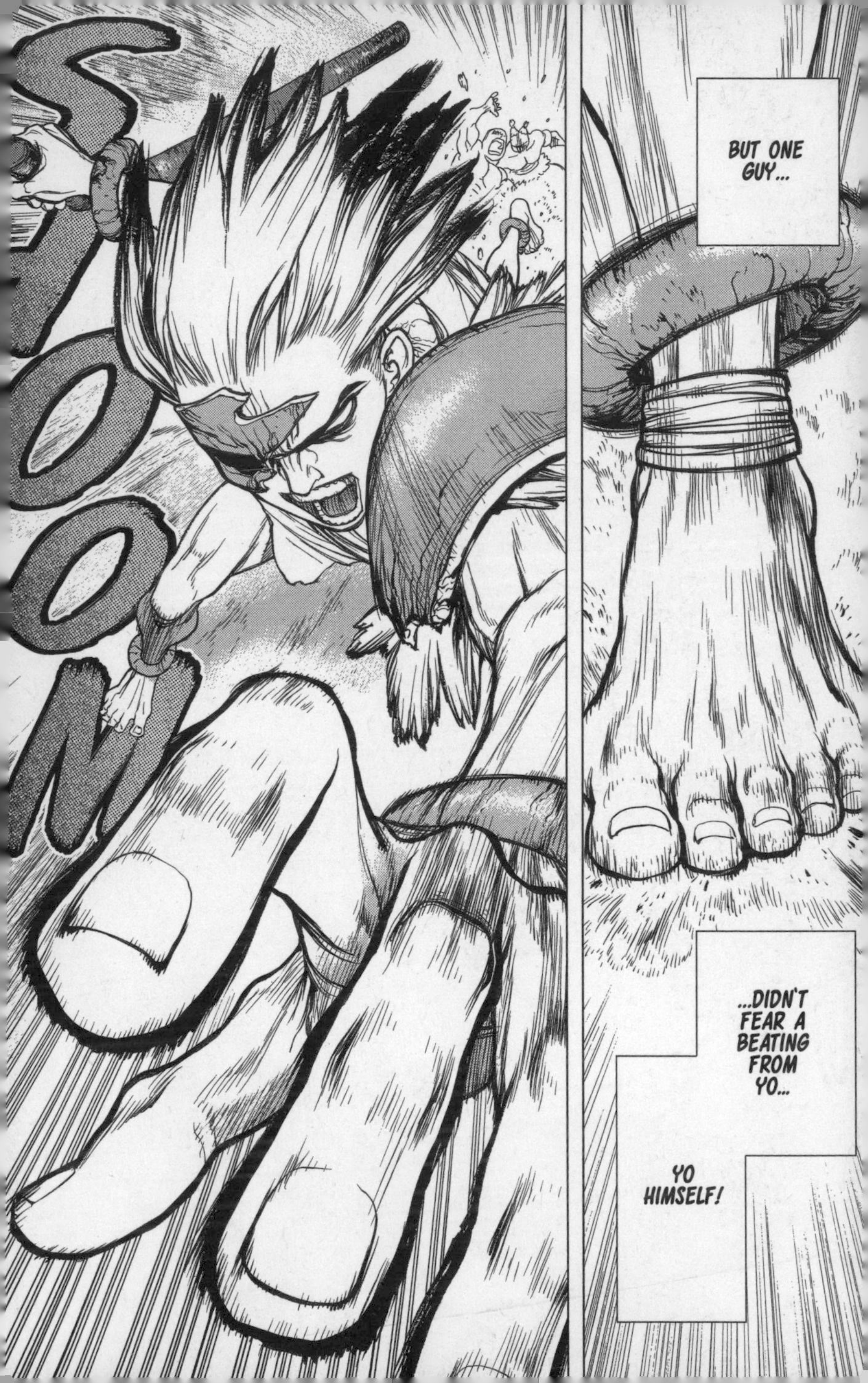
BUT ONE GUY...
...DIDN'T FEAR A BEATING FROM YO...
YO HIMSELF!

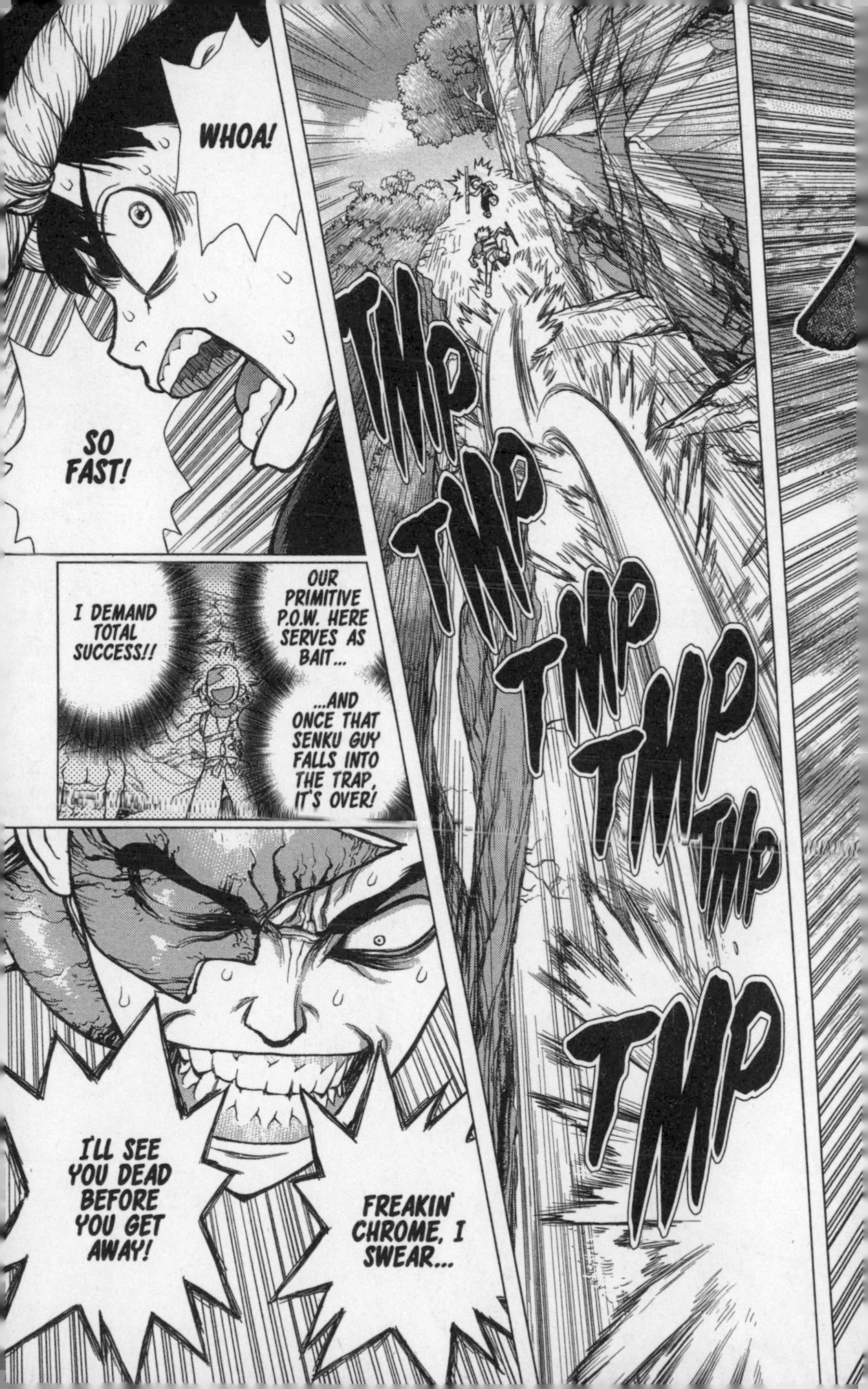
TMP
TMP
TMP
TMP
TMP
TMP
WHOA!
SO FAST!
OUR PRIMITIVE P.O.W. HERE SERVES AS BAIT...
...AND ONCE THAT SENKU GUY FALLS INTO THE TRAP, IT'S OVER!
I DEMAND TOTAL SUCCESS!!
FREAKIN' CHROME, I SWEAR...
I'LL SEE YOU DEAD BEFORE YOU GET AWAY!

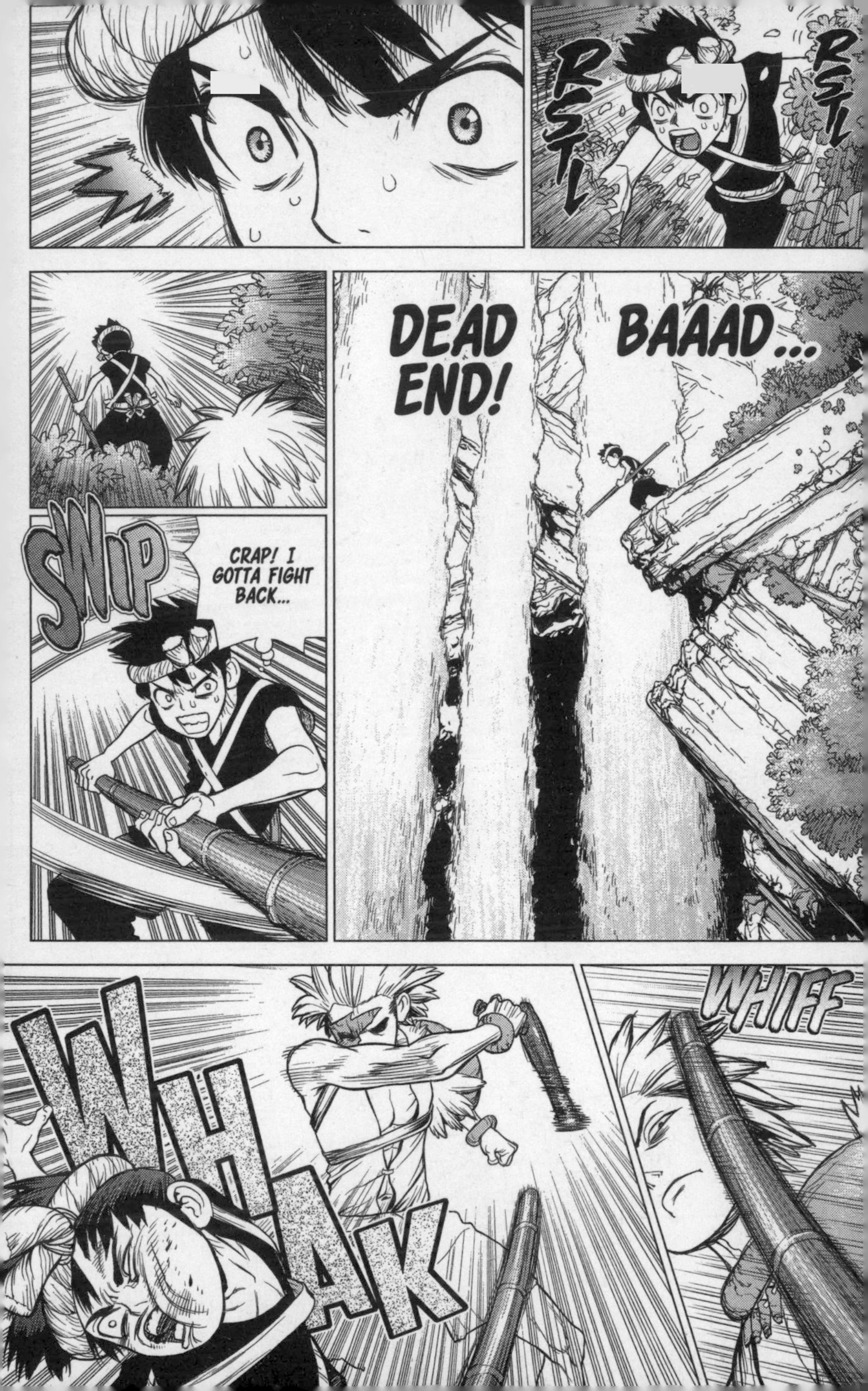
RSTL
RSTL
BAAAD...
DEAD END!
SNIP
CRAP! I GOTTA FIGHT BACK...
WHIFF
WHAK

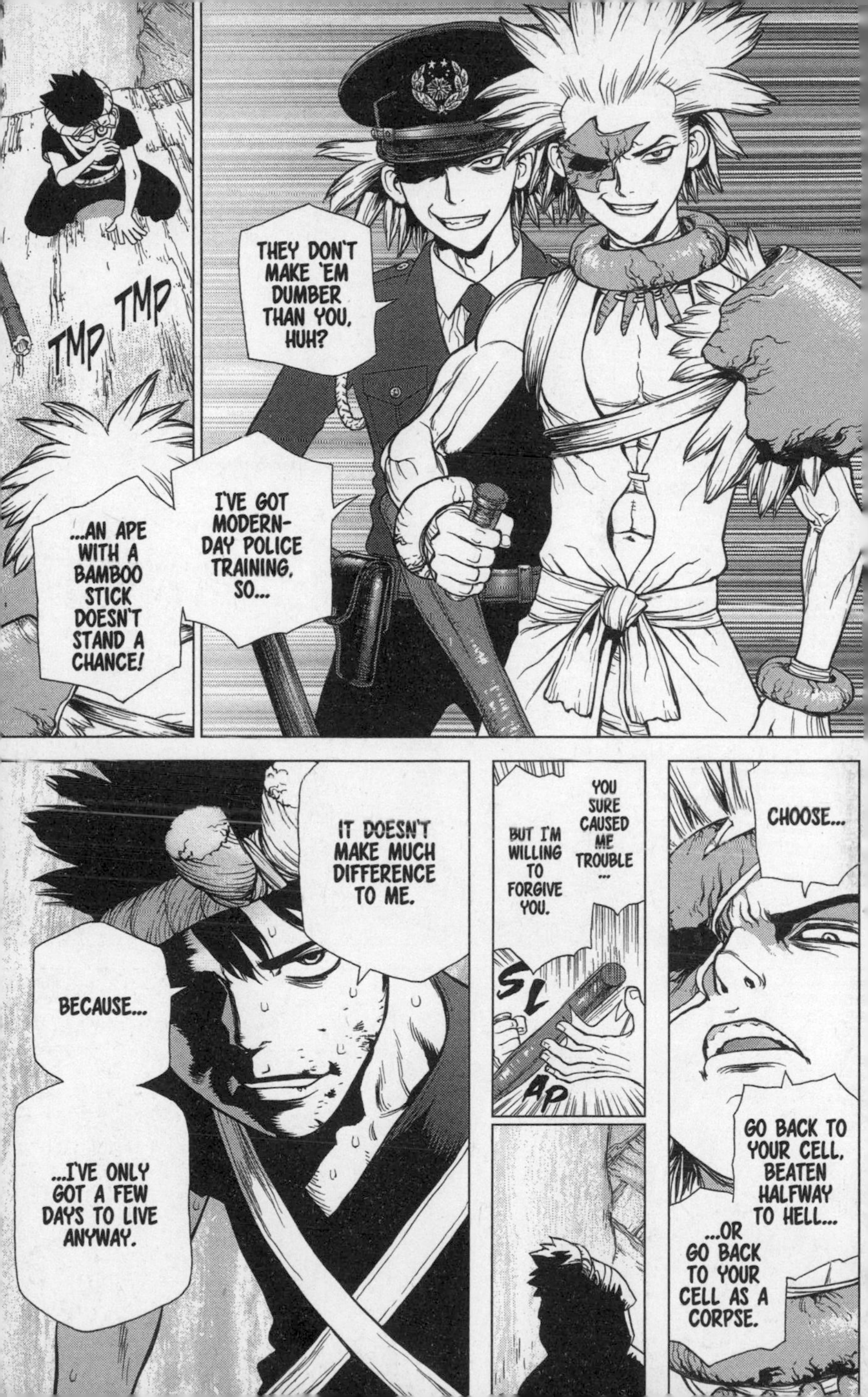
THEY DON'T MAKE 'EM DUMBER THAN YOU, HUH?
I'VE GOT MODERN-DAY POLICE TRAINING, SO...
...AN APE WITH A BAMBOO STICK DOESN'T STAND A CHANCE!
TMP TMP
CHOOSE...
GO BACK TO YOUR CELL, BEATEN HALFWAY TO HELL...
...OR GO BACK TO YOUR CELL AS A CORPSE.
YOU SURE CAUSED ME TROUBLE...
BUT I'M WILLING TO FORGIVE YOU.
SLAP
IT DOESN'T MAKE MUCH DIFFERENCE TO ME.
BECAUSE...
...I'VE ONLY GOT A FEW DAYS TO LIVE ANYWAY.

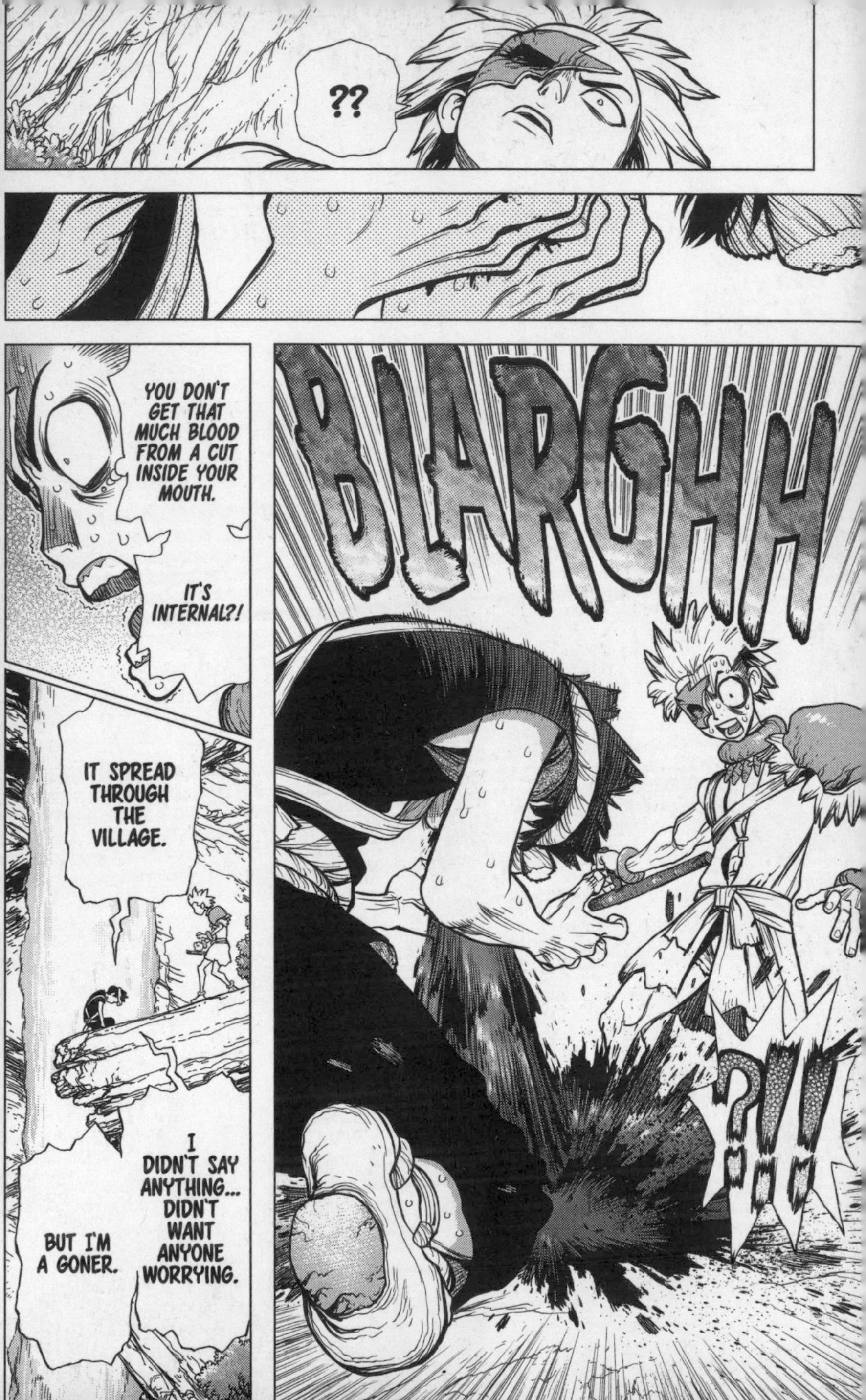
??
BLARGHH
?!!
YOU DON'T GET THAT MUCH BLOOD FROM A CUT INSIDE YOUR MOUTH.
IT'S INTERNAL?!
IT SPREAD THROUGH THE VILLAGE.
I DIDN'T SAY ANYTHING... DIDN'T WANT ANYONE WORRYING.
BUT I'M A GONER.

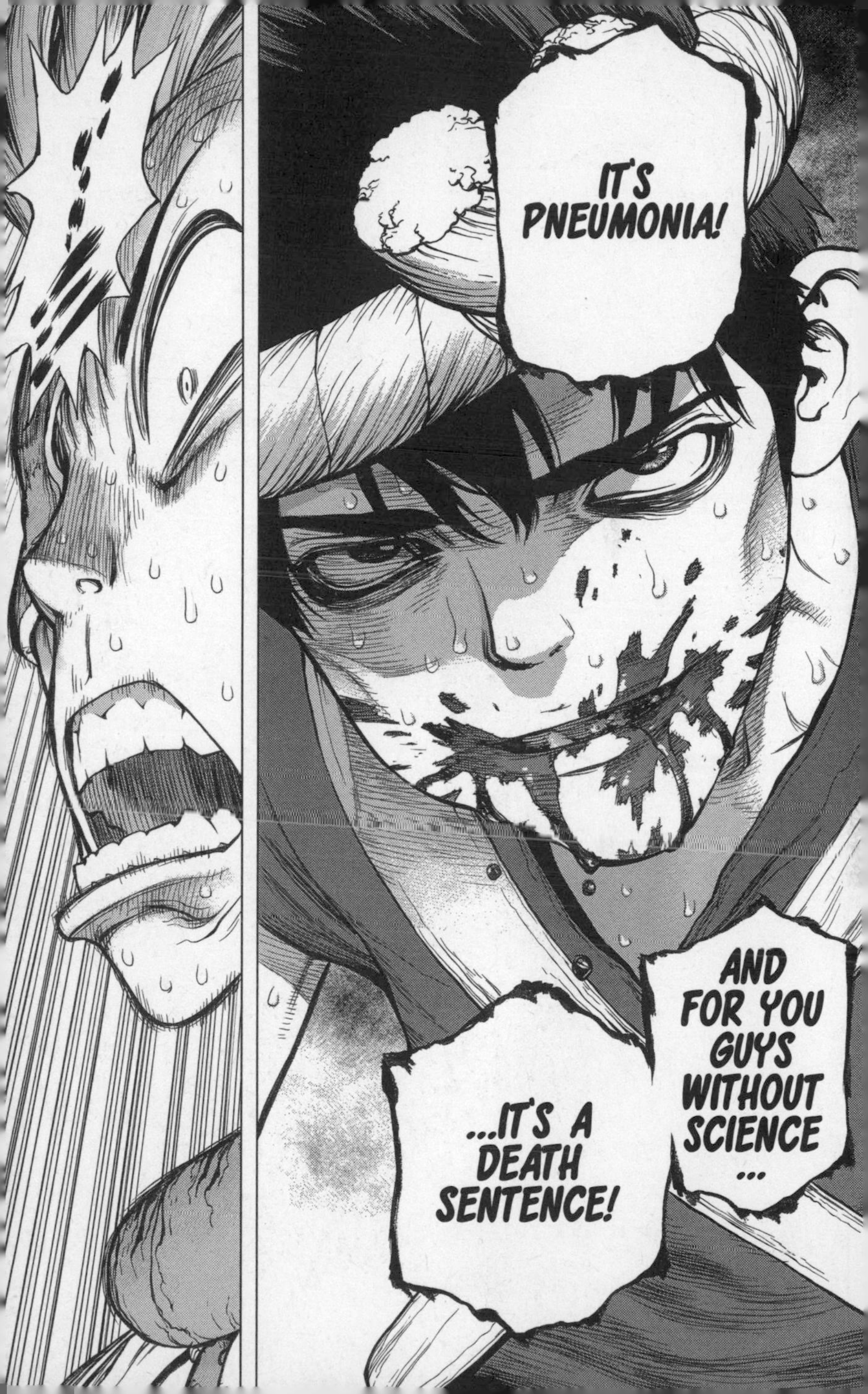
IT'S PNEUMONIA!
AND FOR YOU GUYS WITHOUT SCIENCE ...
...IT'S A DEATH SENTENCE!

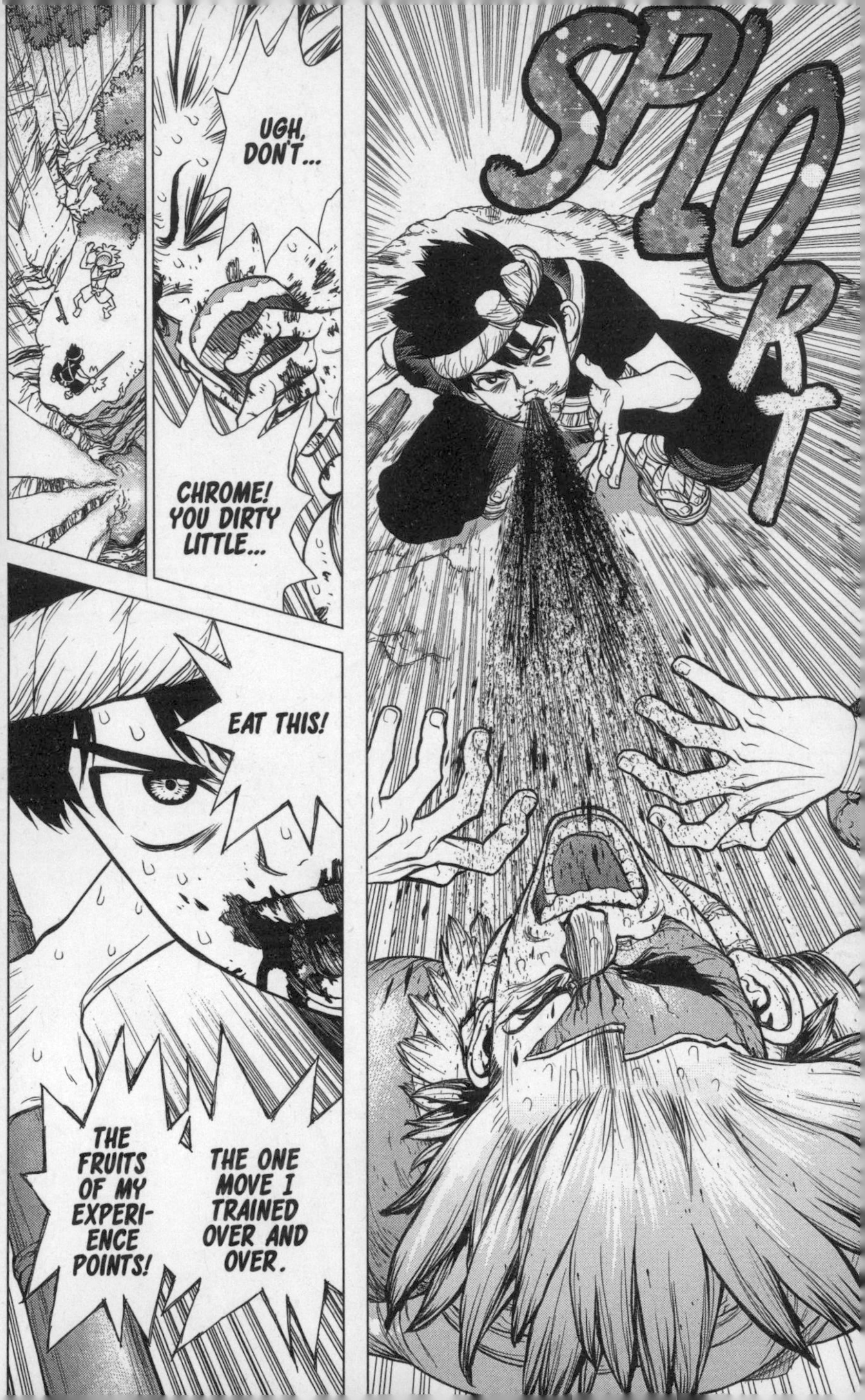
SPLORT
UGH, DON'T...
CHROME! YOU DIRTY LITTLE...
EAT THIS!
THE ONE MOVE I TRAINED OVER AND OVER.
THE FRUITS OF MY EXPERIENCE POINTS!

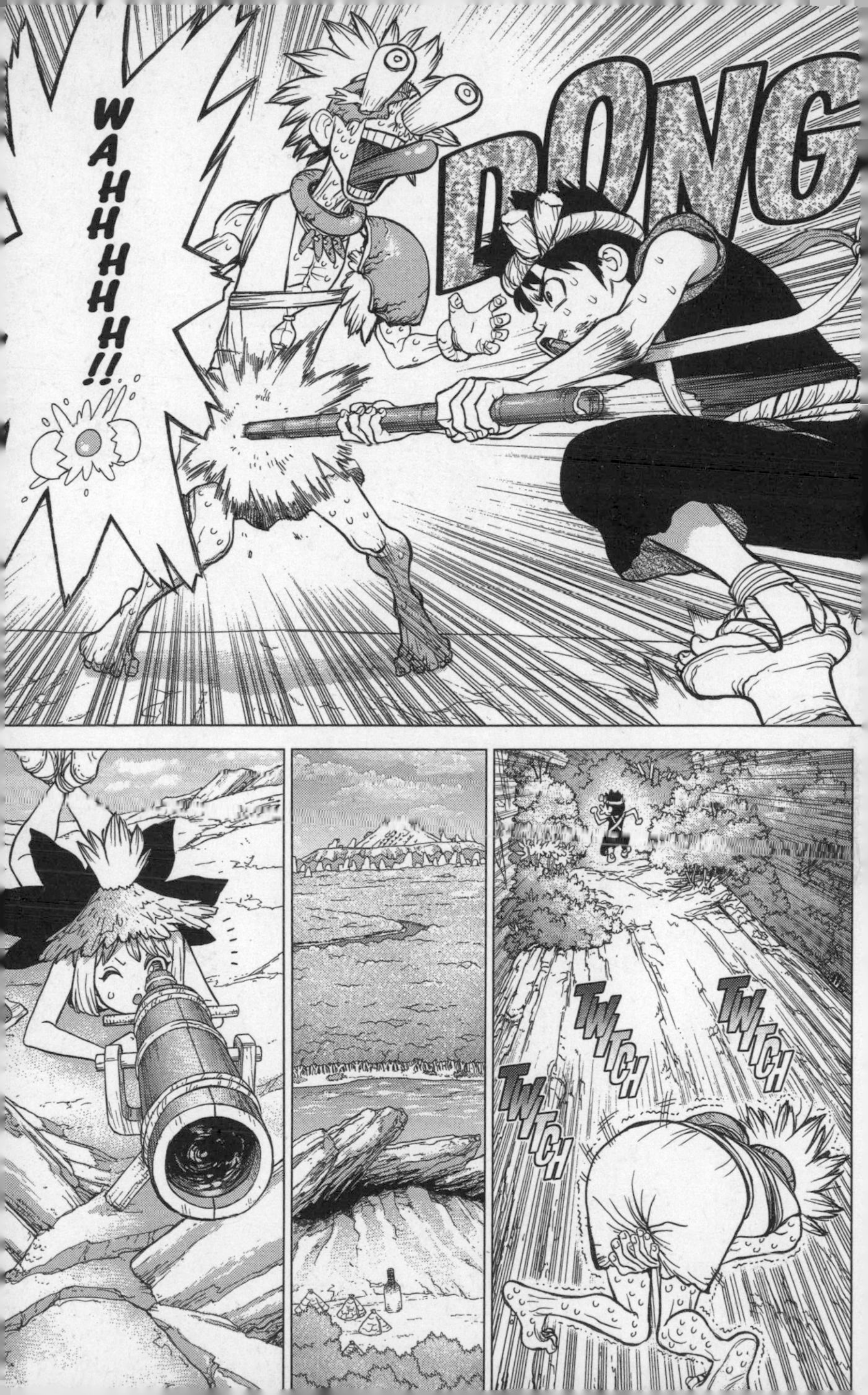
DONG
WAHHHHHH!!
TWITCH
TWITCH
TWITCH

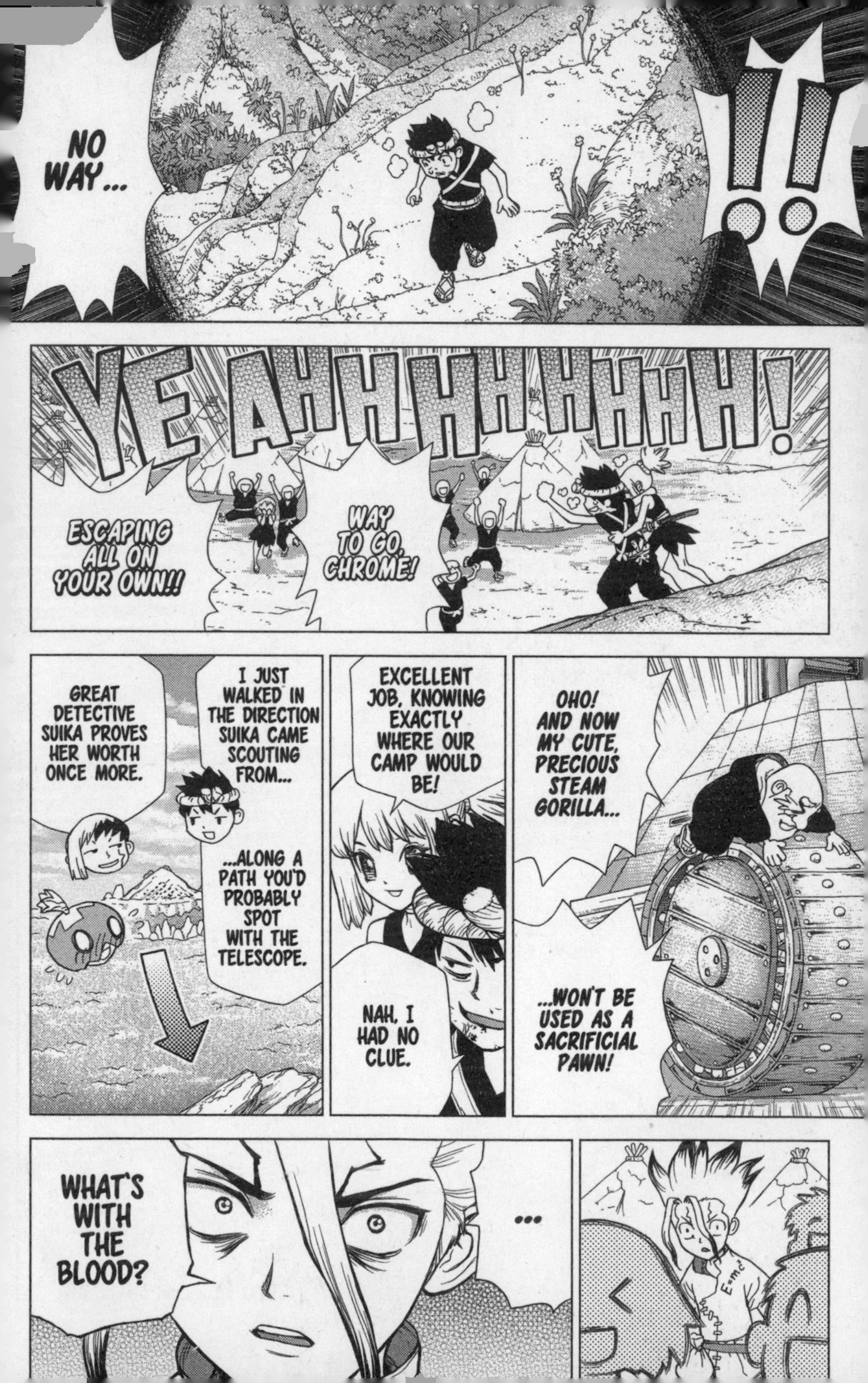
!!
NO WAY...
YEAHHHHHHHHH!
WAY TO GO, CHROME!
ESCAPING ALL ON YOUR OWN!!
OHO! AND NOW MY CUTE, PRECIOUS STEAM GORILLA...
...WON'T BE USED AS A SACRIFICIAL PAWN!
EXCELLENT JOB, KNOWING EXACTLY WHERE OUR CAMP WOULD BE!
NAH, I HAD NO CLUE.
I JUST WALKED IN THE DIRECTION SUIKA CAME SCOUTING FROM...
...ALONG A PATH YOU'D PROBABLY SPOT WITH THE TELESCOPE.
GREAT DETECTIVE SUIKA PROVES HER WORTH ONCE MORE.
...
WHAT'S WITH THE BLOOD?

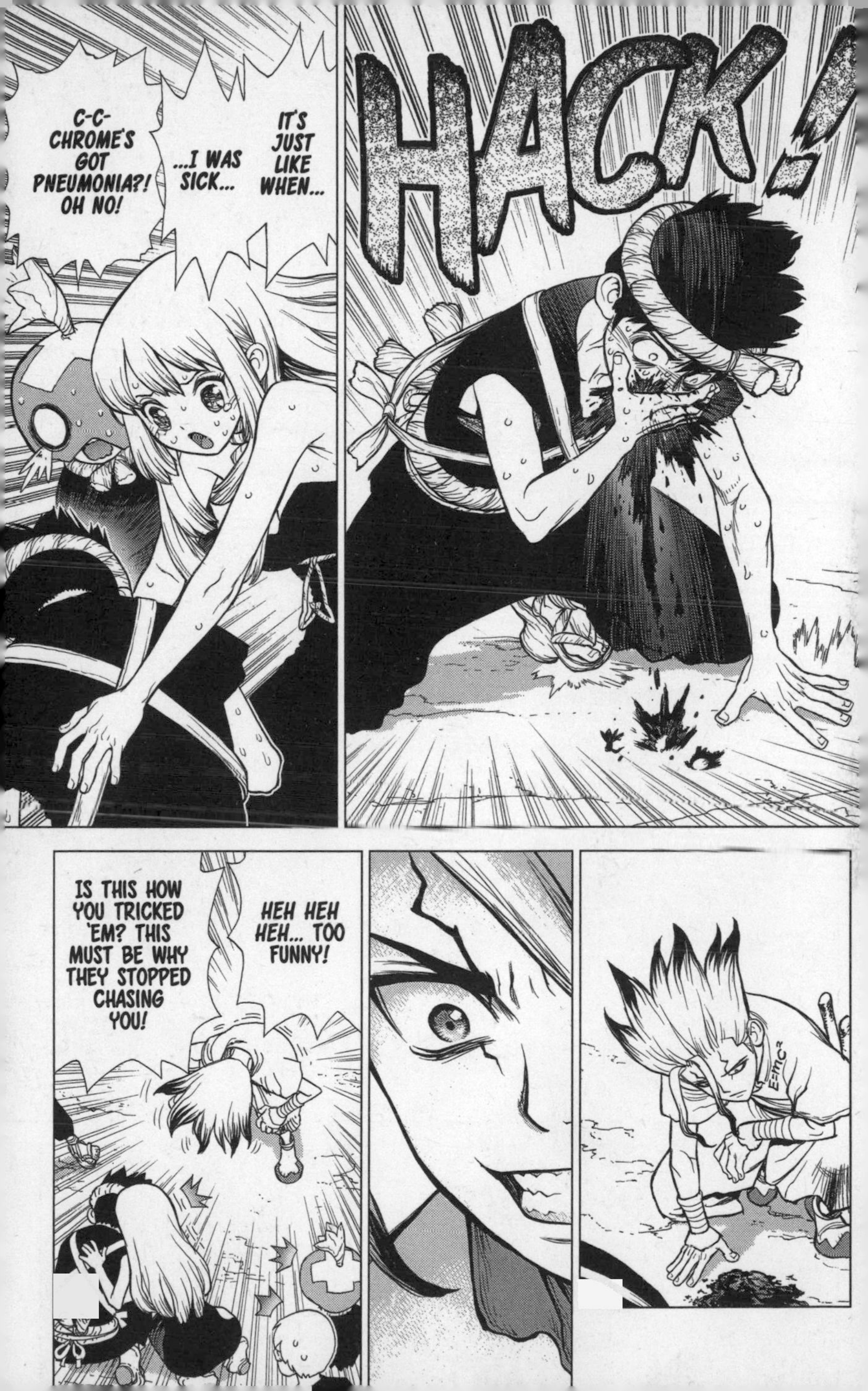
HACK!
IT'S JUST LIKE WHEN...
...I WAS SICK...
C-C-CHROME'S GOT PNEUMONIA?! OH NO!
HEH HEH HEH... TOO FUNNY!
IS THIS HOW YOU TRICKED 'EM? THIS MUST BE WHY THEY STOPPED CHASING YOU!

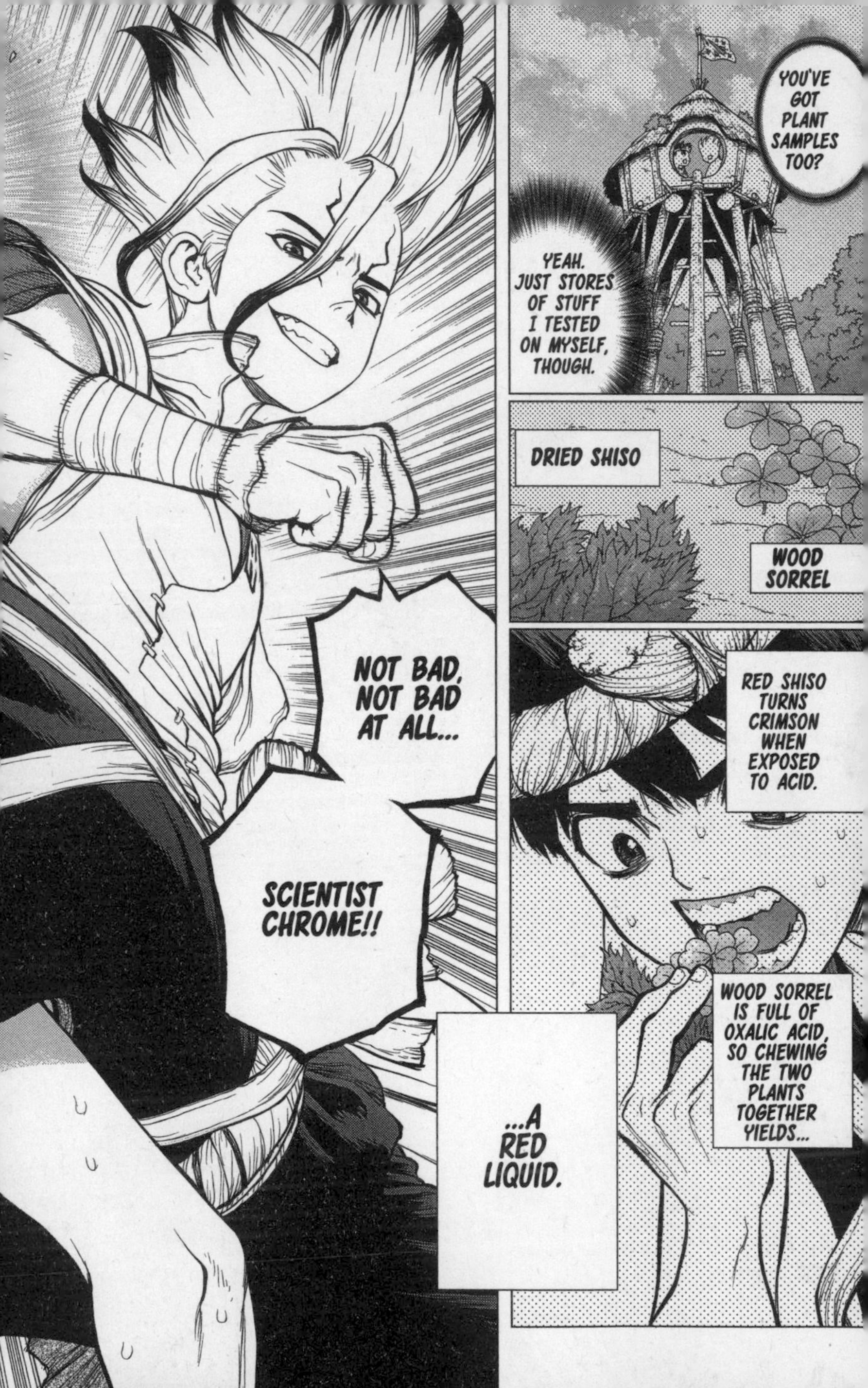
YOU'VE GOT PLANT SAMPLES TOO?
YEAH. JUST STORES OF STUFF I TESTED ON MYSELF, THOUGH.
DRIED SHISO
WOOD SORREL
RED SHISO TURNS CRIMSON WHEN EXPOSED TO ACID.
WOOD SORREL IS FULL OF OXALIC ACID, SO CHEWING THE TWO PLANTS TOGETHER YIELDS...
...A RED LIQUID.
NOT BAD, NOT BAD AT ALL...
SCIENTIST CHROME!!

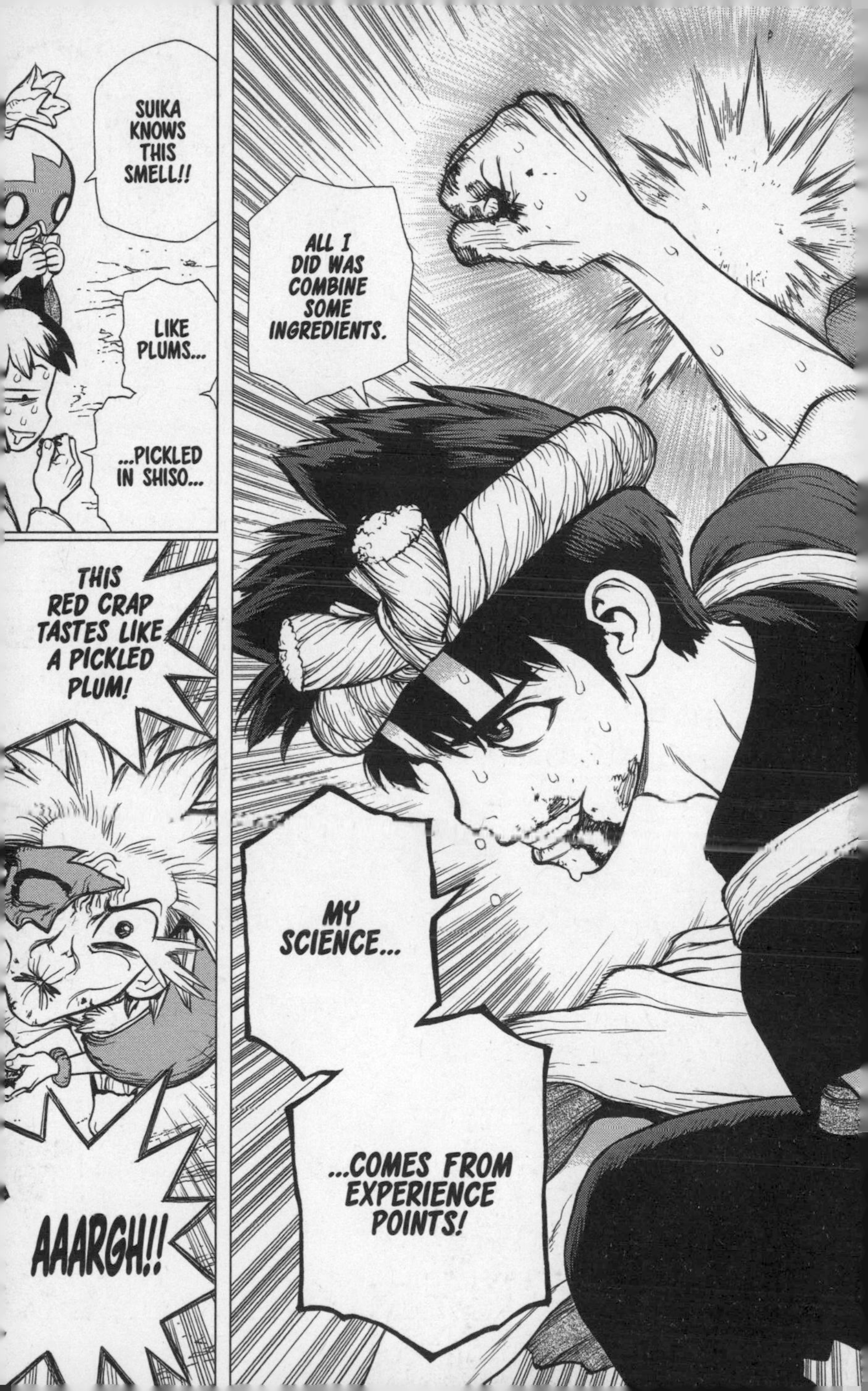
ALL I DID WAS COMBINE SOME INGREDIENTS.
MY SCIENCE...
...COMES FROM EXPERIENCE POINTS!
SUIKA KNOWS THIS SMELL!!
LIKE PLUMS...
...PICKLED IN SHISO...
THIS RED CRAP TASTES LIKE A PICKLED PLUM!
AAARGH!!

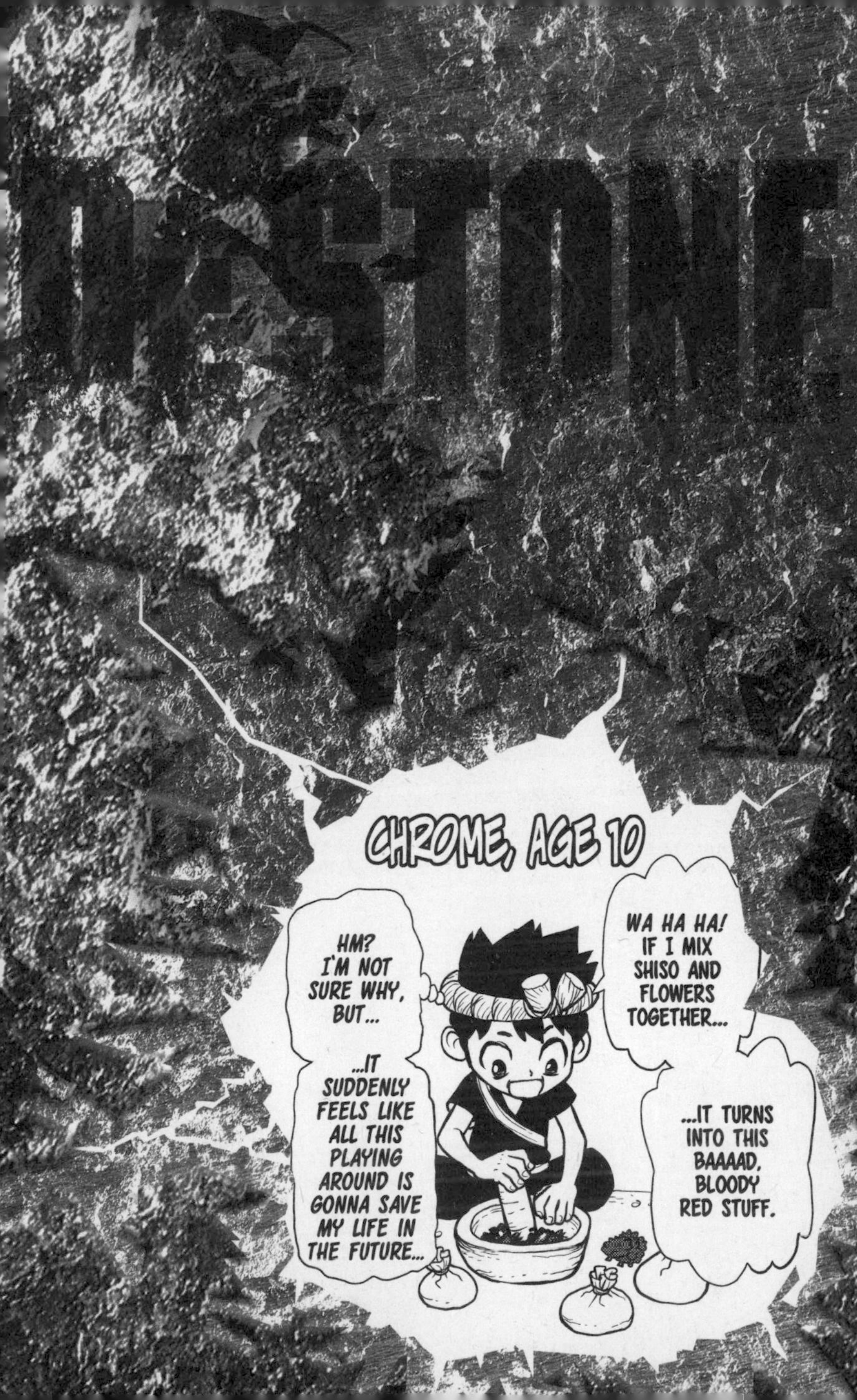
Dr. STONE
CHROME, AGE 10
WA HA HA! IF I MIX SHISO AND FLOWERS TOGETHER...
...IT TURNS INTO THIS BAAAAD, BLOODY RED STUFF.
HM? I'M NOT SURE WHY, BUT...
...IT SUDDENLY FEELS LIKE ALL THIS PLAYING AROUND IS GONNA SAVE MY LIFE IN THE FUTURE...

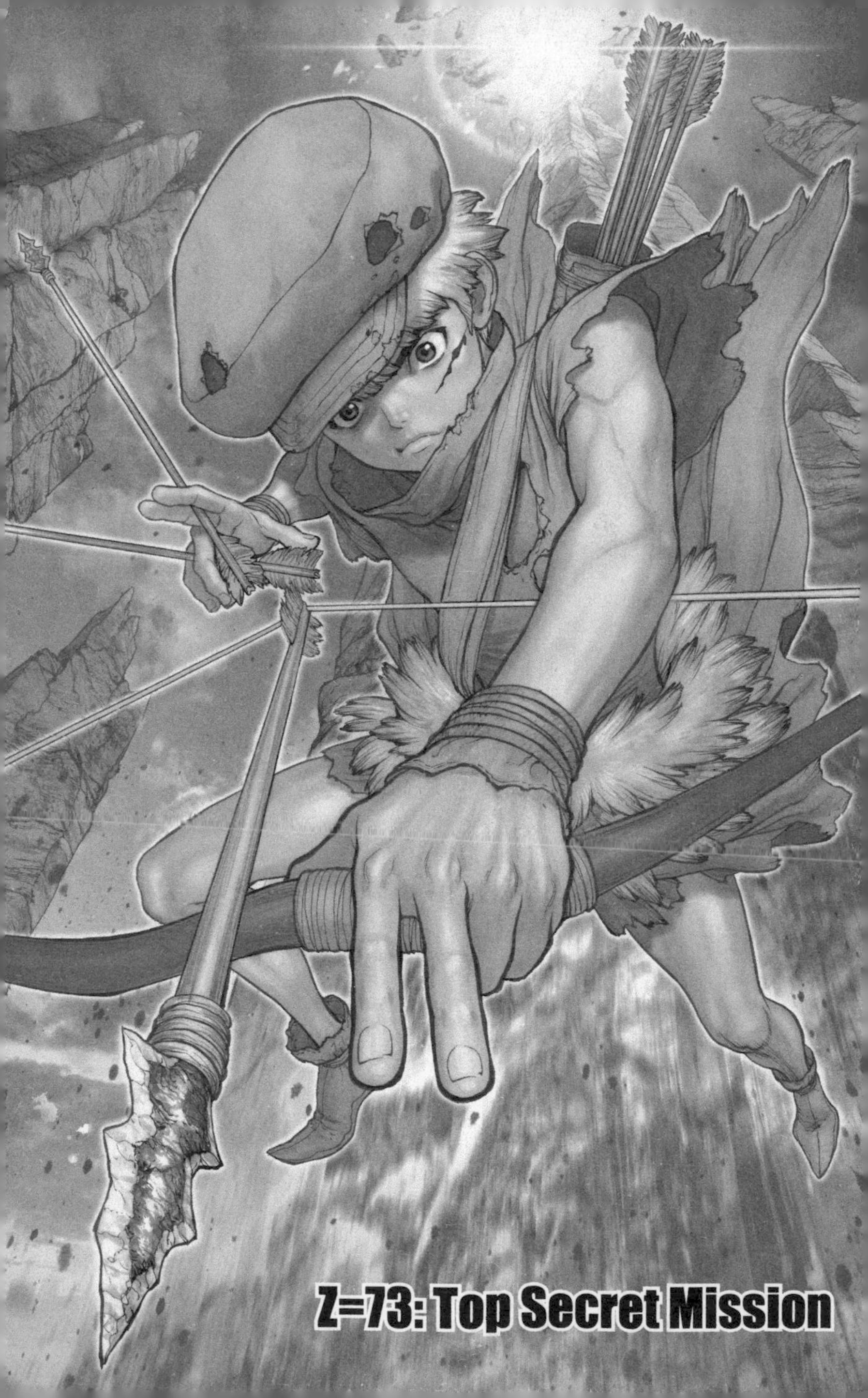
Z=73: Top Secret Mission

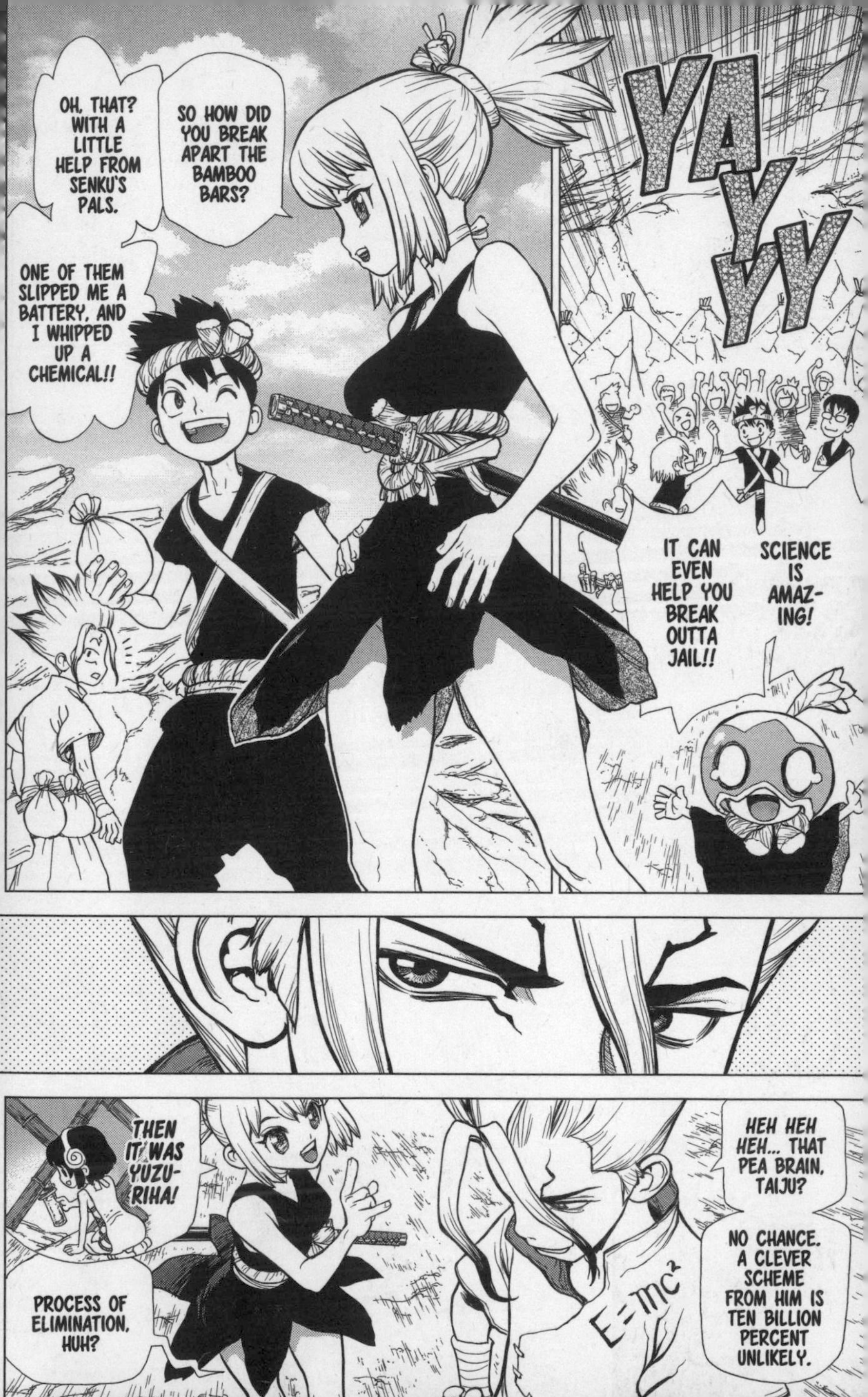
YAYYYY
SCIENCE IS AMAZ-ING!
IT CAN EVEN HELP YOU BREAK OUTTA JAIL!!
SO HOW DID YOU BREAK APART THE BAMBOO BARS?
OH, THAT? WITH A LITTLE HELP FROM SENKU'S PALS.
ONE OF THEM SLIPPED ME A BATTERY, AND I WHIPPED UP A CHEMICAL!!
HEH HEH HEH... THAT PEA BRAIN, TAIJU?
NO CHANCE. A CLEVER SCHEME FROM HIM IS TEN BILLION PERCENT UNLIKELY.
E=mc²
THEN IT WAS YUZURIHA!
PROCESS OF ELIMINATION, HUH?

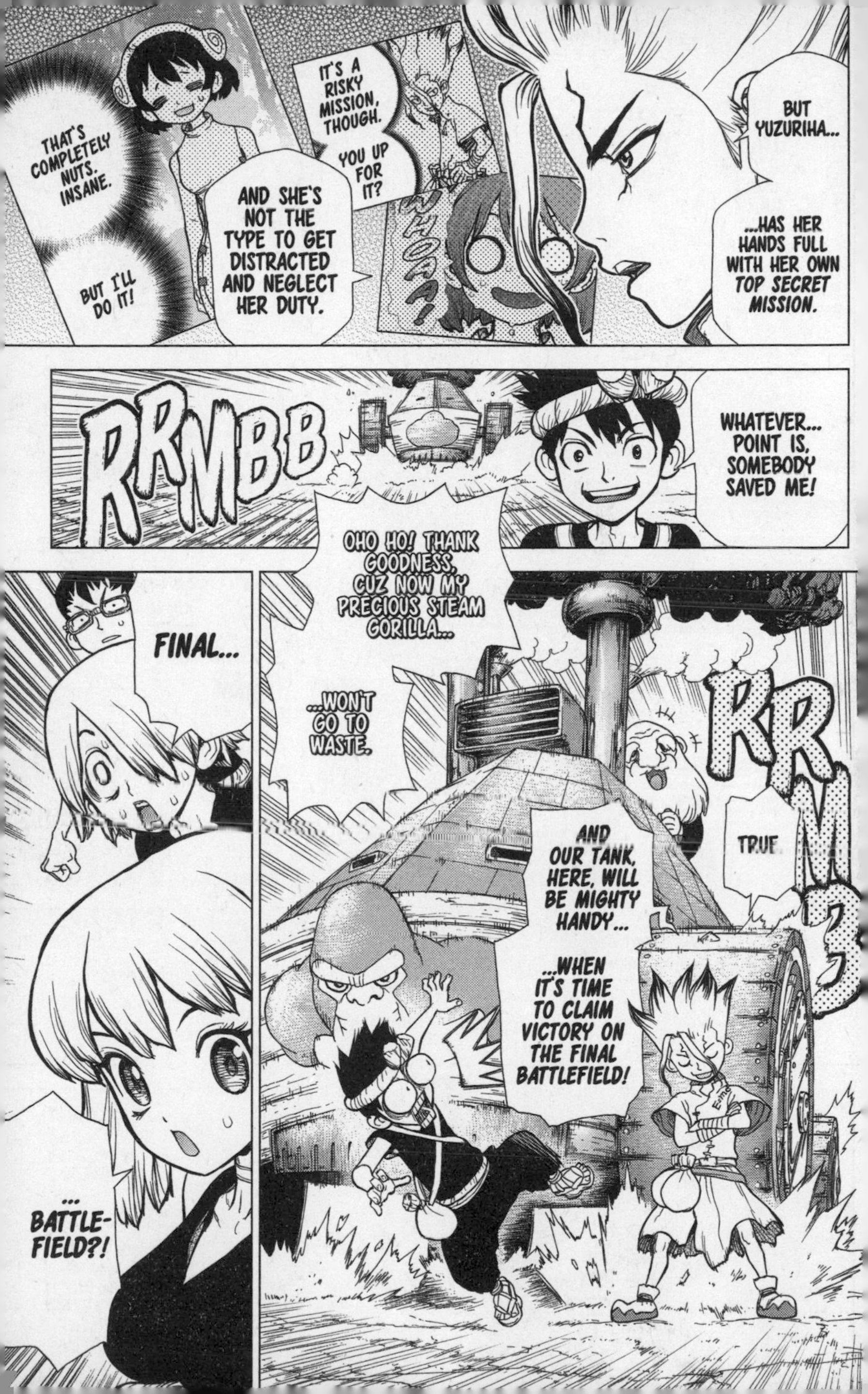

BUT YUZURIHA...
...HAS HER HANDS FULL WITH HER OWN TOP SECRET MISSION.
IT'S A RISKY MISSION, THOUGH.
YOU UP FOR IT?
AND SHE'S NOT THE TYPE TO GET DISTRACTED AND NEGLECT HER DUTY.
THAT'S COMPLETELY NUTS. INSANE.
BUT I'LL DO IT!
WHATEVER... POINT IS, SOMEBODY SAVED ME!
RRMBB
OHO HO! THANK GOODNESS, CUZ NOW MY PRECIOUS STEAM GORILLA...
...WON'T GO TO WASTE.
TRUE.
AND OUR TANK, HERE, WILL BE MIGHTY HANDY...
...WHEN IT'S TIME TO CLAIM VICTORY ON THE FINAL BATTLEFIELD!
FINAL...
...BATTLE-FIELD?!

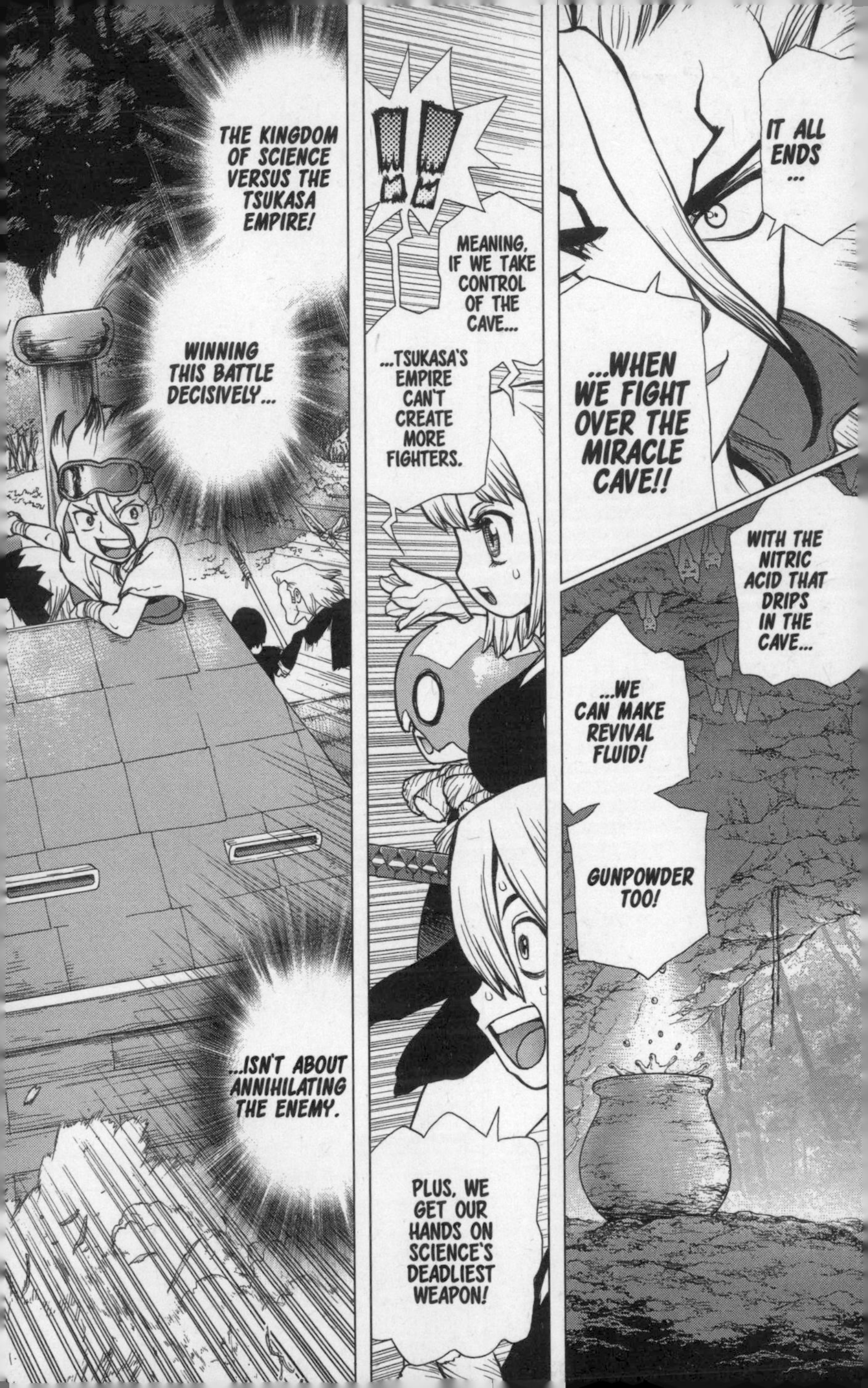
IT ALL ENDS ...
...WHEN WE FIGHT OVER THE MIRACLE CAVE!!
WITH THE NITRIC ACID THAT DRIPS IN THE CAVE...
...WE CAN MAKE REVIVAL FLUID!
GUNPOWDER TOO!
!!
MEANING, IF WE TAKE CONTROL OF THE CAVE...
...TSUKASA'S EMPIRE CAN'T CREATE MORE FIGHTERS.
PLUS, WE GET OUR HANDS ON SCIENCE'S DEADLIEST WEAPON!
THE KINGDOM OF SCIENCE VERSUS THE TSUKASA EMPIRE!
WINNING THIS BATTLE DECISIVELY...
...ISN'T ABOUT ANNIHILATING THE ENEMY.

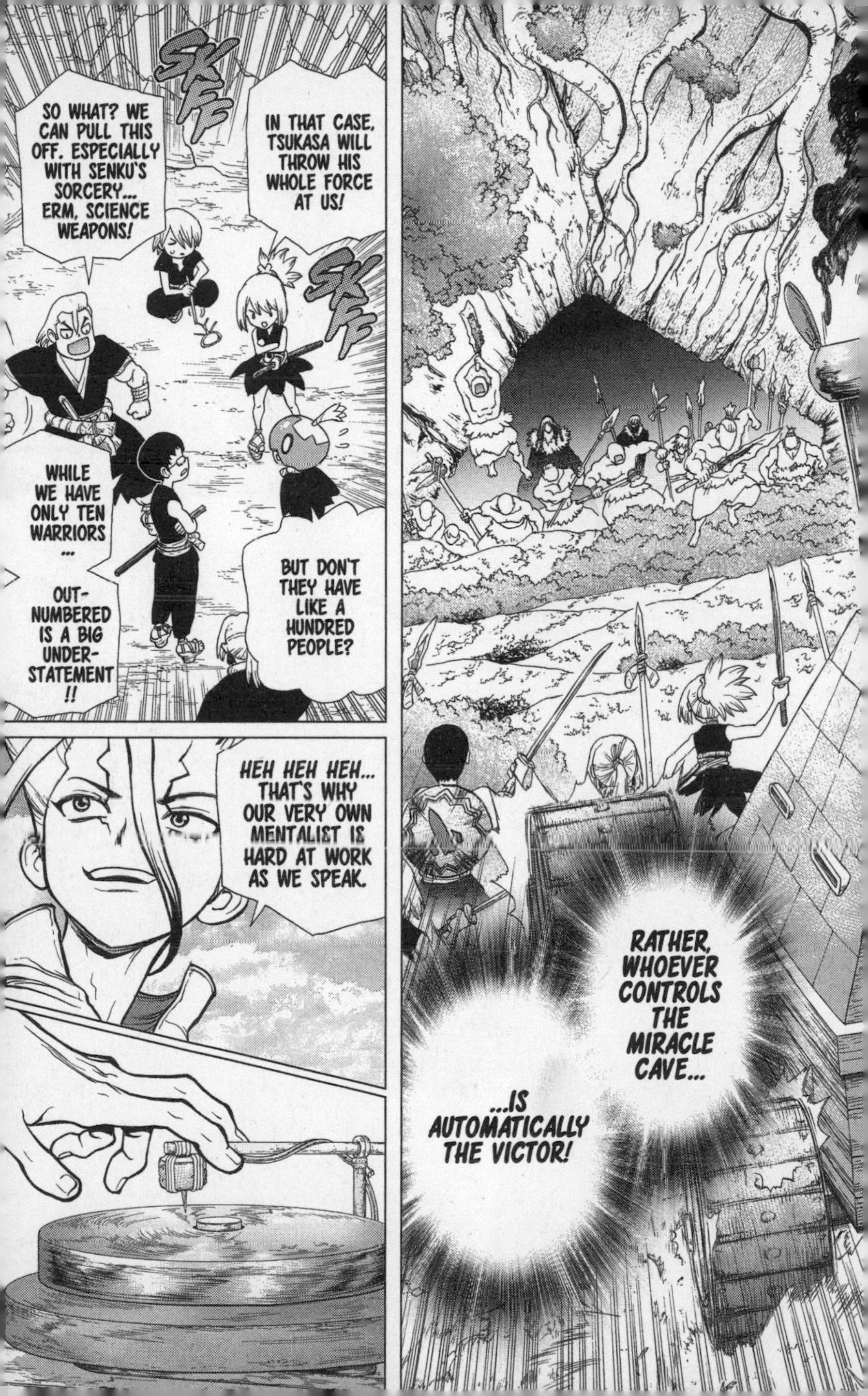
RATHER, WHOEVER CONTROLS THE MIRACLE CAVE...
...IS AUTOMATICALLY THE VICTOR!
IN THAT CASE, TSUKASA WILL THROW HIS WHOLE FORCE AT US!
SKFF
SKFF
SO WHAT? WE CAN PULL THIS OFF. ESPECIALLY WITH SENKU'S SORCERY... ERM, SCIENCE WEAPONS!
BUT DON'T THEY HAVE LIKE A HUNDRED PEOPLE?
WHILE WE HAVE ONLY TEN WARRIORS...
OUT-NUMBERED IS A BIG UNDER-STATEMENT!!
HEH HEH HEH... THAT'S WHY OUR VERY OWN MENTALIST IS HARD AT WORK AS WE SPEAK.

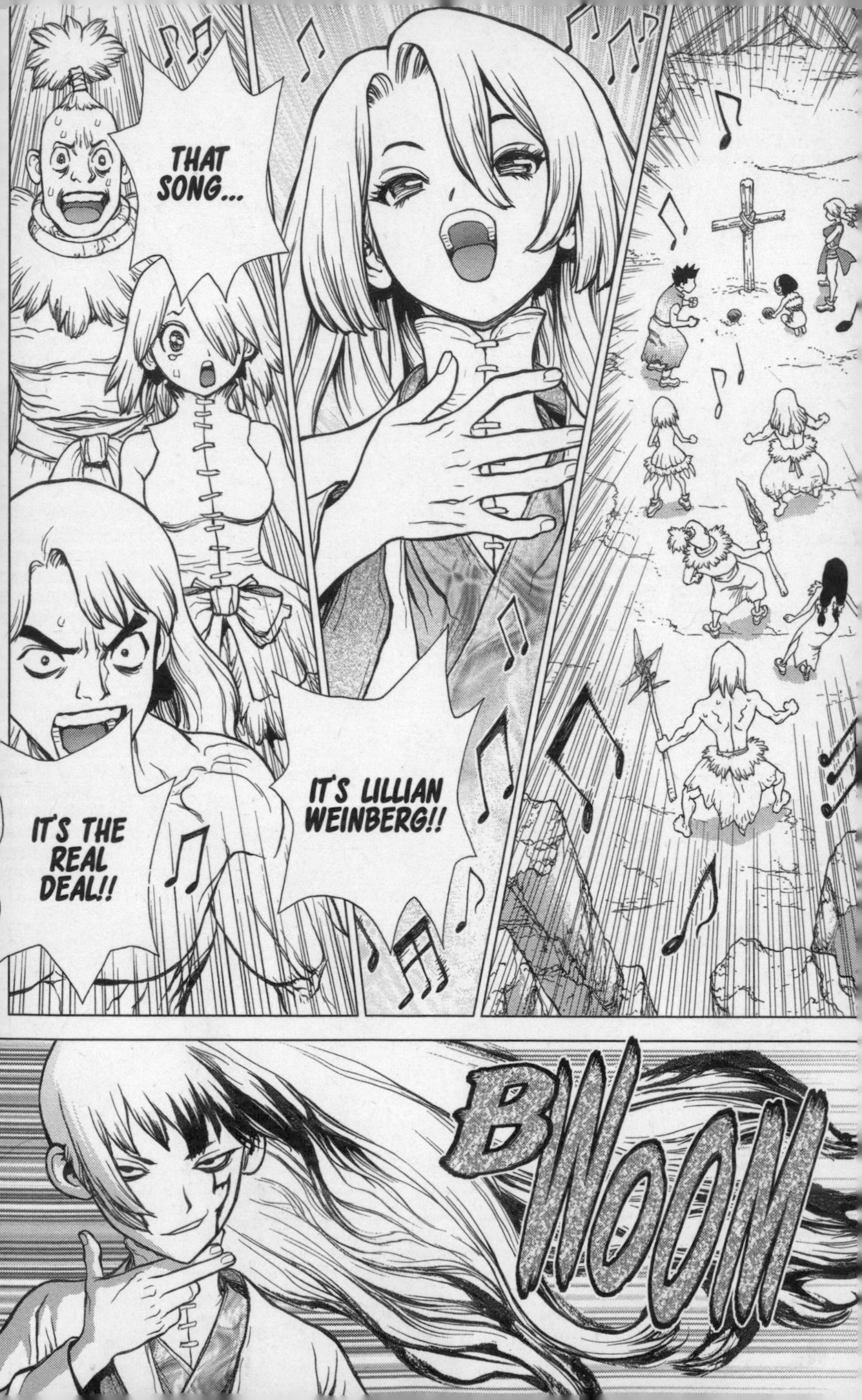
IT'S LILLIAN WEINBERG!!
THAT SONG...
IT'S THE REAL DEAL!!
BWOOM

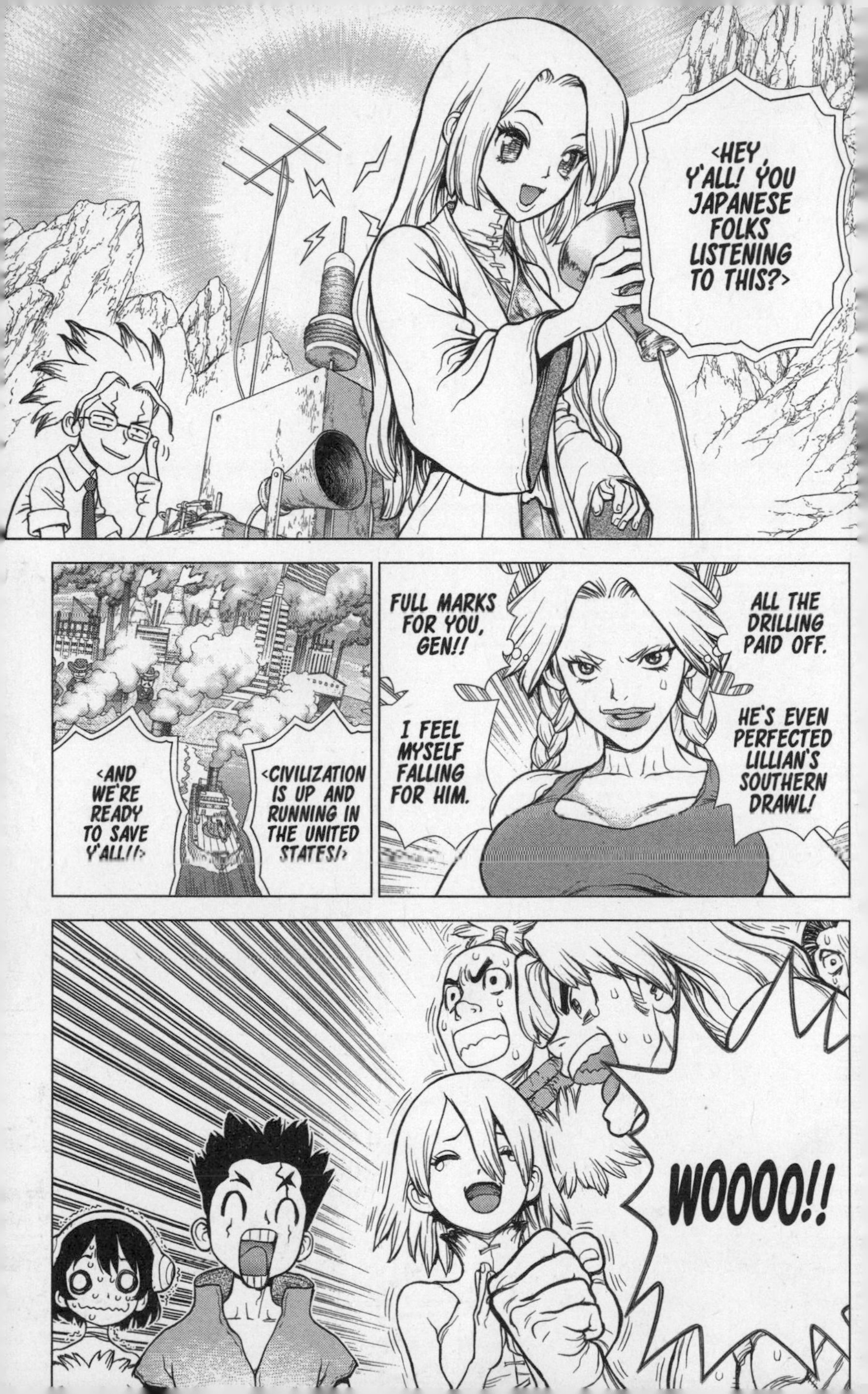
<HEY, Y'ALL! YOU JAPANESE FOLKS LISTENING TO THIS?>
ALL THE DRILLING PAID OFF.
FULL MARKS FOR YOU, GEN!!
HE'S EVEN PERFECTED LILLIAN'S SOUTHERN DRAWL!
I FEEL MYSELF FALLING FOR HIM.
<CIVILIZATION IS UP AND RUNNING IN THE UNITED STATES!>
<AND WE'RE READY TO SAVE Y'ALL!!>
WOOOO!!

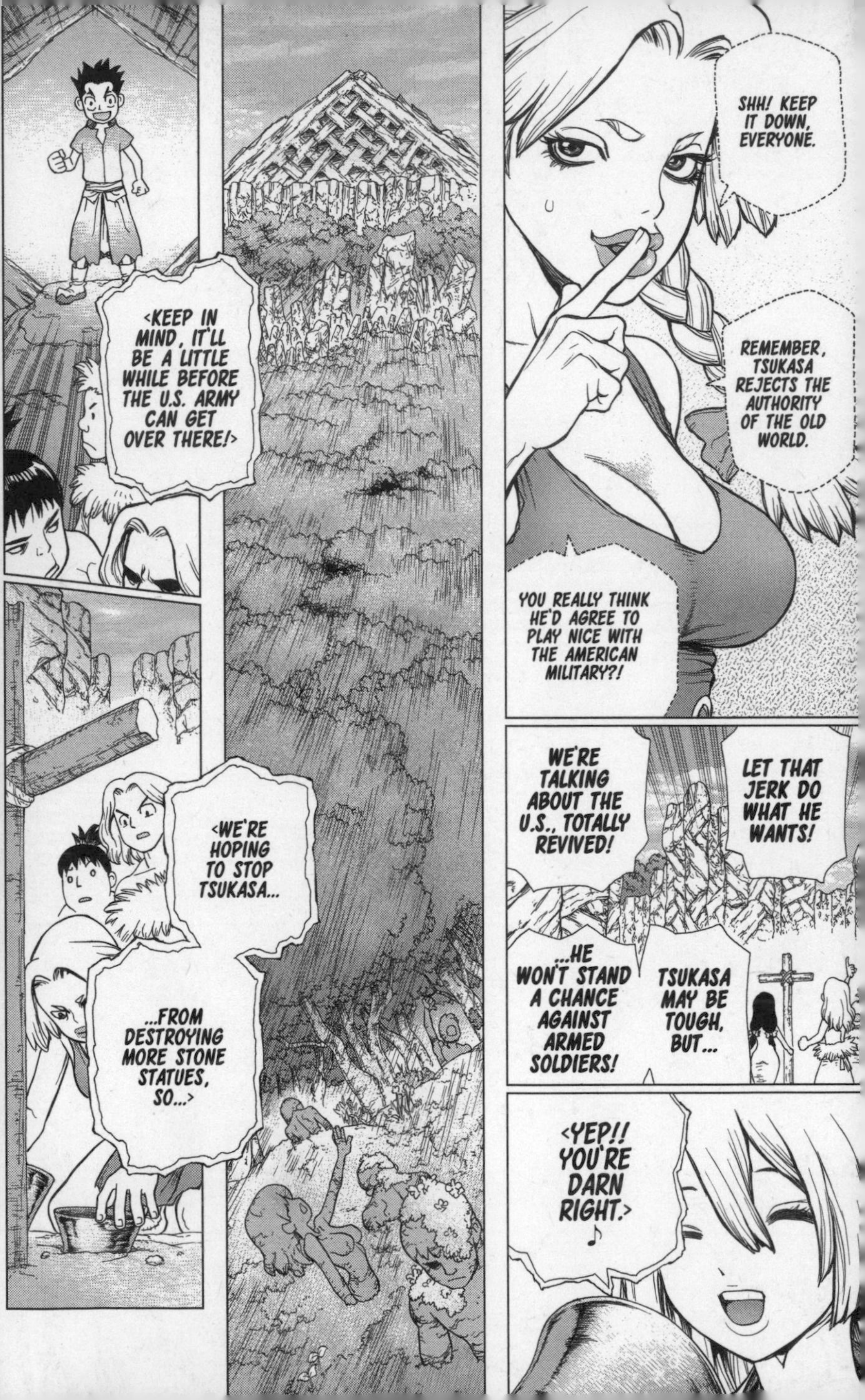
SHH! KEEP IT DOWN, EVERYONE.
REMEMBER, TSUKASA REJECTS THE AUTHORITY OF THE OLD WORLD.
YOU REALLY THINK HE'D AGREE TO PLAY NICE WITH THE AMERICAN MILITARY?!
LET THAT JERK DO WHAT HE WANTS!
WE'RE TALKING ABOUT THE U.S., TOTALLY REVIVED!
TSUKASA MAY BE TOUGH, BUT...
...HE WON'T STAND A CHANCE AGAINST ARMED SOLDIERS!
<YEP!! YOU'RE DARN RIGHT.> ♪
<KEEP IN MIND, IT'LL BE A LITTLE WHILE BEFORE THE U.S. ARMY CAN GET OVER THERE!>
<WE'RE HOPING TO STOP TSUKASA...
...FROM DESTROYING MORE STONE STATUES, SO...>

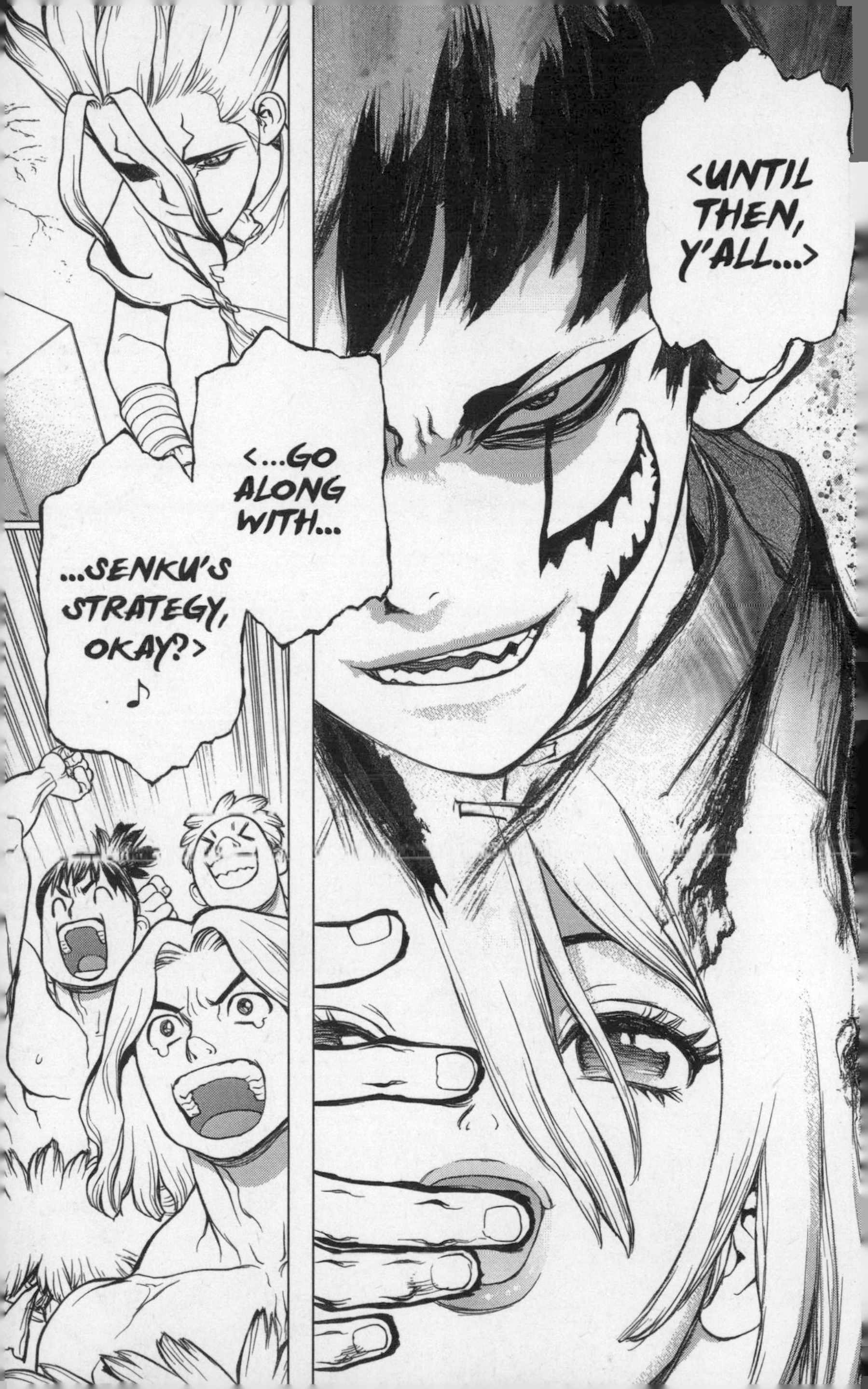
<UNTIL THEN, Y'ALL...>
<...GO ALONG WITH...
...SENKU'S STRATEGY, OKAY?> ♪

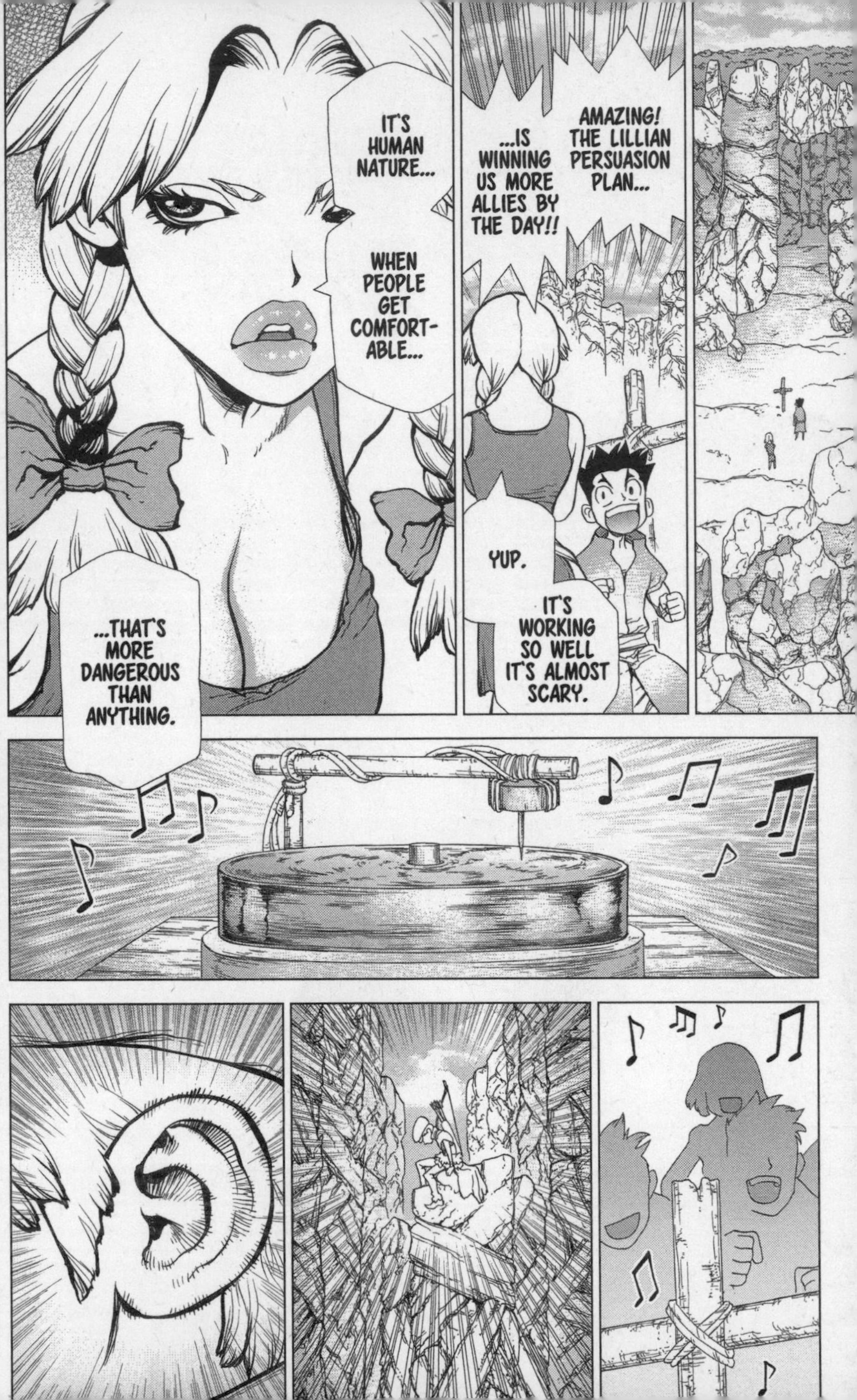
AMAZING! THE LILLIAN PERSUASION PLAN...
...IS WINNING US MORE ALLIES BY THE DAY!!
YUP.
IT'S WORKING SO WELL IT'S ALMOST SCARY.
IT'S HUMAN NATURE...
WHEN PEOPLE GET COMFORTABLE...
...THAT'S MORE DANGEROUS THAN ANYTHING.

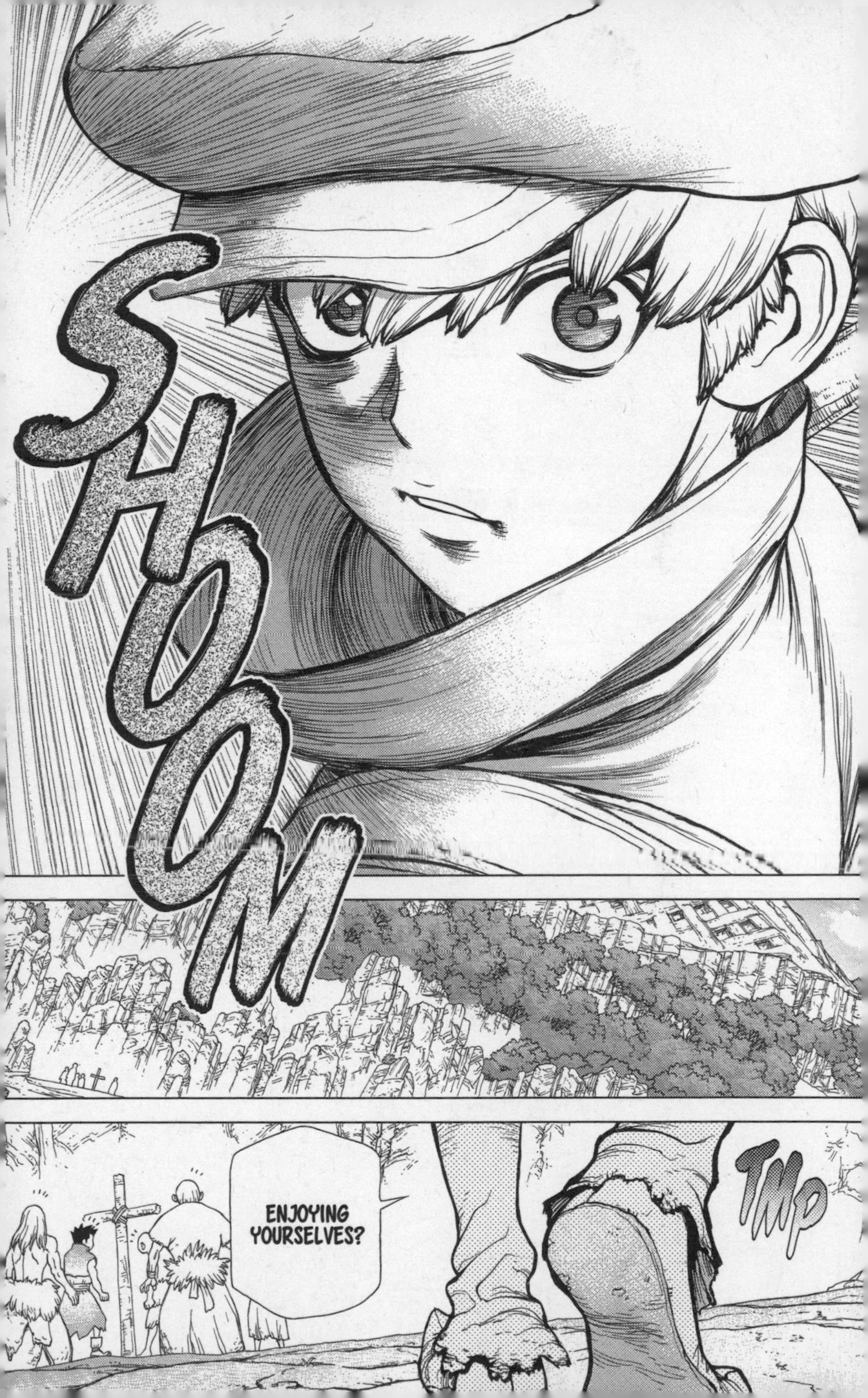
SHOOM
TMP
ENJOYING YOURSELVES?

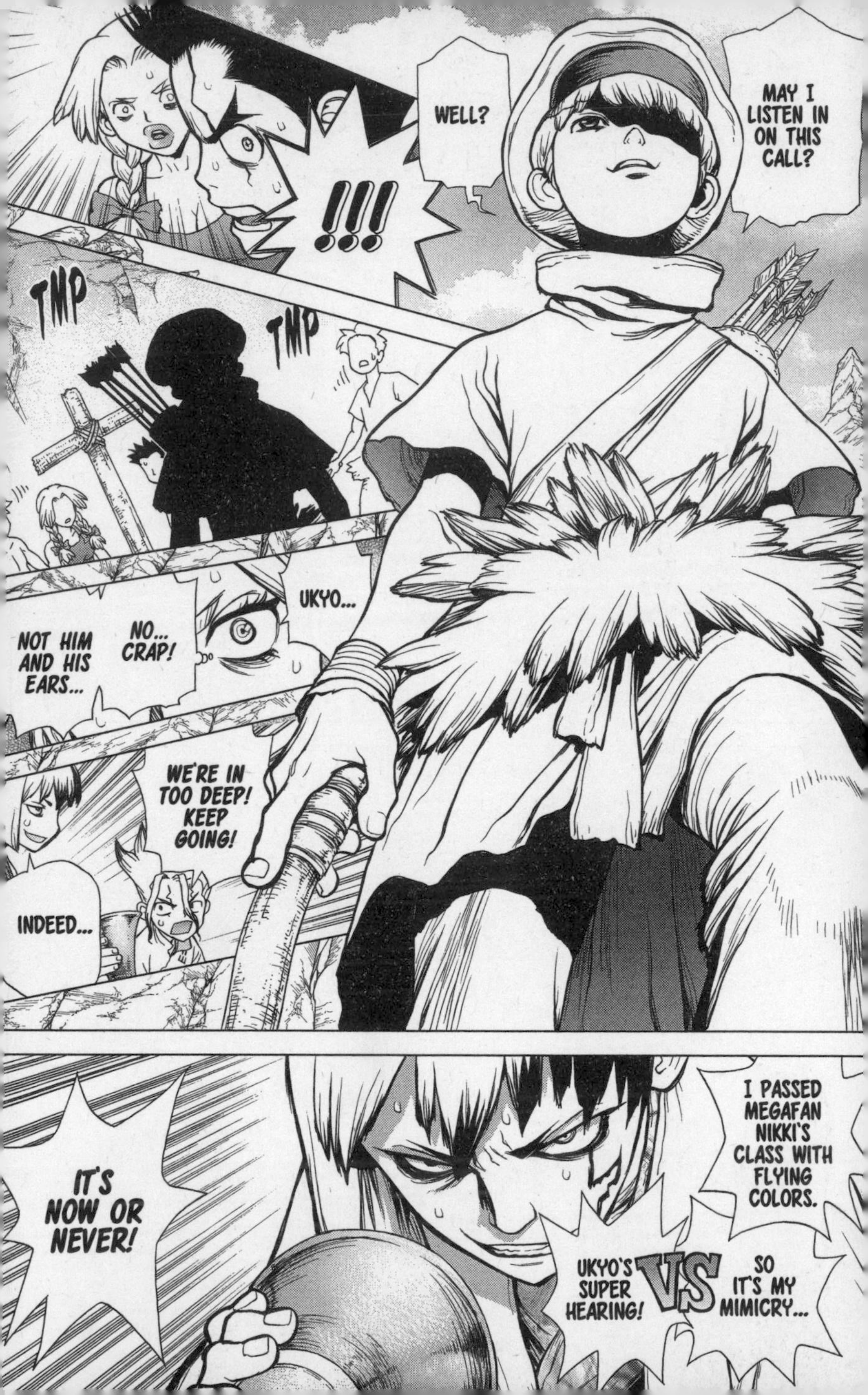
MAY I LISTEN IN ON THIS CALL?
WELL?
!!!
TMP
TMP
UKYO...
NO... CRAP!
NOT HIM AND HIS EARS...
WE'RE IN TOO DEEP! KEEP GOING!
INDEED...
I PASSED MEGAFAN NIKKI'S CLASS WITH FLYING COLORS.
SO IT'S MY MIMICRY...
VS
UKYO'S SUPER HEARING!
IT'S NOW OR NEVER!

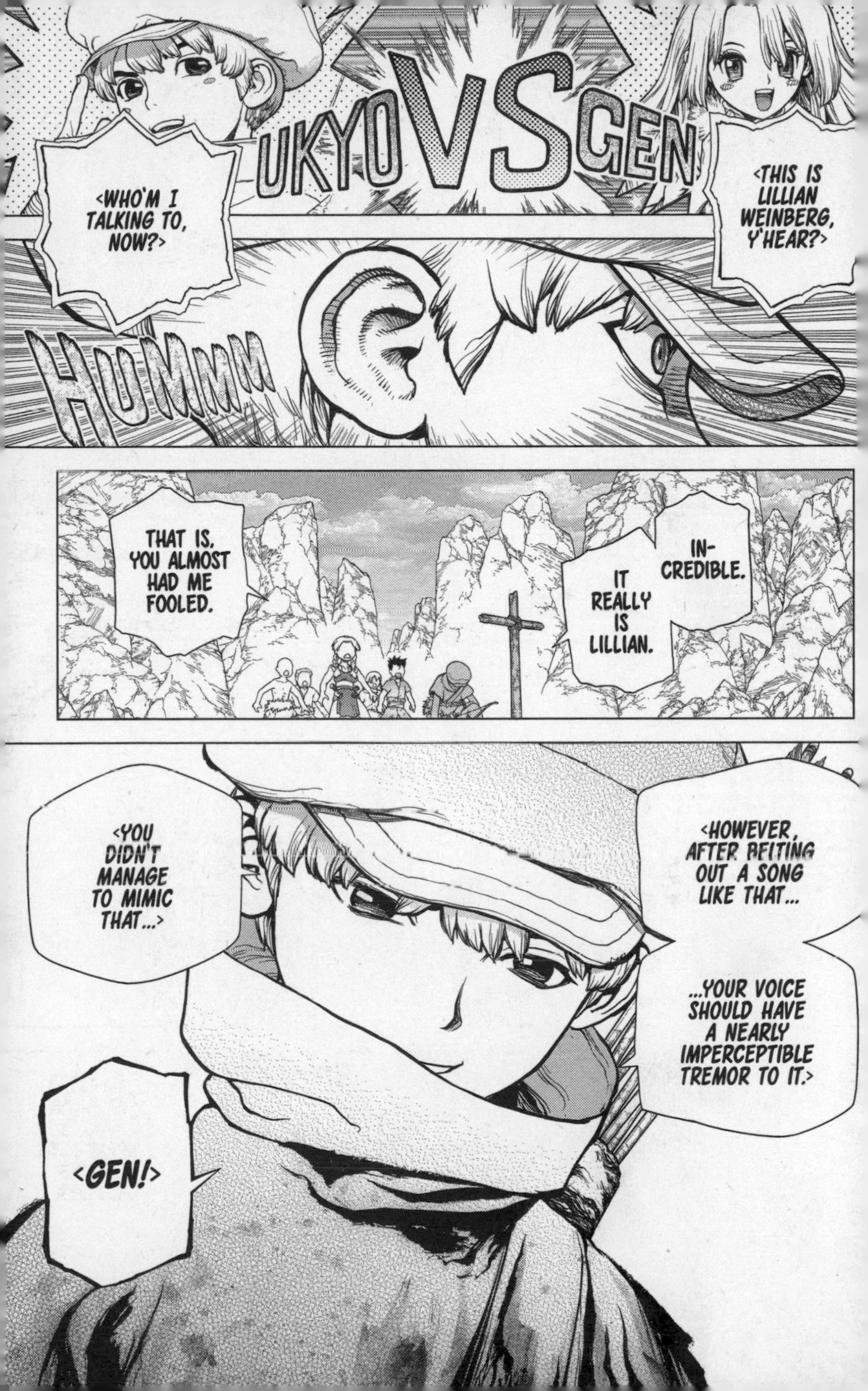
<THIS IS LILLIAN WEINBERG, Y'HEAR?>
UKYO VS GEN
<WHO'M I TALKING TO, NOW?>
HUMMM
IN-CREDIBLE.
IT REALLY IS LILLIAN.
THAT IS, YOU ALMOST HAD ME FOOLED.
<HOWEVER, AFTER BELTING OUT A SONG LIKE THAT...
...YOUR VOICE SHOULD HAVE A NEARLY IMPERCEPTIBLE TREMOR TO IT.>
<YOU DIDN'T MANAGE TO MIMIC THAT...>
<GEN!>

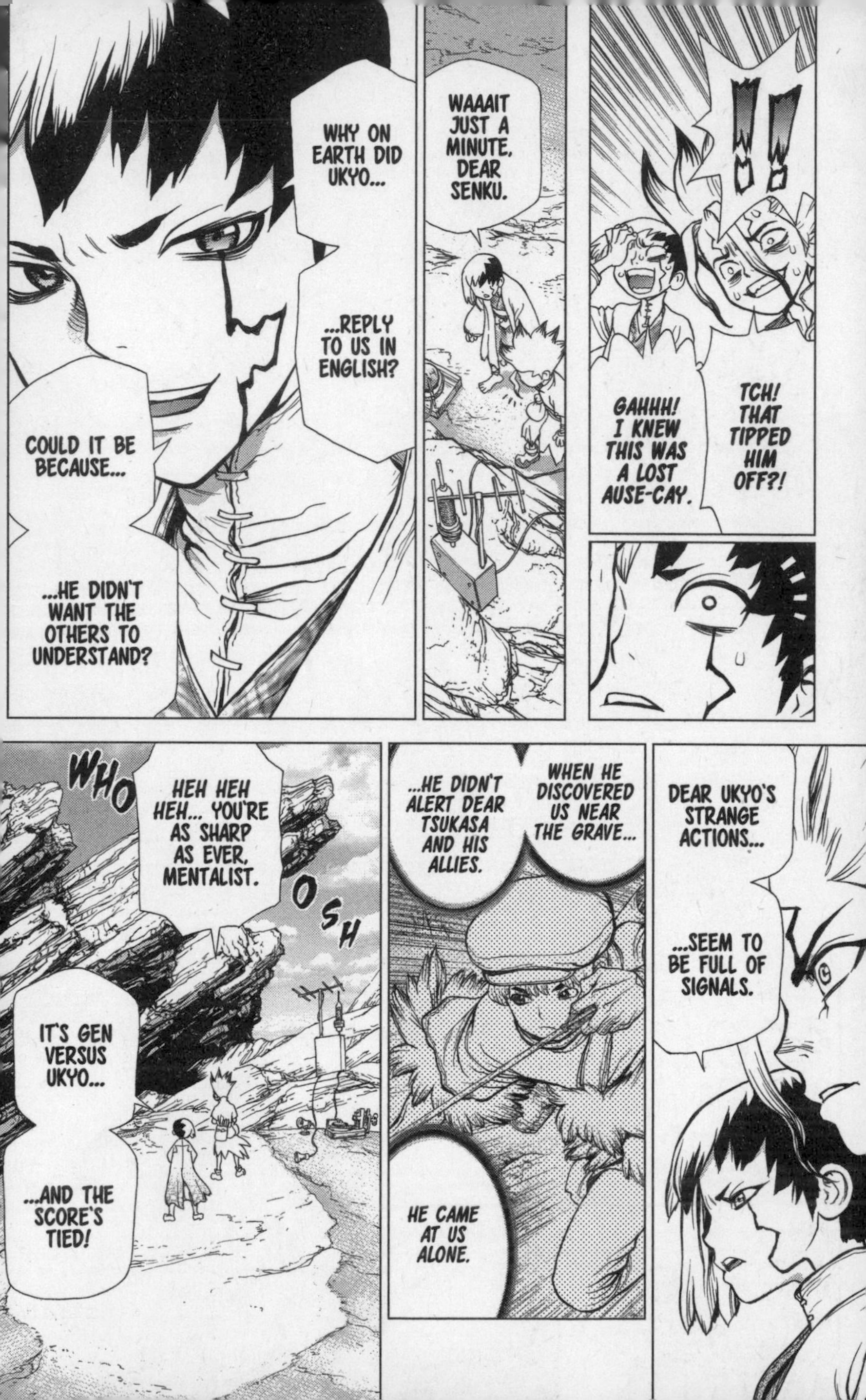
!!
TCH! THAT TIPPED HIM OFF?!
GAHHH! I KNEW THIS WAS A LOST AUSE-CAY.
WAAAIT JUST A MINUTE, DEAR SENKU.
WHY ON EARTH DID UKYO...
...REPLY TO US IN ENGLISH?
COULD IT BE BECAUSE...
...HE DIDN'T WANT THE OTHERS TO UNDERSTAND?
DEAR UKYO'S STRANGE ACTIONS...
...SEEM TO BE FULL OF SIGNALS.
WHEN HE DISCOVERED US NEAR THE GRAVE...
...HE DIDN'T ALERT DEAR TSUKASA AND HIS ALLIES.
HE CAME AT US ALONE.
WHOOSH
HEH HEH HEH... YOU'RE AS SHARP AS EVER, MENTALIST.
IT'S GEN VERSUS UKYO...
...AND THE SCORE'S TIED!

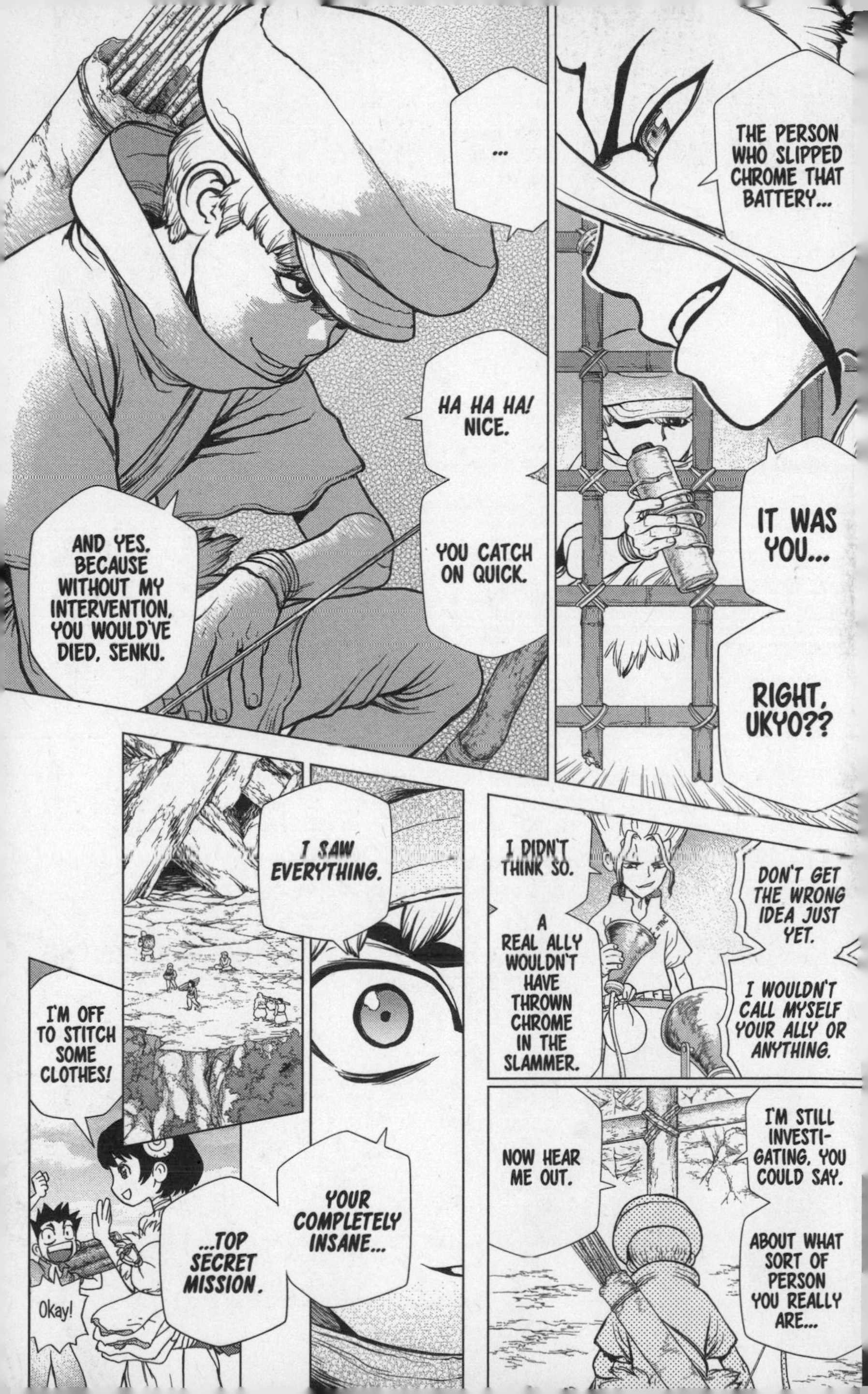
THE PERSON WHO SLIPPED CHROME THAT BATTERY...
IT WAS YOU...
RIGHT, UKYO??
...
HA HA HA! NICE.
YOU CATCH ON QUICK.
AND YES. BECAUSE WITHOUT MY INTERVENTION, YOU WOULD'VE DIED, SENKU.
DON'T GET THE WRONG IDEA JUST YET.
I WOULDN'T CALL MYSELF YOUR ALLY OR ANYTHING.
I DIDN'T THINK SO.
A REAL ALLY WOULDN'T HAVE THROWN CHROME IN THE SLAMMER.
I'M STILL INVESTI-GATING, YOU COULD SAY.
ABOUT WHAT SORT OF PERSON YOU REALLY ARE...
NOW HEAR ME OUT.
I SAW EVERYTHING.
YOUR COMPLETELY INSANE...
...TOP SECRET MISSION.
I'M OFF TO STITCH SOME CLOTHES!
Okay!

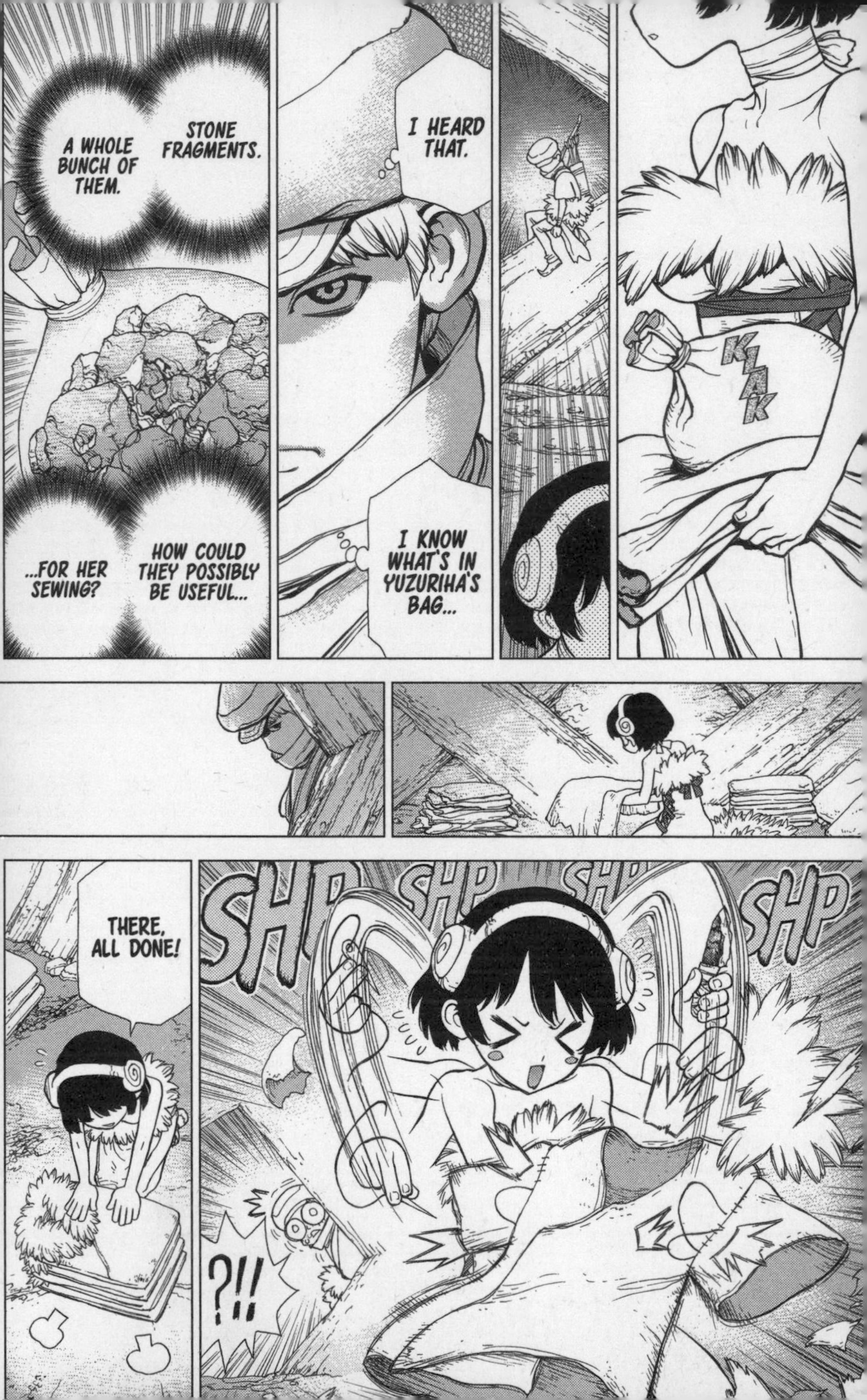
KLAK
I HEARD THAT.
I KNOW WHAT'S IN YUZURIHA'S BAG...
STONE FRAGMENTS.
A WHOLE BUNCH OF THEM.
HOW COULD THEY POSSIBLY BE USEFUL...
...FOR HER SEWING?
SHP SHP SHP SHP
?!!
THERE, ALL DONE!

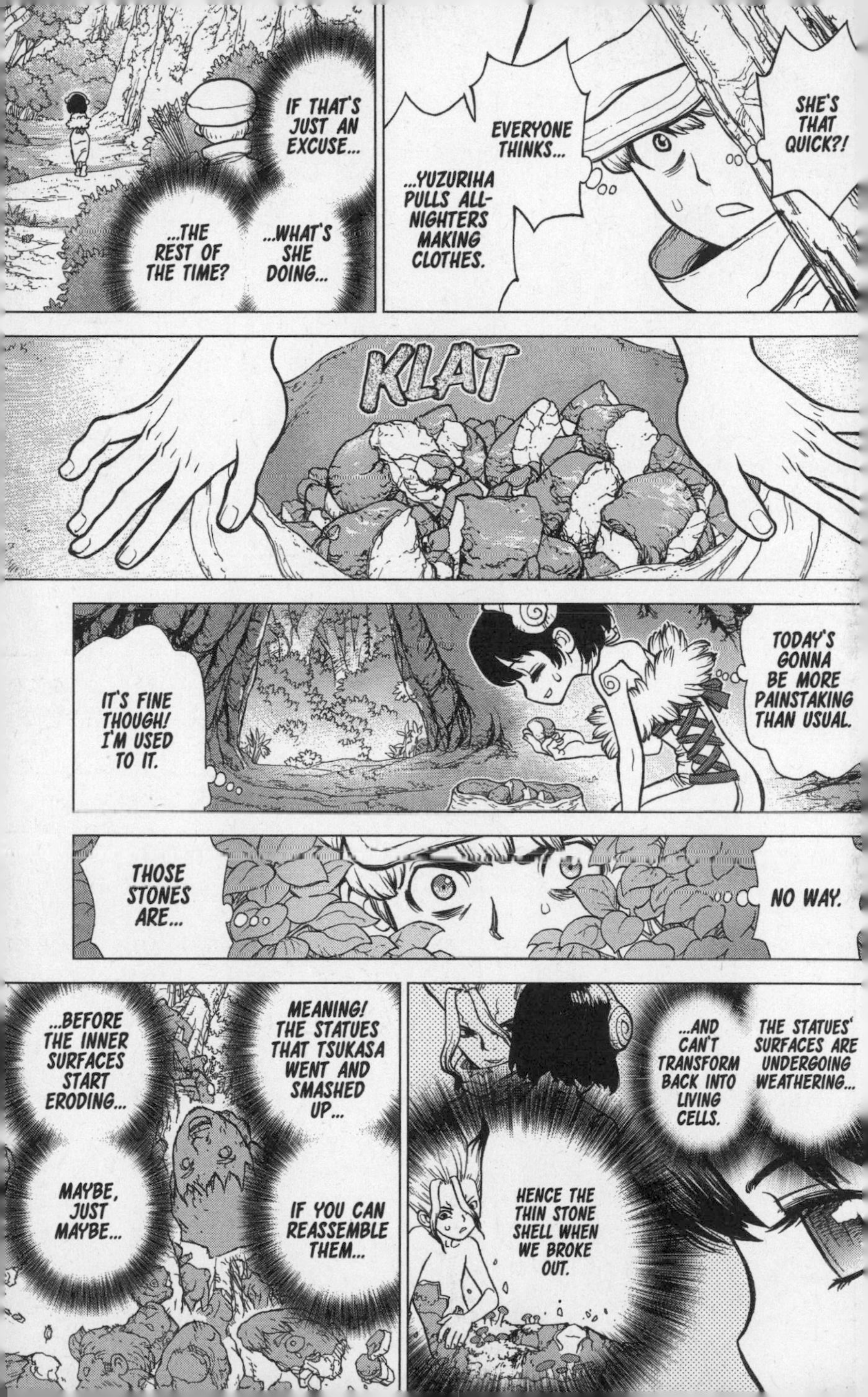
SHE'S THAT QUICK?!
EVERYONE THINKS...
...YUZURIHA PULLS ALL-NIGHTERS MAKING CLOTHES.
IF THAT'S JUST AN EXCUSE...
...WHAT'S SHE DOING...
...THE REST OF THE TIME?
KLAT
TODAY'S GONNA BE MORE PAINSTAKING THAN USUAL.
IT'S FINE THOUGH! I'M USED TO IT.
NO WAY.
THOSE STONES ARE...
THE STATUES' SURFACES ARE UNDERGOING WEATHERING...
...AND CAN'T TRANSFORM BACK INTO LIVING CELLS.
HENCE THE THIN STONE SHELL WHEN WE BROKE OUT.
MEANING! THE STATUES THAT TSUKASA WENT AND SMASHED UP...
...BEFORE THE INNER SURFACES START ERODING...
IF YOU CAN REASSEMBLE THEM...
MAYBE, JUST MAYBE...

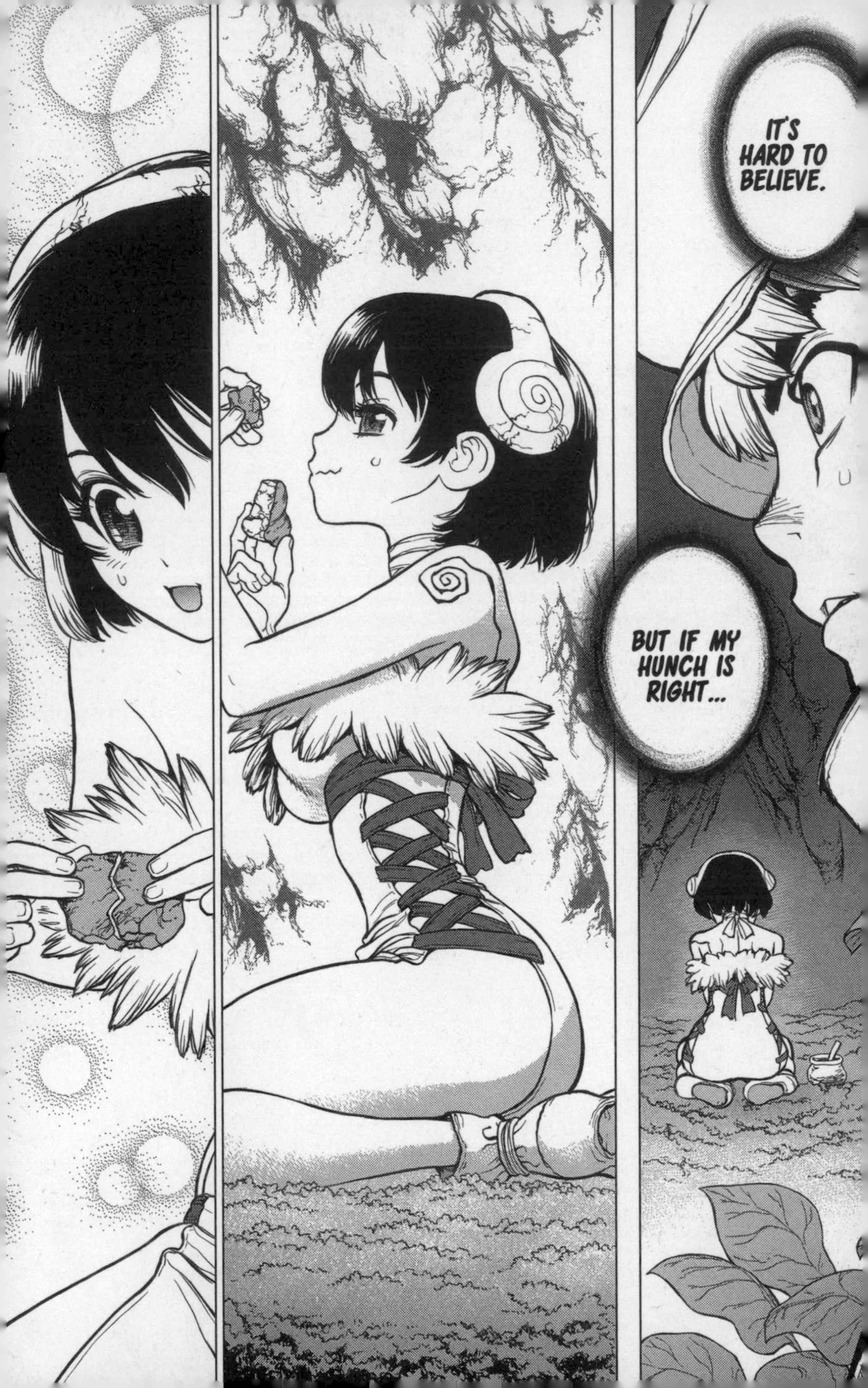
IT'S HARD TO BELIEVE.
BUT IF MY HUNCH IS RIGHT...

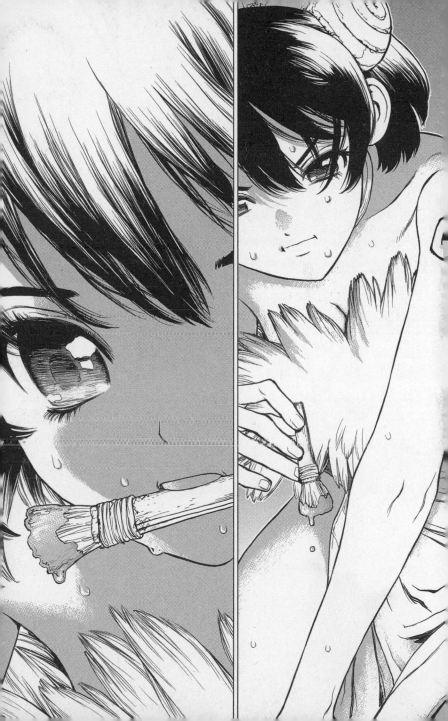

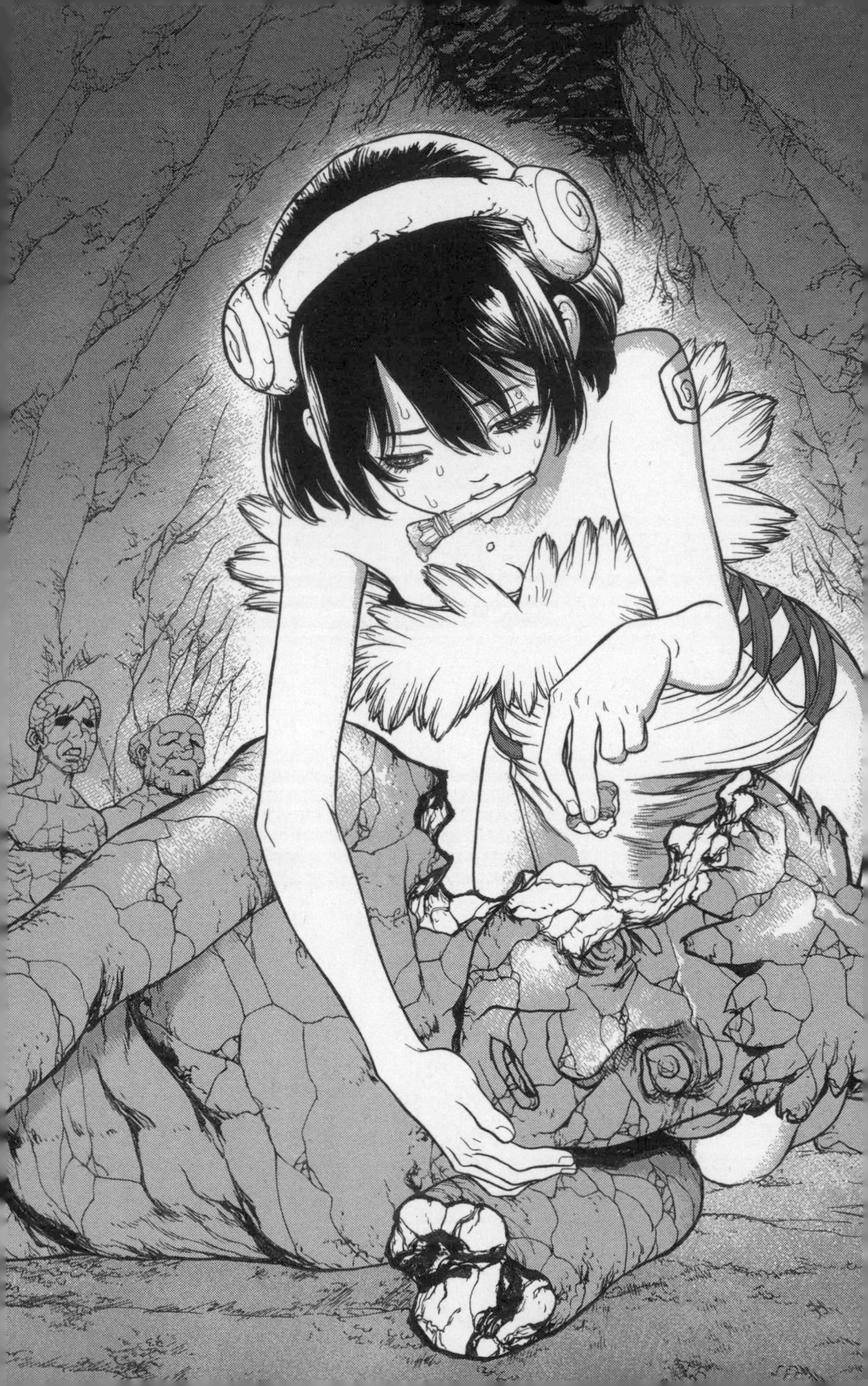

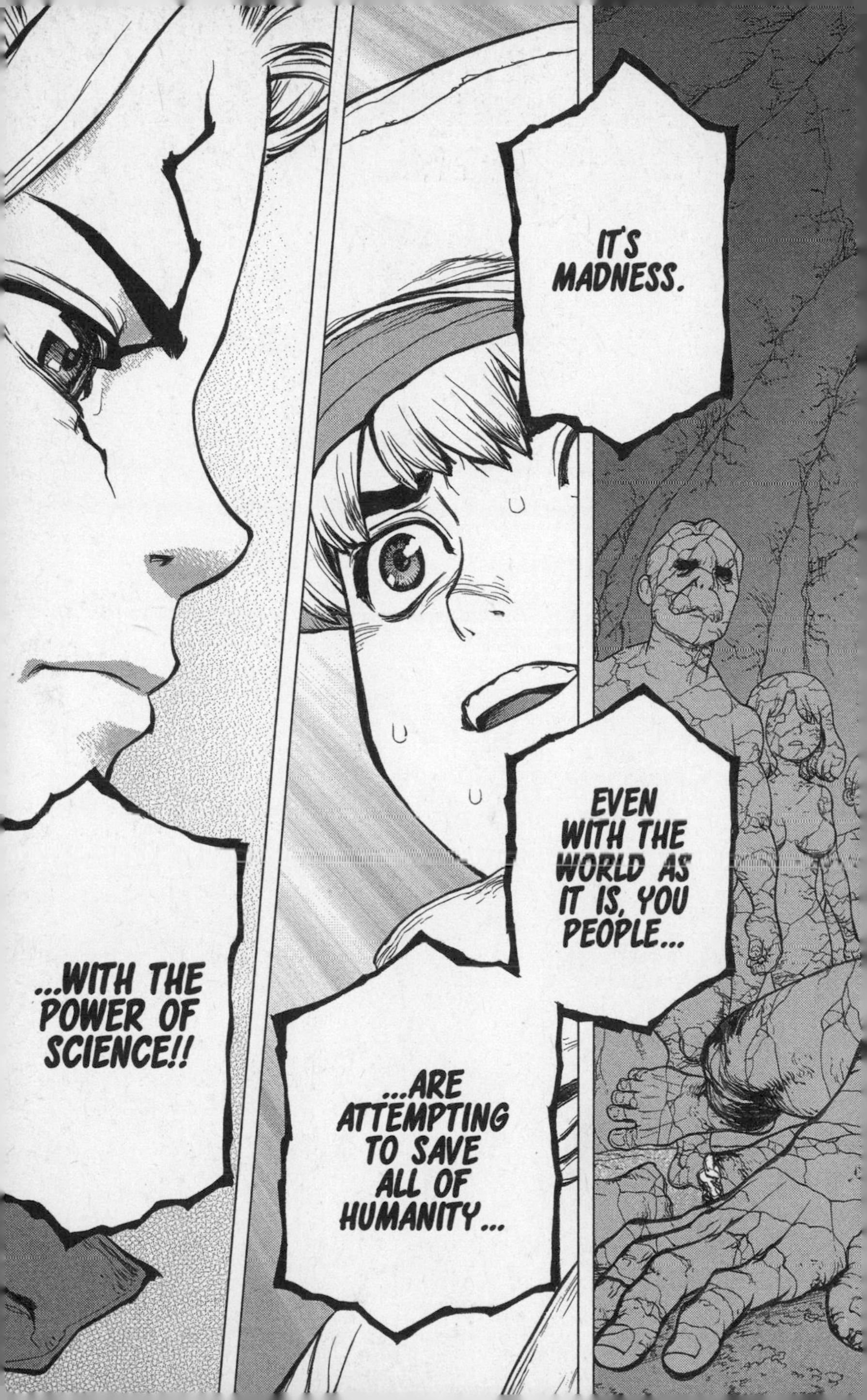
IT'S MADNESS.
EVEN WITH THE WORLD AS IT IS, YOU PEOPLE...
...ARE ATTEMPTING TO SAVE ALL OF HUMANITY...
...WITH THE POWER OF SCIENCE!!

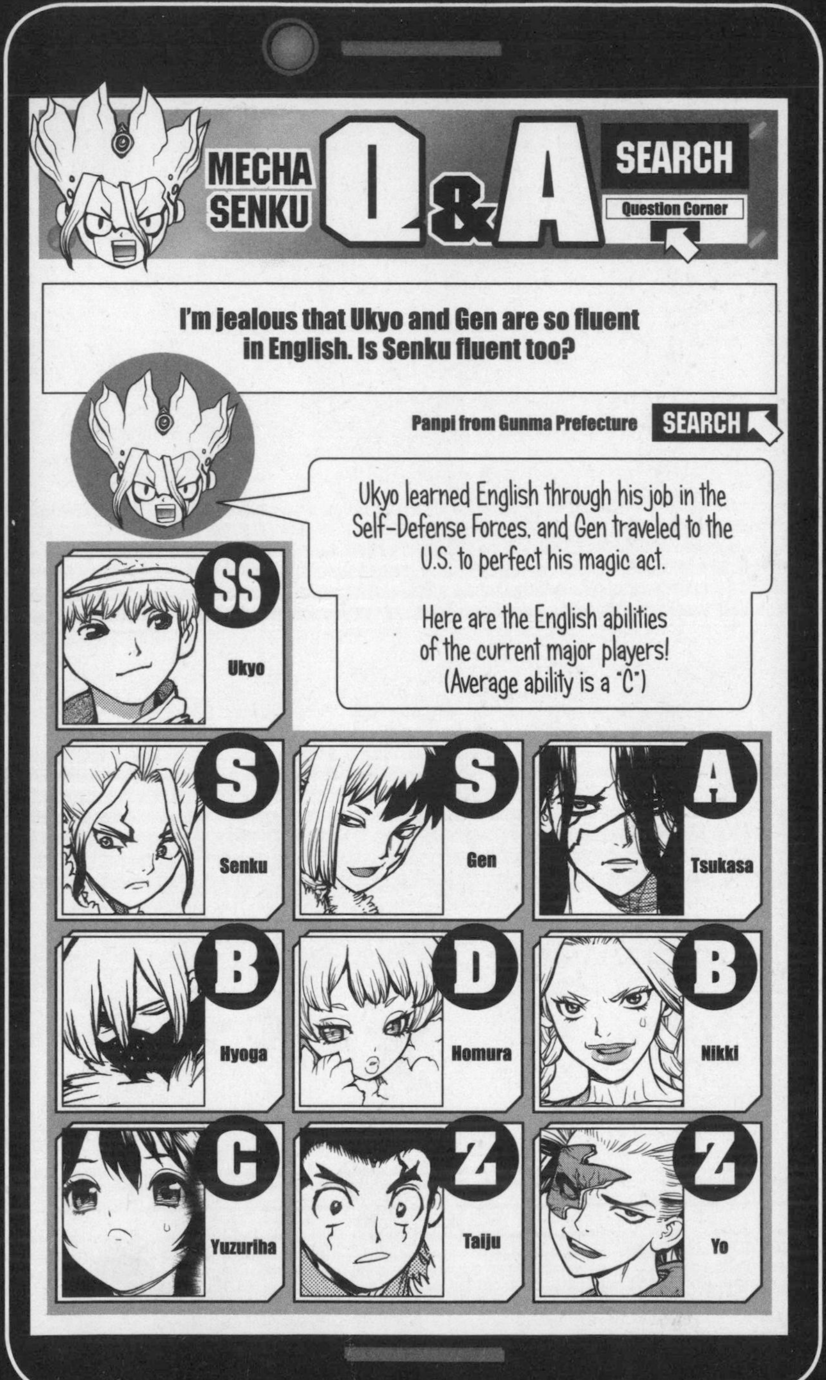
MECHA SENKU
Q&A
SEARCH
Question Corner
I'm jealous that Ukyo and Gen are so fluent in English. Is Senku fluent too?
Panpi from Gunma Prefecture
SEARCH
Ukyo learned English through his job in the Self-Defense Forces, and Gen traveled to the U.S. to perfect his magic act.
Here are the English abilities of the current major players! (Average ability is a "C")
SS
Ukyo
S
Senku
S
Gen
A
Tsukasa
B
Hyoga
D
Homura
B
Nikki
C
Yuzuriha
Z
Taiju
Z
Yo

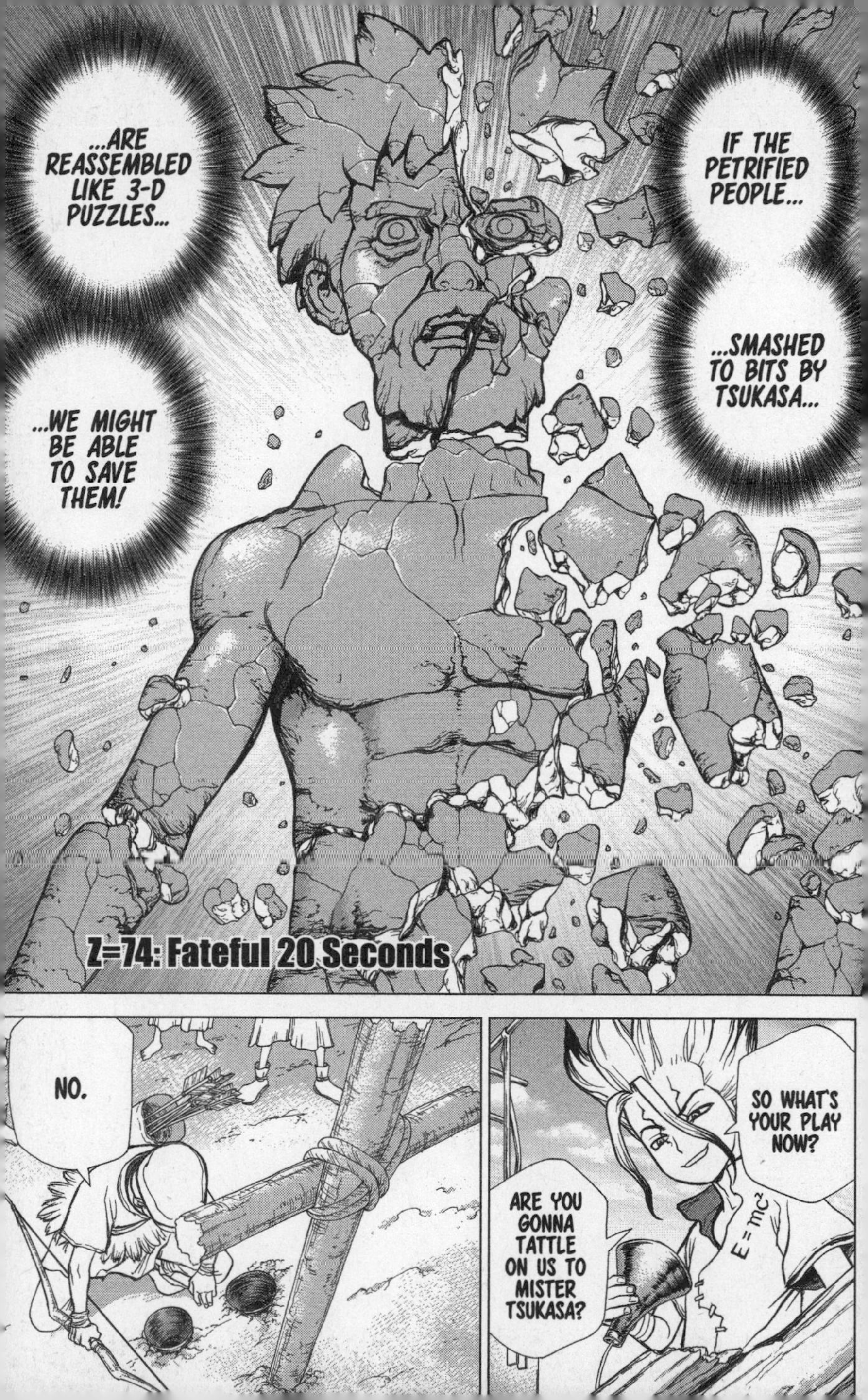
IF THE PETRIFIED PEOPLE...
...SMASHED TO BITS BY TSUKASA...
...ARE REASSEMBLED LIKE 3-D PUZZLES...
...WE MIGHT BE ABLE TO SAVE THEM!
Z=74: Fateful 20 Seconds
SO WHAT'S YOUR PLAY NOW?
ARE YOU GONNA TATTLE ON US TO MISTER TSUKASA?
E=mc²
NO.

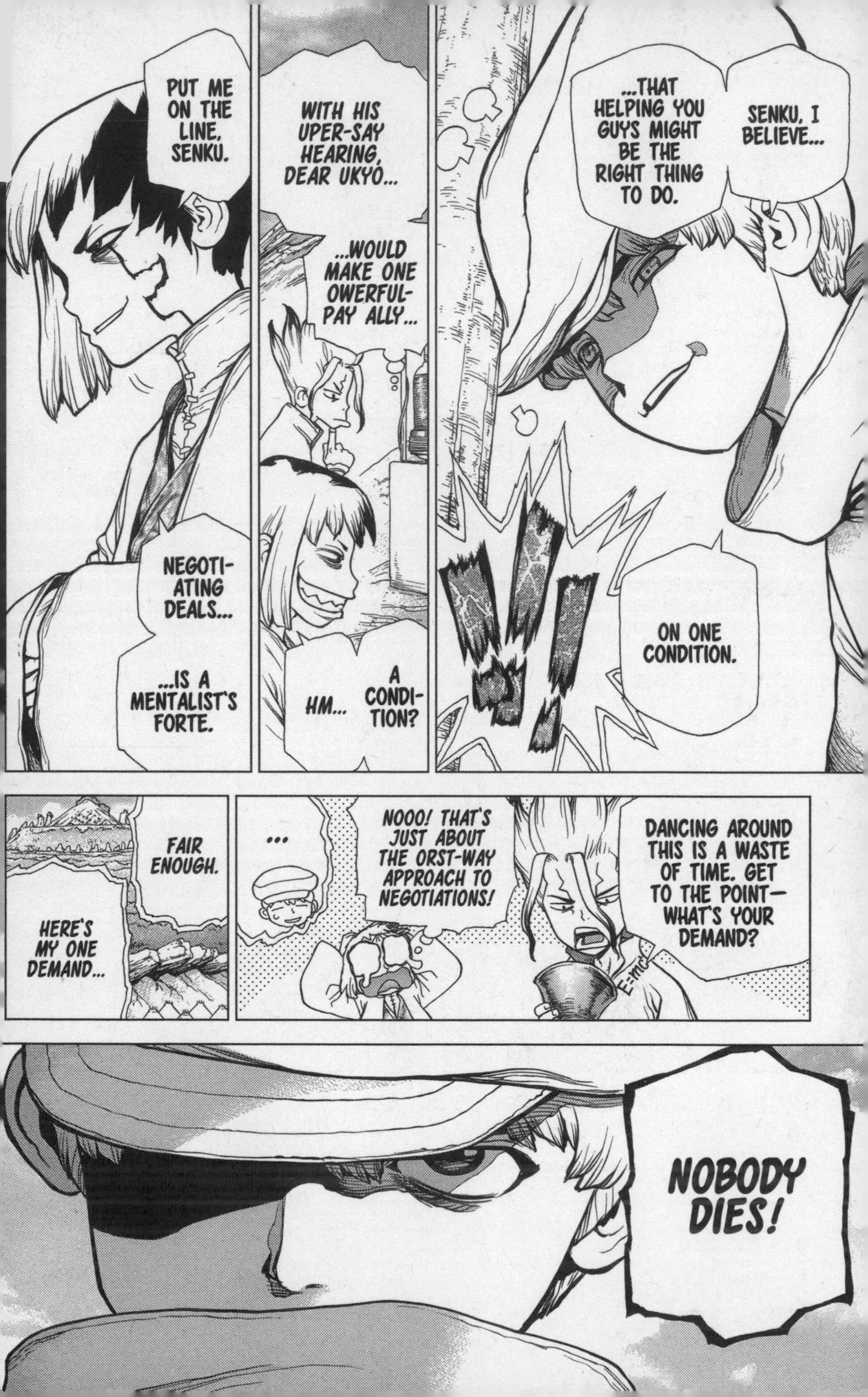
SENKU, I BELIEVE...
...THAT HELPING YOU GUYS MIGHT BE THE RIGHT THING TO DO.
ON ONE CONDITION.
WITH HIS UPER-SAY HEARING, DEAR UKYŌ...
...WOULD MAKE ONE OWERFUL-PAY ALLY...
A CONDITION?
HM...
PUT ME ON THE LINE, SENKU.
NEGOTIATING DEALS...
...IS A MENTALIST'S FORTE.
DANCING AROUND THIS IS A WASTE OF TIME. GET TO THE POINT— WHAT'S YOUR DEMAND?
NOOO! THAT'S JUST ABOUT THE ORST-WAY APPROACH TO NEGOTIATIONS!
...
FAIR ENOUGH.
HERE'S MY ONE DEMAND...
NOBODY DIES!

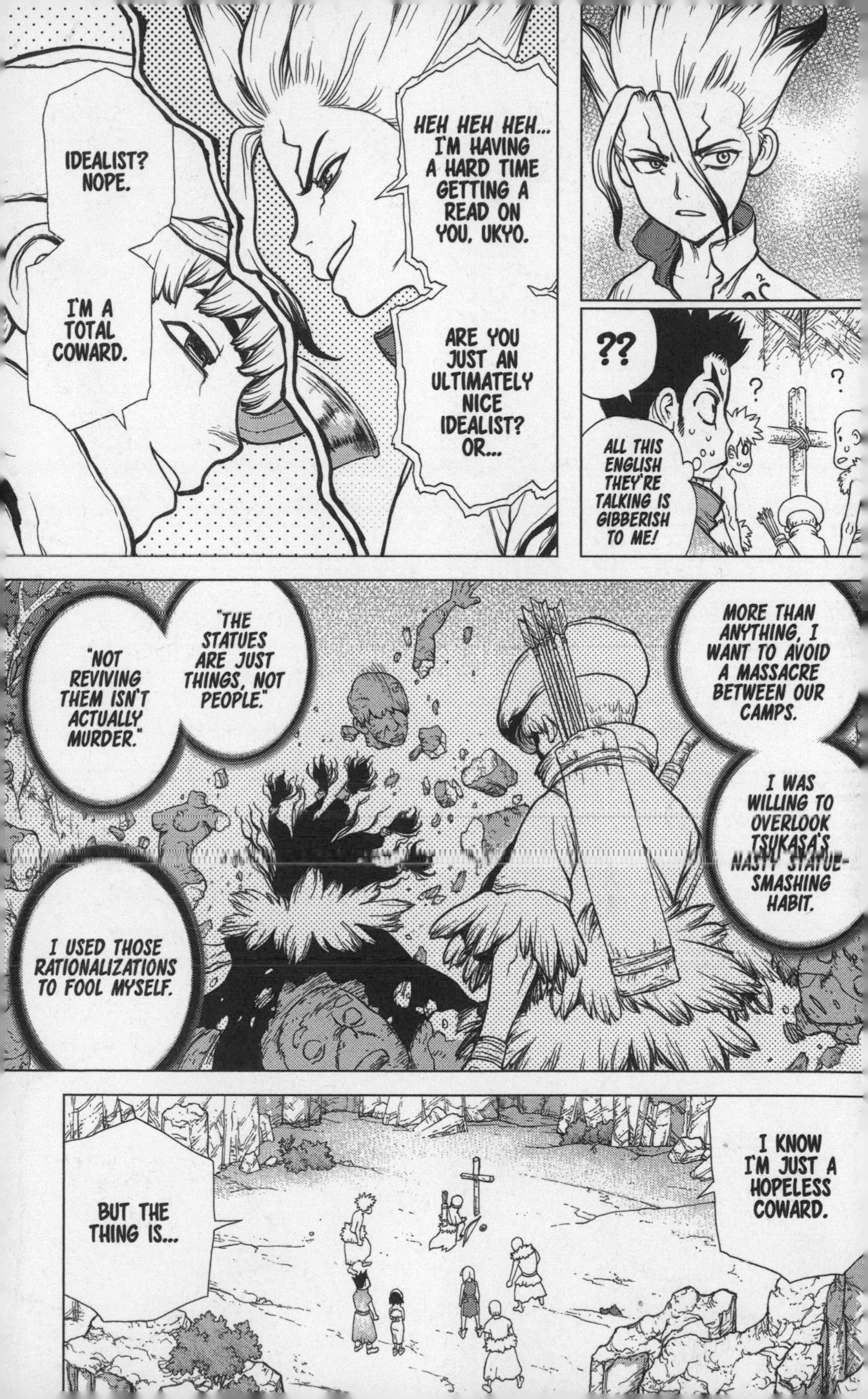
??
ALL THIS ENGLISH THEY'RE TALKING IS GIBBERISH TO ME!
HEH HEH HEH... I'M HAVING A HARD TIME GETTING A READ ON YOU, UKYO.
ARE YOU JUST AN ULTIMATELY NICE IDEALIST? OR...
IDEALIST? NOPE.
I'M A TOTAL COWARD.
MORE THAN ANYTHING, I WANT TO AVOID A MASSACRE BETWEEN OUR CAMPS.
I WAS WILLING TO OVERLOOK TSUKASA'S NASTY STATUE-SMASHING HABIT.
"THE STATUES ARE JUST THINGS, NOT PEOPLE."
"NOT REVIVING THEM ISN'T ACTUALLY MURDER."
I USED THOSE RATIONALIZATIONS TO FOOL MYSELF.
I KNOW I'M JUST A HOPELESS COWARD.
BUT THE THING IS...

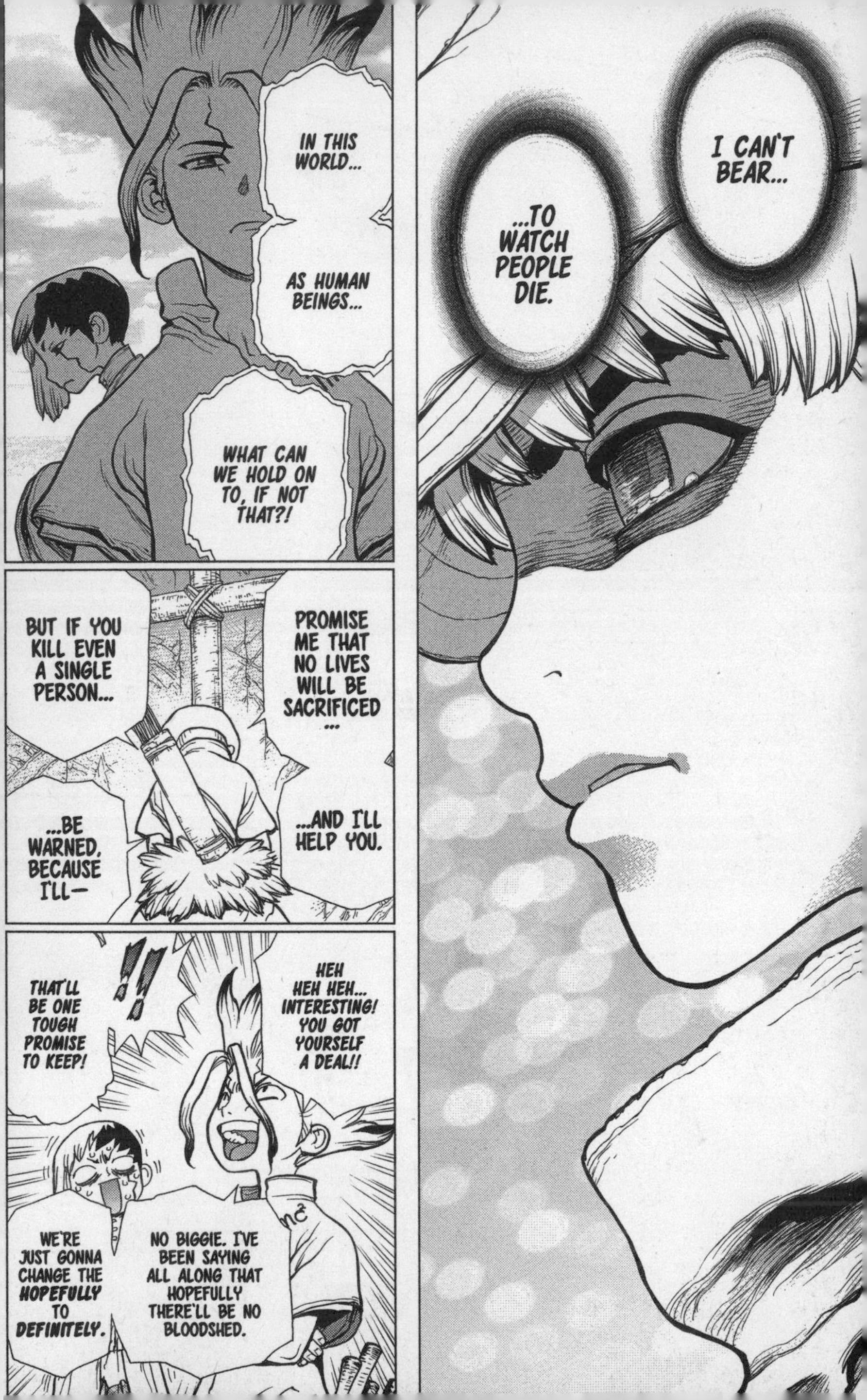
I CAN'T BEAR...
...TO WATCH PEOPLE DIE.
IN THIS WORLD...
AS HUMAN BEINGS...
WHAT CAN WE HOLD ON TO, IF NOT THAT?!
PROMISE ME THAT NO LIVES WILL BE SACRIFICED...
...AND I'LL HELP YOU.
BUT IF YOU KILL EVEN A SINGLE PERSON...
...BE WARNED, BECAUSE I'LL—
HEH HEH HEH... INTERESTING! YOU GOT YOURSELF A DEAL!!
!!
THAT'LL BE ONE TOUGH PROMISE TO KEEP!
NO BIGGIE. I'VE BEEN SAYING ALL ALONG THAT HOPEFULLY THERE'LL BE NO BLOODSHED.
WE'RE JUST GONNA CHANGE THE **HOPEFULLY** TO **DEFINITELY**.

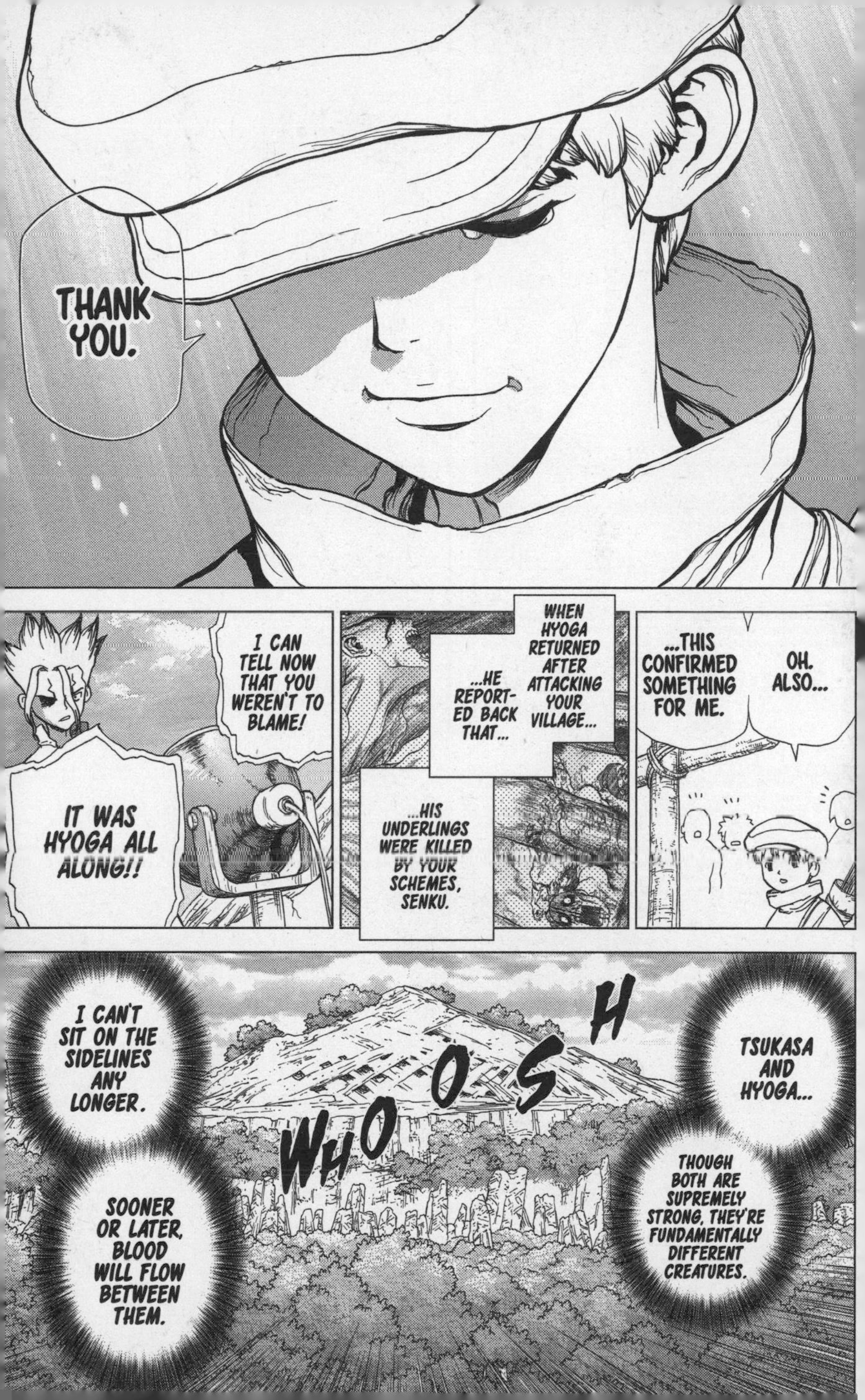
THANK YOU.
OH. ALSO...
...THIS CONFIRMED SOMETHING FOR ME.
WHEN HYOGA RETURNED AFTER ATTACKING YOUR VILLAGE...
...HE REPORT-ED BACK THAT...
...HIS UNDERLINGS WERE KILLED BY YOUR SCHEMES, SENKU.
I CAN TELL NOW THAT YOU WEREN'T TO BLAME!
IT WAS HYOGA ALL ALONG!!
TSUKASA AND HYOGA...
THOUGH BOTH ARE SUPREMELY STRONG, THEY'RE FUNDAMENTALLY DIFFERENT CREATURES.
WHOOSH
I CAN'T SIT ON THE SIDELINES ANY LONGER.
SOONER OR LATER, BLOOD WILL FLOW BETWEEN THEM.

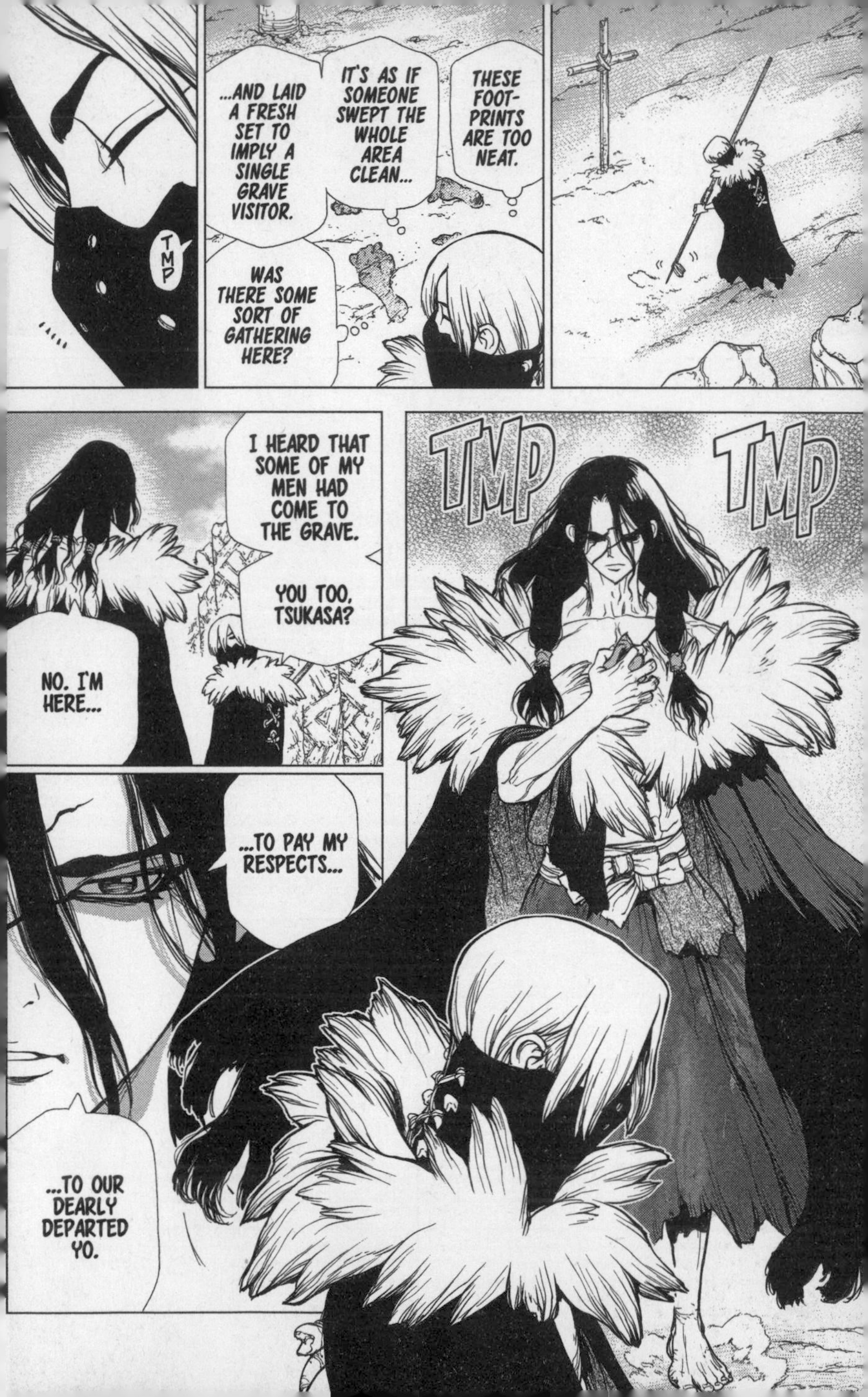

THESE FOOT-PRINTS ARE TOO NEAT.
IT'S AS IF SOMEONE SWEPT THE WHOLE AREA CLEAN...
...AND LAID A FRESH SET TO IMPLY A SINGLE GRAVE VISITOR.
WAS THERE SOME SORT OF GATHERING HERE?
TMP
TMP
TMP
I HEARD THAT SOME OF MY MEN HAD COME TO THE GRAVE.
YOU TOO, TSUKASA?
NO. I'M HERE...
...TO PAY MY RESPECTS...
...TO OUR DEARLY DEPARTED YO.

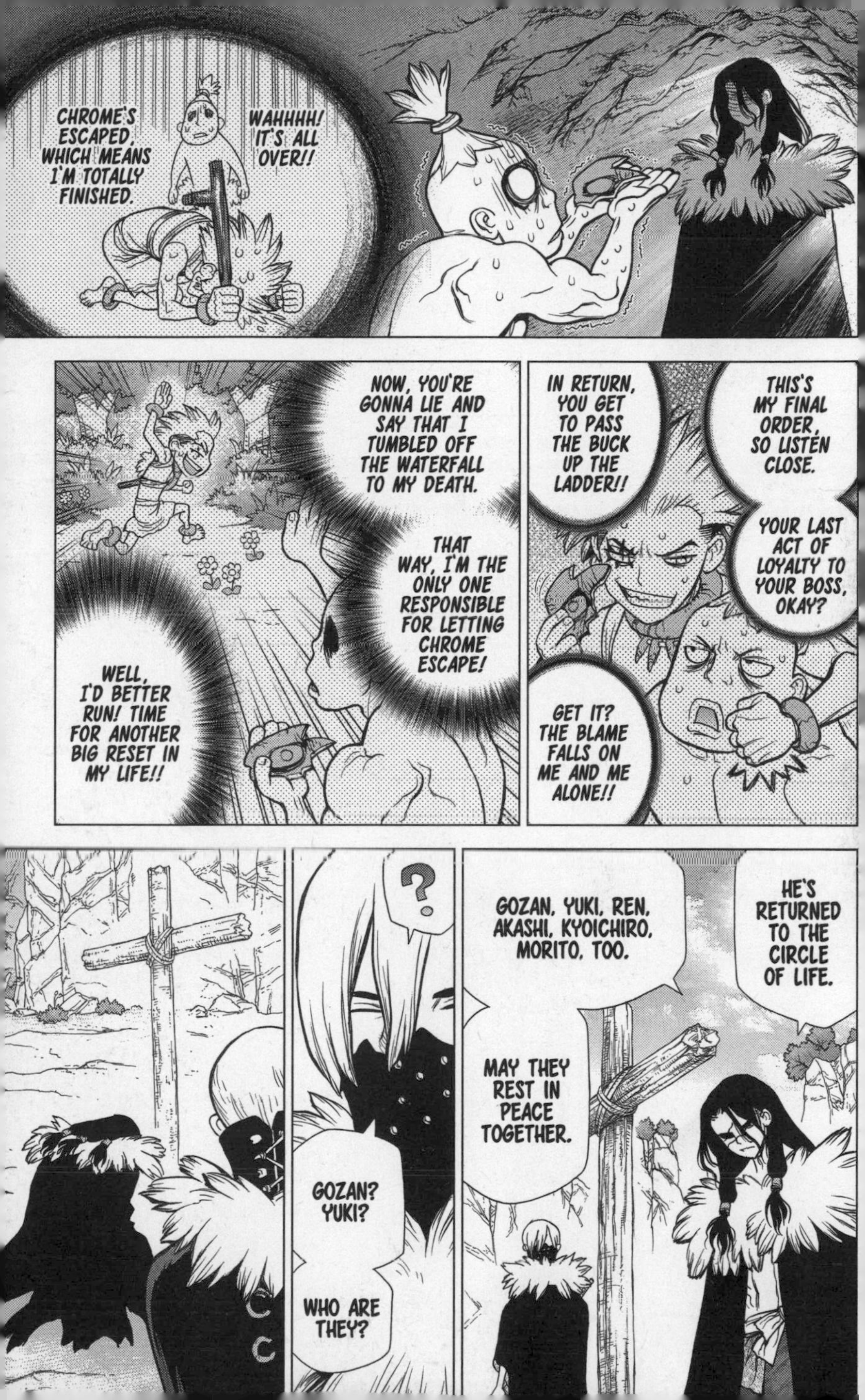
WAHHHH! IT'S ALL OVER!!
CHROME'S ESCAPED, WHICH MEANS I'M TOTALLY FINISHED.
THIS'S MY FINAL ORDER, SO LISTEN CLOSE.
IN RETURN, YOU GET TO PASS THE BUCK UP THE LADDER!!
YOUR LAST ACT OF LOYALTY TO YOUR BOSS, OKAY?
GET IT? THE BLAME FALLS ON ME AND ME ALONE!!
NOW, YOU'RE GONNA LIE AND SAY THAT I TUMBLED OFF THE WATERFALL TO MY DEATH.
THAT WAY, I'M THE ONLY ONE RESPONSIBLE FOR LETTING CHROME ESCAPE!
WELL, I'D BETTER RUN! TIME FOR ANOTHER BIG RESET IN MY LIFE!!
HE'S RETURNED TO THE CIRCLE OF LIFE.
GOZAN, YUKI, REN, AKASHI, KYOICHIRO, MORITO, TOO.
MAY THEY REST IN PEACE TOGETHER.
?
GOZAN? YUKI?
WHO ARE THEY?

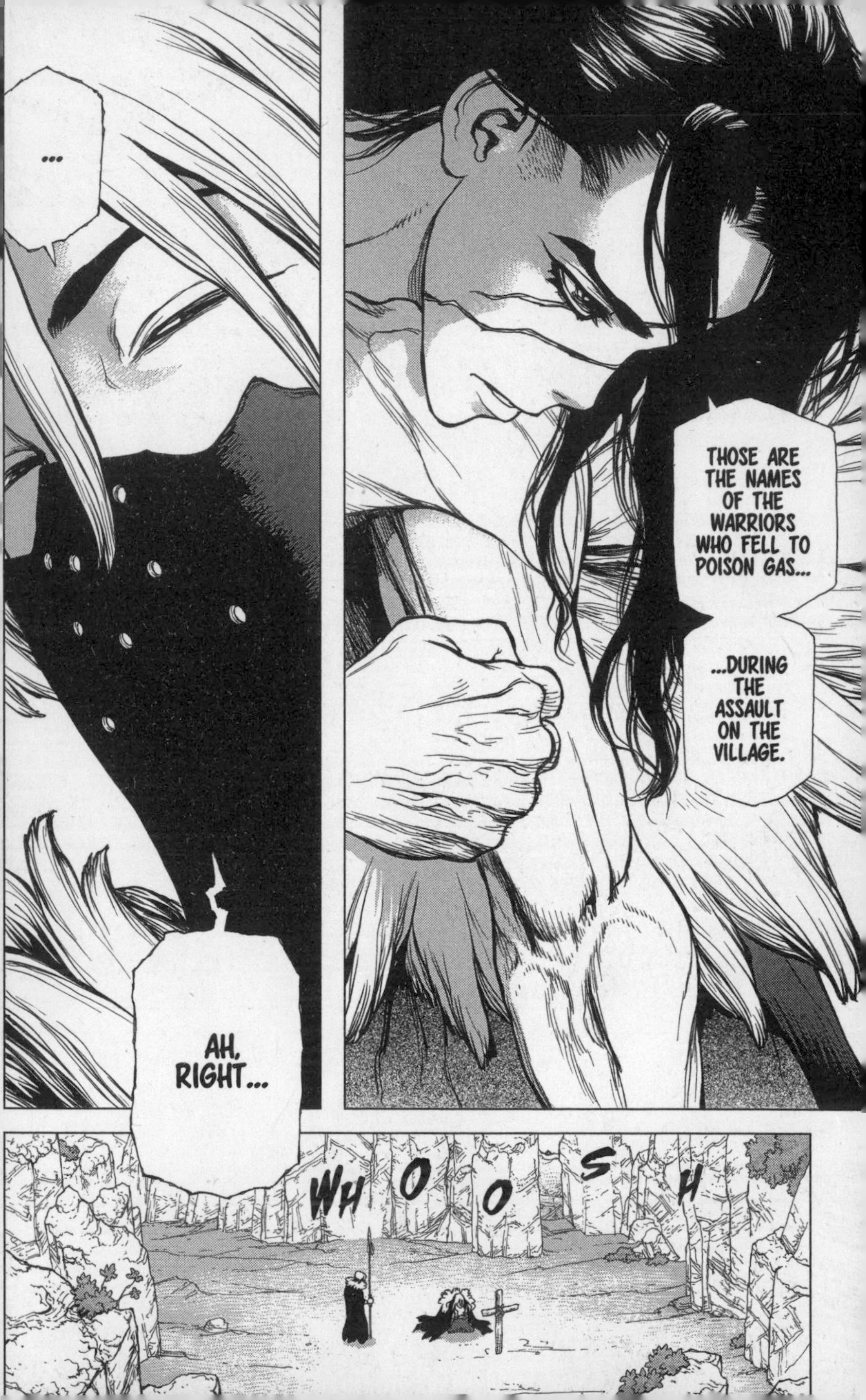
THOSE ARE THE NAMES OF THE WARRIORS WHO FELL TO POISON GAS...
...DURING THE ASSAULT ON THE VILLAGE.
...
AH, RIGHT...
WHOOSH

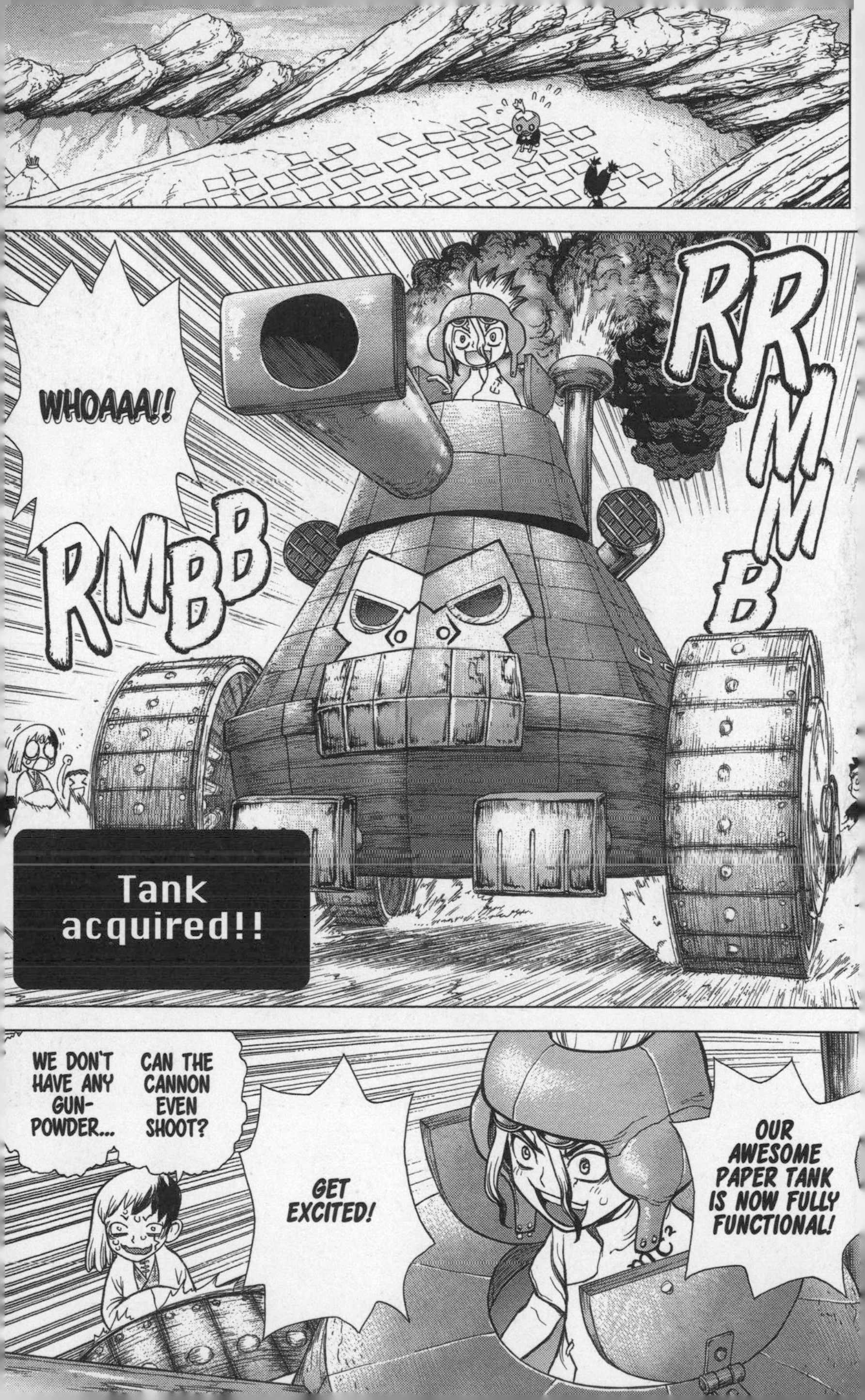
RRMMB
WHOAAA!!
RMBB
Tank acquired!!
OUR AWESOME PAPER TANK IS NOW FULLY FUNCTIONAL!
GET EXCITED!
CAN THE CANNON EVEN SHOOT?
WE DON'T HAVE ANY GUN-POWDER...

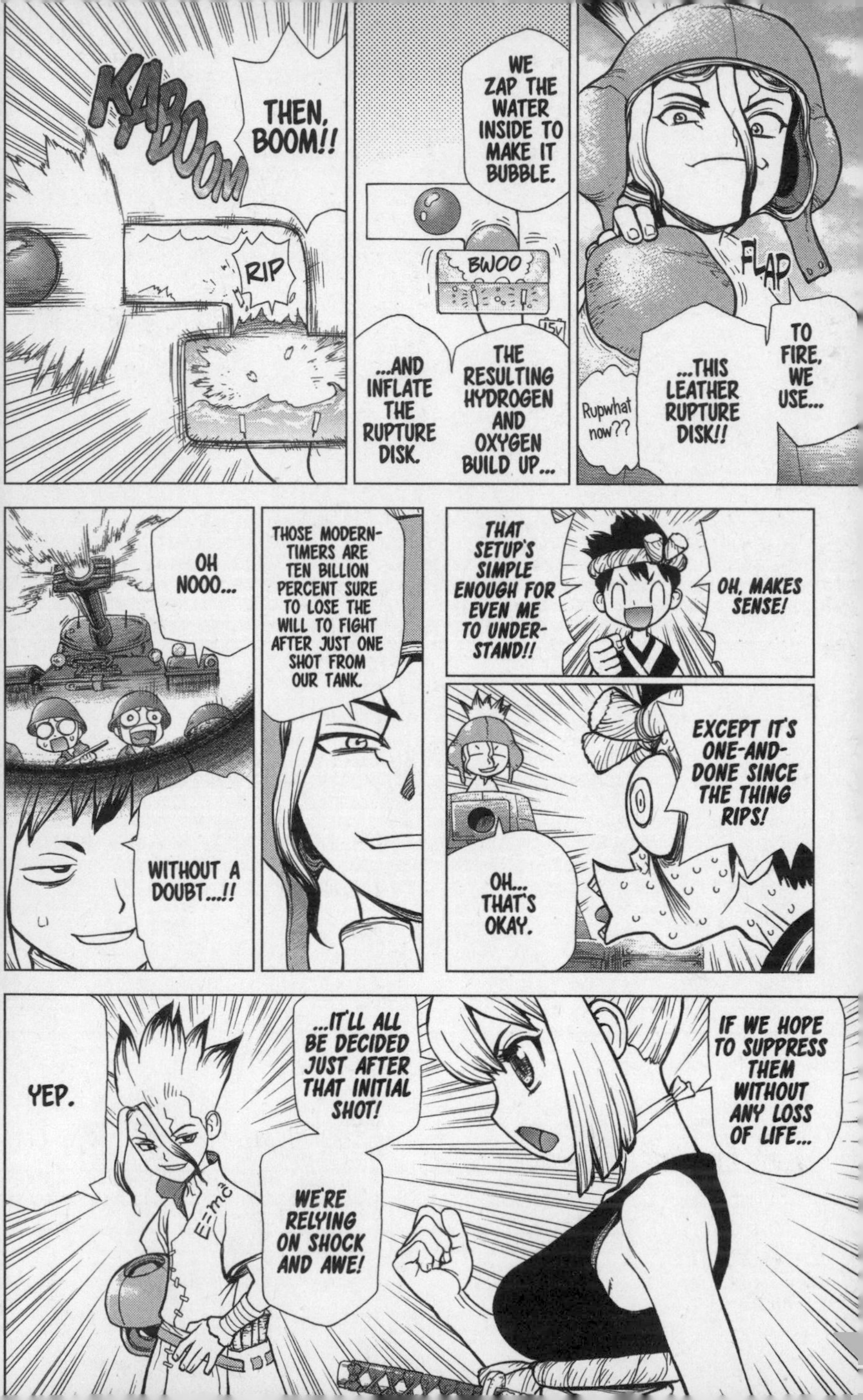
TO FIRE, WE USE...
...THIS LEATHER RUPTURE DISK!!
FLAP
Rupwhat now??
WE ZAP THE WATER INSIDE TO MAKE IT BUBBLE.
BWOO
15V
THE RESULTING HYDROGEN AND OXYGEN BUILD UP...
...AND INFLATE THE RUPTURE DISK.
THEN, BOOM!!
KABOOM
RIP
OH, MAKES SENSE!
THAT SETUP'S SIMPLE ENOUGH FOR EVEN ME TO UNDERSTAND!!
EXCEPT IT'S ONE-AND-DONE SINCE THE THING RIPS!
OH... THAT'S OKAY.
THOSE MODERN-TIMERS ARE TEN BILLION PERCENT SURE TO LOSE THE WILL TO FIGHT AFTER JUST ONE SHOT FROM OUR TANK.
OH NOOO...
WITHOUT A DOUBT...!!
IF WE HOPE TO SUPPRESS THEM WITHOUT ANY LOSS OF LIFE...
...IT'LL ALL BE DECIDED JUST AFTER THAT INITIAL SHOT!
WE'RE RELYING ON SHOCK AND AWE!
YEP.
$E=mc^2$

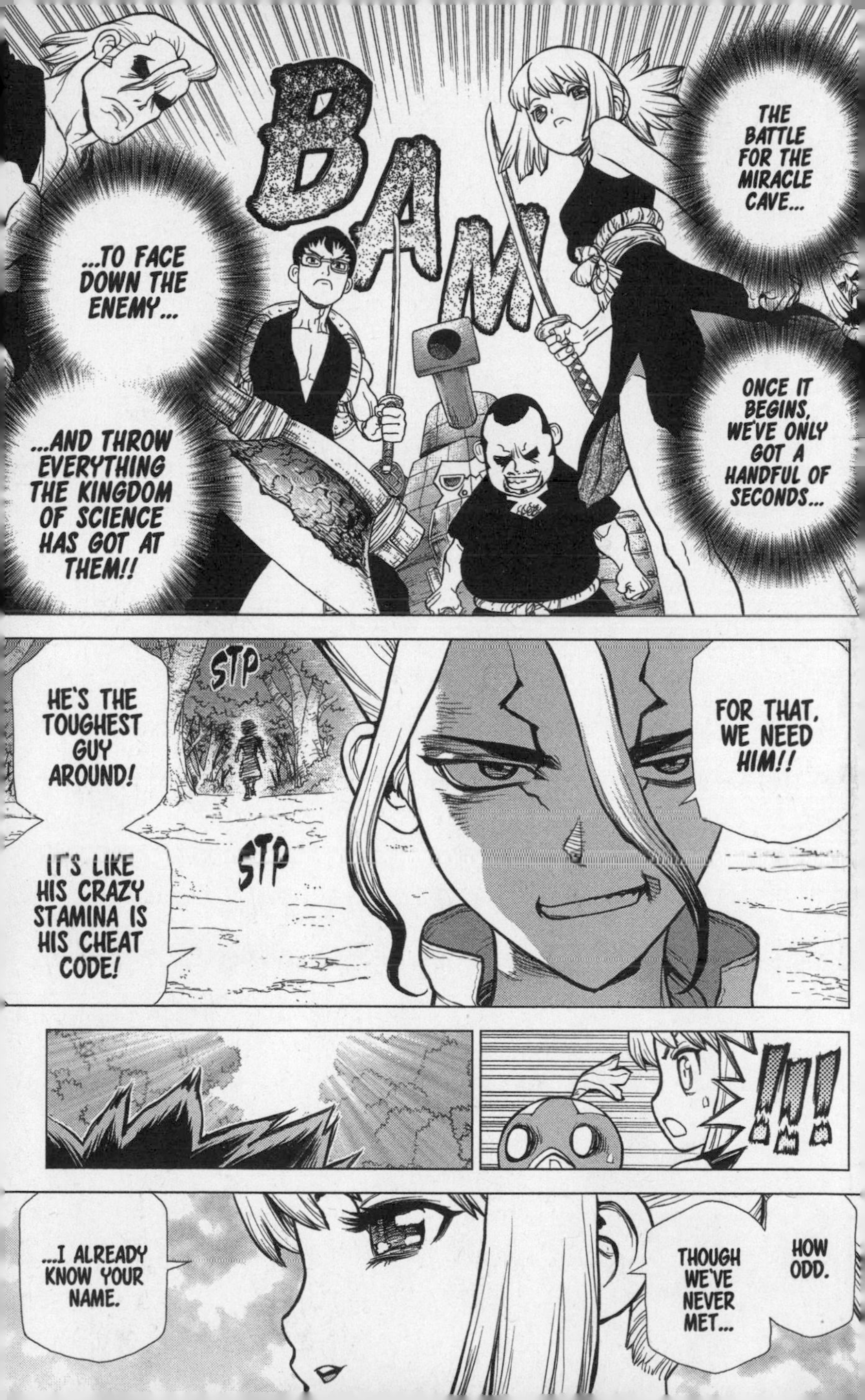
THE BATTLE FOR THE MIRACLE CAVE...
BAM
ONCE IT BEGINS, WE'VE ONLY GOT A HANDFUL OF SECONDS...
...TO FACE DOWN THE ENEMY...
...AND THROW EVERYTHING THE KINGDOM OF SCIENCE HAS GOT AT THEM!!
FOR THAT, WE NEED HIM!!
STP
HE'S THE TOUGHEST GUY AROUND!
STP
IT'S LIKE HIS CRAZY STAMINA IS HIS CHEAT CODE!
!!!
HOW ODD.
THOUGH WE'VE NEVER MET...
...I ALREADY KNOW YOUR NAME.

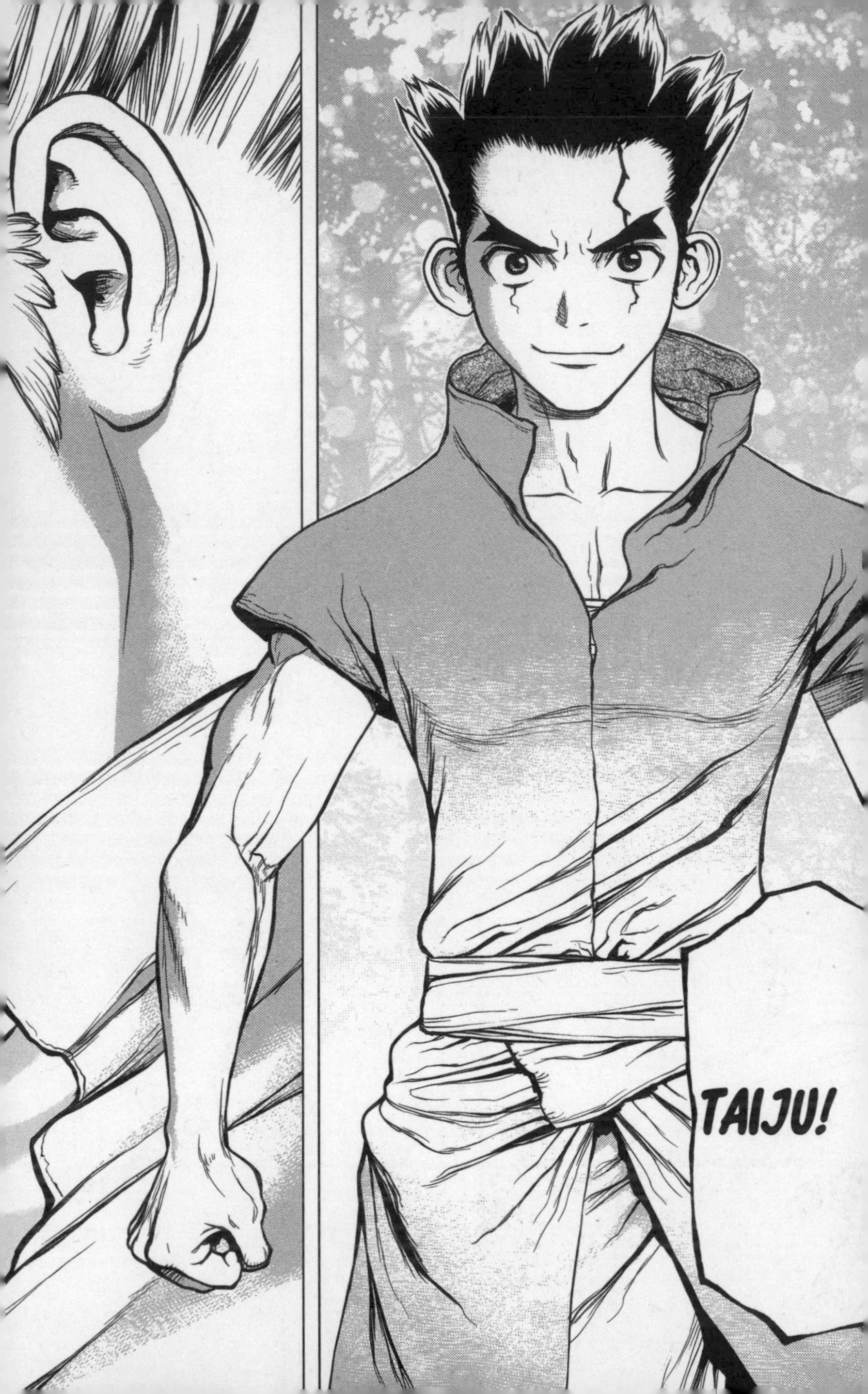
TAIJU!

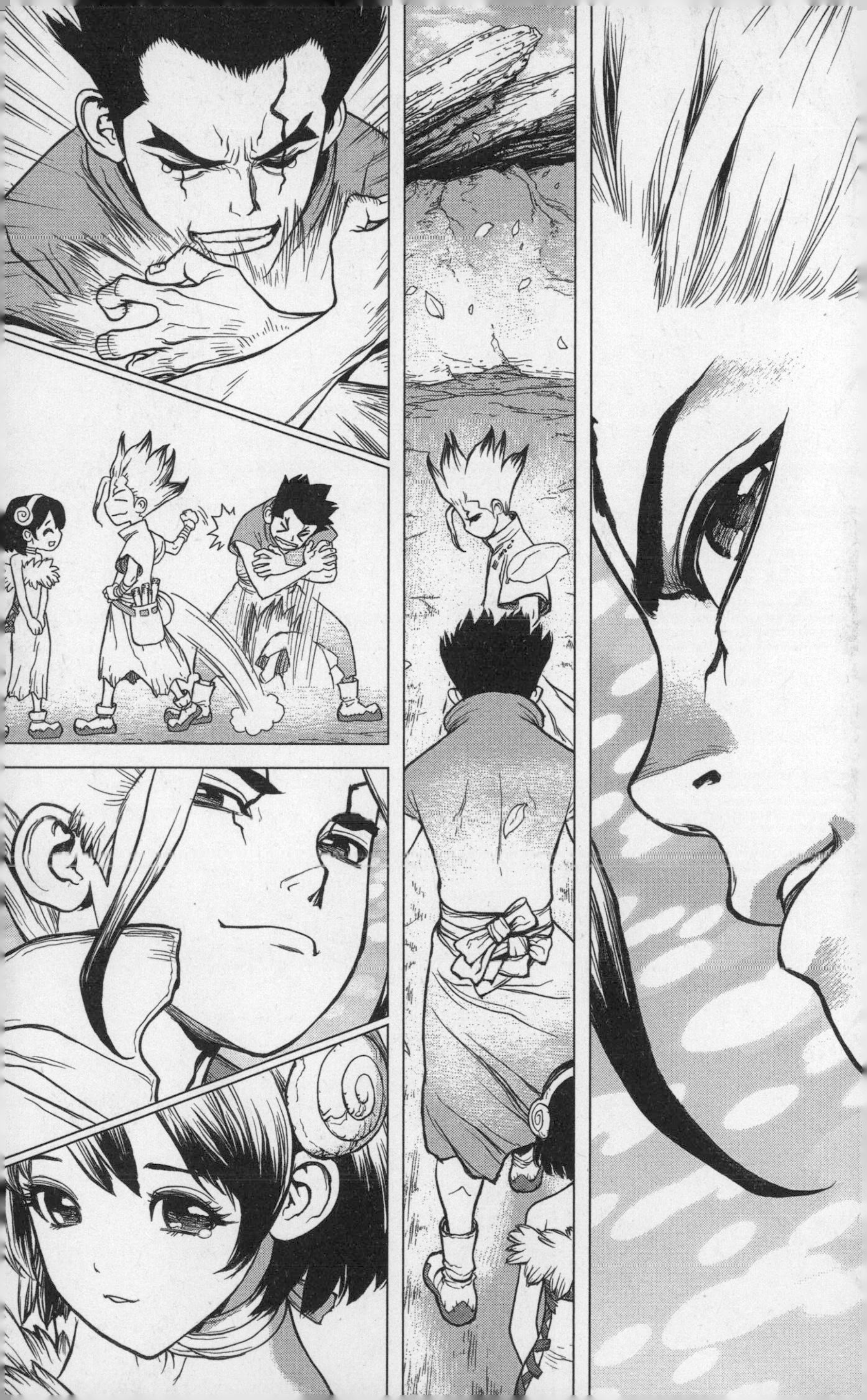

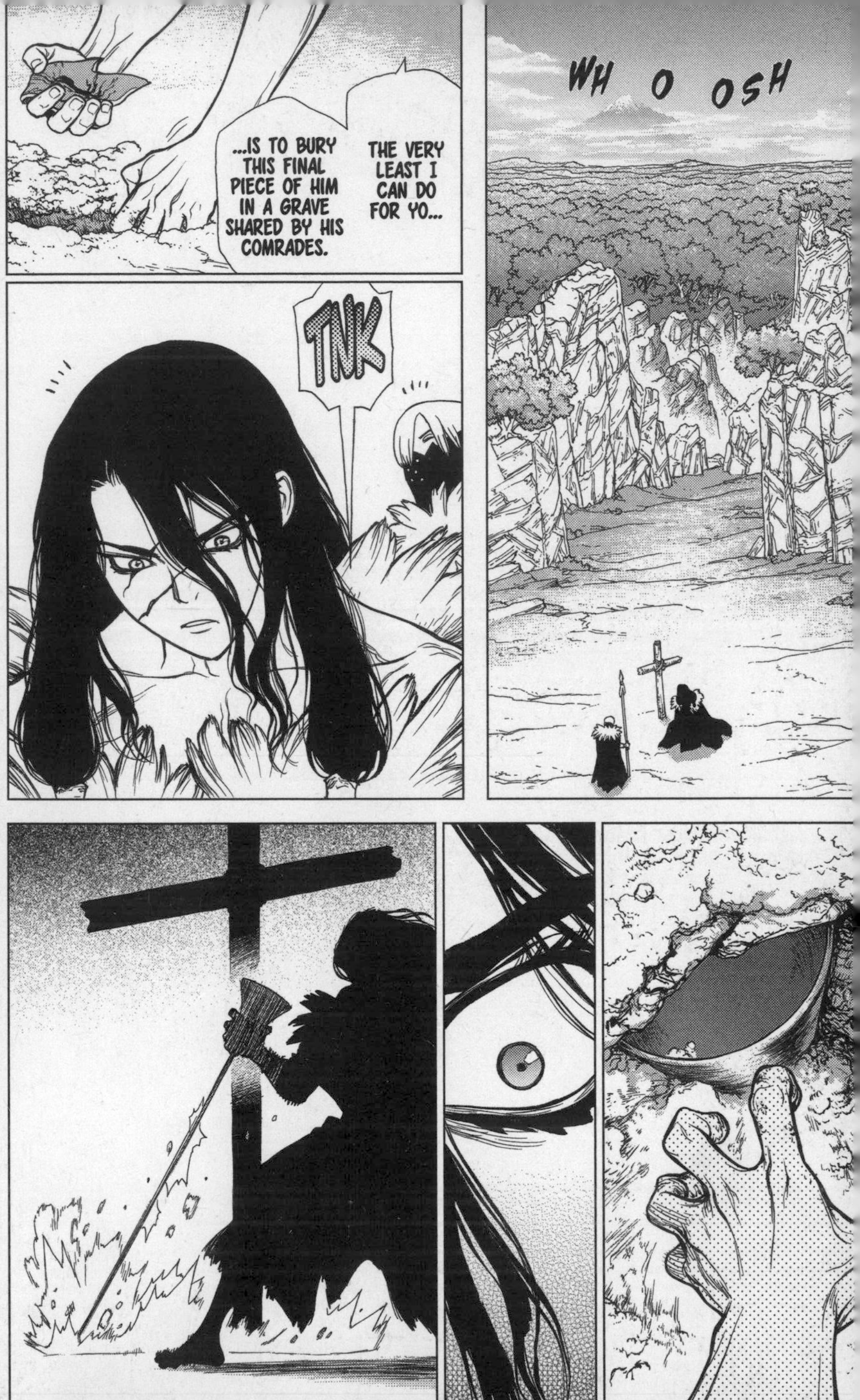
WHOOOSH
THE VERY LEAST I CAN DO FOR YO...
...IS TO BURY THIS FINAL PIECE OF HIM IN A GRAVE SHARED BY HIS COMRADES.
TNK

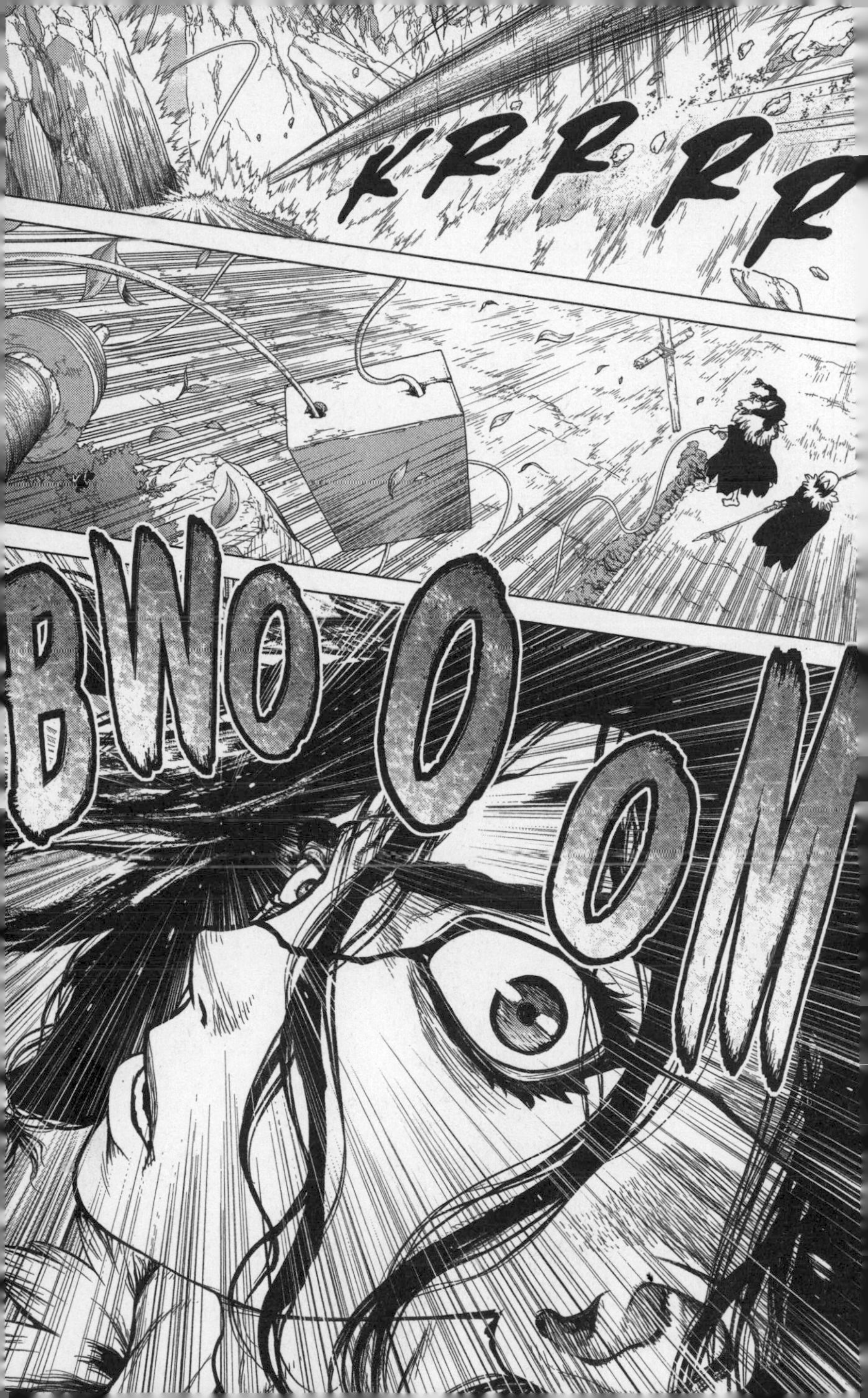
KRRRR
BWOOOOM

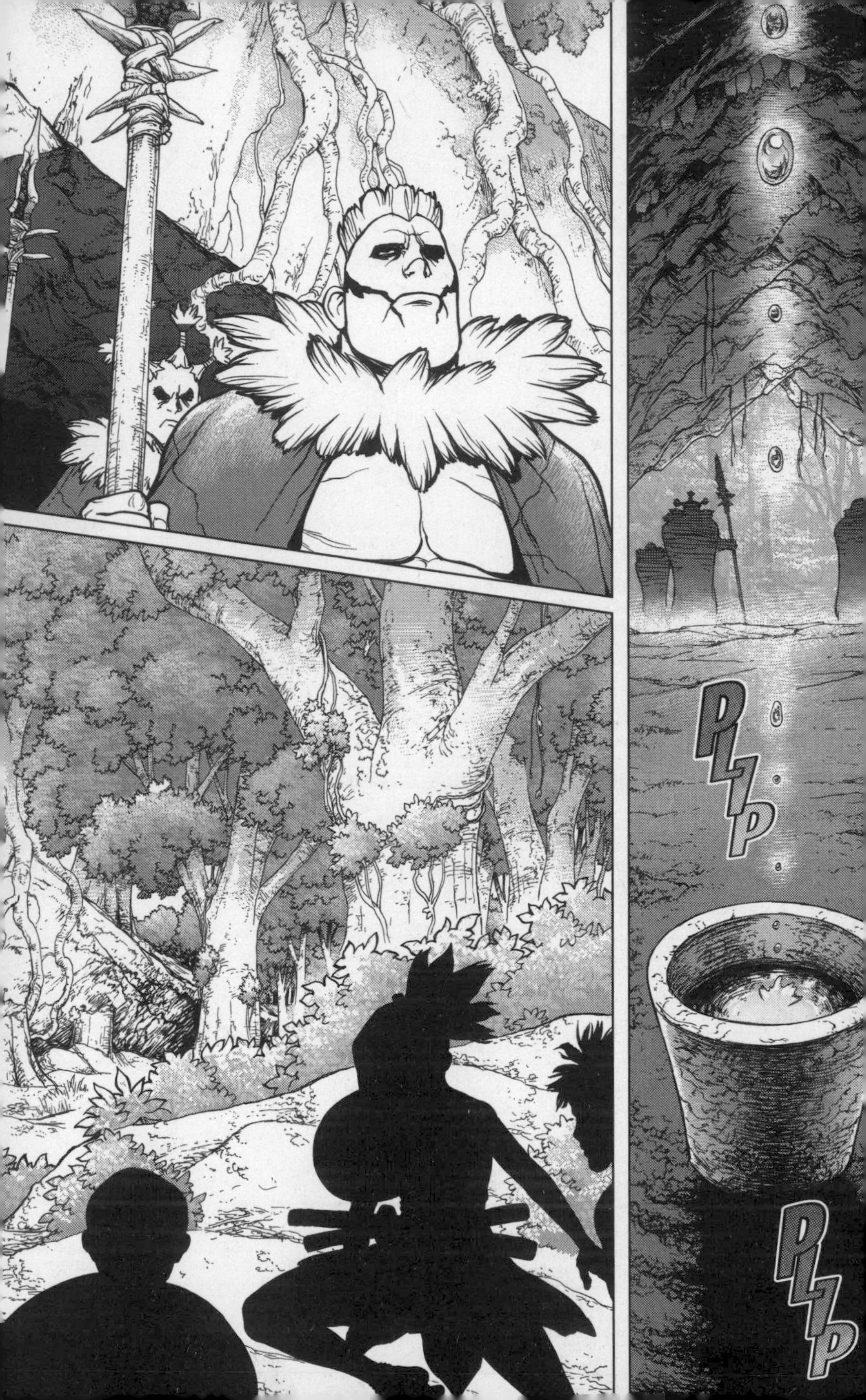
PLIP
PLIP

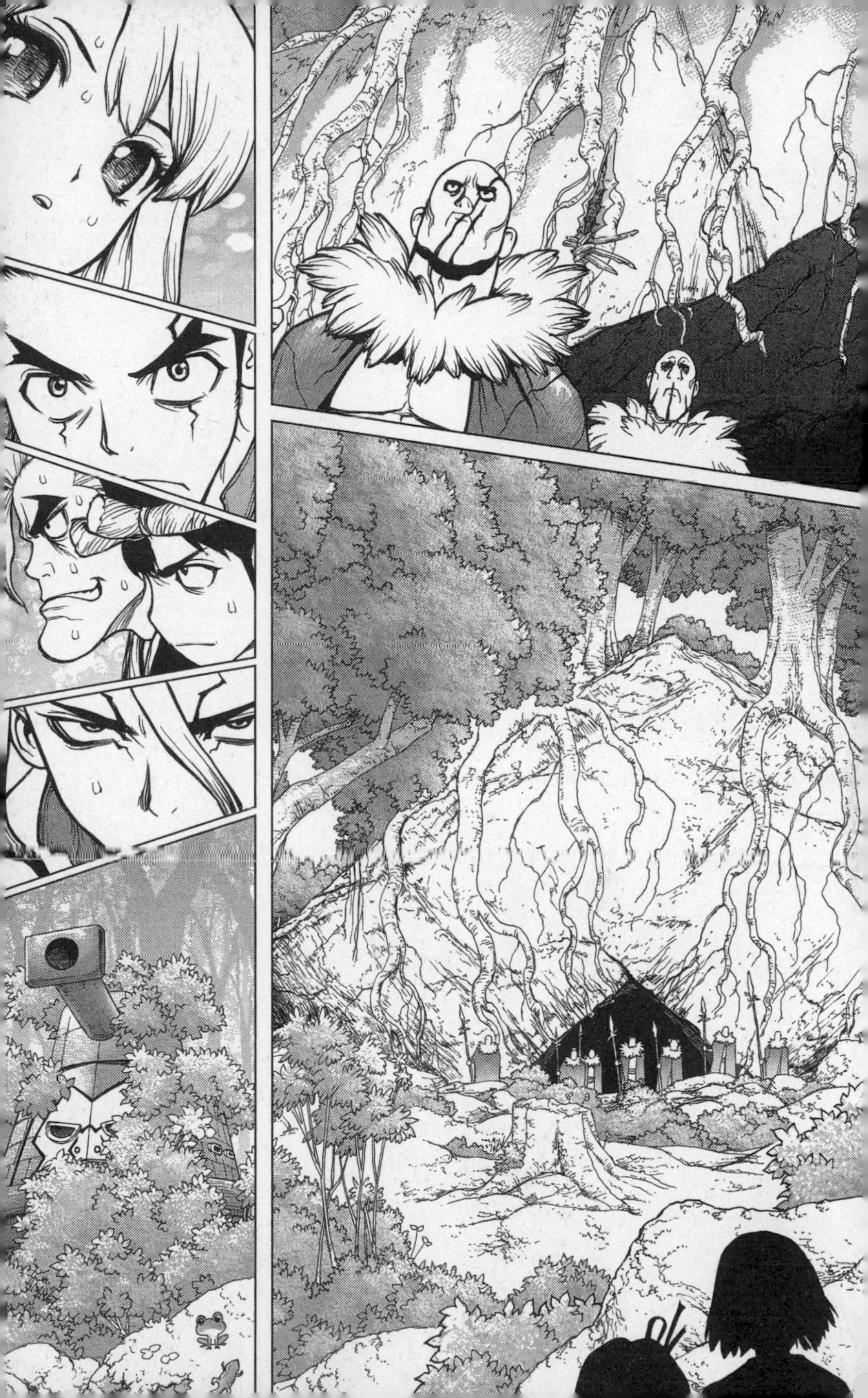

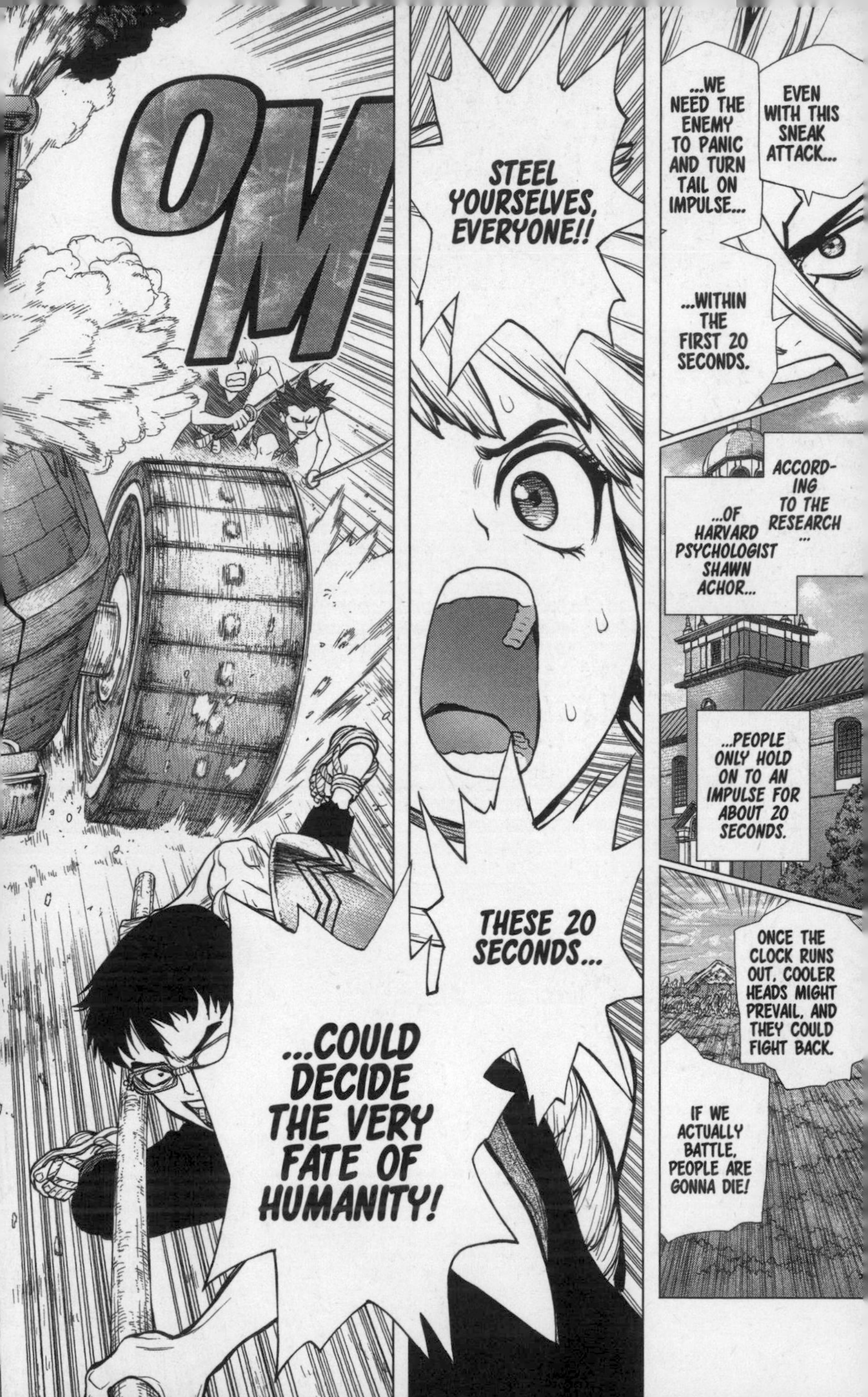
EVEN WITH THIS SNEAK ATTACK...
...WE NEED THE ENEMY TO PANIC AND TURN TAIL ON IMPULSE...
...WITHIN THE FIRST 20 SECONDS.
ACCORDING TO THE RESEARCH...
...OF HARVARD PSYCHOLOGIST SHAWN ACHOR...
...PEOPLE ONLY HOLD ON TO AN IMPULSE FOR ABOUT 20 SECONDS.
ONCE THE CLOCK RUNS OUT, COOLER HEADS MIGHT PREVAIL, AND THEY COULD FIGHT BACK.
IF WE ACTUALLY BATTLE, PEOPLE ARE GONNA DIE!
STEEL YOURSELVES, EVERYONE!!
THESE 20 SECONDS...
OM
...COULD DECIDE THE VERY FATE OF HUMANITY!

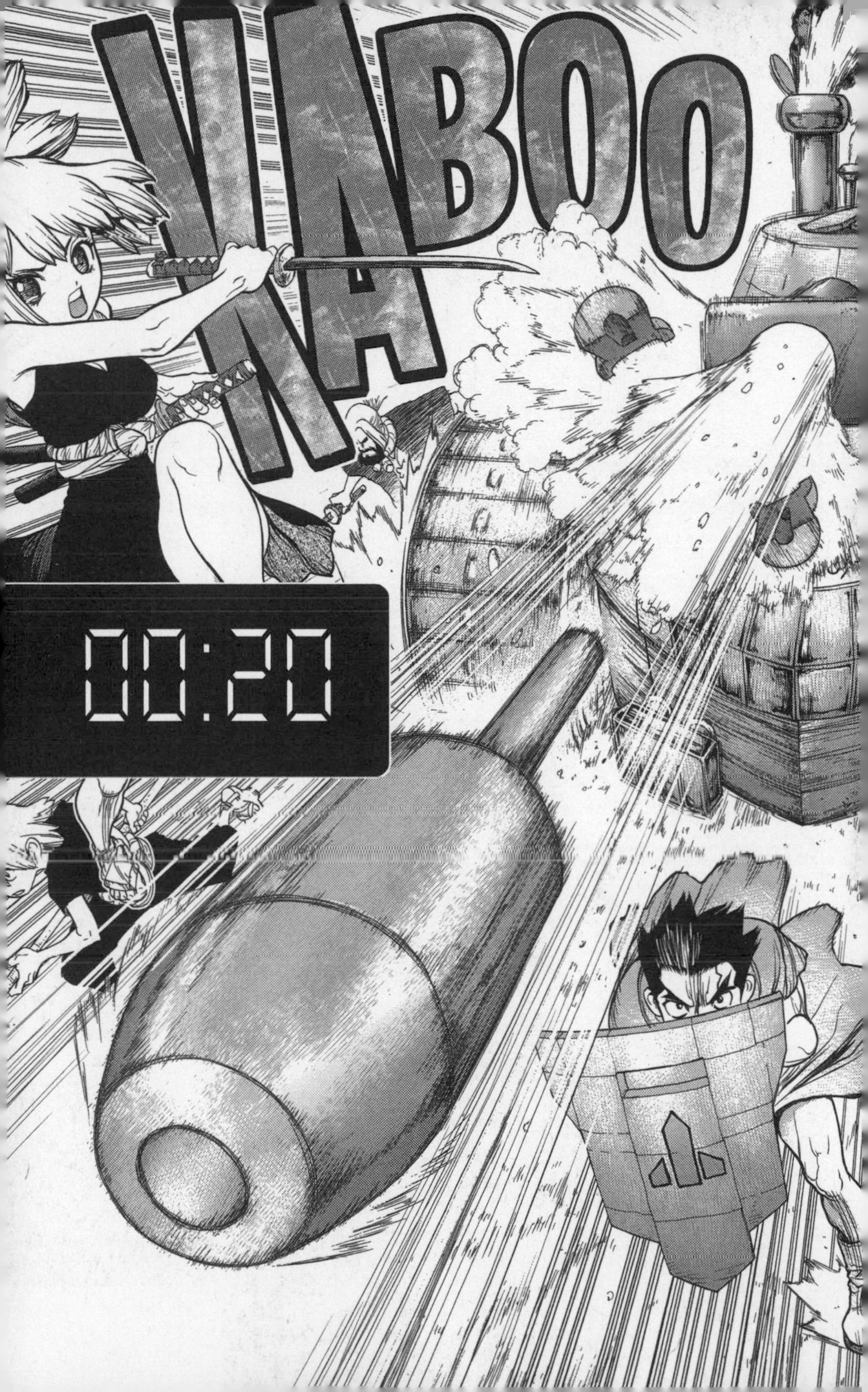
WABOO
00:20

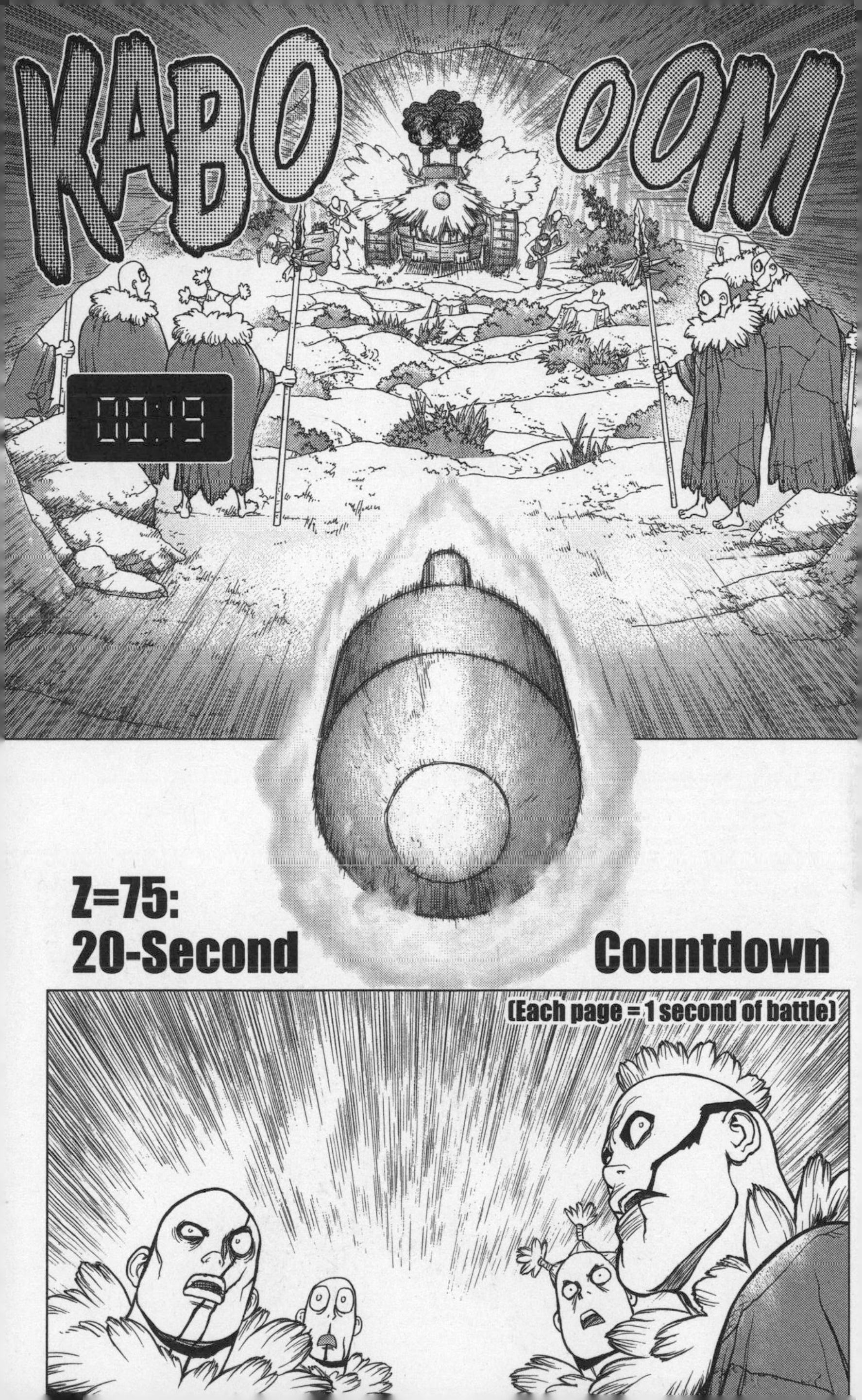
KABOOOM
00:19
Z=75:
20-Second Countdown
(Each page = 1 second of battle)

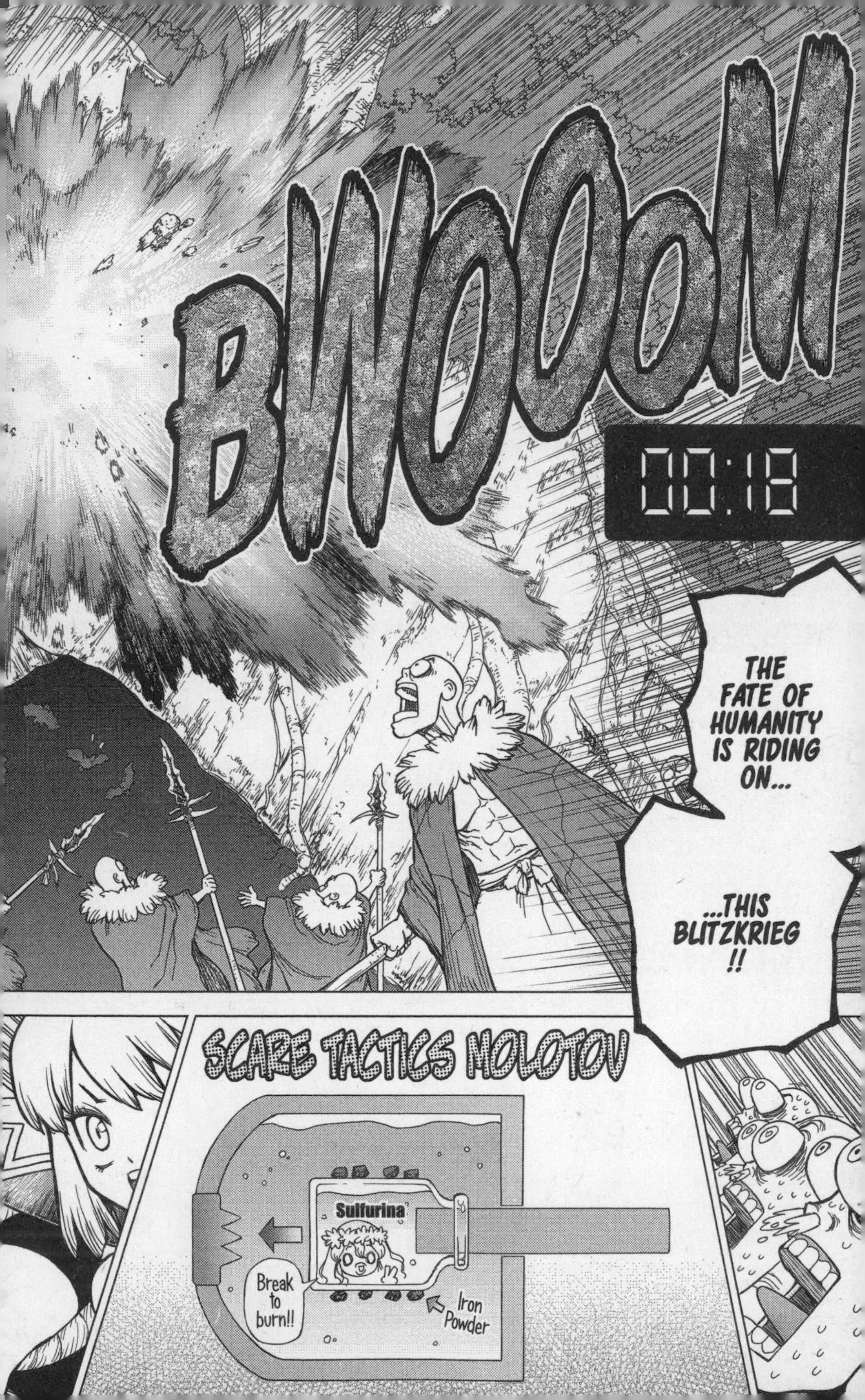
BWOOOM
00:18
THE FATE OF HUMANITY IS RIDING ON...
...THIS BLITZKRIEG!!
SCARE TACTICS MOLOTOV
Sulfurina
Break to burn!!
Iron Powder

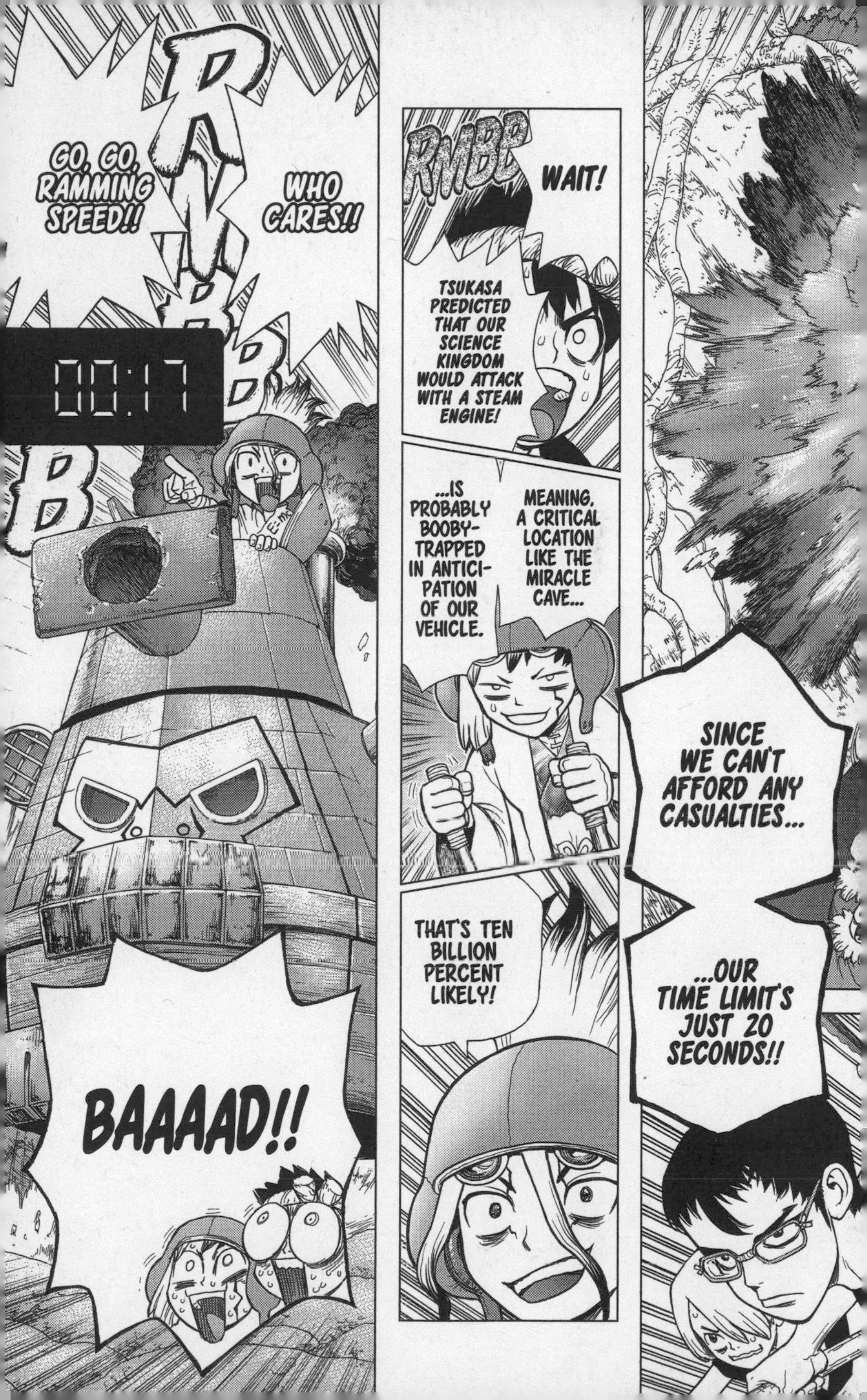
SINCE WE CAN'T AFFORD ANY CASUALTIES...
...OUR TIME LIMIT'S JUST 20 SECONDS!!
RMBB
WAIT!
TSUKASA PREDICTED THAT OUR SCIENCE KINGDOM WOULD ATTACK WITH A STEAM ENGINE!
MEANING, A CRITICAL LOCATION LIKE THE MIRACLE CAVE...
...IS PROBABLY BOOBY-TRAPPED IN ANTICIPATION OF OUR VEHICLE.
THAT'S TEN BILLION PERCENT LIKELY!
WHO CARES!!
GO, GO, RAMMING SPEED!!
00:17
BAAAAD!!

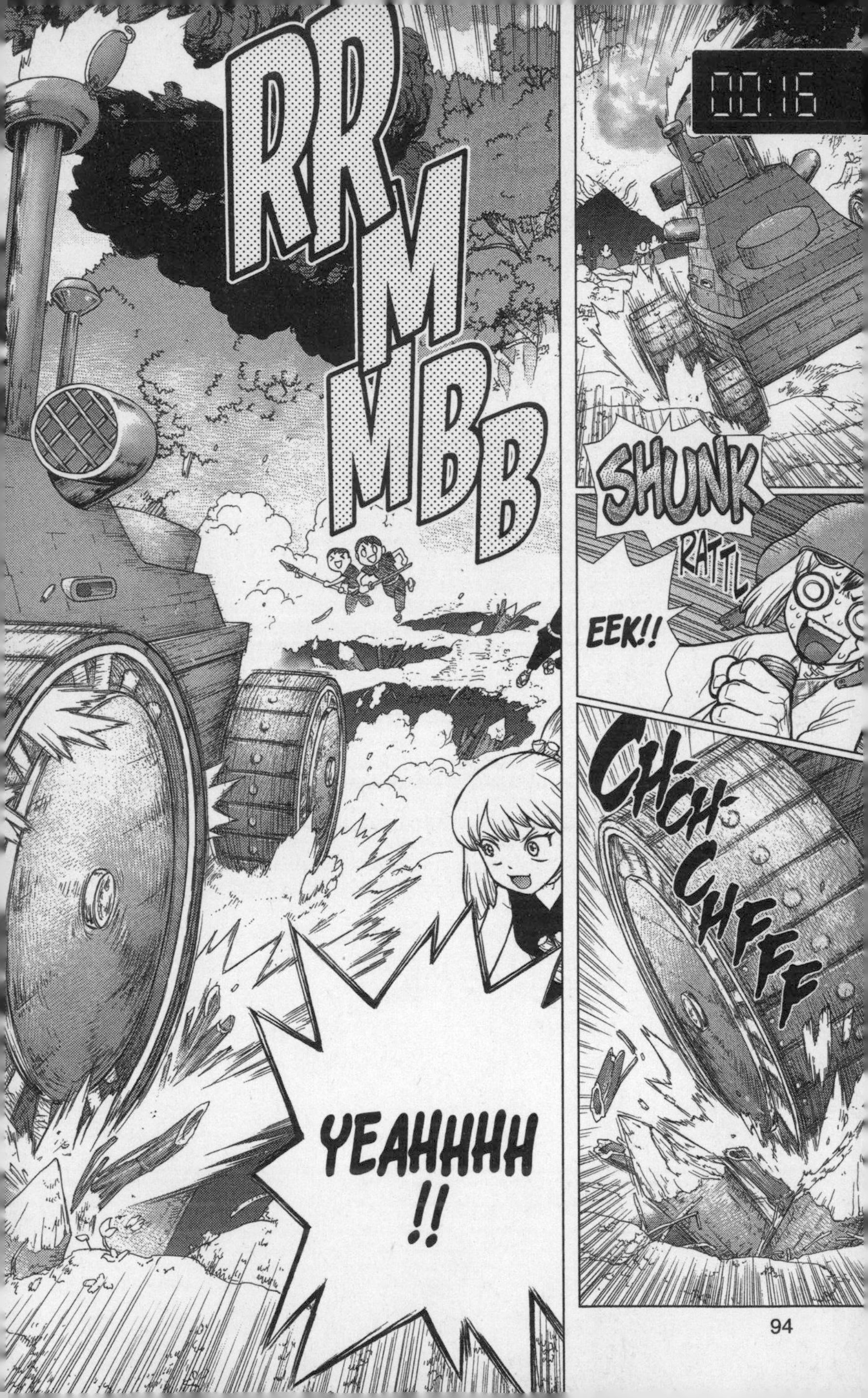
00:16
SHUNK
RATTL
EEK!!
CHCH-CHFFF
RRMMBB
YEAHHHH!!

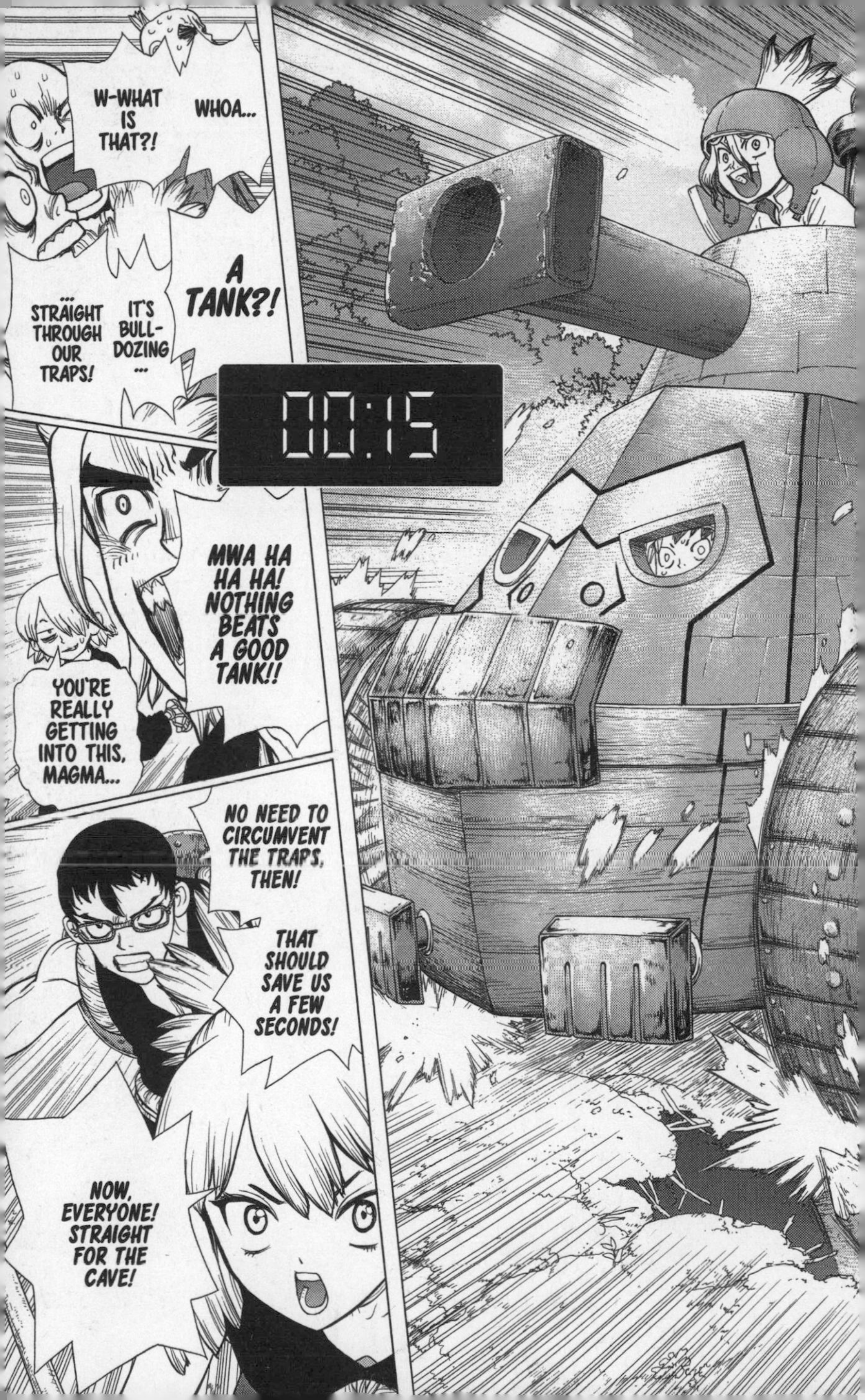
00:15
WHOA...
W-WHAT IS THAT?!
A TANK?!
IT'S BULLDOZING...
...STRAIGHT THROUGH OUR TRAPS!
MWA HA HA HA! NOTHING BEATS A GOOD TANK!!
YOU'RE REALLY GETTING INTO THIS, MAGMA...
NO NEED TO CIRCUMVENT THE TRAPS, THEN!
THAT SHOULD SAVE US A FEW SECONDS!
NOW, EVERYONE! STRAIGHT FOR THE CAVE!

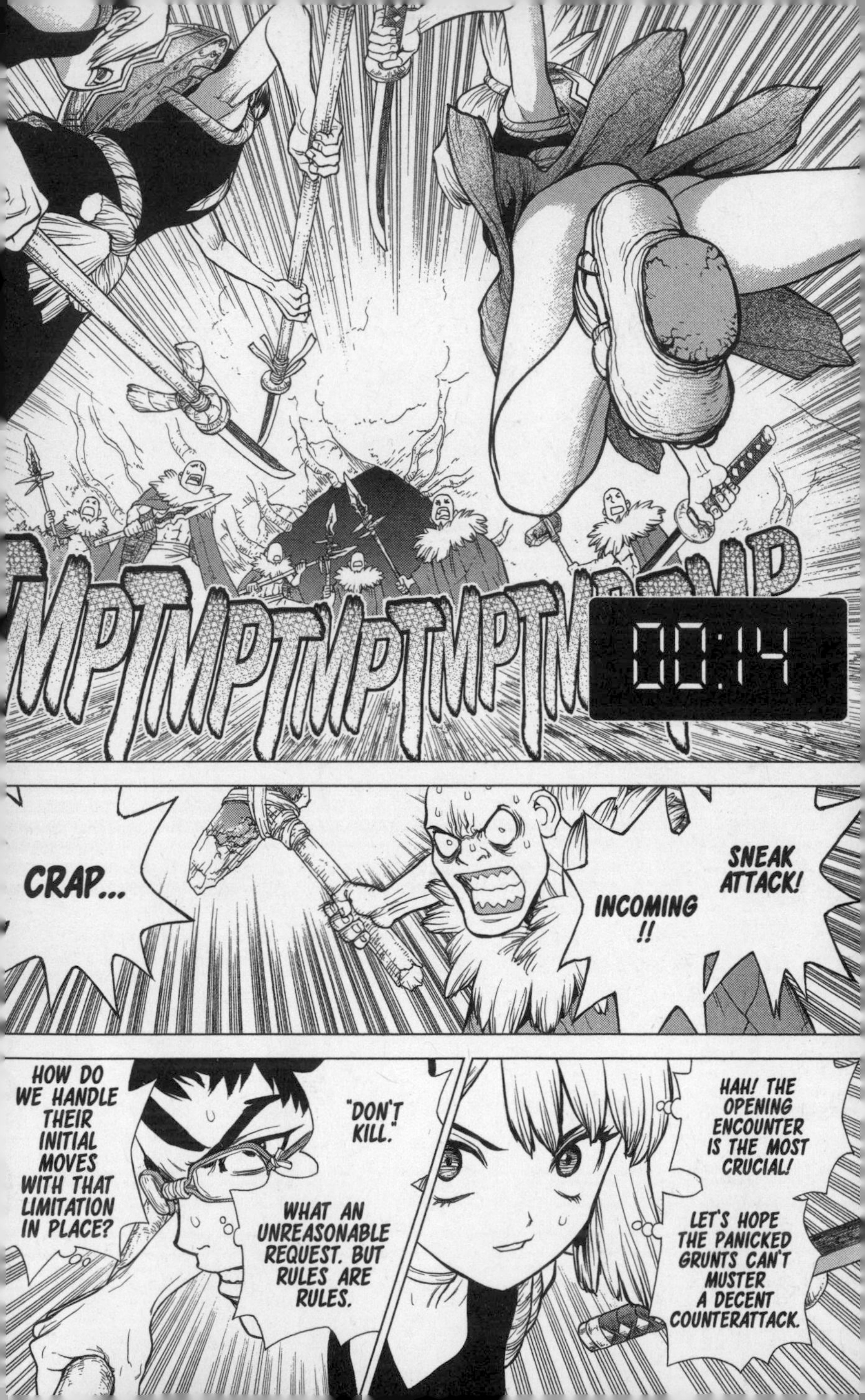
TMPTMPTMPTMPTM
00:14
SNEAK ATTACK!
INCOMING !!
CRAP...
HAH! THE OPENING ENCOUNTER IS THE MOST CRUCIAL!
LET'S HOPE THE PANICKED GRUNTS CAN'T MUSTER A DECENT COUNTERATTACK.
"DON'T KILL."
WHAT AN UNREASONABLE REQUEST. BUT RULES ARE RULES.
HOW DO WE HANDLE THEIR INITIAL MOVES WITH THAT LIMITATION IN PLACE?

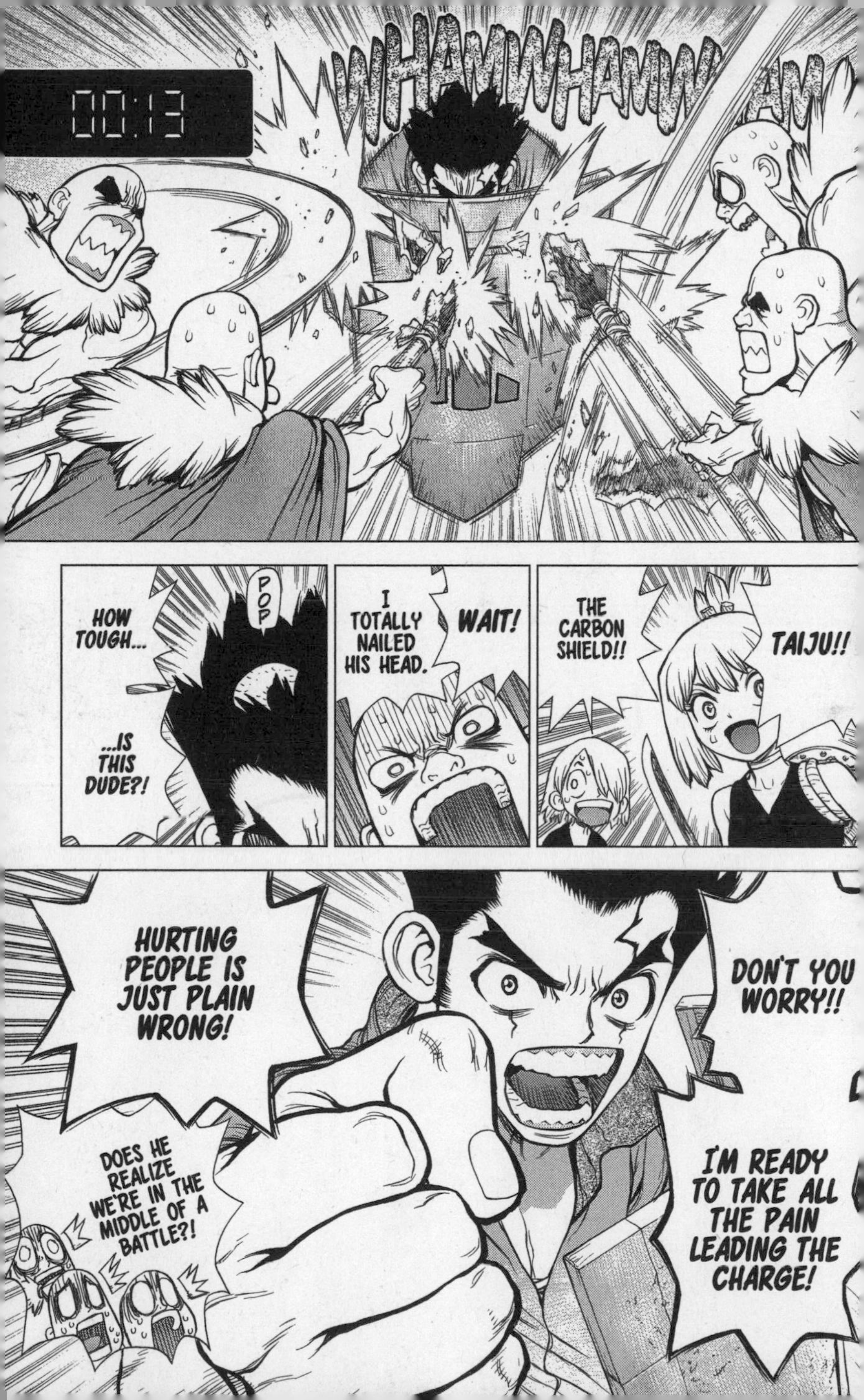

00:13
WHAMWHAMW AM
TAIJU!!
THE CARBON SHIELD!!
WAIT!
I TOTALLY NAILED HIS HEAD.
POP
HOW TOUGH...
...IS THIS DUDE?!
DON'T YOU WORRY!!
I'M READY TO TAKE ALL THE PAIN LEADING THE CHARGE!
HURTING PEOPLE IS JUST PLAIN WRONG!
DOES HE REALIZE WE'RE IN THE MIDDLE OF A BATTLE?!

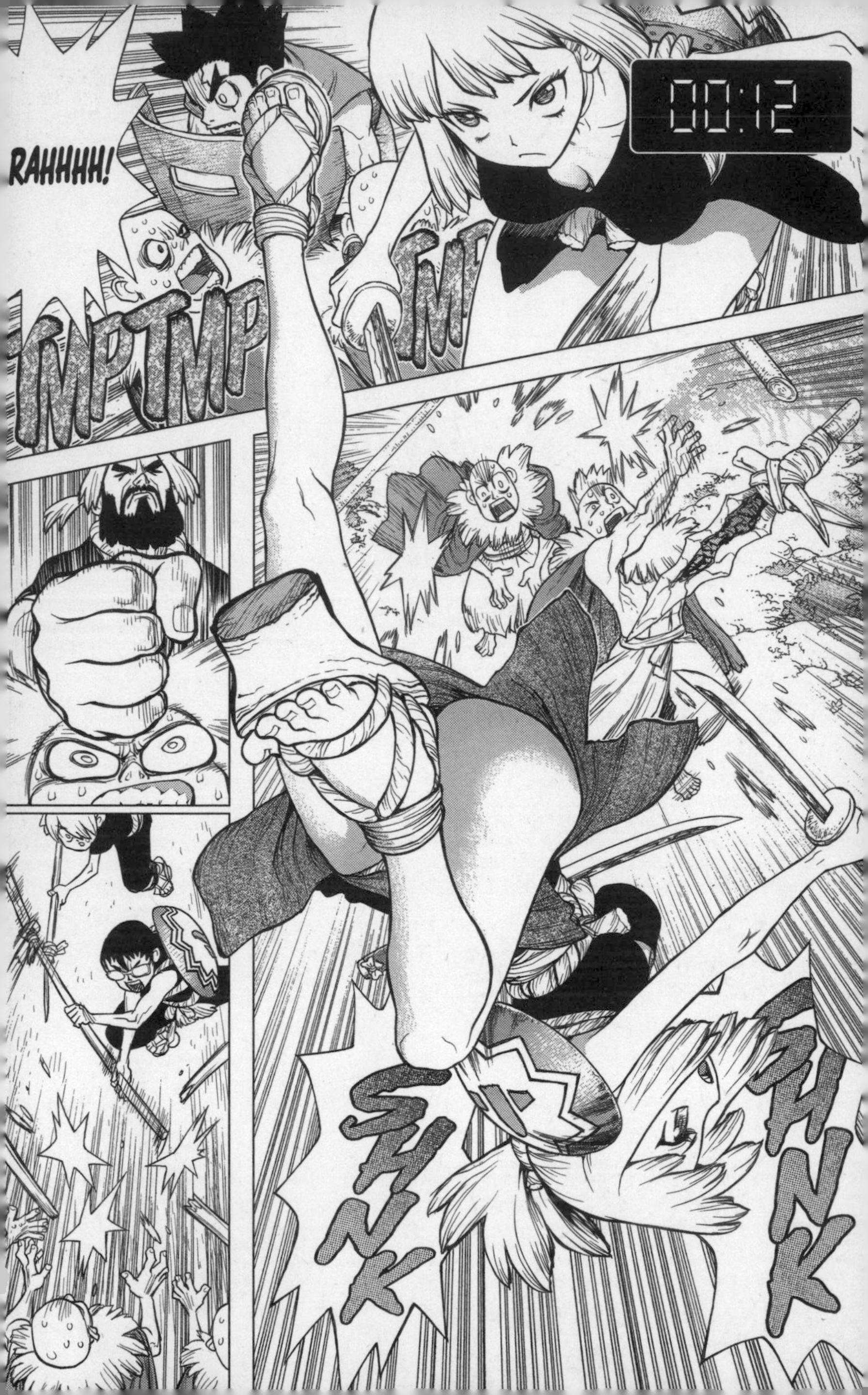

00:12
TMPTMPTMP
RAHHHH!
SHNK
SHNK

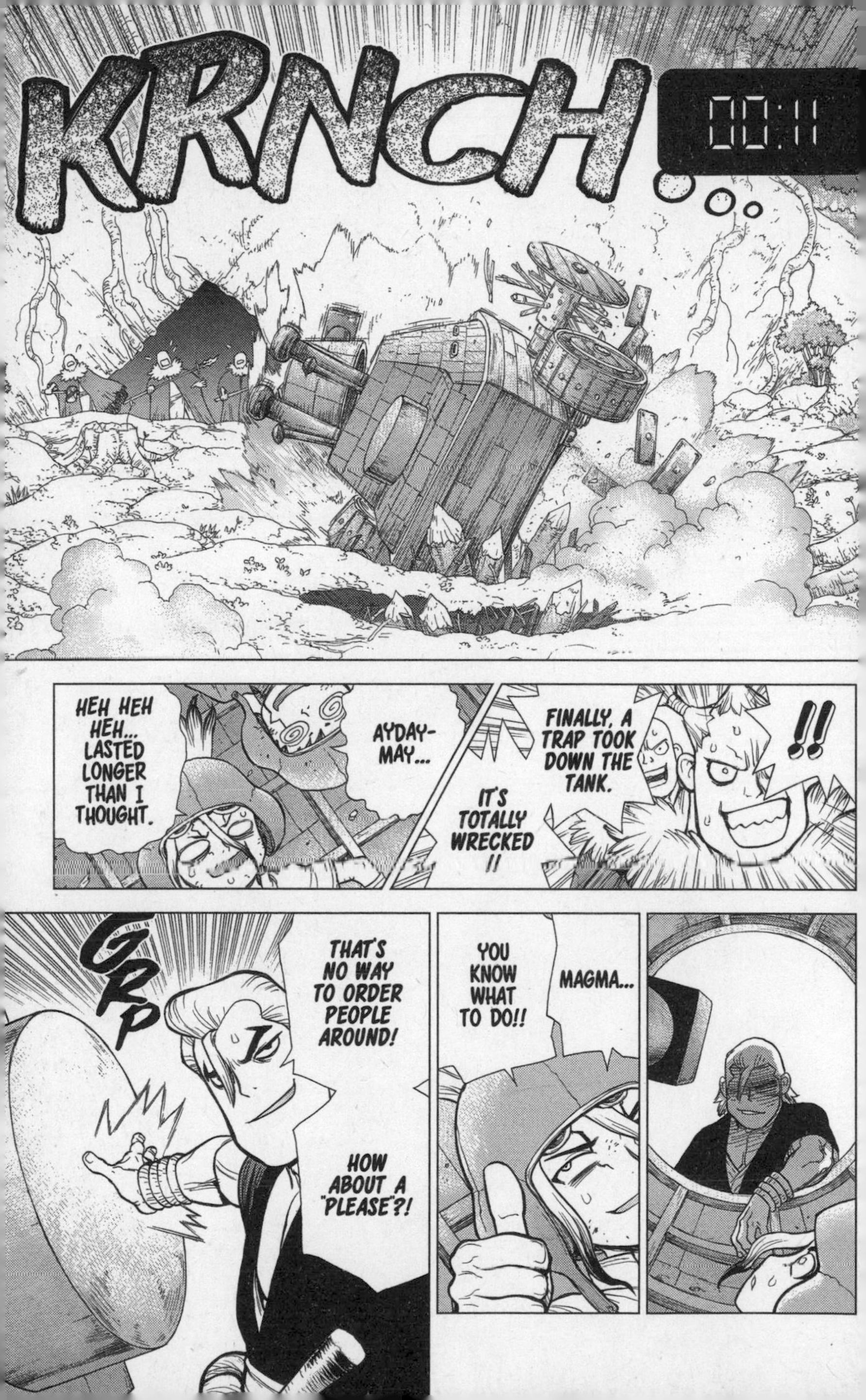
00:11
KRNCH
FINALLY, A TRAP TOOK DOWN THE TANK.
!!
IT'S TOTALLY WRECKED!!
AYDAY-MAY...
HEH HEH HEH... LASTED LONGER THAN I THOUGHT.
MAGMA...
YOU KNOW WHAT TO DO!!
THAT'S NO WAY TO ORDER PEOPLE AROUND!
GRP
HOW ABOUT A "PLEASE"?!

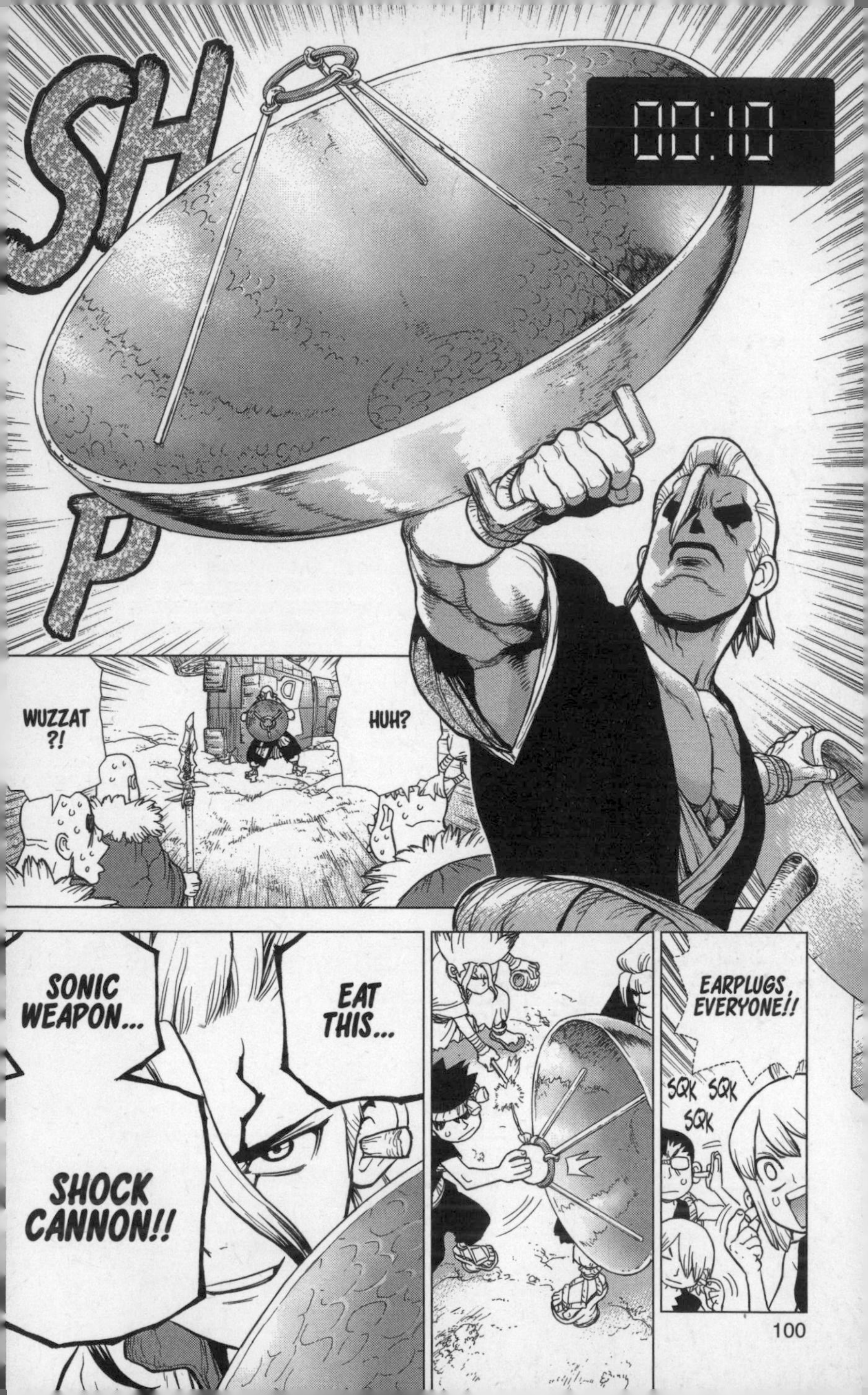
00:10
SHP
HUH?
WUZZAT?!
EARPLUGS, EVERYONE!!
SQK SQK SQK
EAT THIS...
SONIC WEAPON...
SHOCK CANNON!!

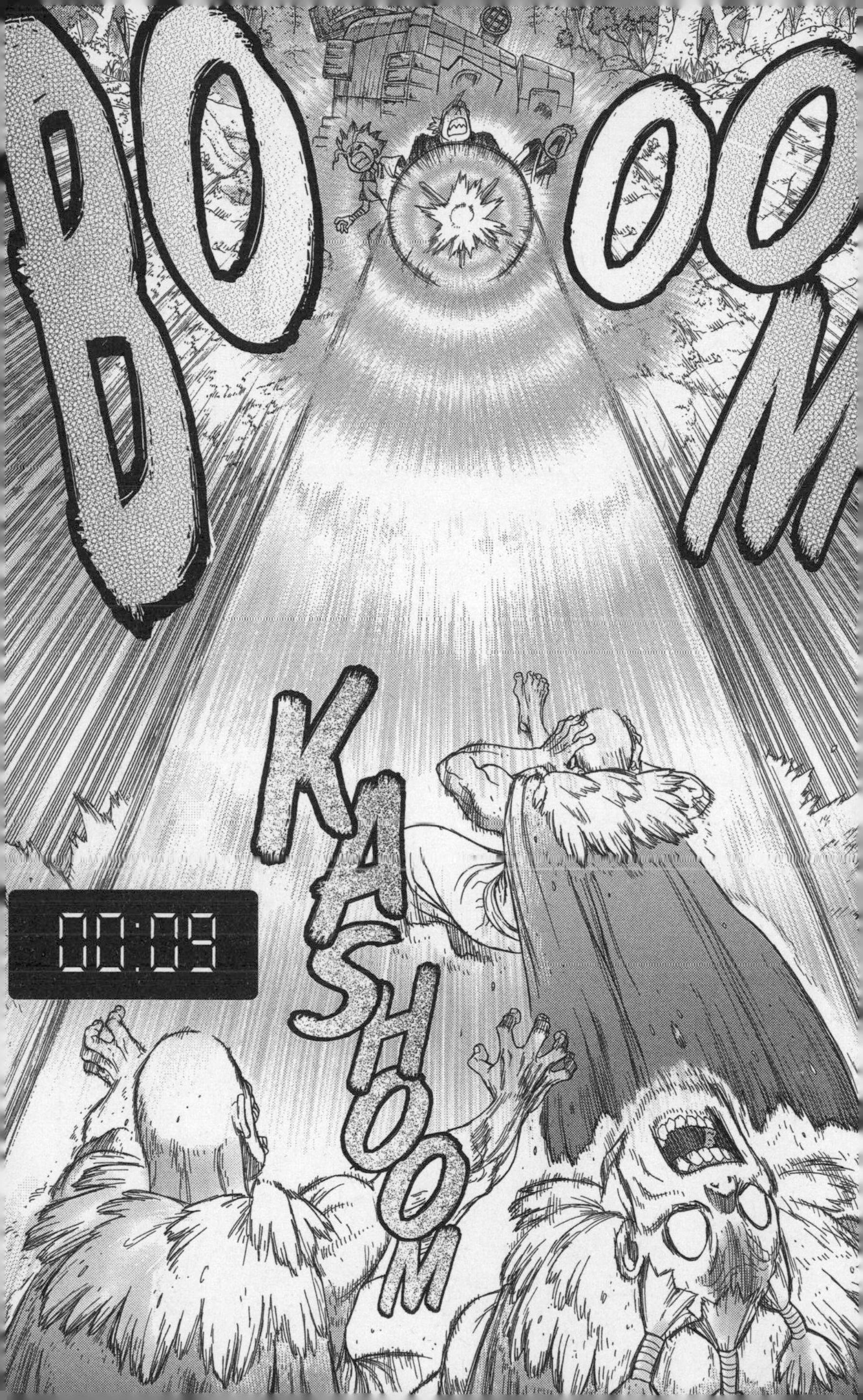
BOOOOM
00:09
KASHOOM

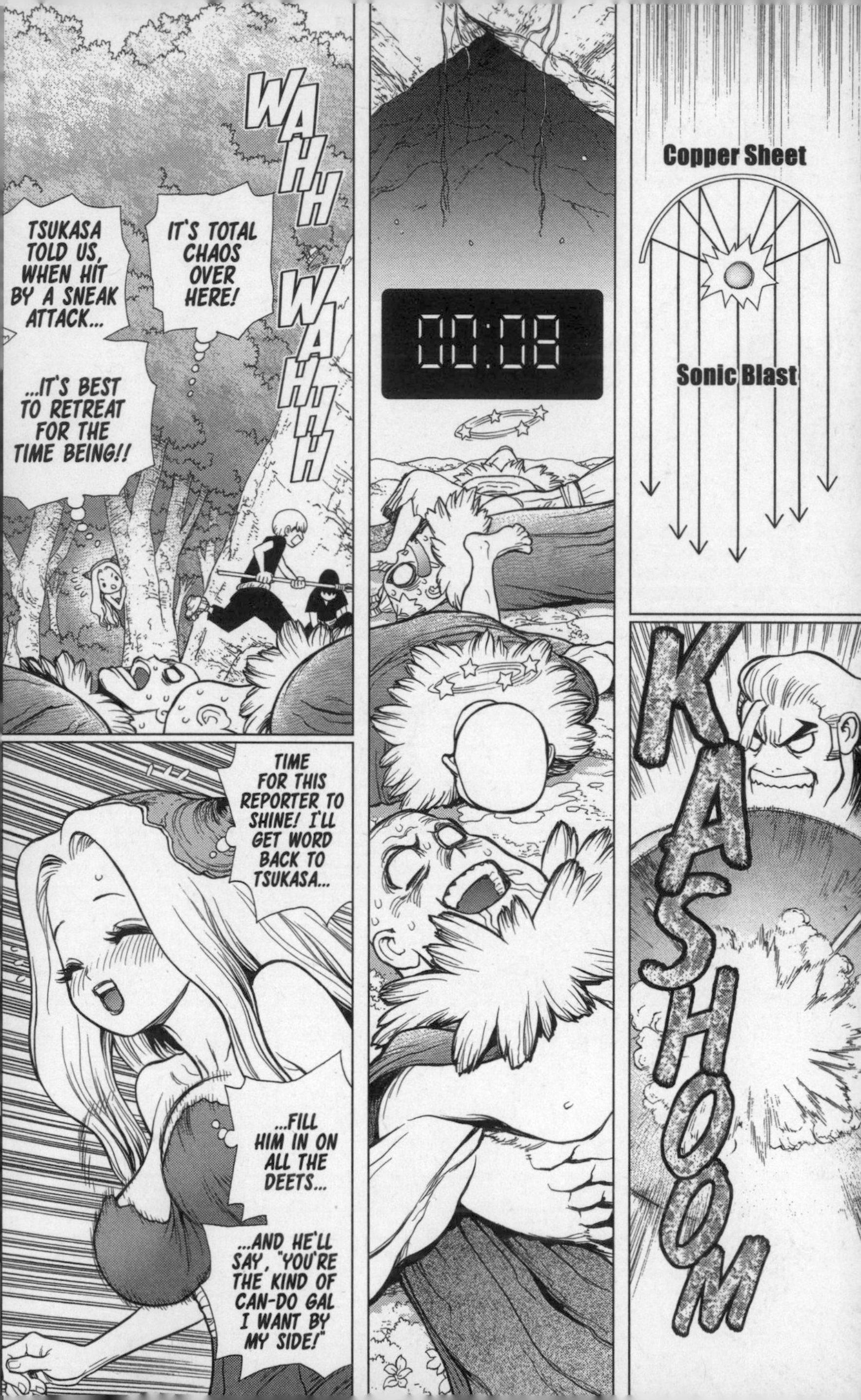
Copper Sheet
Sonic Blast
KASHOOM
00:08
WAHHH
WAHHHH
IT'S TOTAL CHAOS OVER HERE!
TSUKASA TOLD US, WHEN HIT BY A SNEAK ATTACK...
...IT'S BEST TO RETREAT FOR THE TIME BEING!!
TIME FOR THIS REPORTER TO SHINE! I'LL GET WORD BACK TO TSUKASA...
...FILL HIM IN ON ALL THE DEETS...
...AND HE'LL SAY, "YOU'RE THE KIND OF CAN-DO GAL I WANT BY MY SIDE!"

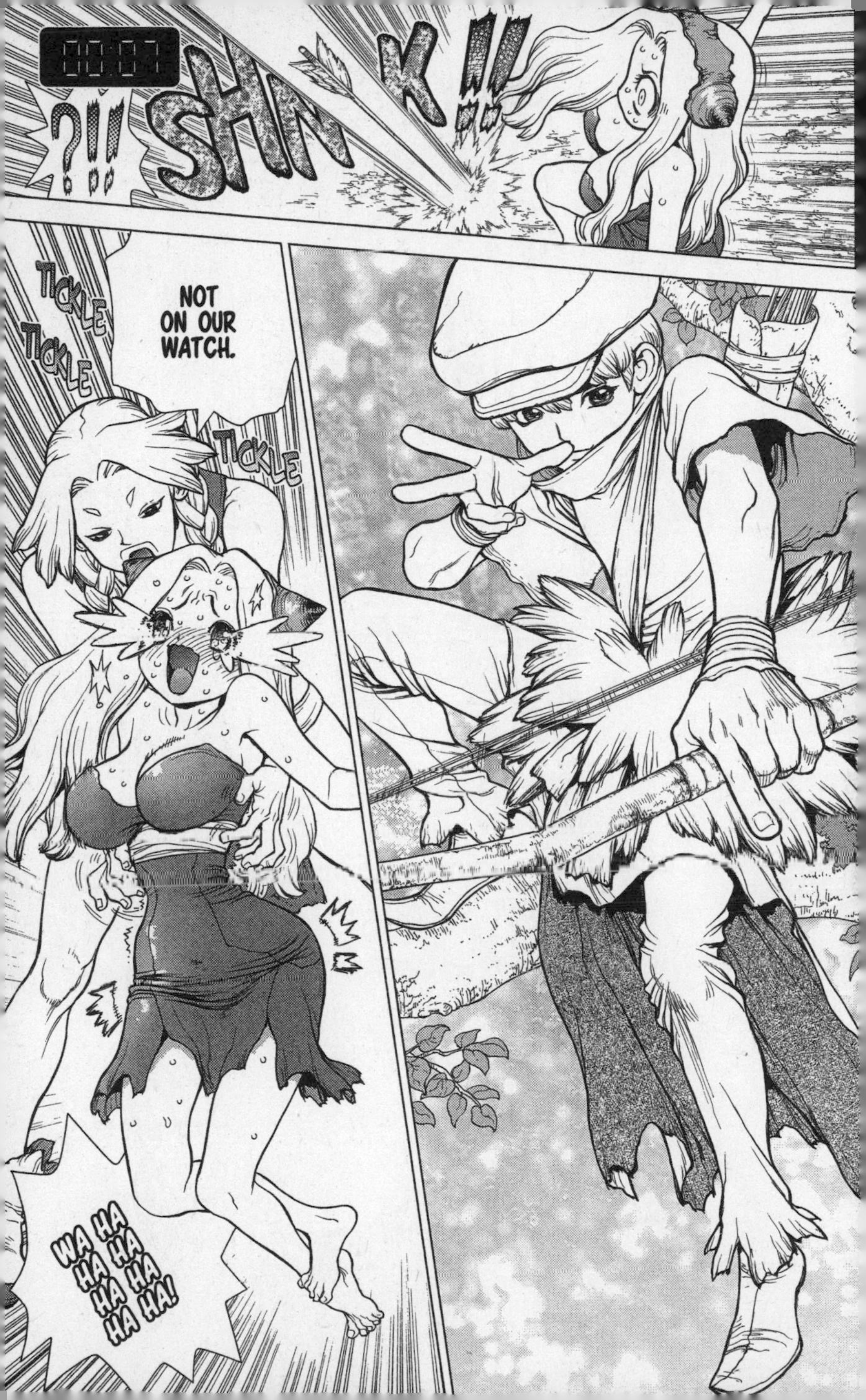
00:07
SHINK!!
?!!
NOT ON OUR WATCH.
TICKLE TICKLE
TICKLE
WA HA HA HA HA HA HA HA HA HA!

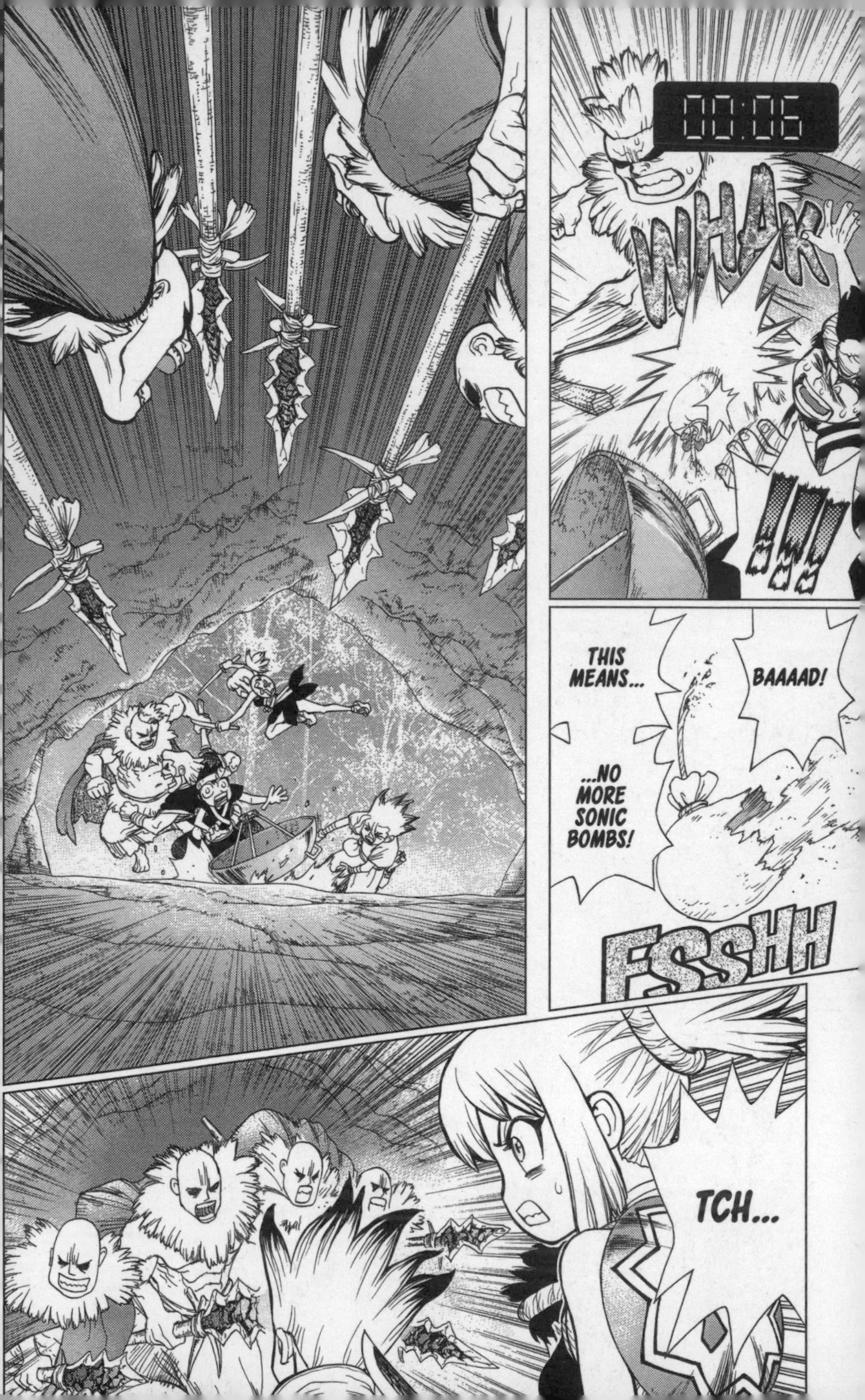
00:06
WHAK
!!!
BAAAAD!
THIS MEANS...
...NO MORE SONIC BOMBS!
FSSHH
TCH...

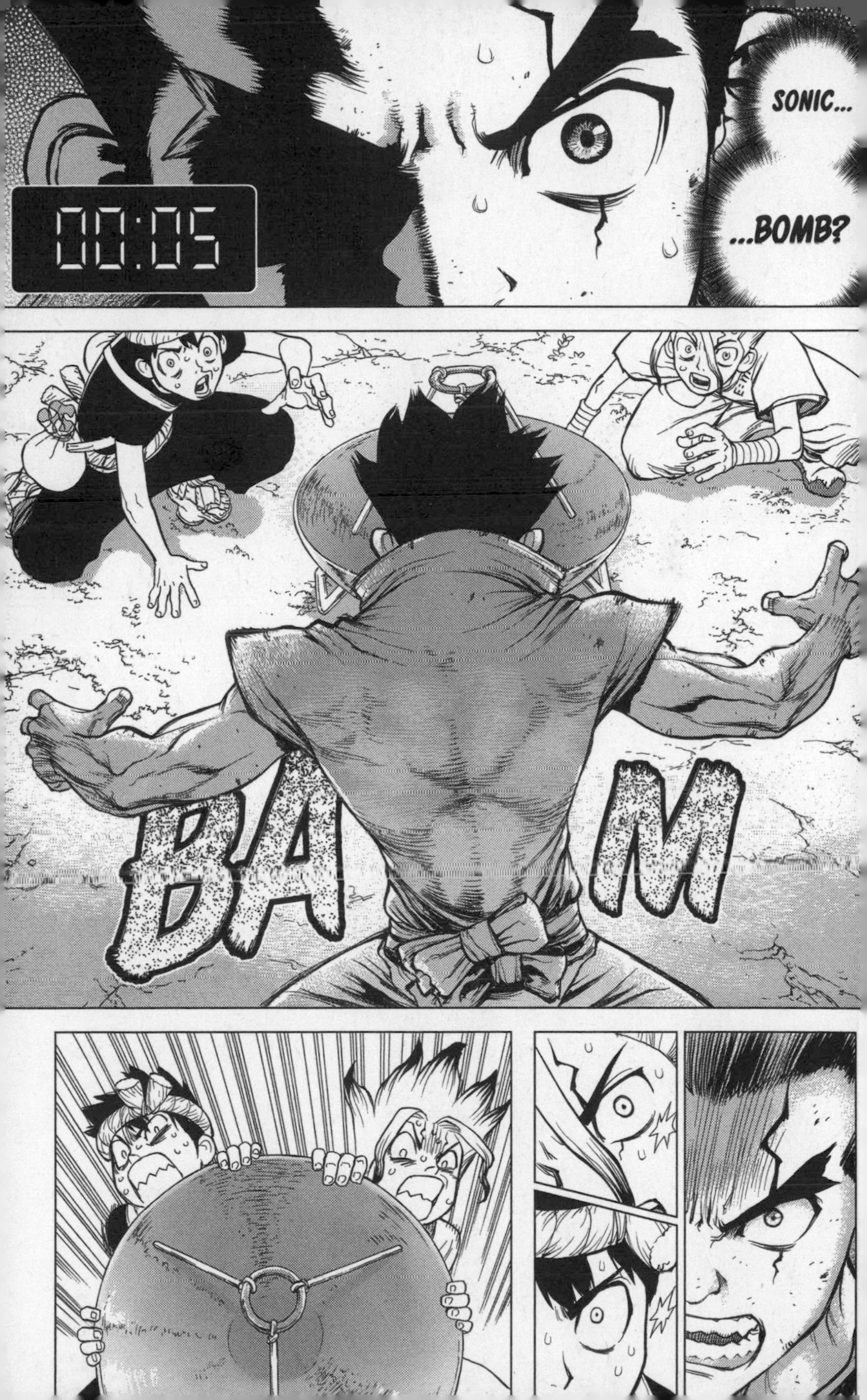
SONIC...
...BOMB?
00:05
BAM

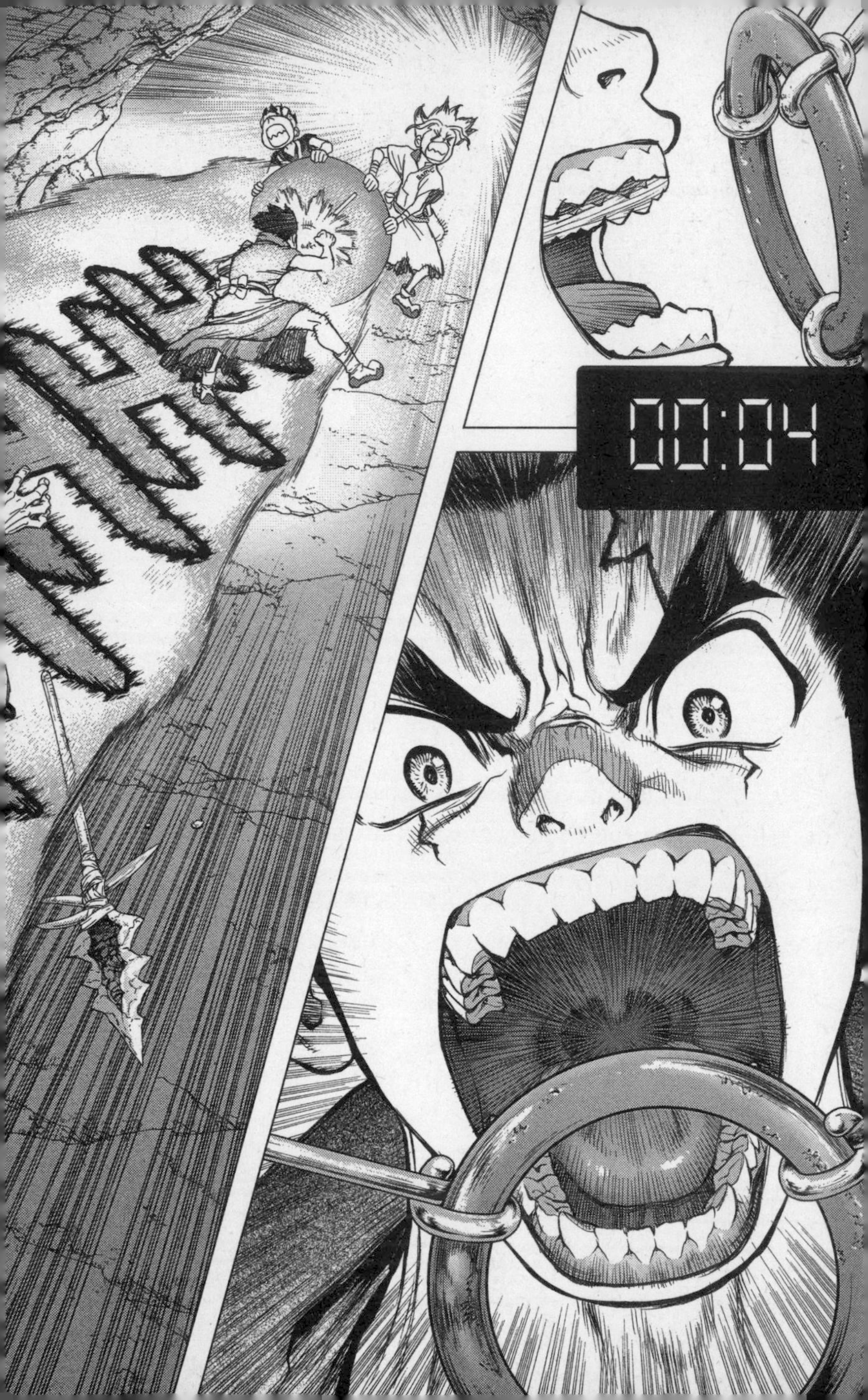
00:04

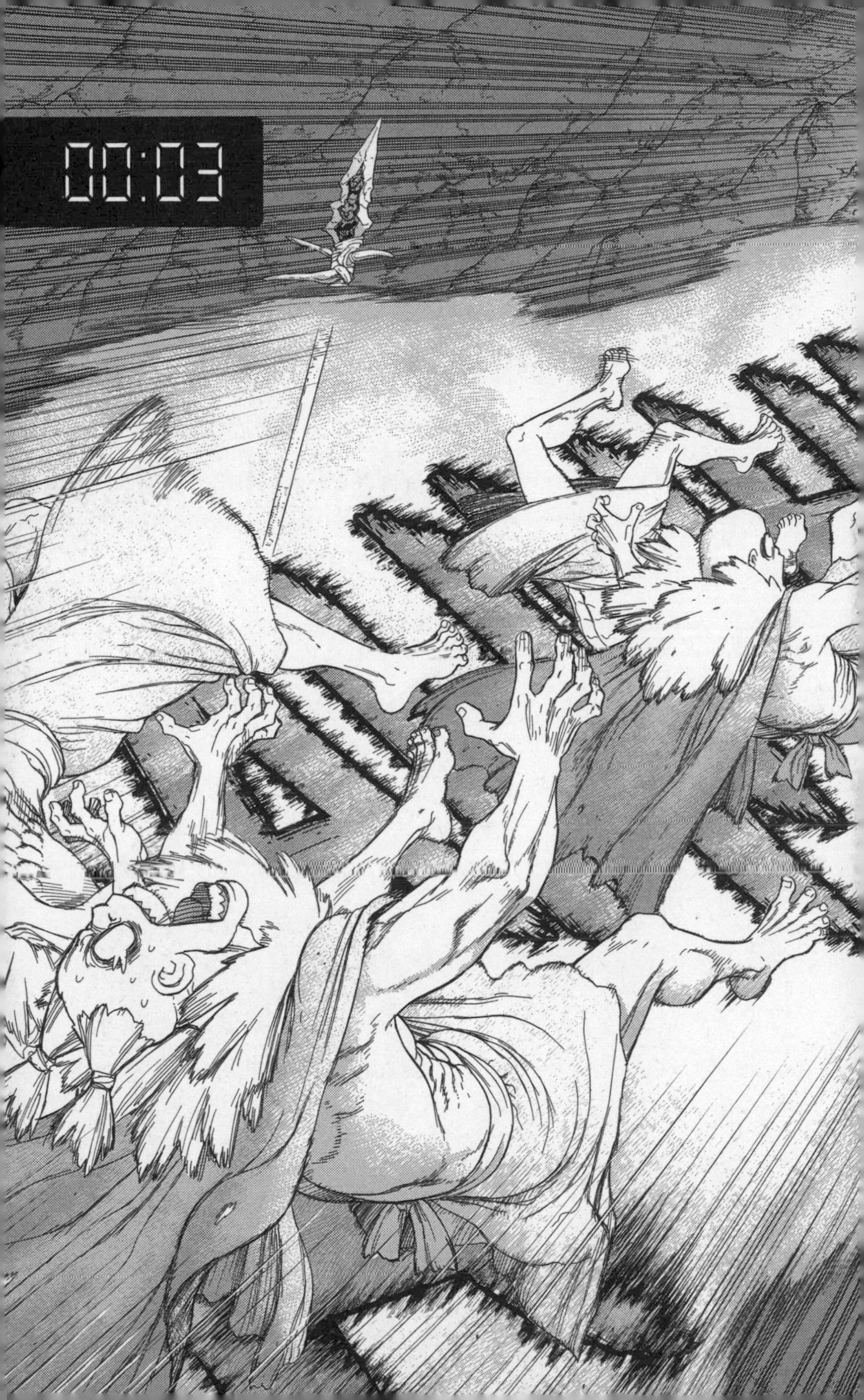
00:03

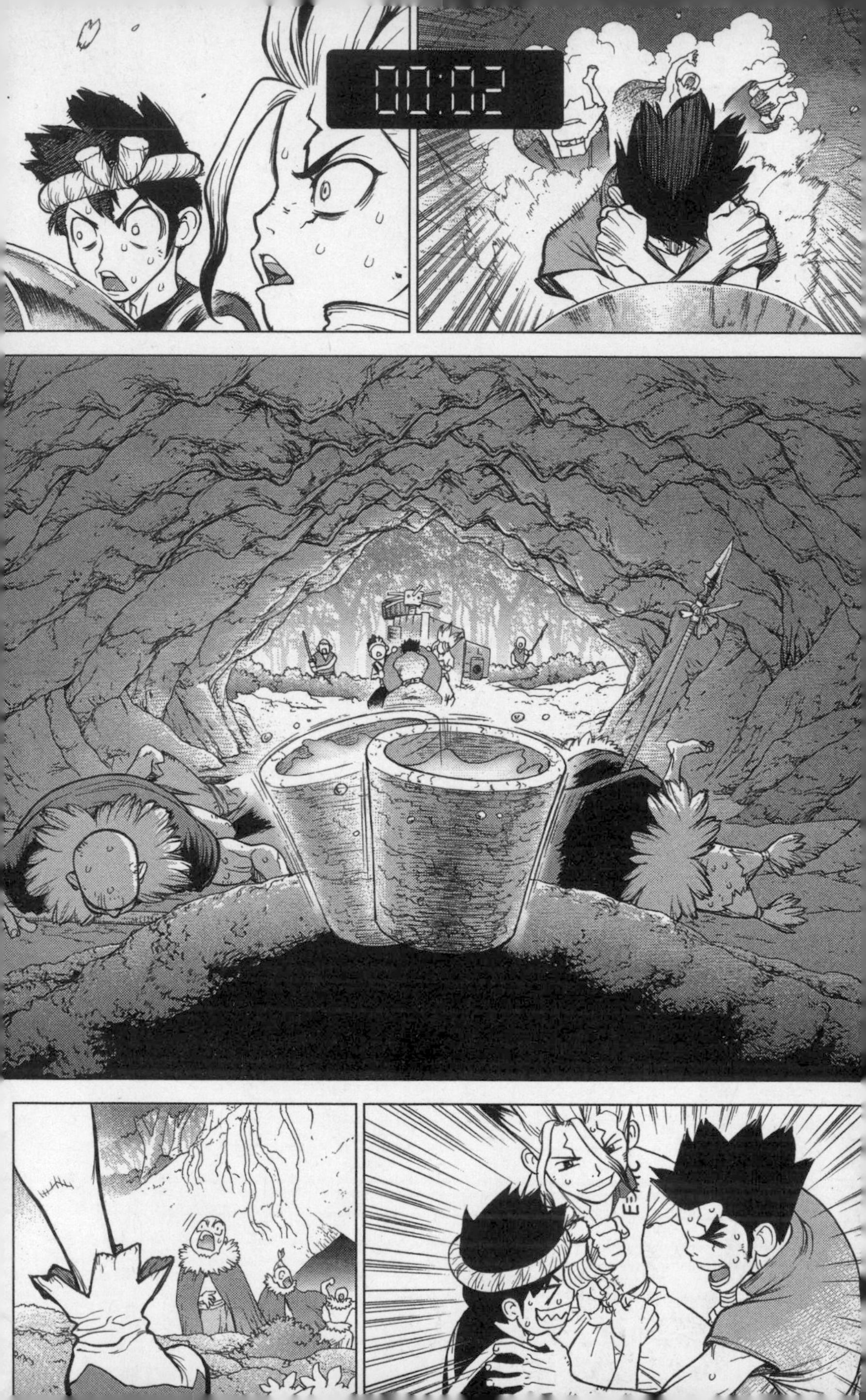
00:02

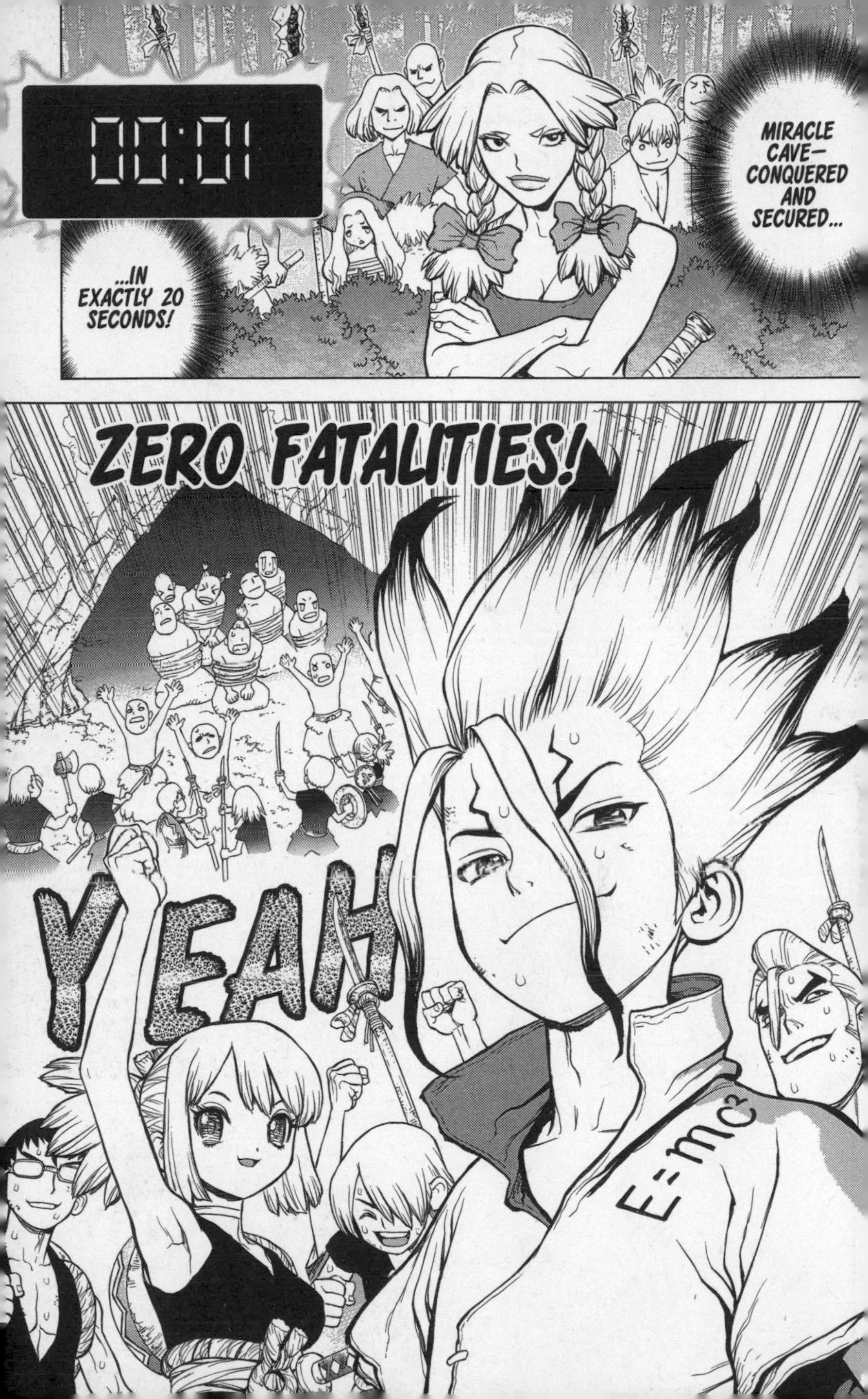
MIRACLE CAVE— CONQUERED AND SECURED...
00:01
...IN EXACTLY 20 SECONDS!
ZERO FATALITIES!
YEAH

Tsukasa Empire

FIGHTER FILE 5

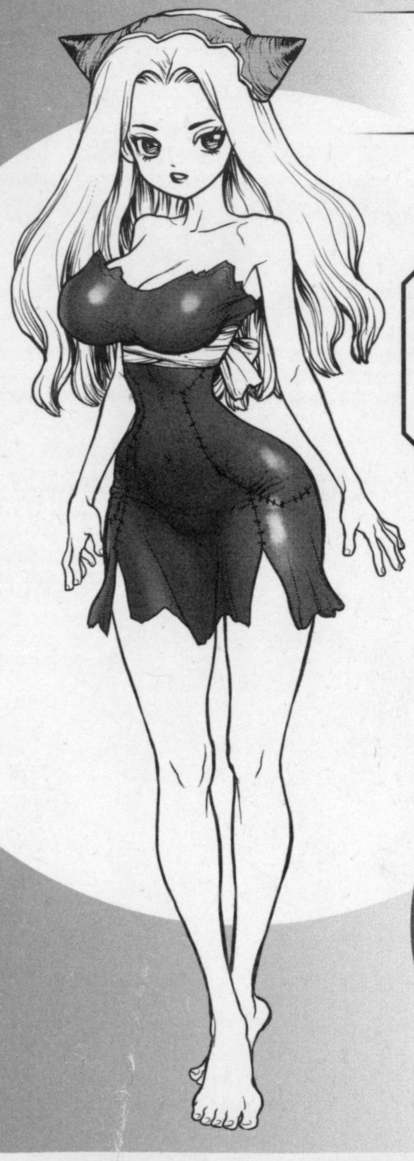

Reporter

Fighting Skills:	☆
Writing Skills:	☆☆☆
Researching Skills:	☆☆☆☆☆

Full Name: Minami Hokutozai

Height: 166 cm

A former newspaper reporter known for her extensive network of connections and her reputation for hunting down every last detail of a story. In Japanese name order, the kanji in her full name are "North, East, West, South," which spells out NEWS, so perhaps she felt the pull of destiny toward this career path. She takes pride in her work and would never use her sex appeal as a tool for seducing people into giving her a scoop.

Z=76: Final Battle

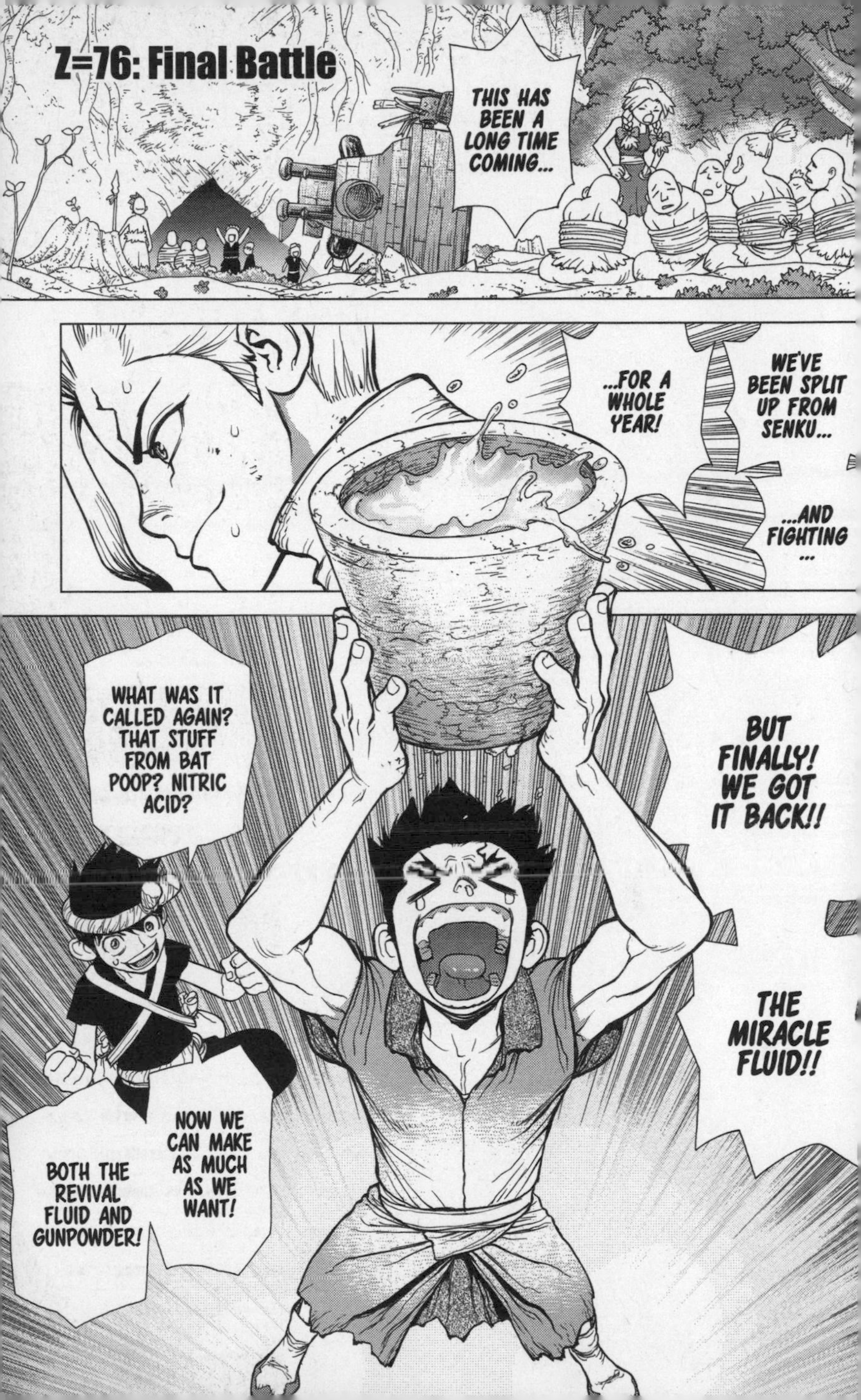
THIS HAS BEEN A LONG TIME COMING...
WE'VE BEEN SPLIT UP FROM SENKU...
...AND FIGHTING...
...FOR A WHOLE YEAR!
BUT FINALLY! WE GOT IT BACK!!
THE MIRACLE FLUID!!
WHAT WAS IT CALLED AGAIN? THAT STUFF FROM BAT POOP? NITRIC ACID?
NOW WE CAN MAKE AS MUCH AS WE WANT!
BOTH THE REVIVAL FLUID AND GUNPOWDER!

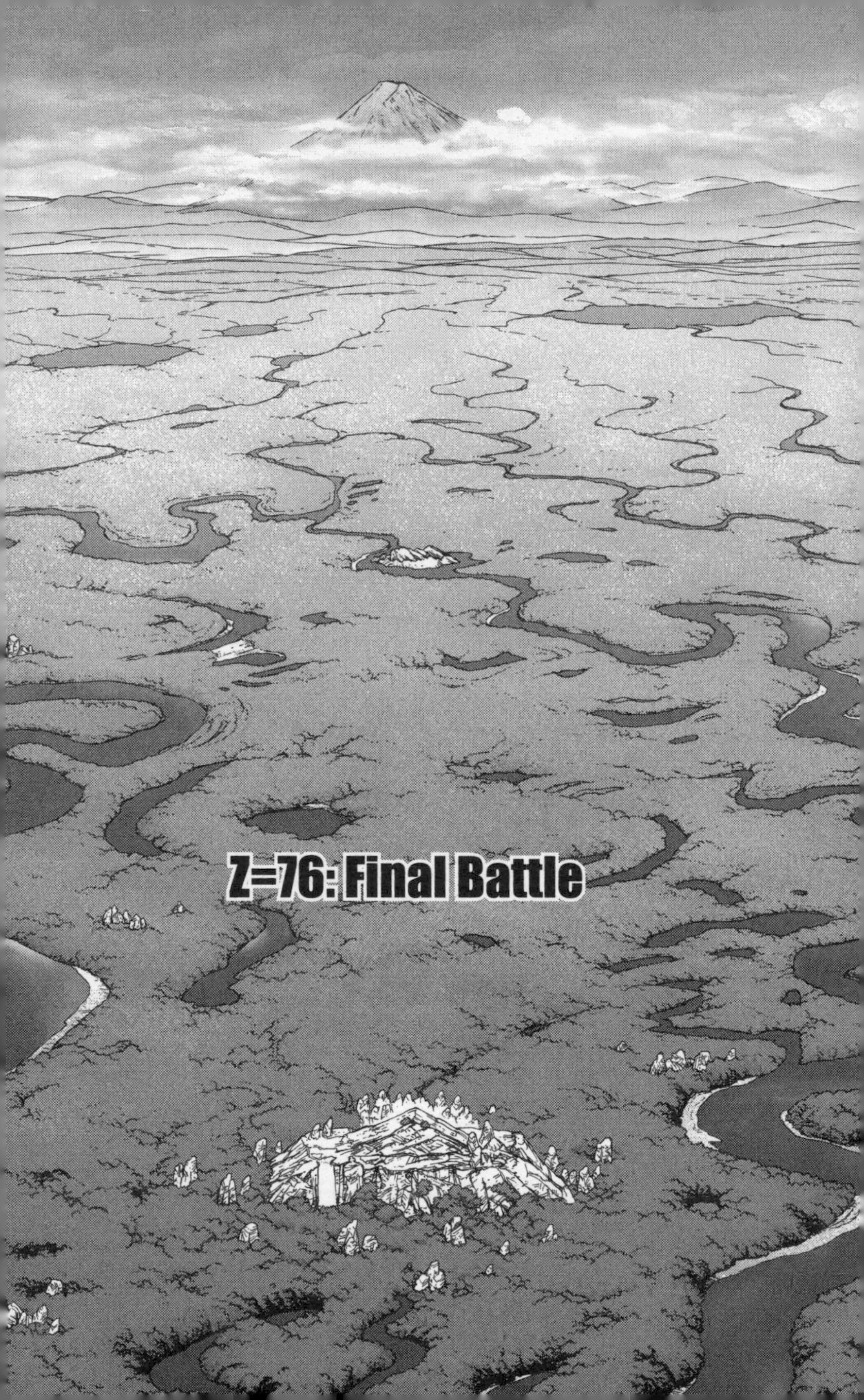
Z=76: Final Battle

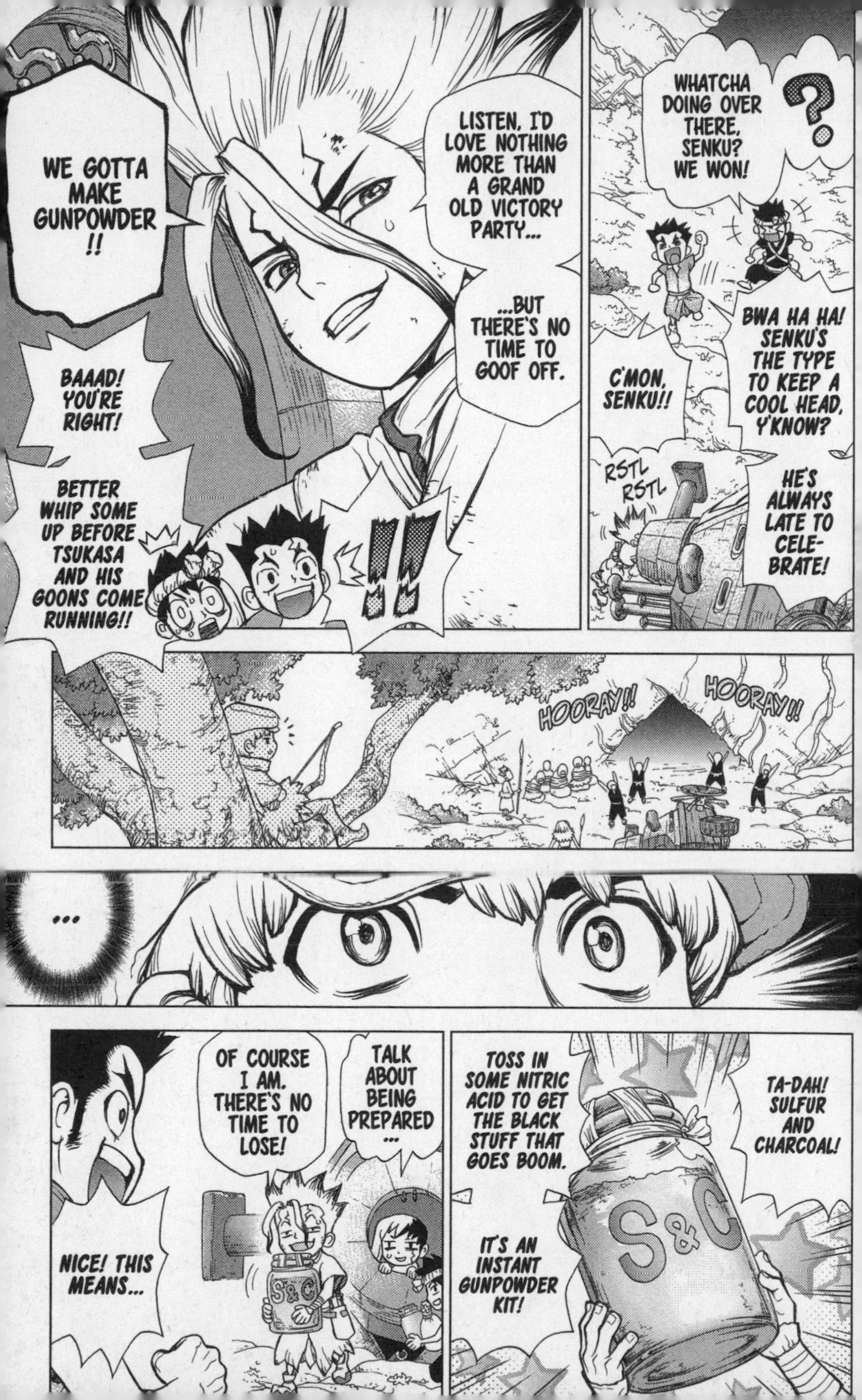
WHATCHA DOING OVER THERE, SENKU? WE WON!
?
BWA HA HA! SENKU'S THE TYPE TO KEEP A COOL HEAD, Y'KNOW?
C'MON, SENKU!!
RSTL RSTL
HE'S ALWAYS LATE TO CELE-BRATE!
LISTEN, I'D LOVE NOTHING MORE THAN A GRAND OLD VICTORY PARTY...
...BUT THERE'S NO TIME TO GOOF OFF.
WE GOTTA MAKE GUNPOWDER !!
!!
BAAAD! YOU'RE RIGHT!
BETTER WHIP SOME UP BEFORE TSUKASA AND HIS GOONS COME RUNNING!!
HOORAY!!
HOORAY!!
...
TA-DAH! SULFUR AND CHARCOAL!
TOSS IN SOME NITRIC ACID TO GET THE BLACK STUFF THAT GOES BOOM.
IT'S AN INSTANT GUNPOWDER KIT!
S&C
TALK ABOUT BEING PREPARED ...
OF COURSE I AM. THERE'S NO TIME TO LOSE!
NICE! THIS MEANS...

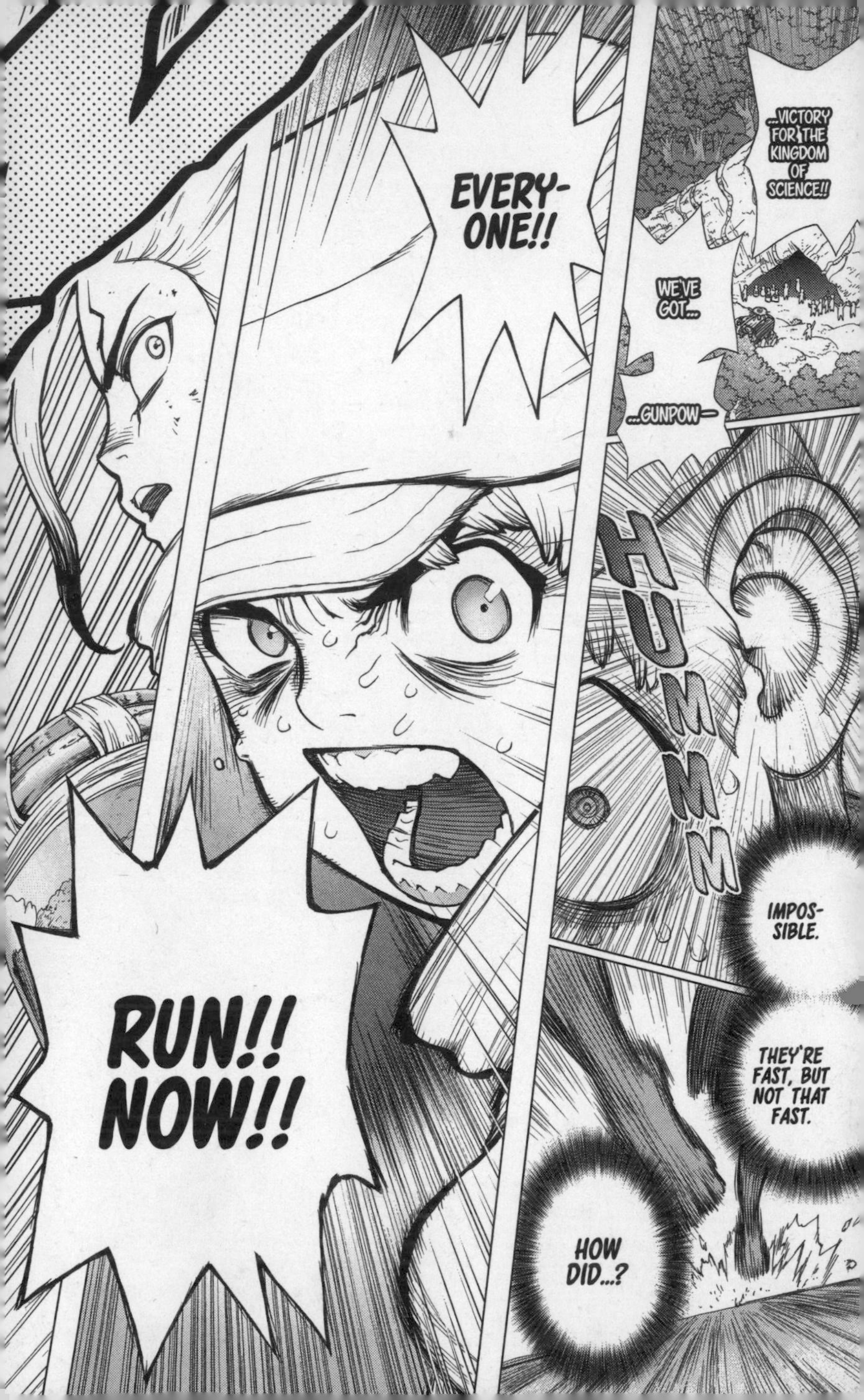
...VICTORY FOR THE KINGDOM OF SCIENCE!!
WE'VE GOT...
...GUNPOW—
HUMMMM
IMPOSSIBLE.
THEY'RE FAST, BUT NOT THAT FAST.
HOW DID...?
EVERY-ONE!!
RUN!! NOW!!

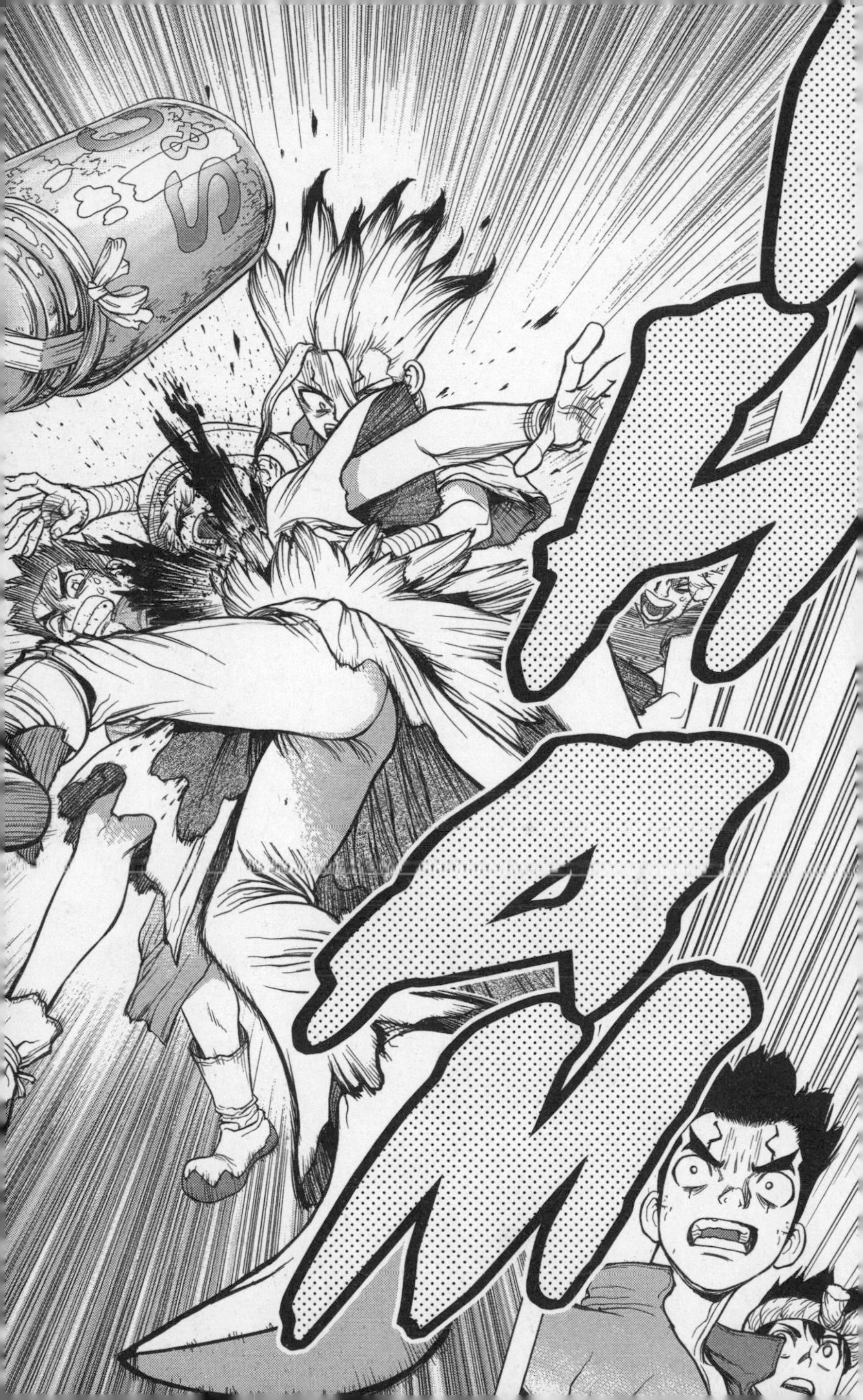

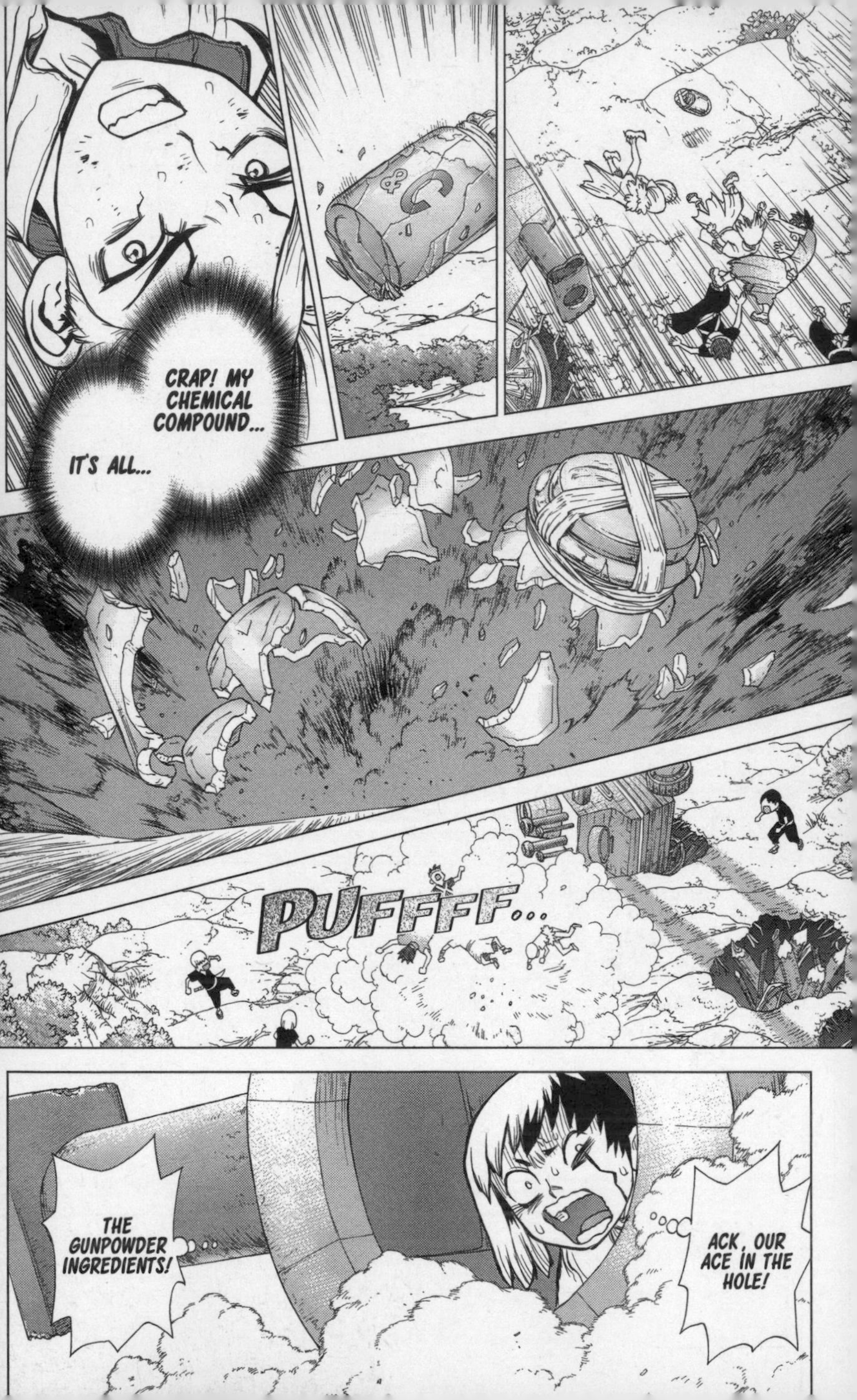
CRAP! MY CHEMICAL COMPOUND...
IT'S ALL...
PUFFFF...
ACK, OUR ACE IN THE HOLE!
THE GUNPOWDER INGREDIENTS!

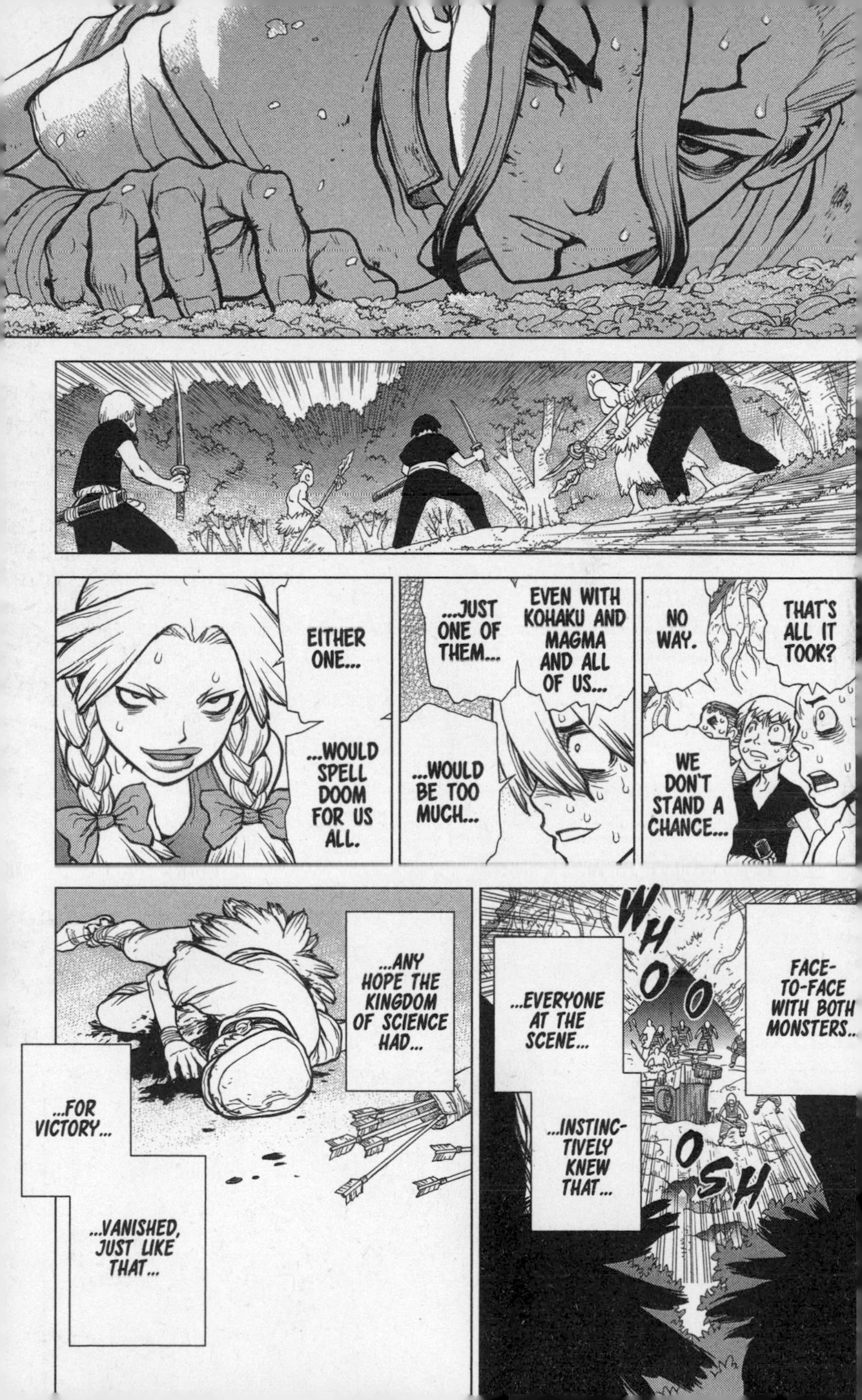
THAT'S ALL IT TOOK?
NO WAY.
WE DON'T STAND A CHANCE...
EVEN WITH KOHAKU AND MAGMA AND ALL OF US...
...JUST ONE OF THEM...
...WOULD BE TOO MUCH...
EITHER ONE...
...WOULD SPELL DOOM FOR US ALL.
FACE-TO-FACE WITH BOTH MONSTERS...
WHOOOOSH
...EVERYONE AT THE SCENE...
...INSTINCTIVELY KNEW THAT...
...ANY HOPE THE KINGDOM OF SCIENCE HAD...
...FOR VICTORY...
...VANISHED, JUST LIKE THAT...

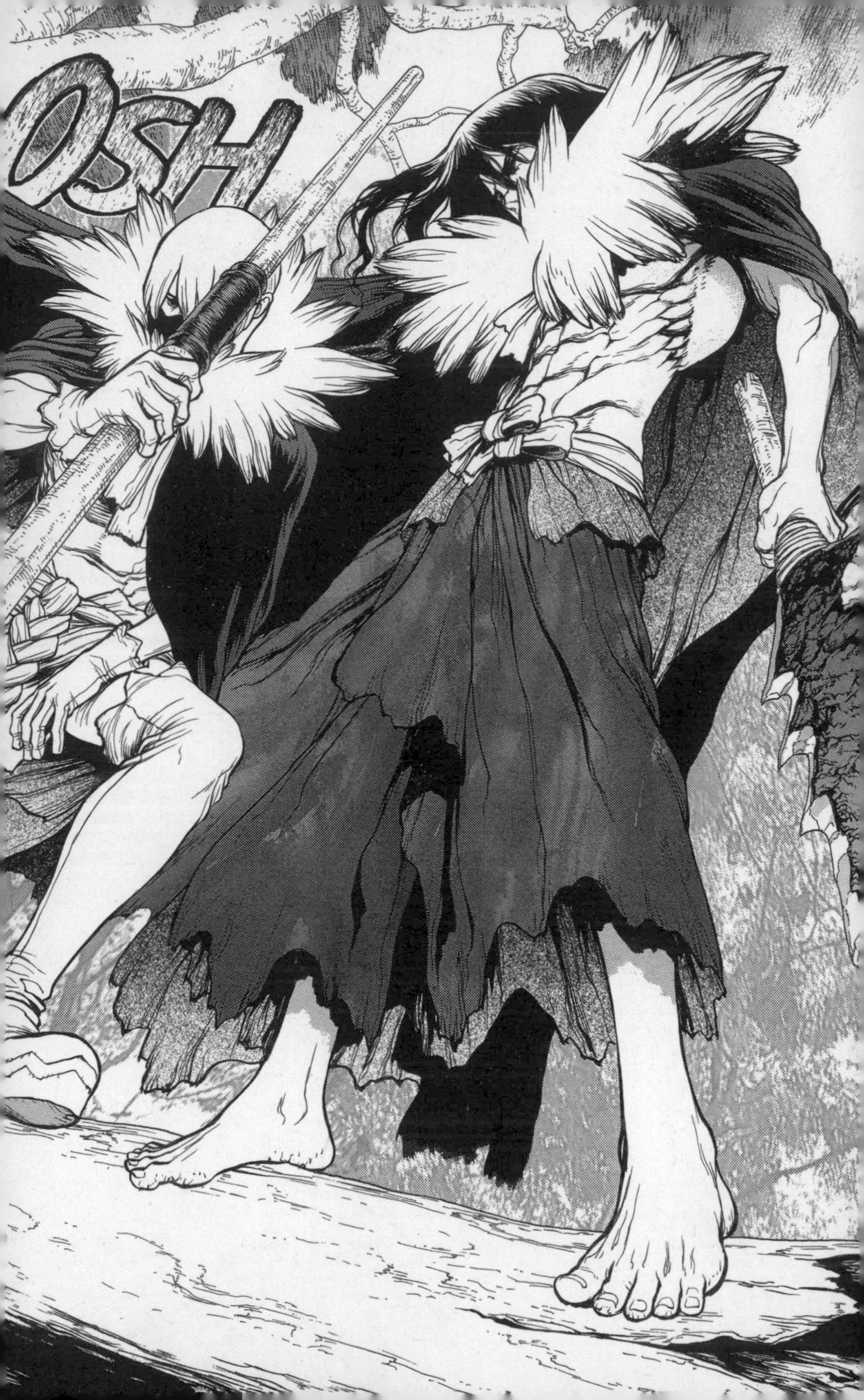
OSH

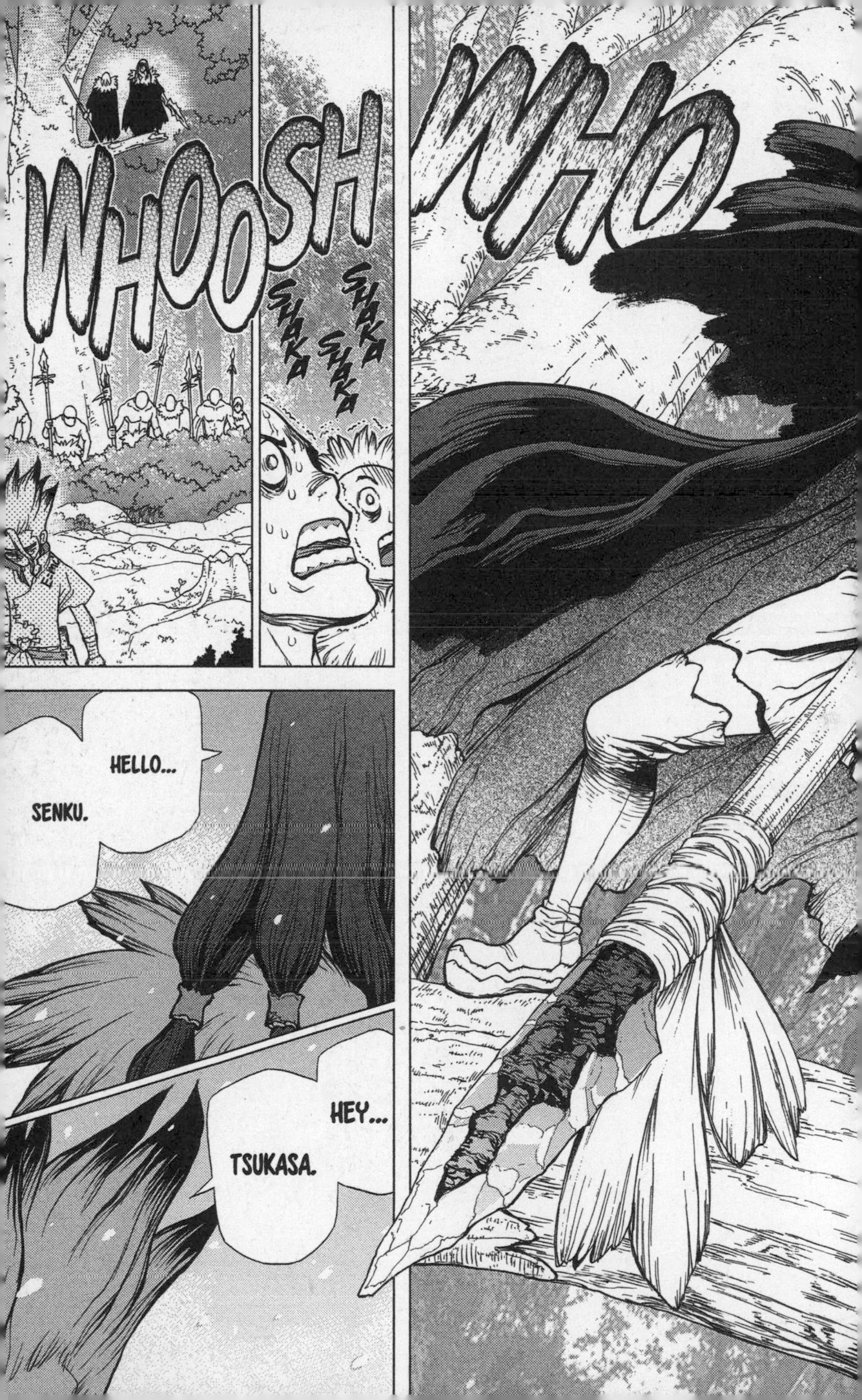

WHO
WHOOSH
SHAKA SHAKA
SHAKA SHAKA
HELLO...
SENKU.
HEY...
TSUKASA.

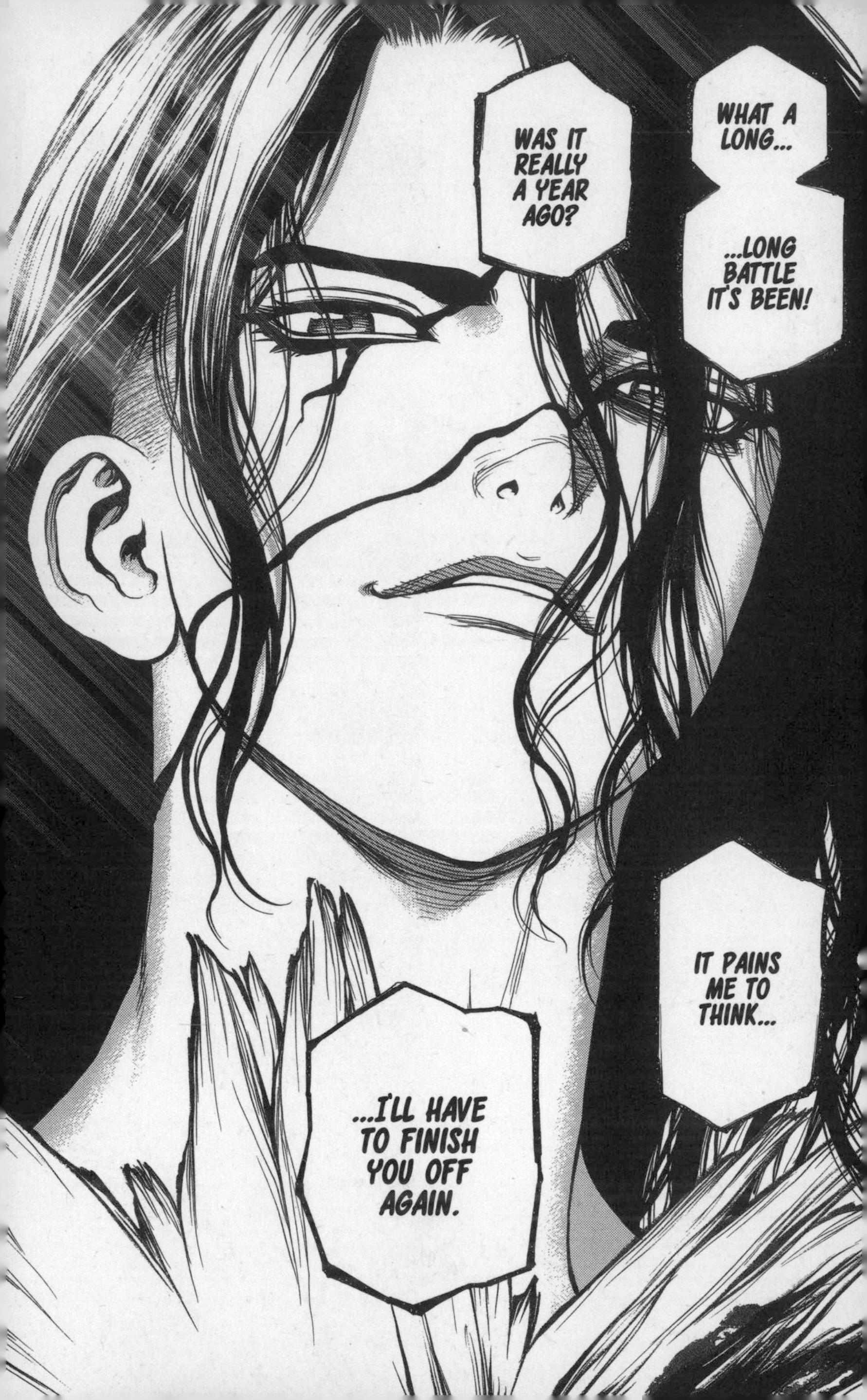
WHAT A LONG...
...LONG BATTLE IT'S BEEN!
WAS IT REALLY A YEAR AGO?
IT PAINS ME TO THINK...
...I'LL HAVE TO FINISH YOU OFF AGAIN.

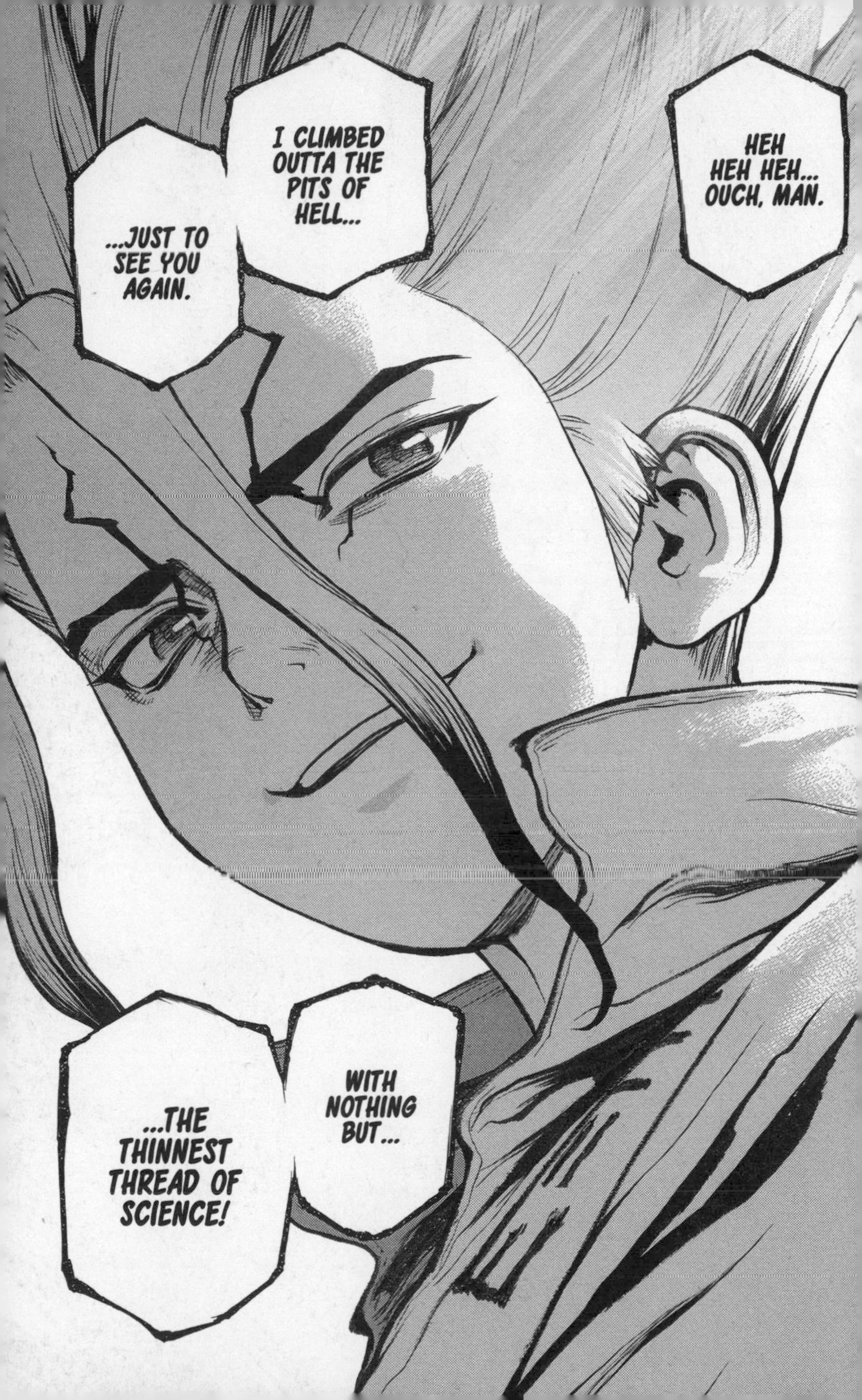
HEH HEH HEH... OUCH, MAN.
I CLIMBED OUTTA THE PITS OF HELL...
...JUST TO SEE YOU AGAIN.
WITH NOTHING BUT...
...THE THINNEST THREAD OF SCIENCE!

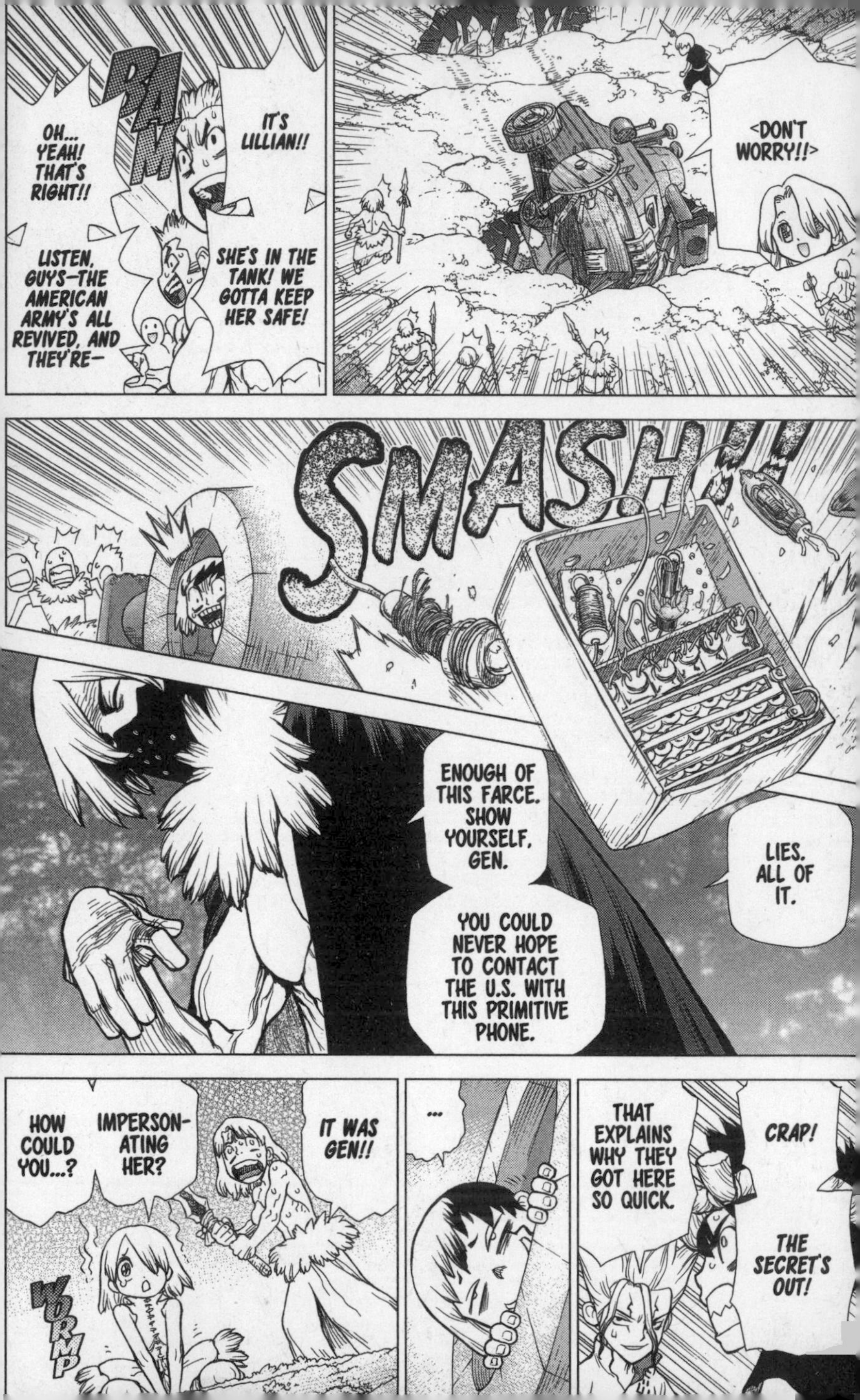
<DON'T WORRY!!>
IT'S LILLIAN!!
BAM
OH... YEAH! THAT'S RIGHT!!
SHE'S IN THE TANK! WE GOTTA KEEP HER SAFE!
LISTEN, GUYS—THE AMERICAN ARMY'S ALL REVIVED, AND THEY'RE—
SMASH!!
LIES. ALL OF IT.
ENOUGH OF THIS FARCE. SHOW YOURSELF, GEN.
YOU COULD NEVER HOPE TO CONTACT THE U.S. WITH THIS PRIMITIVE PHONE.
CRAP!
THAT EXPLAINS WHY THEY GOT HERE SO QUICK.
THE SECRET'S OUT!
...
IT WAS GEN!!
IMPERSON-ATING HER?
HOW COULD YOU...?
WORMP

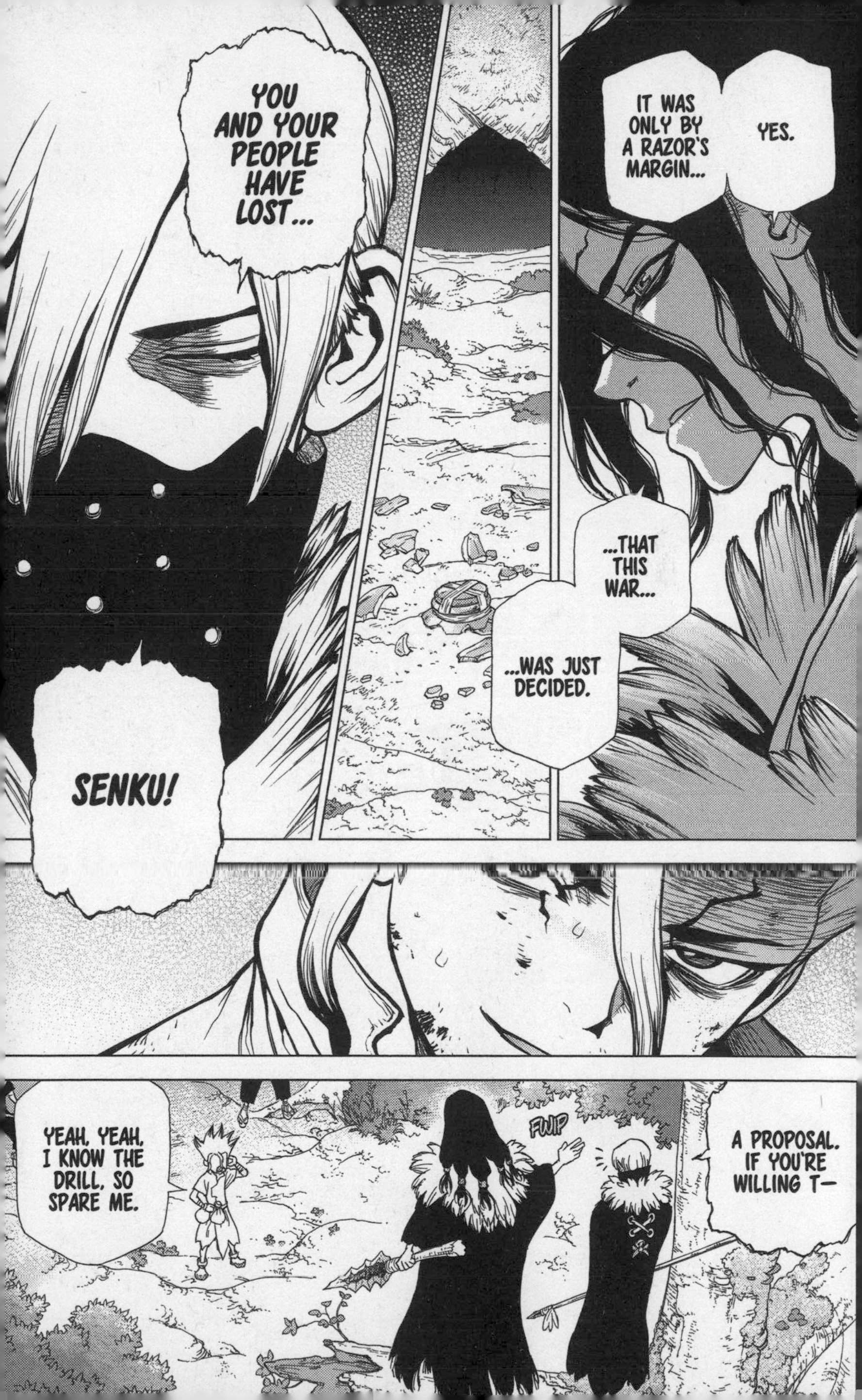
YES.
IT WAS ONLY BY A RAZOR'S MARGIN...
...THAT THIS WAR...
...WAS JUST DECIDED.
YOU AND YOUR PEOPLE HAVE LOST...
SENKU!
A PROPOSAL. IF YOU'RE WILLING T—
FWIP
YEAH, YEAH, I KNOW THE DRILL, SO SPARE ME.

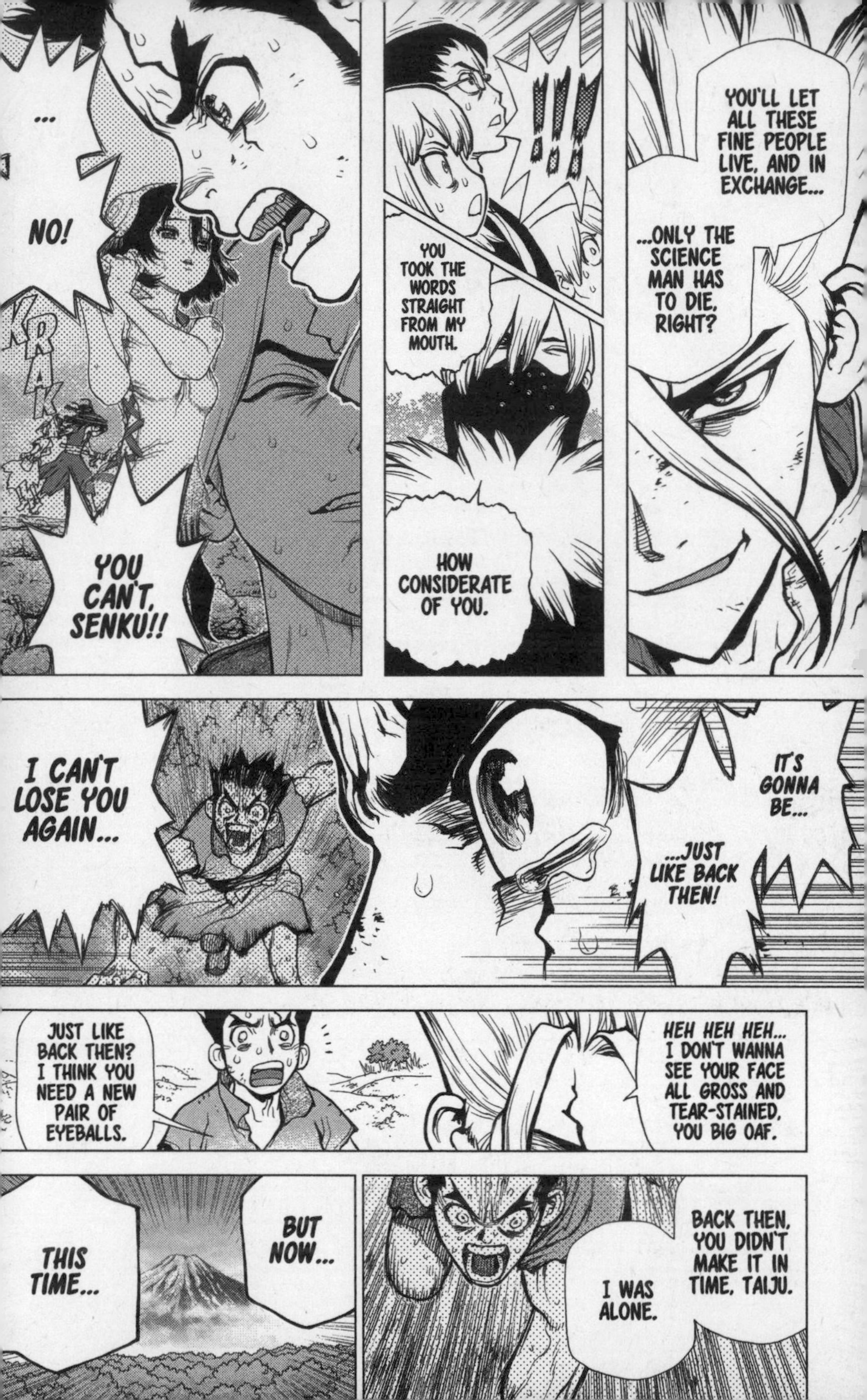

YOU'LL LET ALL THESE FINE PEOPLE LIVE, AND IN EXCHANGE...
...ONLY THE SCIENCE MAN HAS TO DIE, RIGHT?
!!!
YOU TOOK THE WORDS STRAIGHT FROM MY MOUTH.
HOW CONSIDERATE OF YOU.
...
NO!
KRAK
YOU CAN'T, SENKU!!
IT'S GONNA BE...
...JUST LIKE BACK THEN!
I CAN'T LOSE YOU AGAIN...
HEH HEH HEH... I DON'T WANNA SEE YOUR FACE ALL GROSS AND TEAR-STAINED, YOU BIG OAF.
JUST LIKE BACK THEN? I THINK YOU NEED A NEW PAIR OF EYEBALLS.
BACK THEN, YOU DIDN'T MAKE IT IN TIME, TAIJU.
I WAS ALONE.
BUT NOW...
THIS TIME...

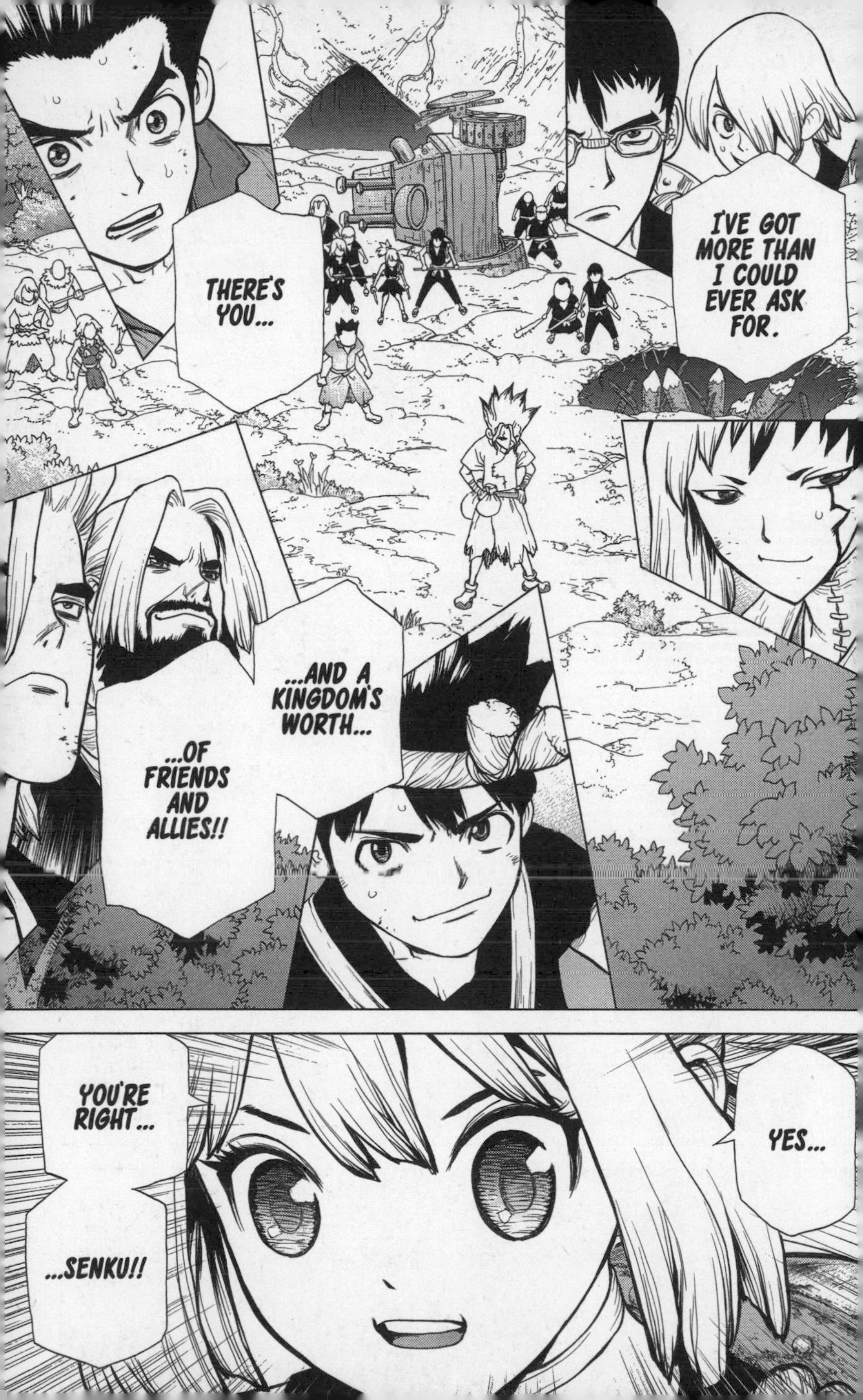
I'VE GOT MORE THAN I COULD EVER ASK FOR.
THERE'S YOU...
...AND A KINGDOM'S WORTH...
...OF FRIENDS AND ALLIES!!
YES...
YOU'RE RIGHT...
...SENKU!!

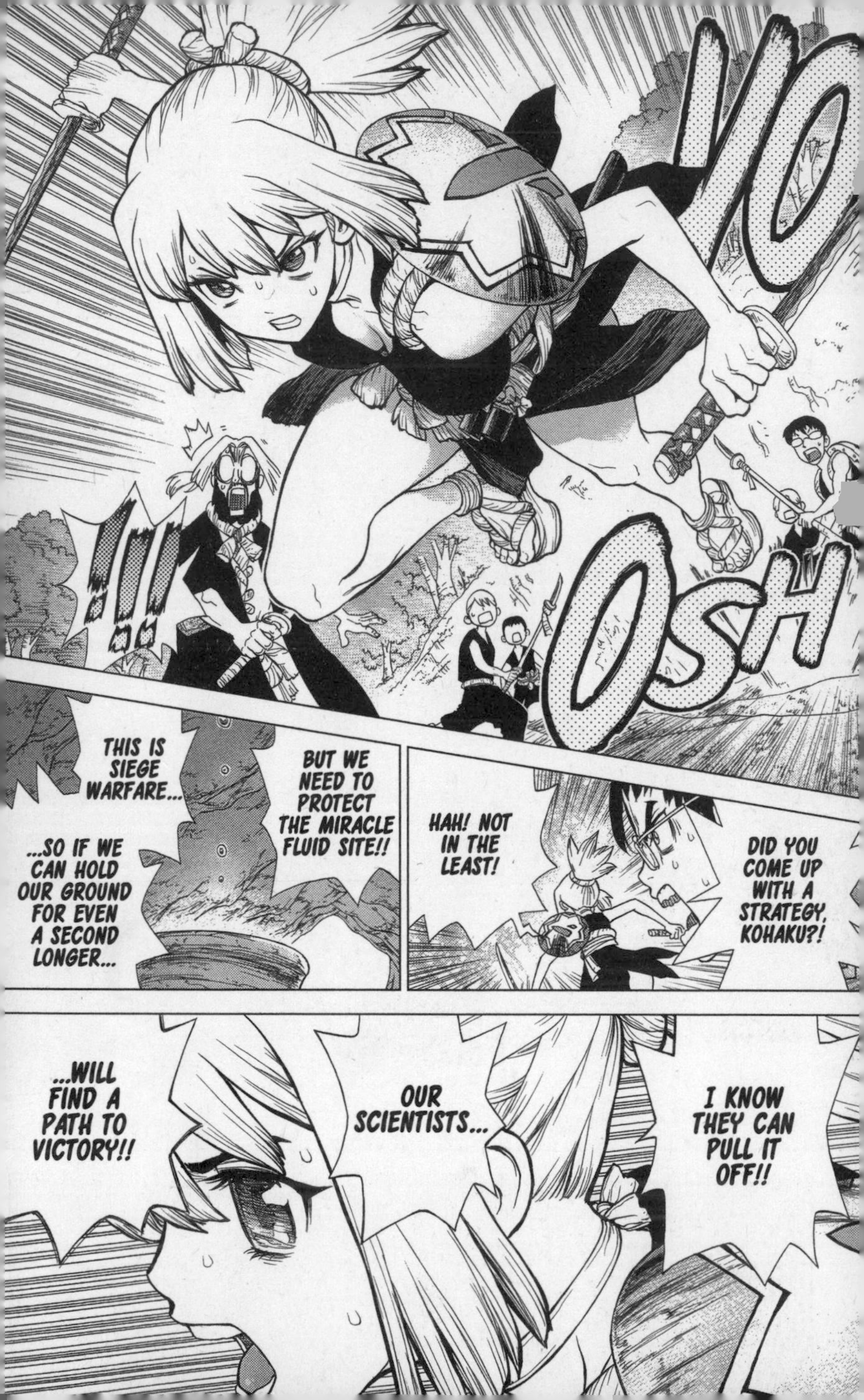
HOOSH
!!!
DID YOU COME UP WITH A STRATEGY, KOHAKU?!
HAH! NOT IN THE LEAST!
BUT WE NEED TO PROTECT THE MIRACLE FLUID SITE!!
THIS IS SIEGE WARFARE...
...SO IF WE CAN HOLD OUR GROUND FOR EVEN A SECOND LONGER...
I KNOW THEY CAN PULL IT OFF!!
OUR SCIENTISTS...
...WILL FIND A PATH TO VICTORY!!

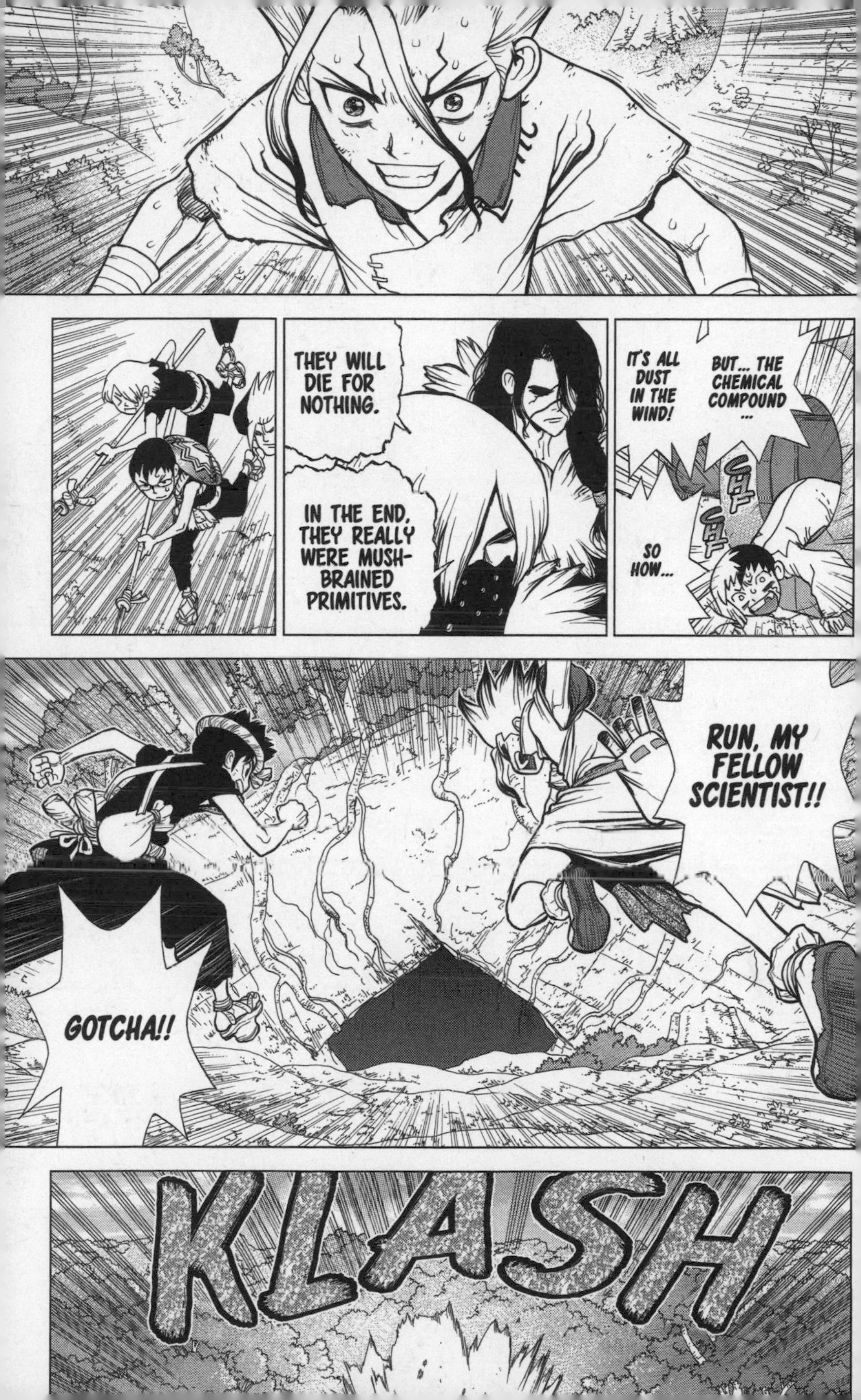
BUT... THE CHEMICAL COMPOUND ...
IT'S ALL DUST IN THE WIND!
CHF
CHF
SO HOW...
THEY WILL DIE FOR NOTHING.
IN THE END, THEY REALLY WERE MUSH-BRAINED PRIMITIVES.
RUN, MY FELLOW SCIENTIST!!
GOTCHA!!
KLASH

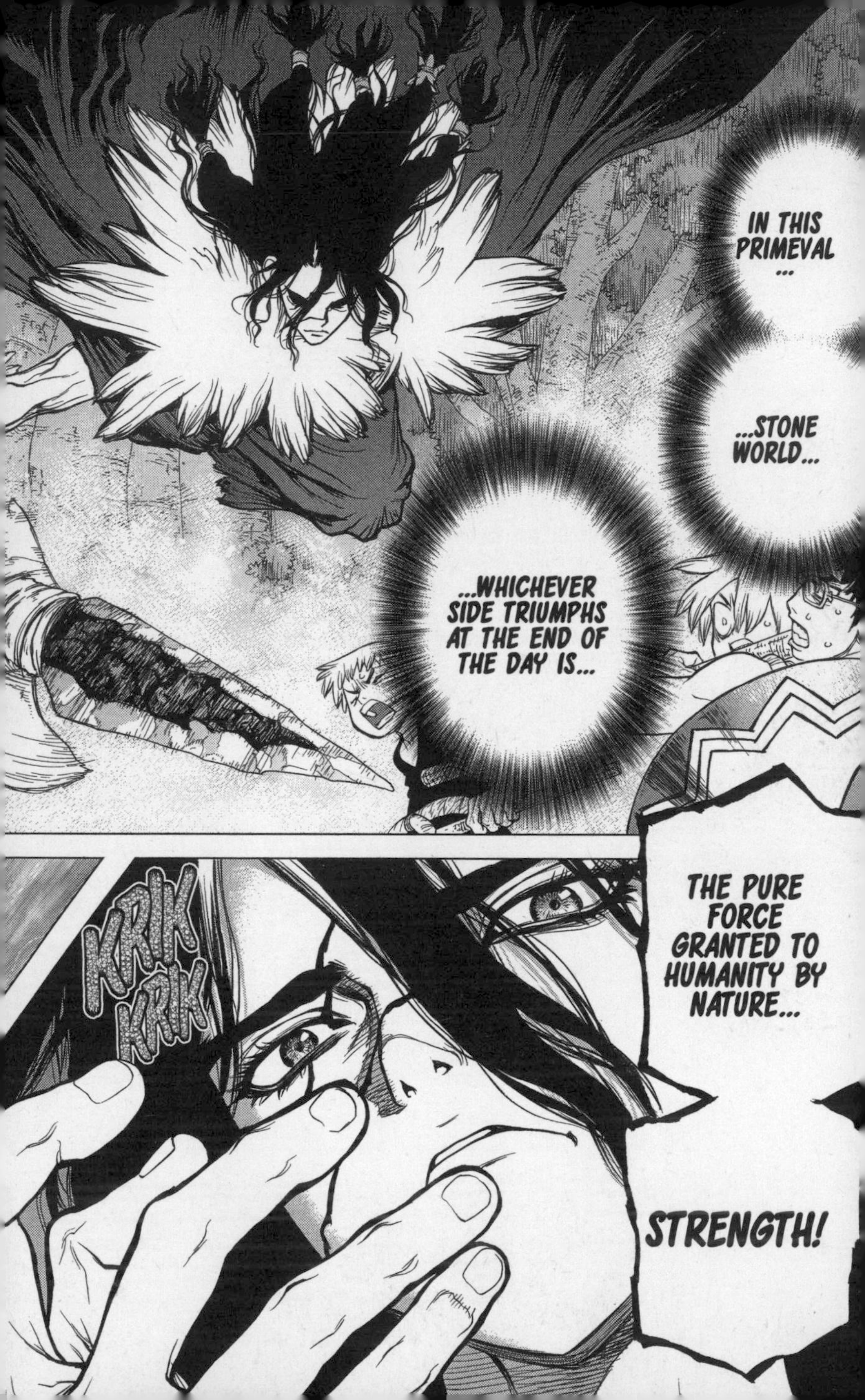
IN THIS PRIMEVAL...
...STONE WORLD...
...WHICHEVER SIDE TRIUMPHS AT THE END OF THE DAY IS...
THE PURE FORCE GRANTED TO HUMANITY BY NATURE...
STRENGTH!
KRIK KRIK

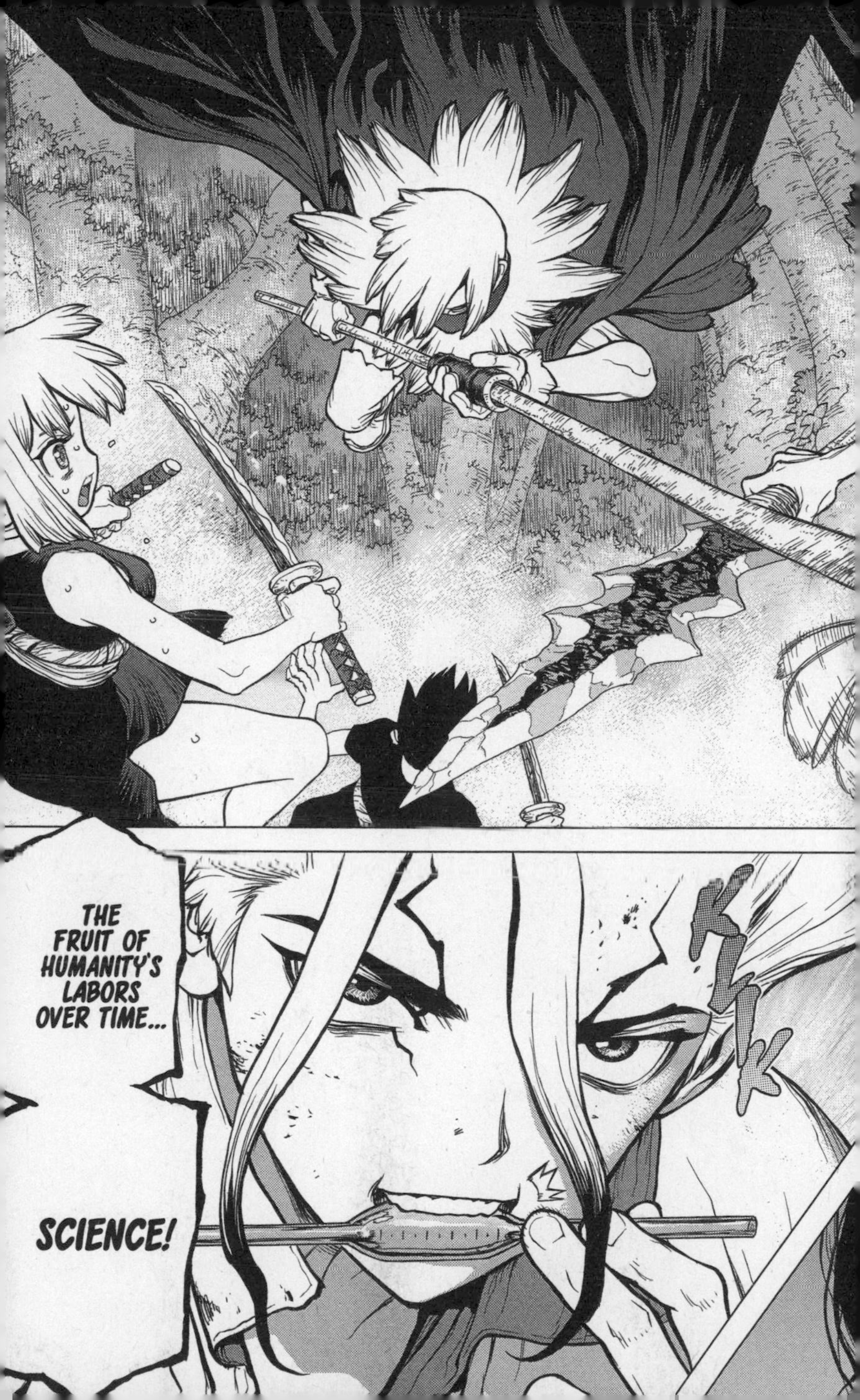
THE FRUIT OF HUMANITY'S LABORS OVER TIME...
SCIENCE!

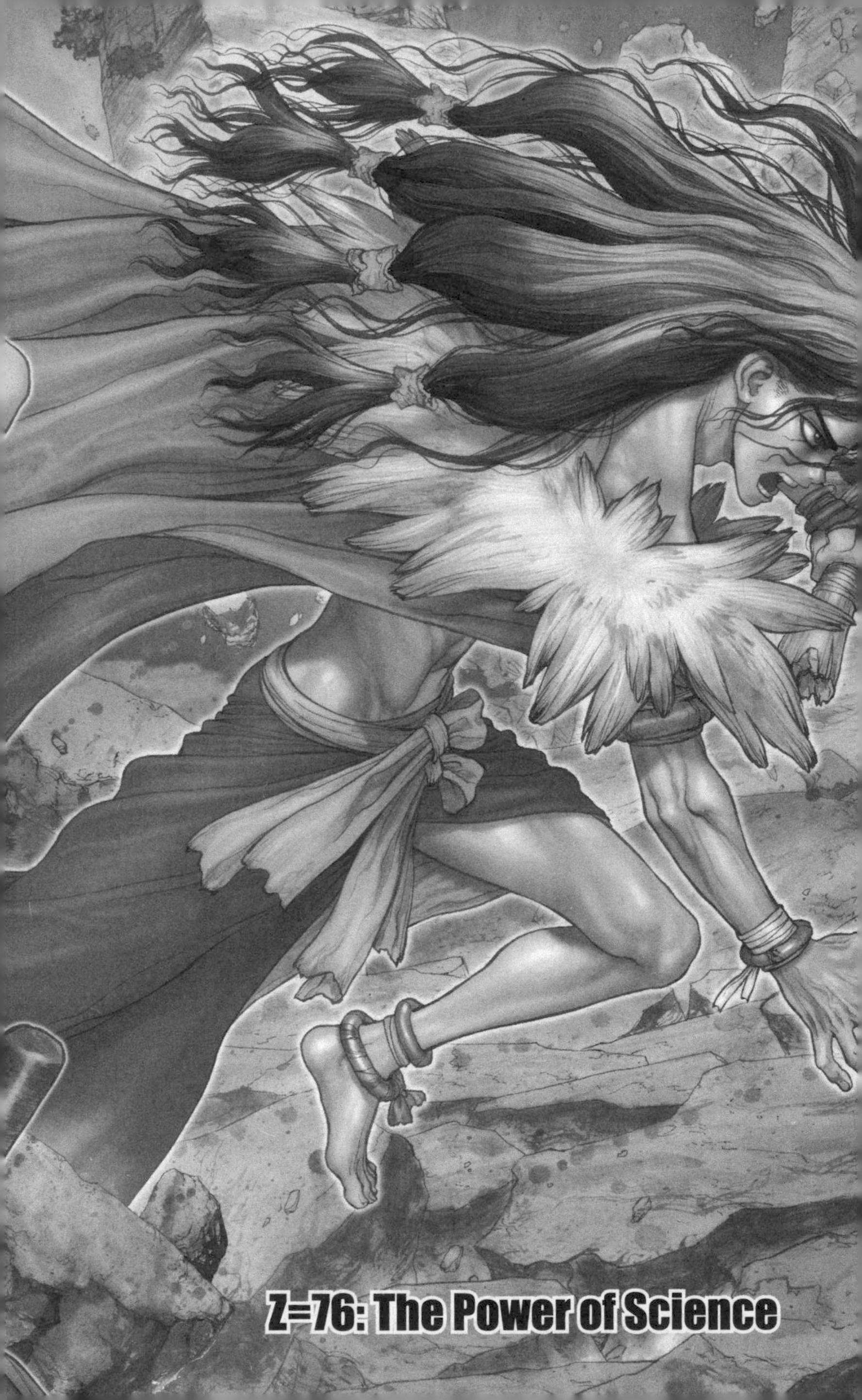
Z=76: The Power of Science

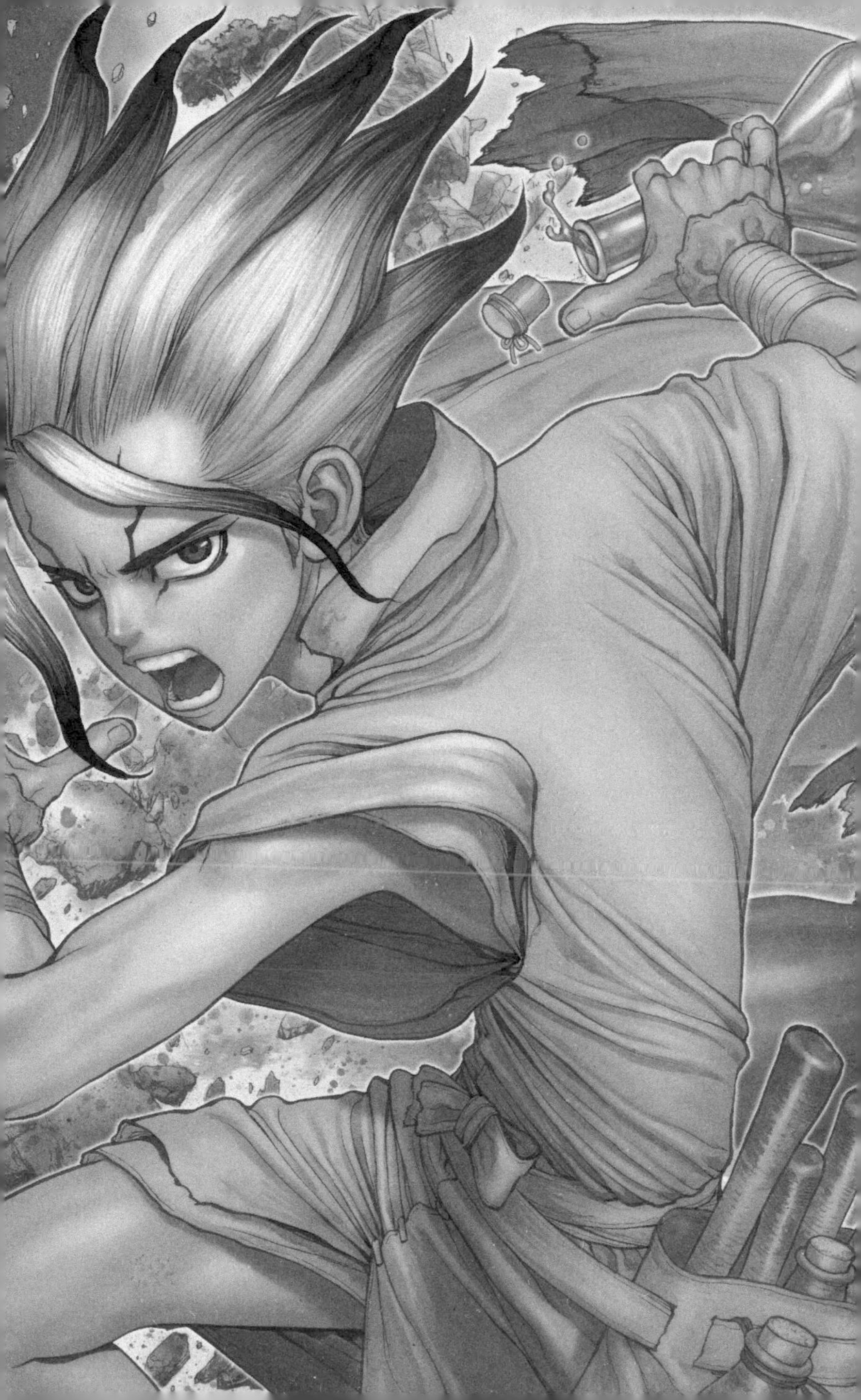

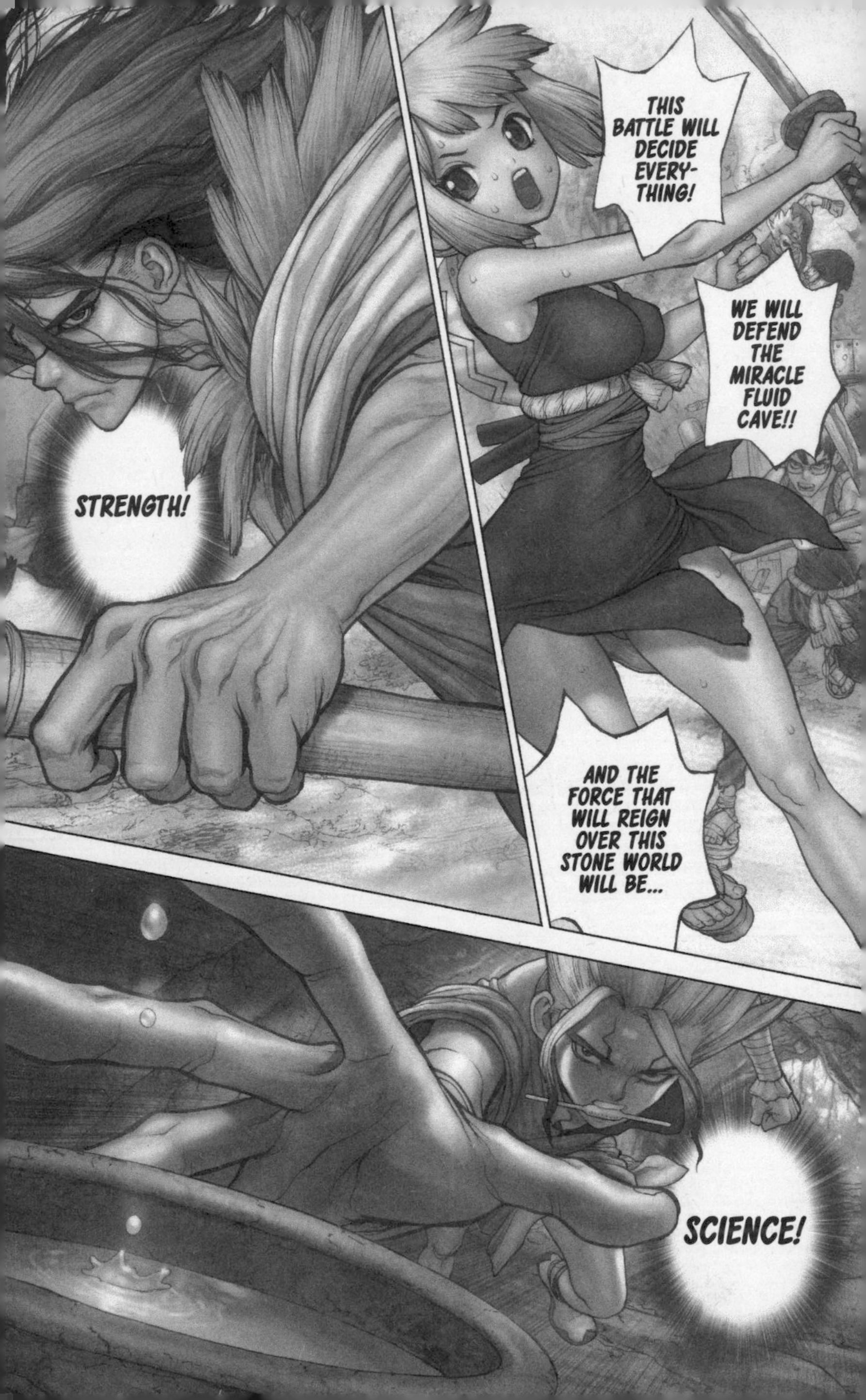
THIS BATTLE WILL DECIDE EVERYTHING!
WE WILL DEFEND THE MIRACLE FLUID CAVE!!
AND THE FORCE THAT WILL REIGN OVER THIS STONE WORLD WILL BE...
STRENGTH!
SCIENCE!

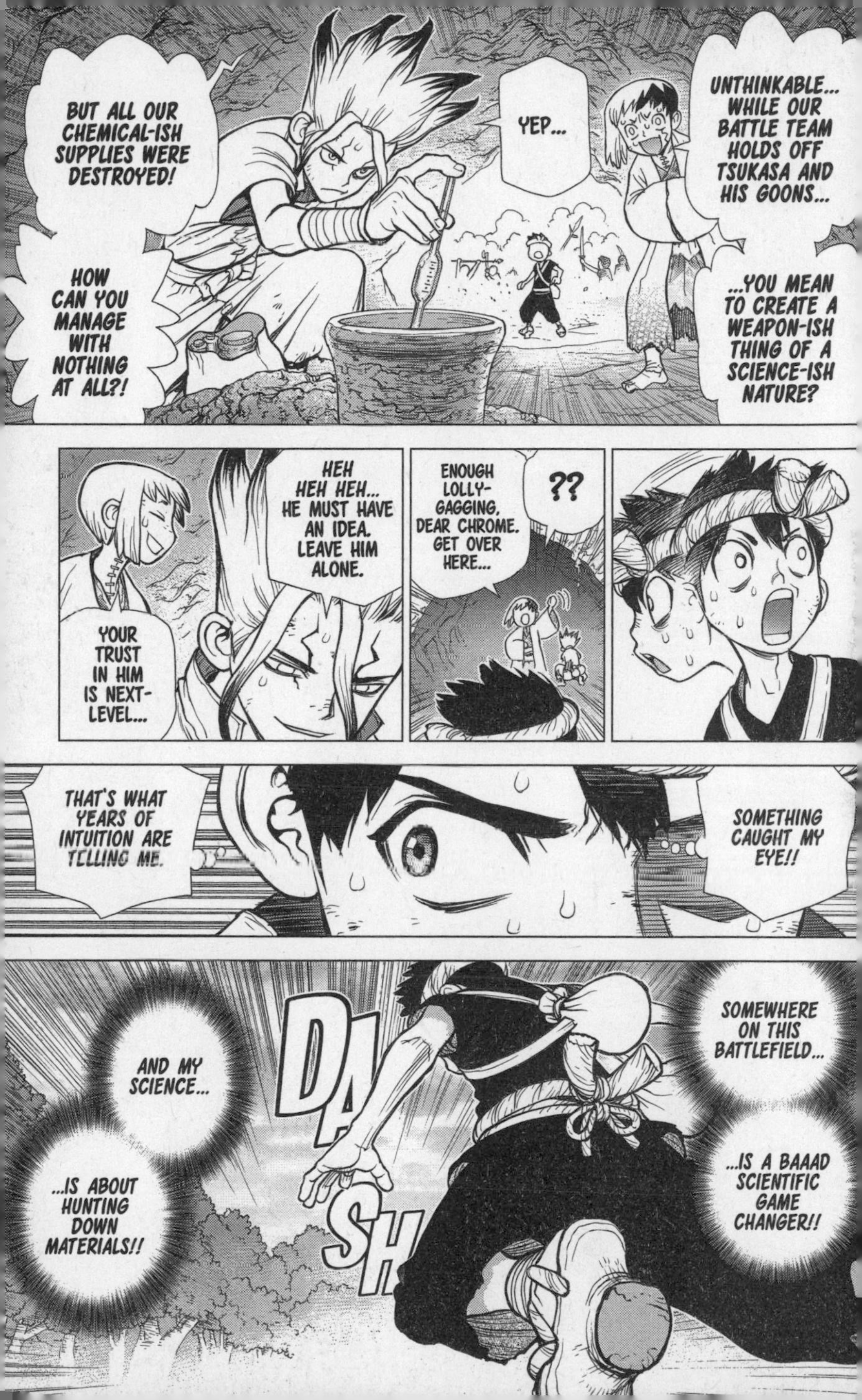
UNTHINKABLE... WHILE OUR BATTLE TEAM HOLDS OFF TSUKASA AND HIS GOONS...
...YOU MEAN TO CREATE A WEAPON-ISH THING OF A SCIENCE-ISH NATURE?
YEP...
BUT ALL OUR CHEMICAL-ISH SUPPLIES WERE DESTROYED!
HOW CAN YOU MANAGE WITH NOTHING AT ALL?!
??
ENOUGH LOLLY-GAGGING, DEAR CHROME. GET OVER HERE...
HEH HEH HEH... HE MUST HAVE AN IDEA. LEAVE HIM ALONE.
YOUR TRUST IN HIM IS NEXT-LEVEL...
SOMETHING CAUGHT MY EYE!!
THAT'S WHAT YEARS OF INTUITION ARE TELLING ME.
SOMEWHERE ON THIS BATTLEFIELD...
...IS A BAAAD SCIENTIFIC GAME CHANGER!!
DASH
AND MY SCIENCE...
...IS ABOUT HUNTING DOWN MATERIALS!!

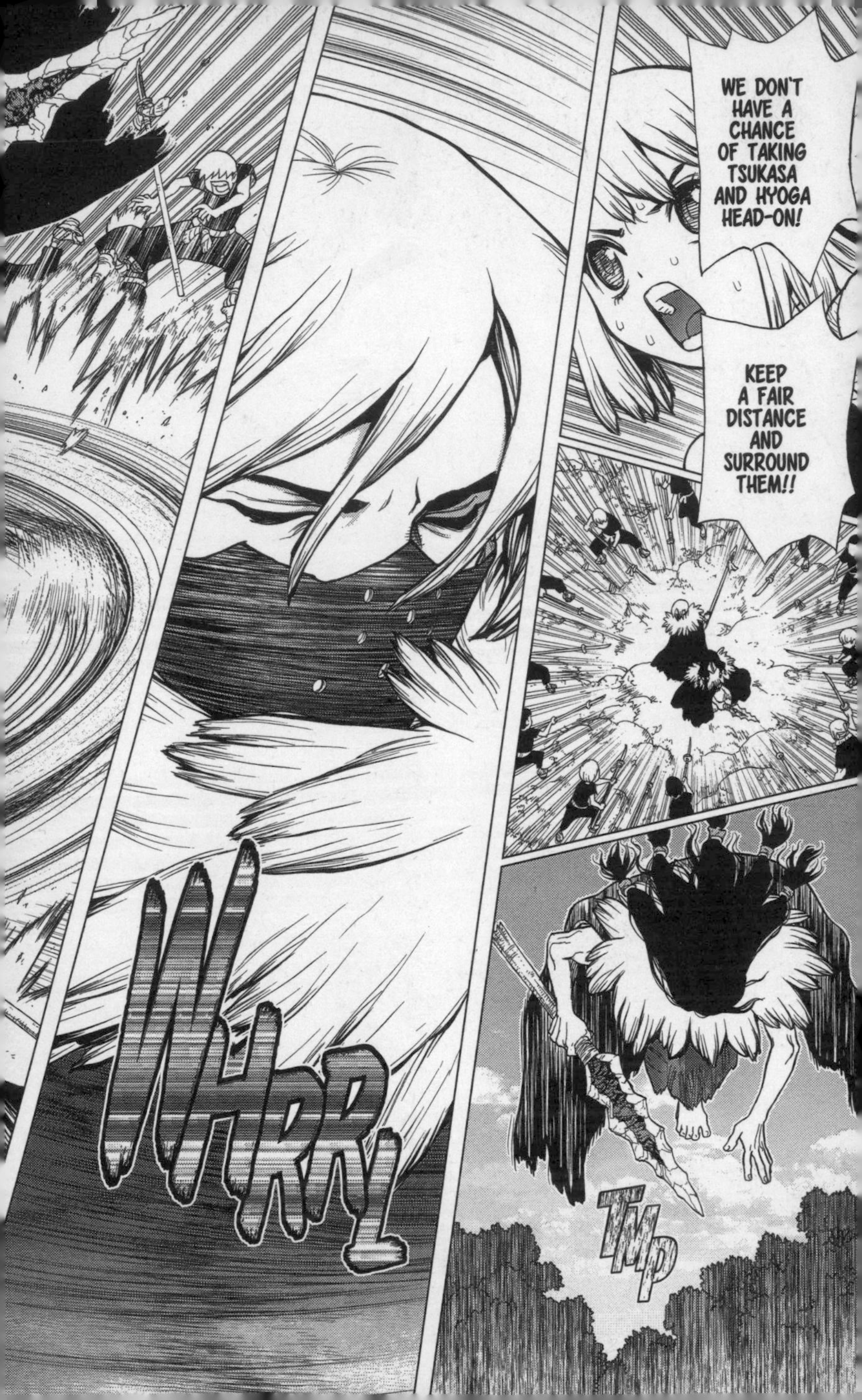
WE DON'T HAVE A CHANCE OF TAKING TSUKASA AND HYOGA HEAD-ON!
KEEP A FAIR DISTANCE AND SURROUND THEM!!
TMP
WHRR

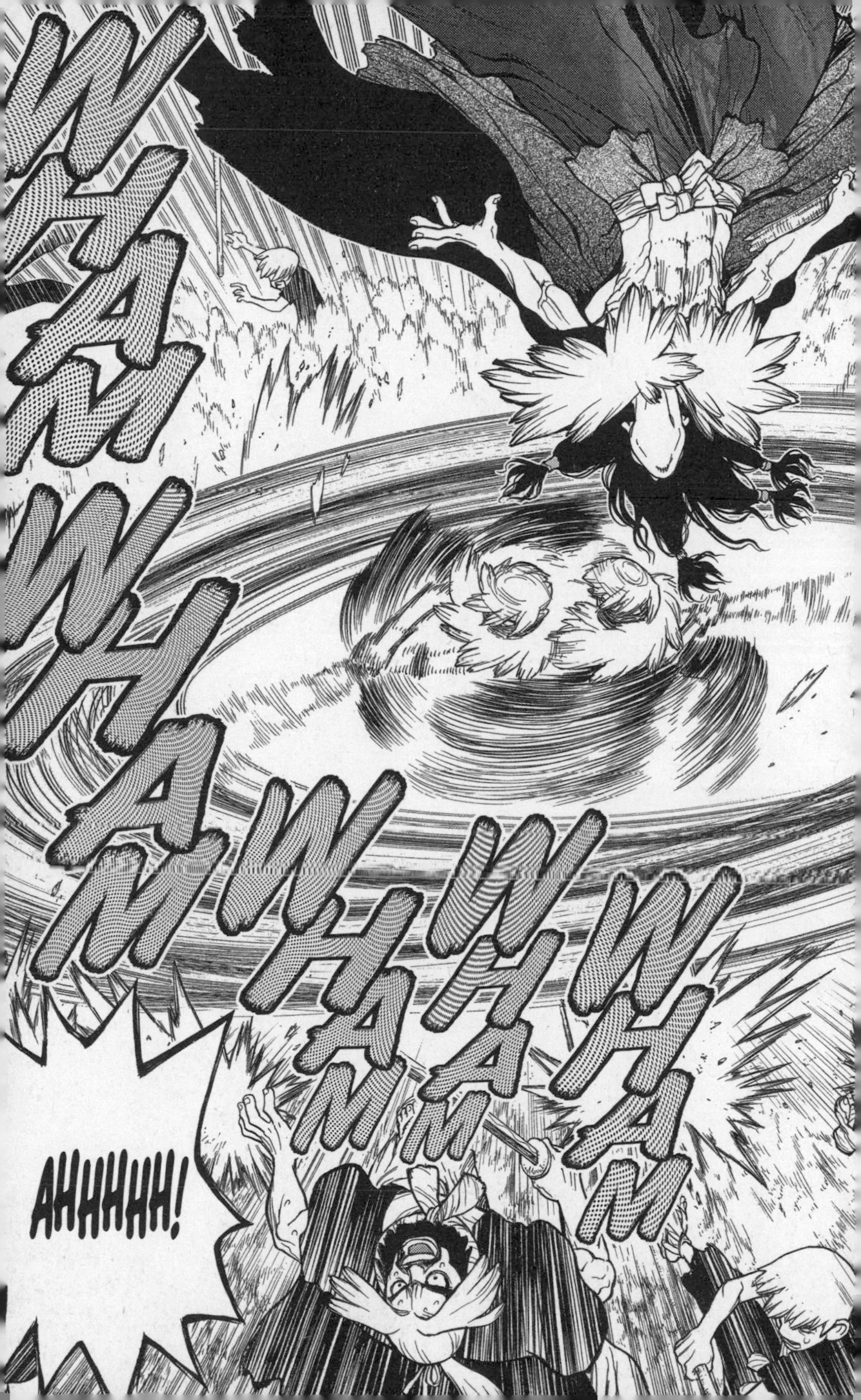
WHAAAAAM
WHAAM
WHAAM
WHAAM
AHHHHH!

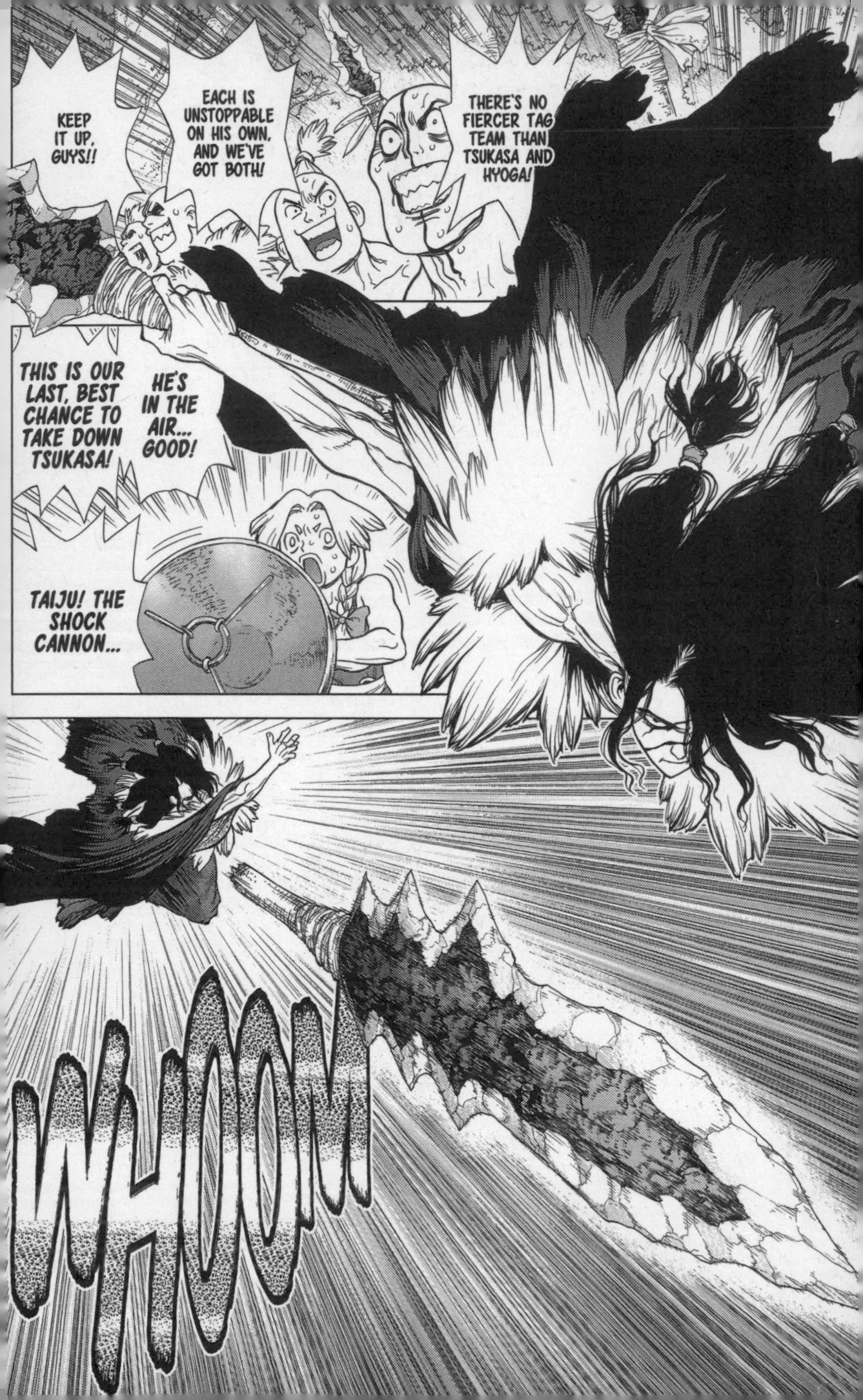
THERE'S NO FIERCER TAG TEAM THAN TSUKASA AND HYOGA!
EACH IS UNSTOPPABLE ON HIS OWN, AND WE'VE GOT BOTH!
KEEP IT UP, GUYS!!
HE'S IN THE AIR... GOOD!
THIS IS OUR LAST, BEST CHANCE TO TAKE DOWN TSUKASA!
TAIJU! THE SHOCK CANNON...
WHOOM

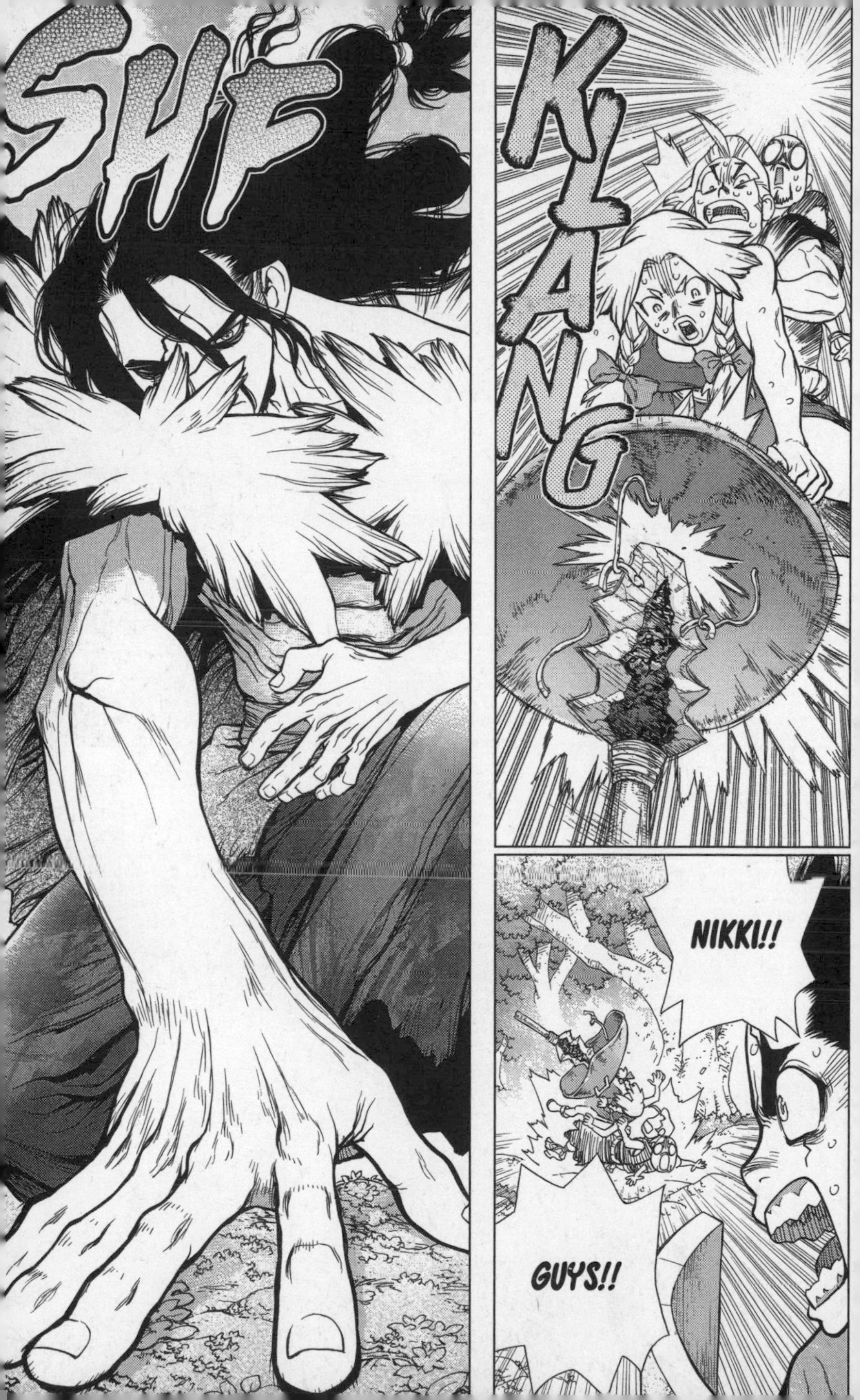
KLANG
NIKKI!!
GUYS!!
SHF

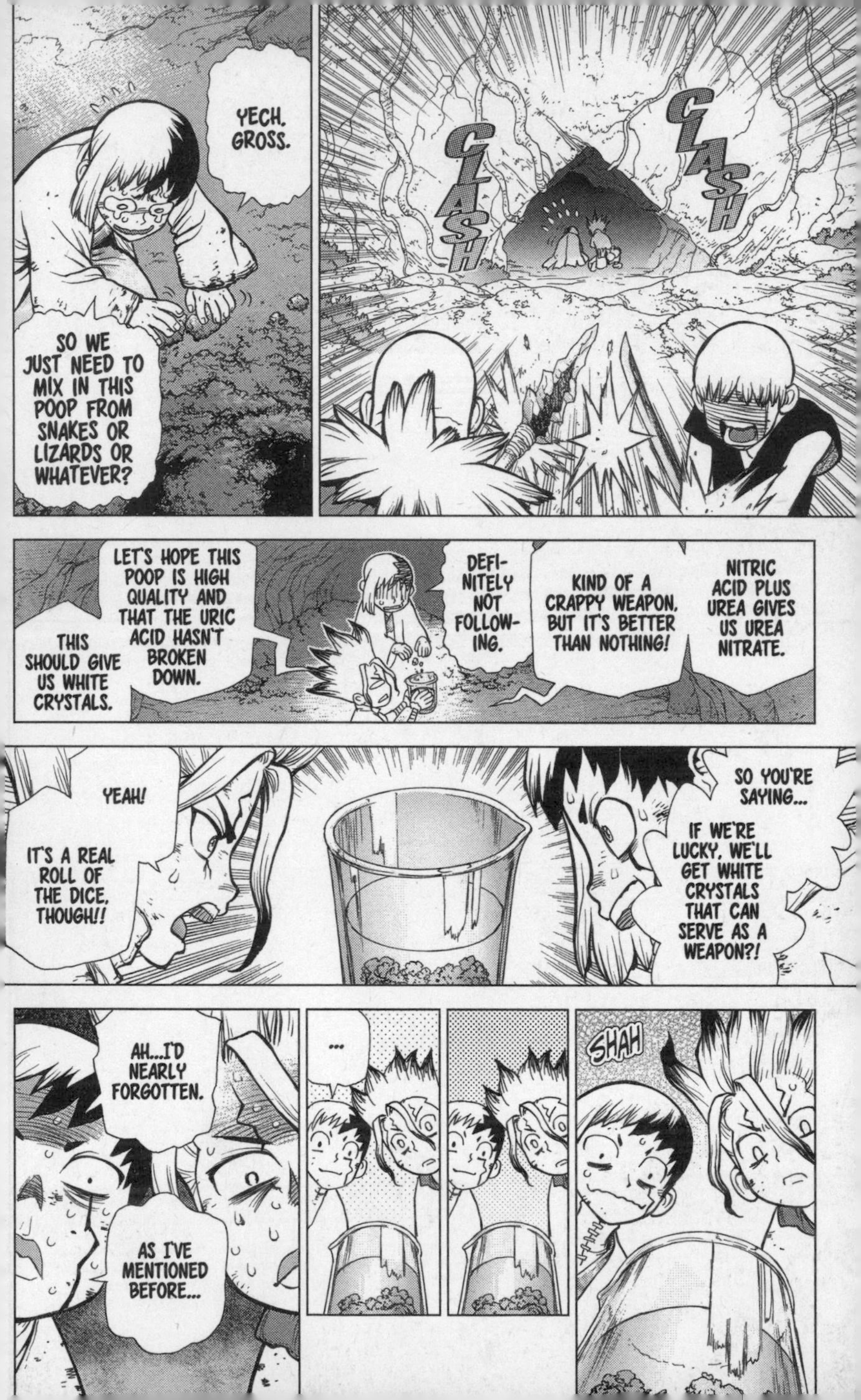
CLASH
CLASH
YECH. GROSS.
SO WE JUST NEED TO MIX IN THIS POOP FROM SNAKES OR LIZARDS OR WHATEVER?
NITRIC ACID PLUS UREA GIVES US UREA NITRATE.
KIND OF A CRAPPY WEAPON, BUT IT'S BETTER THAN NOTHING!
DEFI-NITELY NOT FOLLOW-ING.
LET'S HOPE THIS POOP IS HIGH QUALITY AND THAT THE URIC ACID HASN'T BROKEN DOWN.
THIS SHOULD GIVE US WHITE CRYSTALS.
SO YOU'RE SAYING...
IF WE'RE LUCKY, WE'LL GET WHITE CRYSTALS THAT CAN SERVE AS A WEAPON?!
YEAH!
IT'S A REAL ROLL OF THE DICE, THOUGH!!
SHAH
...
AH...I'D NEARLY FORGOTTEN.
AS I'VE MENTIONED BEFORE...

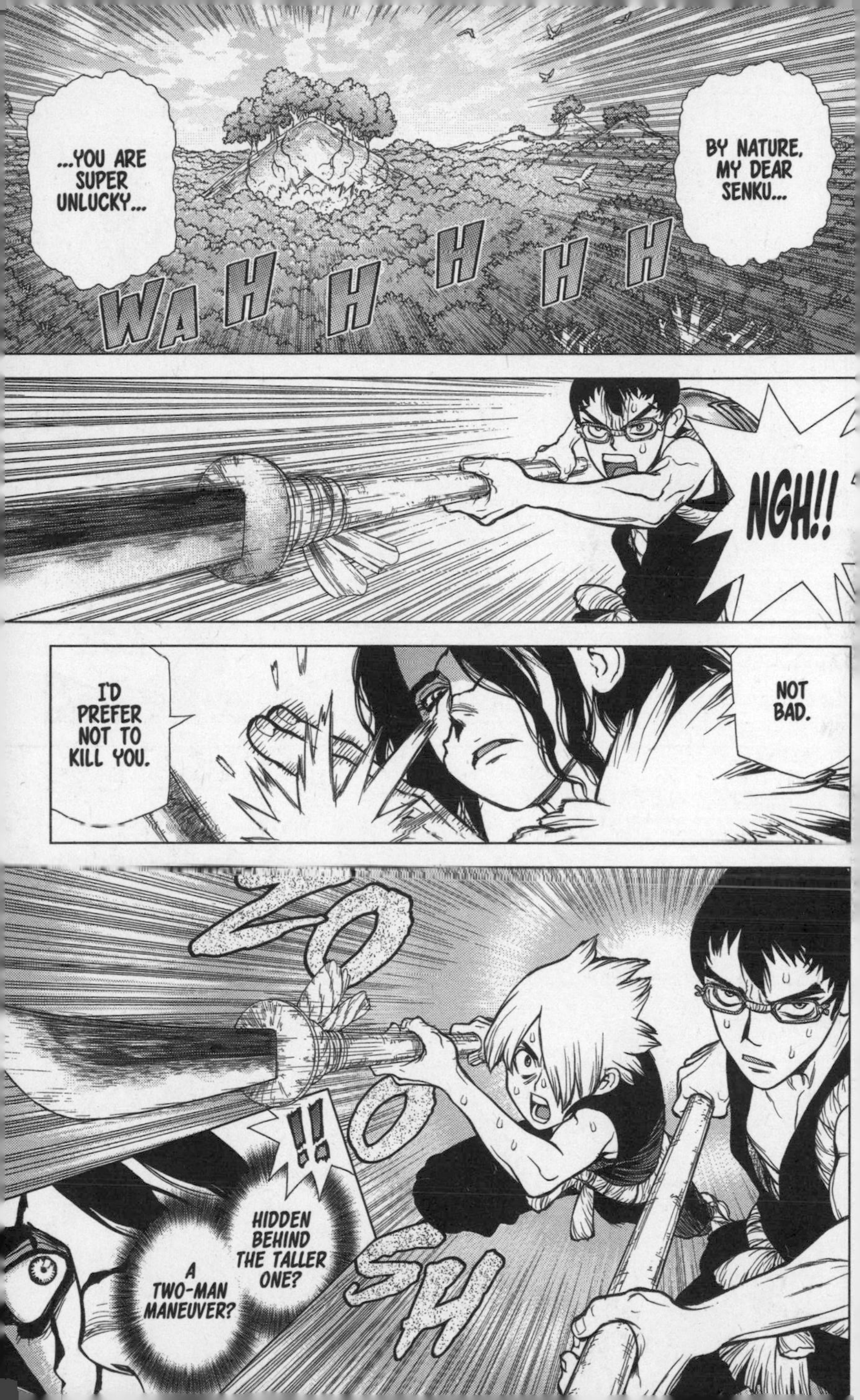
BY NATURE, MY DEAR SENKU...
...YOU ARE SUPER UNLUCKY...
WAHHHHHH
NGH!!
NOT BAD.
I'D PREFER NOT TO KILL YOU.
ZOOOSH
!!
HIDDEN BEHIND THE TALLER ONE?
A TWO-MAN MANEUVER?

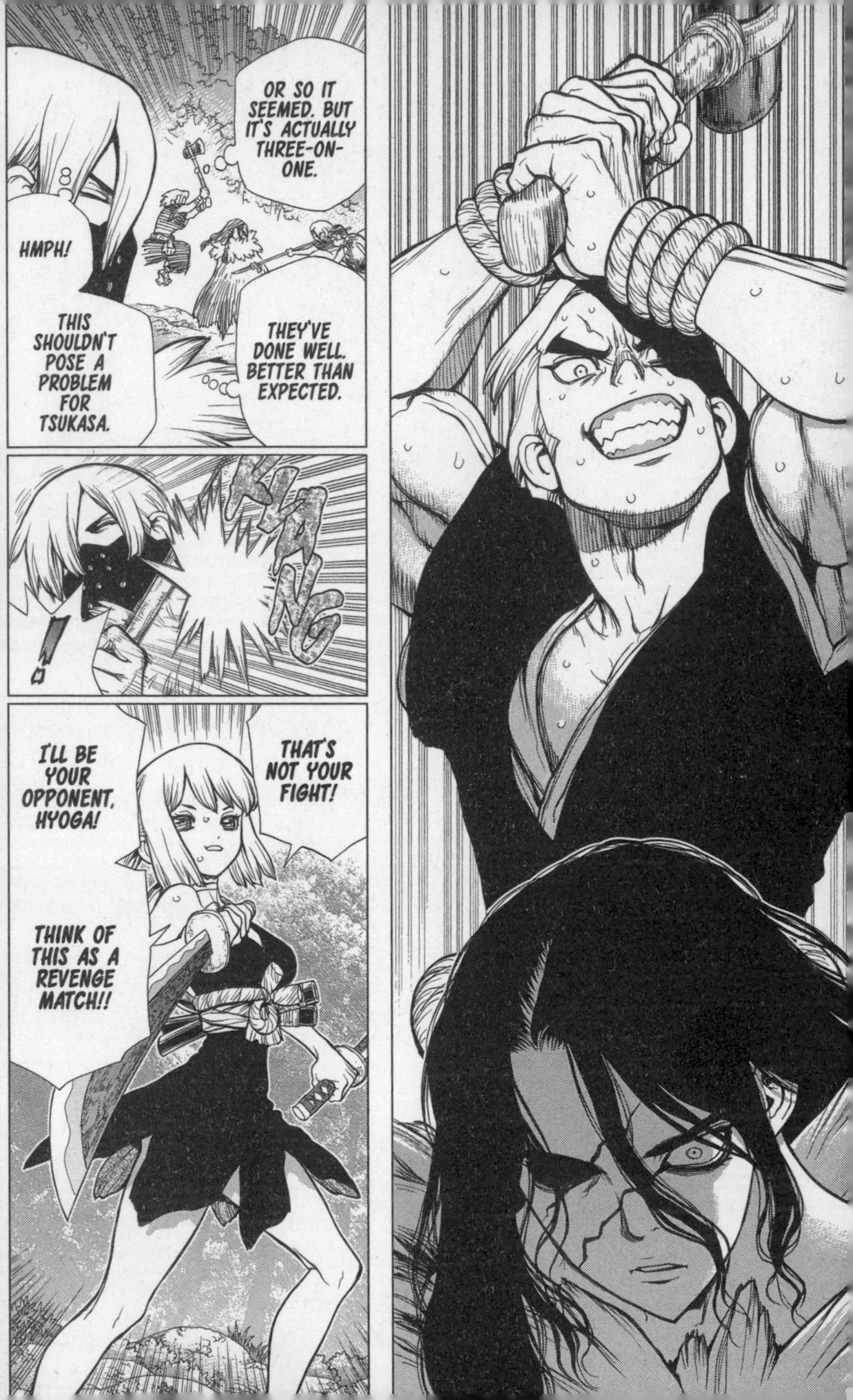
OR SO IT SEEMED. BUT IT'S ACTUALLY THREE-ON-ONE.
HMPH!
THEY'VE DONE WELL. BETTER THAN EXPECTED.
THIS SHOULDN'T POSE A PROBLEM FOR TSUKASA.
KLANG
!
THAT'S NOT YOUR FIGHT!
I'LL BE YOUR OPPONENT, HYOGA!
THINK OF THIS AS A REVENGE MATCH!!

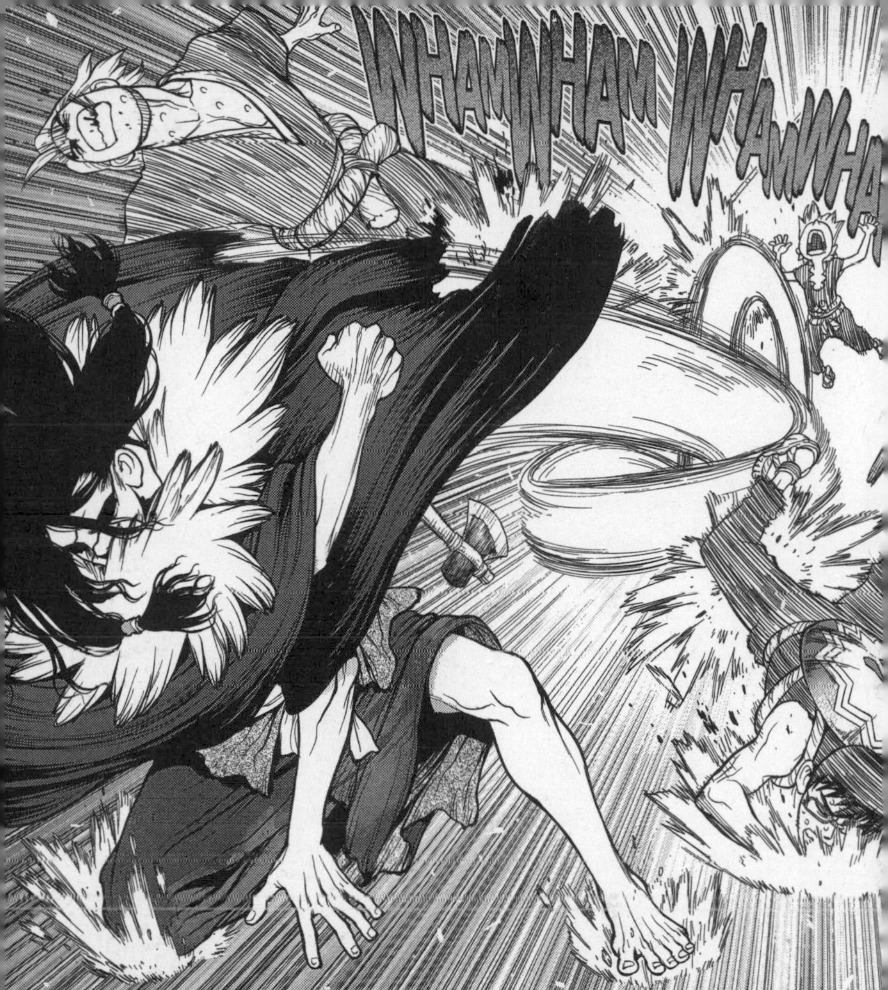
WHAMWHAM WHAMWHA

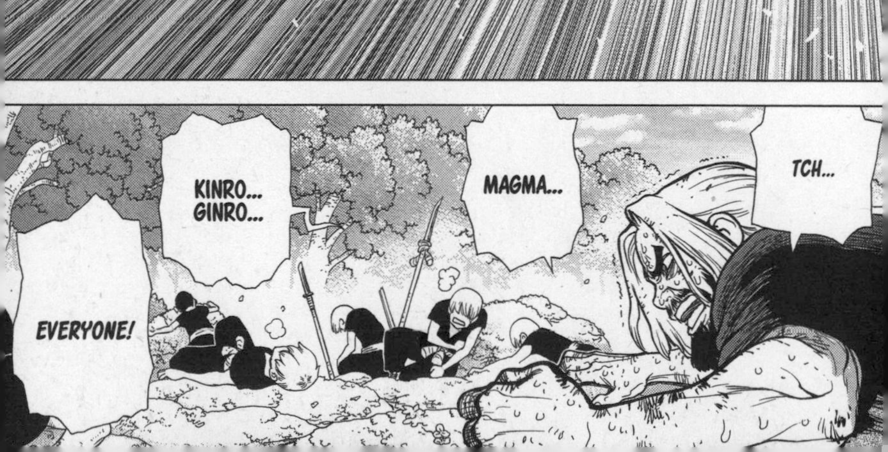
TCH...
MAGMA...
KINRO... GINRO...
EVERYONE!

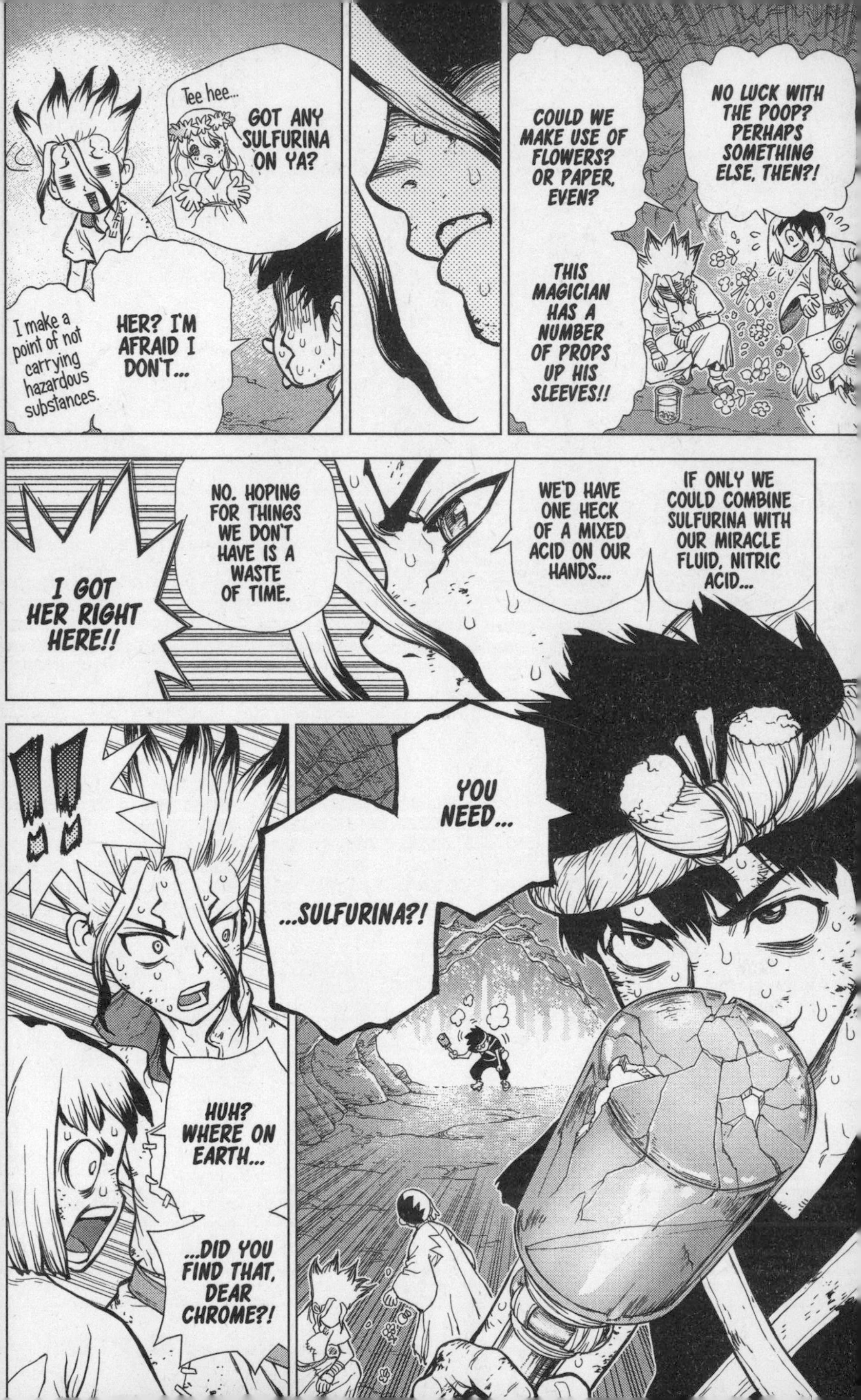
NO LUCK WITH THE POOP? PERHAPS SOMETHING ELSE, THEN?!
COULD WE MAKE USE OF FLOWERS? OR PAPER, EVEN?
THIS MAGICIAN HAS A NUMBER OF PROPS UP HIS SLEEVES!!
Tee hee...
GOT ANY SULFURINA ON YA?
HER? I'M AFRAID I DON'T...
I make a point of not carrying hazardous substances.
IF ONLY WE COULD COMBINE SULFURINA WITH OUR MIRACLE FLUID, NITRIC ACID...
WE'D HAVE ONE HECK OF A MIXED ACID ON OUR HANDS...
NO. HOPING FOR THINGS WE DON'T HAVE IS A WASTE OF TIME.
I GOT HER RIGHT HERE!!
YOU NEED...
...SULFURINA?!
!!
HUH? WHERE ON EARTH...
...DID YOU FIND THAT, DEAR CHROME?!

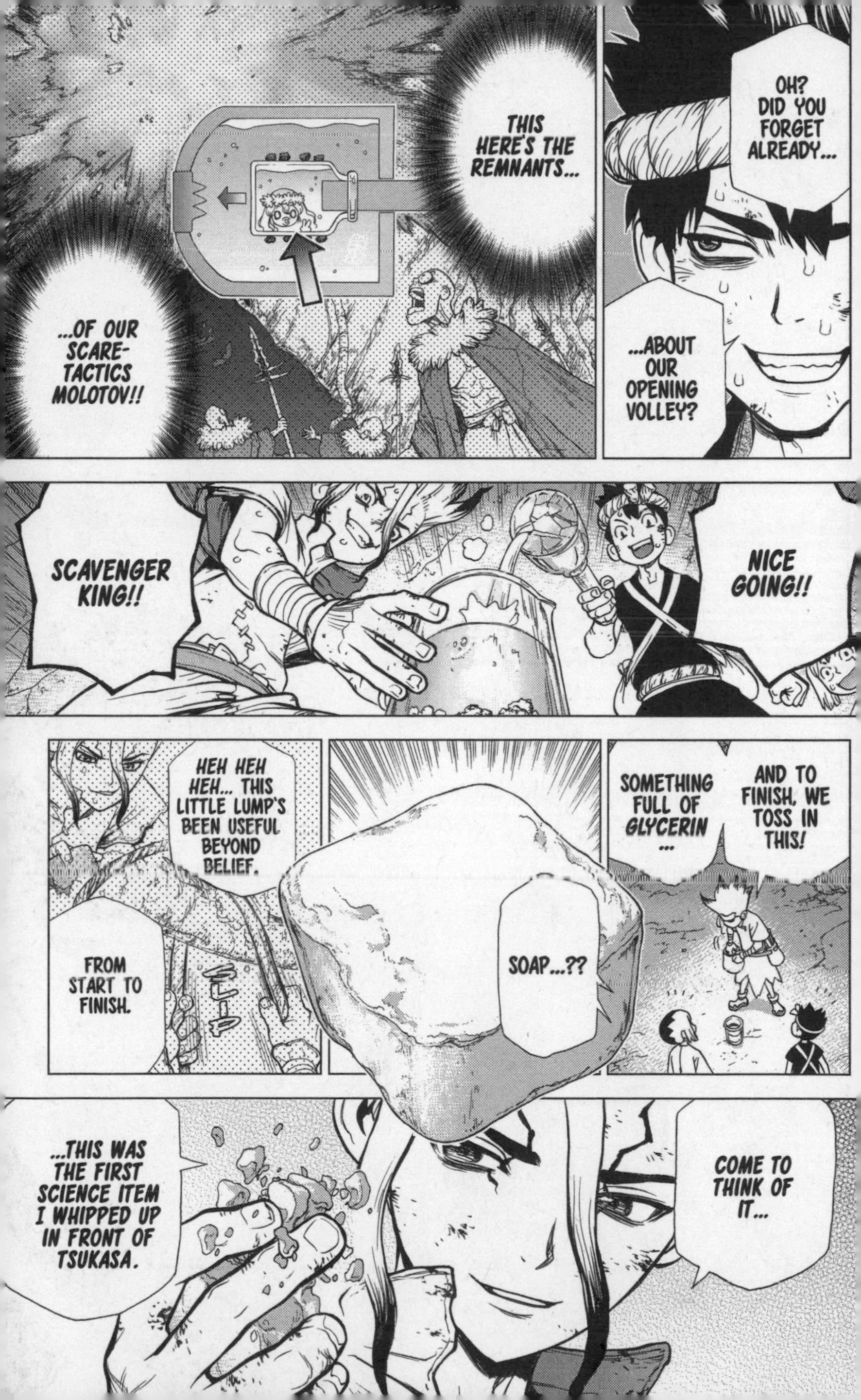
OH? DID YOU FORGET ALREADY...
...ABOUT OUR OPENING VOLLEY?
THIS HERE'S THE REMNANTS...
...OF OUR SCARE-TACTICS MOLOTOV!!
NICE GOING!!
SCAVENGER KING!!
AND TO FINISH, WE TOSS IN THIS!
SOMETHING FULL OF GLYCERIN ...
SOAP...??
HEH HEH HEH... THIS LITTLE LUMP'S BEEN USEFUL BEYOND BELIEF.
FROM START TO FINISH.
COME TO THINK OF IT...
...THIS WAS THE FIRST SCIENCE ITEM I WHIPPED UP IN FRONT OF TSUKASA.

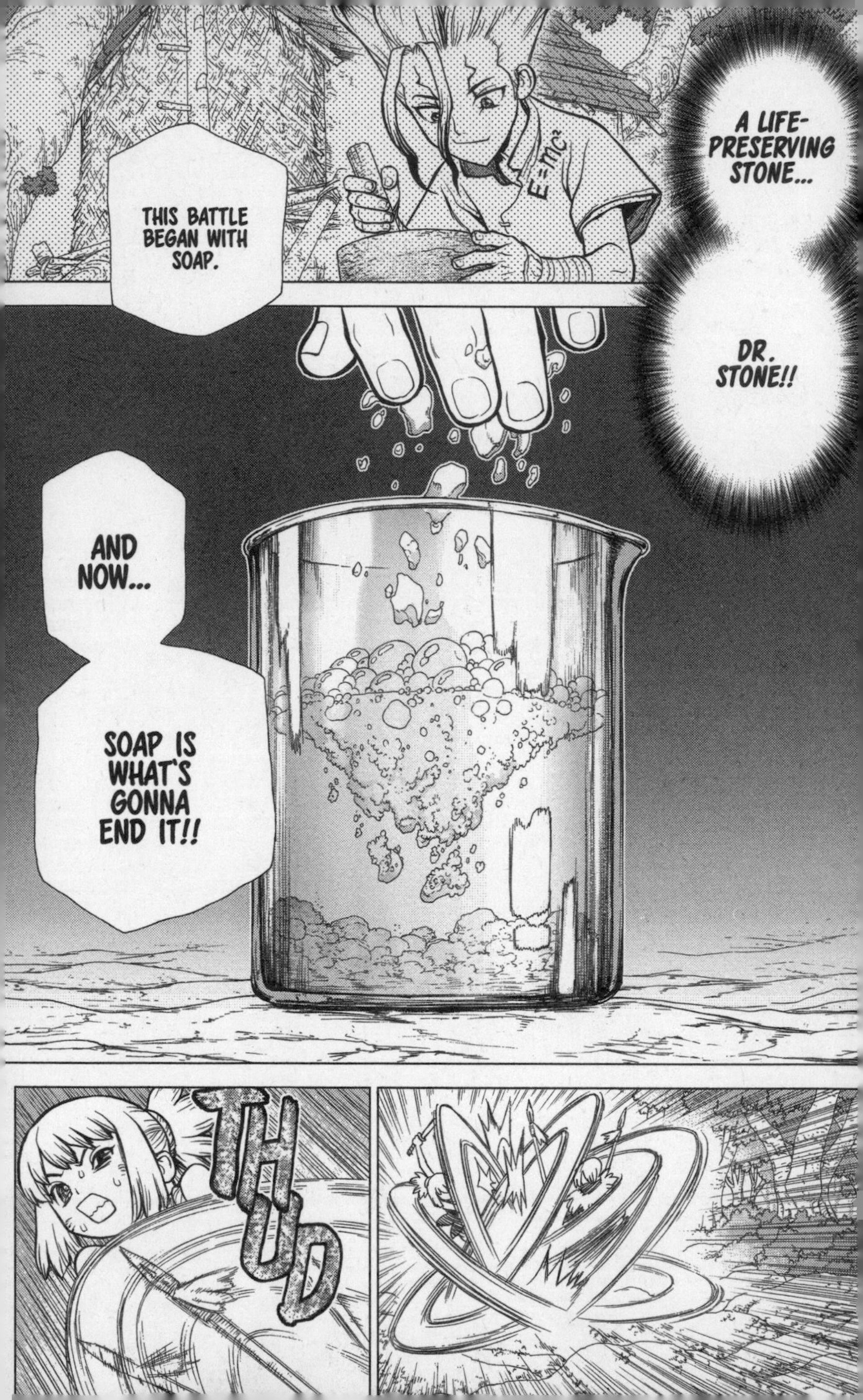
A LIFE-PRESERVING STONE...
DR. STONE!!
THIS BATTLE BEGAN WITH SOAP.
AND NOW...
SOAP IS WHAT'S GONNA END IT!!
THUD

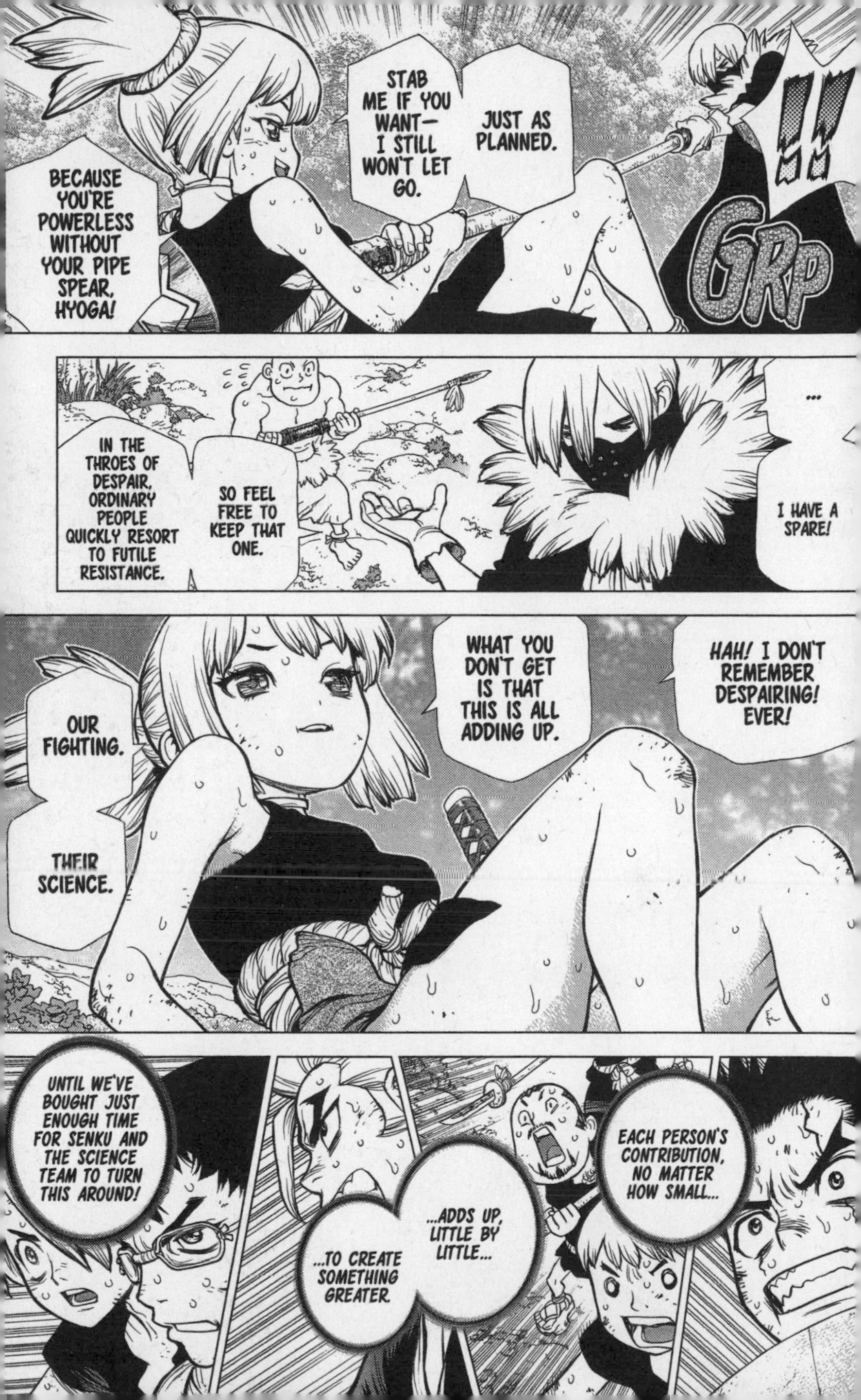
!!
GRP
JUST AS PLANNED.
STAB ME IF YOU WANT— I STILL WON'T LET GO.
BECAUSE YOU'RE POWERLESS WITHOUT YOUR PIPE SPEAR, HYOGA!
...
I HAVE A SPARE!
SO FEEL FREE TO KEEP THAT ONE.
IN THE THROES OF DESPAIR, ORDINARY PEOPLE QUICKLY RESORT TO FUTILE RESISTANCE.
HAH! I DON'T REMEMBER DESPAIRING! EVER!
WHAT YOU DON'T GET IS THAT THIS IS ALL ADDING UP.
OUR FIGHTING.
THEIR SCIENCE.
EACH PERSON'S CONTRIBUTION, NO MATTER HOW SMALL...
...ADDS UP, LITTLE BY LITTLE...
...TO CREATE SOMETHING GREATER.
UNTIL WE'VE BOUGHT JUST ENOUGH TIME FOR SENKU AND THE SCIENCE TEAM TO TURN THIS AROUND!

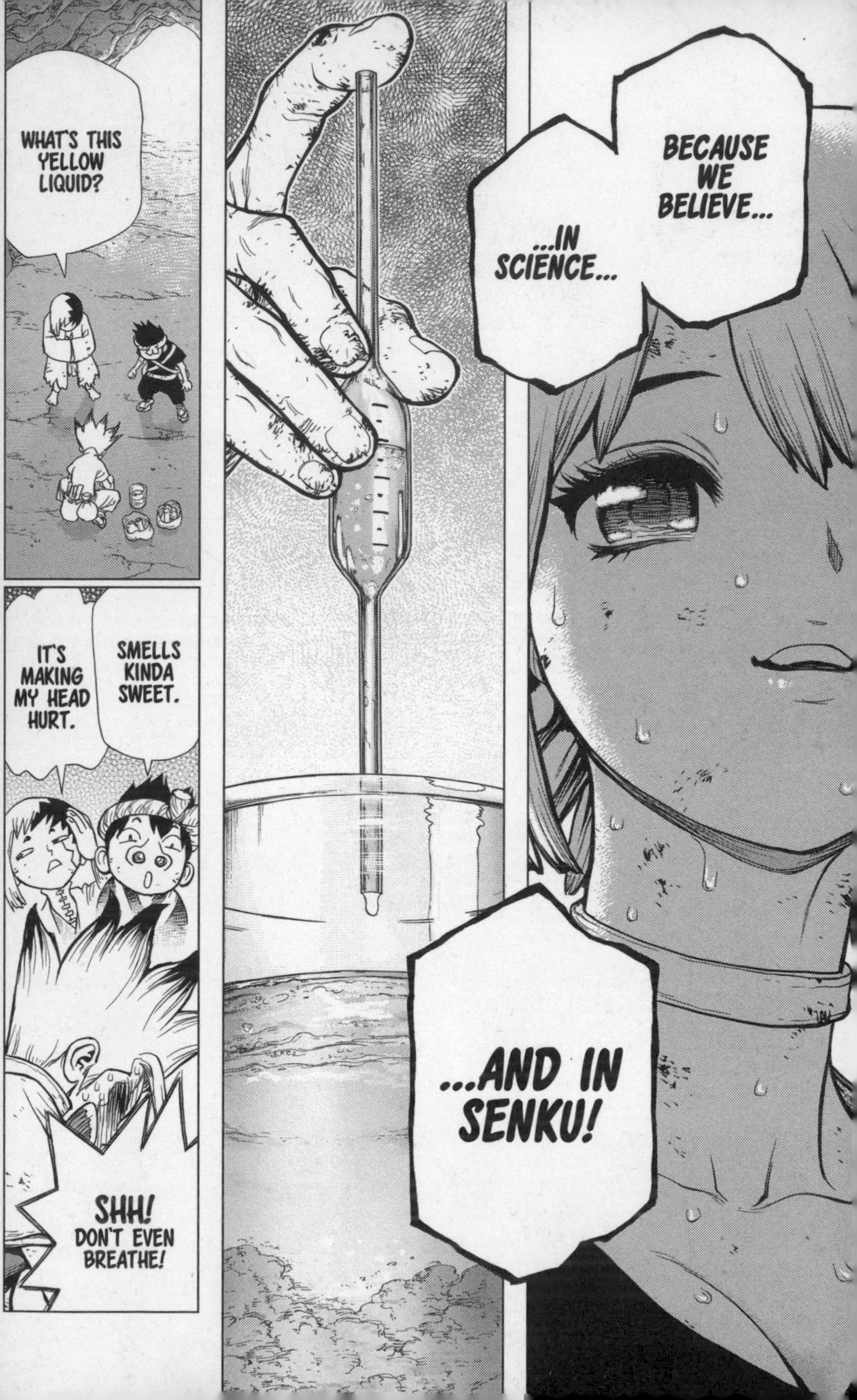
BECAUSE WE BELIEVE...
...IN SCIENCE...
...AND IN SENKU!
WHAT'S THIS YELLOW LIQUID?
SMELLS KINDA SWEET.
IT'S MAKING MY HEAD HURT.
SHH! DON'T EVEN BREATHE!

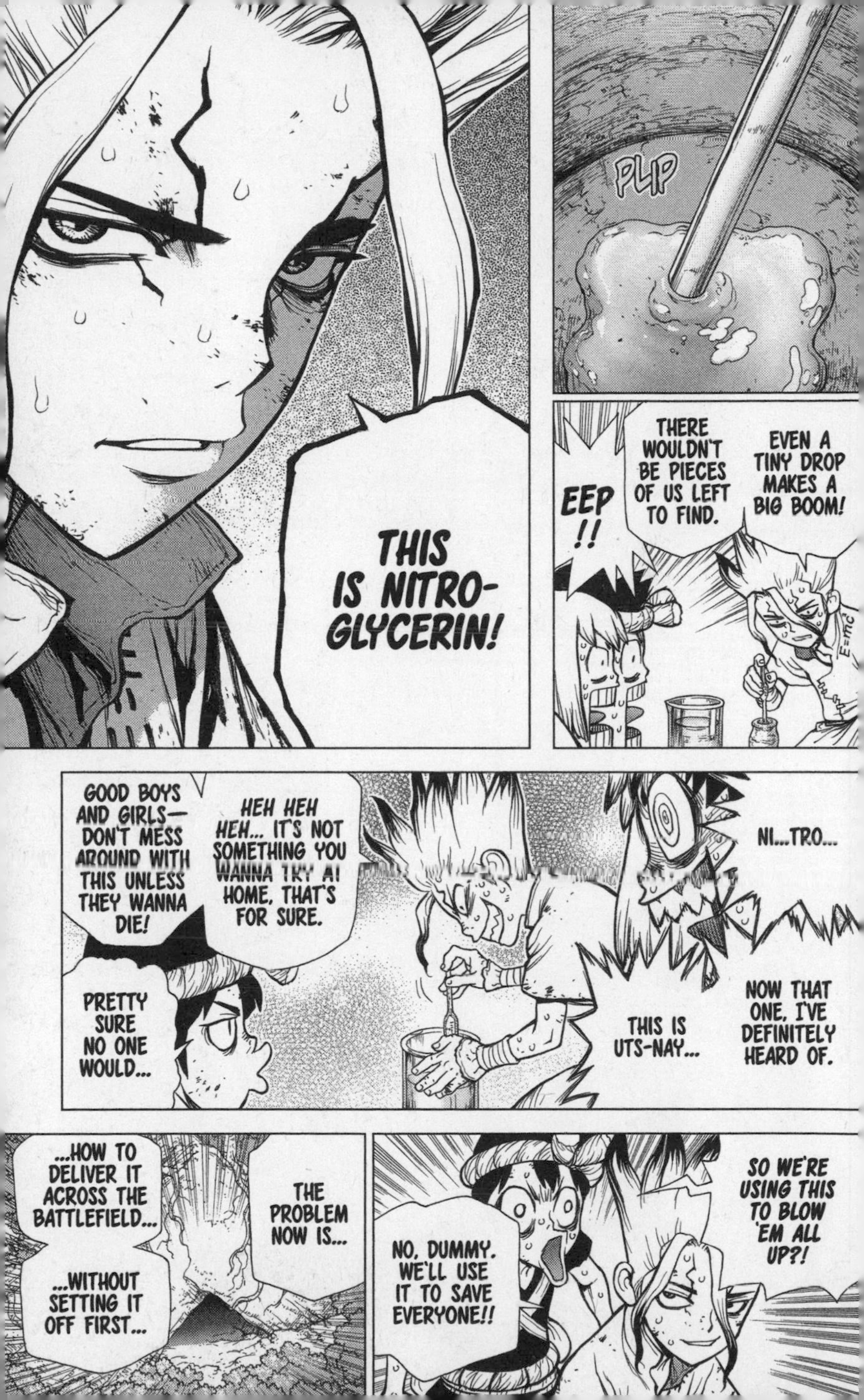
PLIP
EVEN A TINY DROP MAKES A BIG BOOM!
THERE WOULDN'T BE PIECES OF US LEFT TO FIND.
EEP!!
THIS IS NITRO-GLYCERIN!
NI...TRO...
NOW THAT ONE, I'VE DEFINITELY HEARD OF.
THIS IS UTS-NAY...
HEH HEH HEH... IT'S NOT SOMETHING YOU WANNA TRY AT HOME, THAT'S FOR SURE.
GOOD BOYS AND GIRLS— DON'T MESS AROUND WITH THIS UNLESS THEY WANNA DIE!
PRETTY SURE NO ONE WOULD...
SO WE'RE USING THIS TO BLOW 'EM ALL UP?!
NO, DUMMY. WE'LL USE IT TO SAVE EVERYONE!!
THE PROBLEM NOW IS...
...HOW TO DELIVER IT ACROSS THE BATTLEFIELD...
...WITHOUT SETTING IT OFF FIRST...

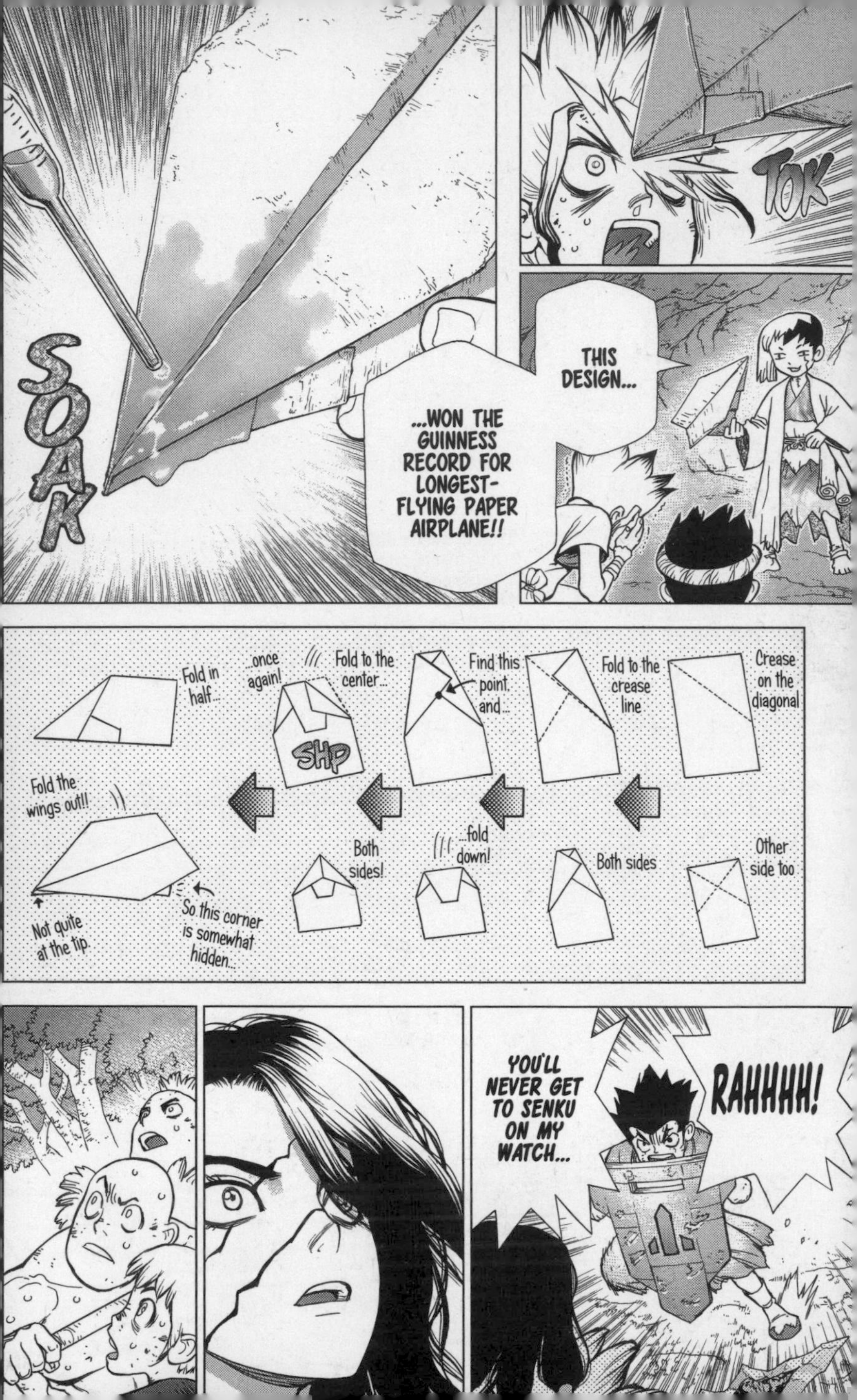
TOK
THIS DESIGN...
...WON THE GUINNESS RECORD FOR LONGEST-FLYING PAPER AIRPLANE!!
SOAK
Crease on the diagonal
Other side too
Fold to the crease line
Both sides
Find this point, and...
...fold down!
Fold to the center...
Both sides!
...once again!
SHP
Fold in half...
Fold the wings out!!
So this corner is somewhat hidden...
Not quite at the tip.
RAHHHH!
YOU'LL NEVER GET TO SENKU ON MY WATCH...

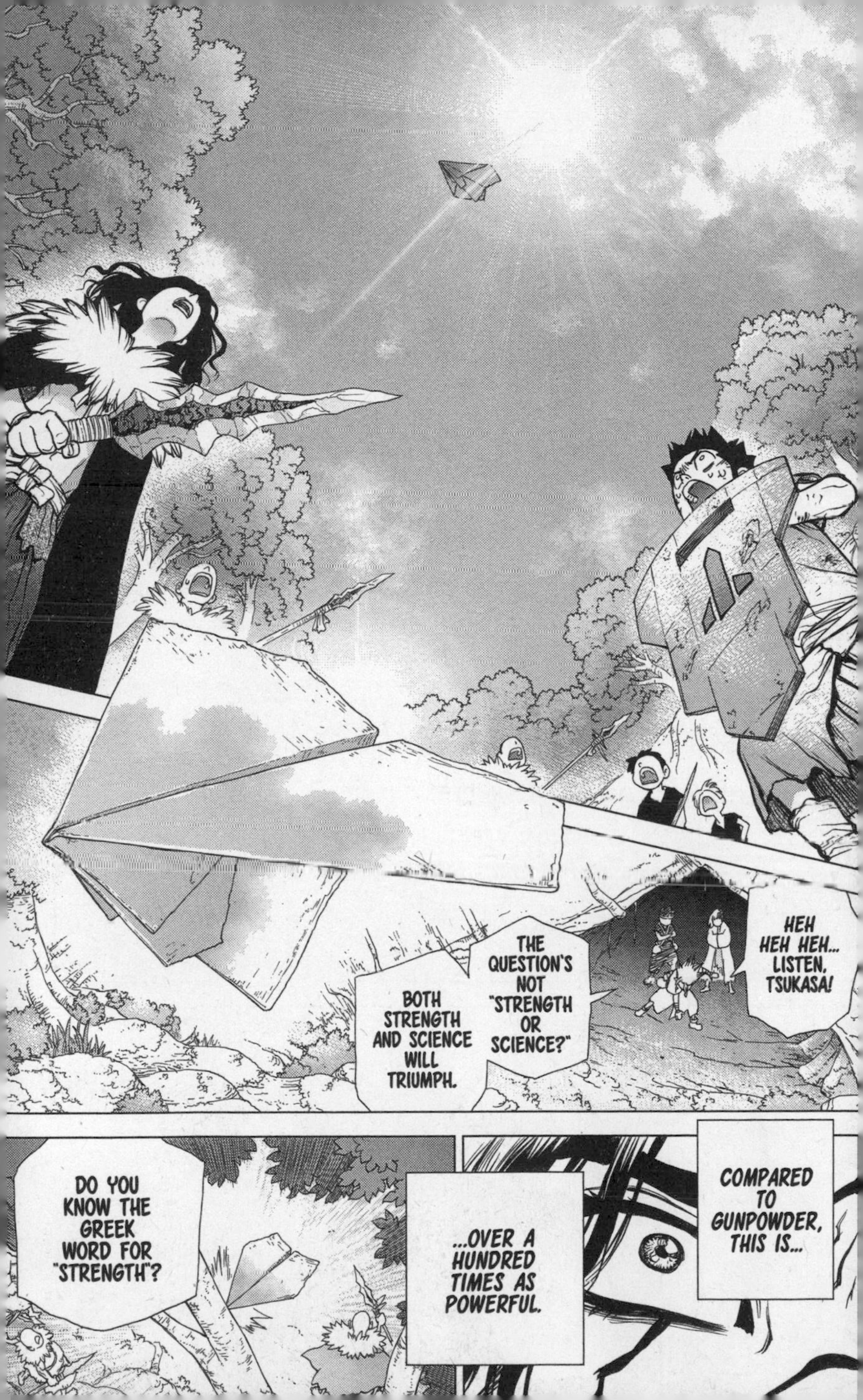
HEH HEH HEH... LISTEN, TSUKASA!
THE QUESTION'S NOT "STRENGTH OR SCIENCE?"
BOTH STRENGTH AND SCIENCE WILL TRIUMPH.
COMPARED TO GUNPOWDER, THIS IS...
...OVER A HUNDRED TIMES AS POWERFUL.
DO YOU KNOW THE GREEK WORD FOR "STRENGTH"?

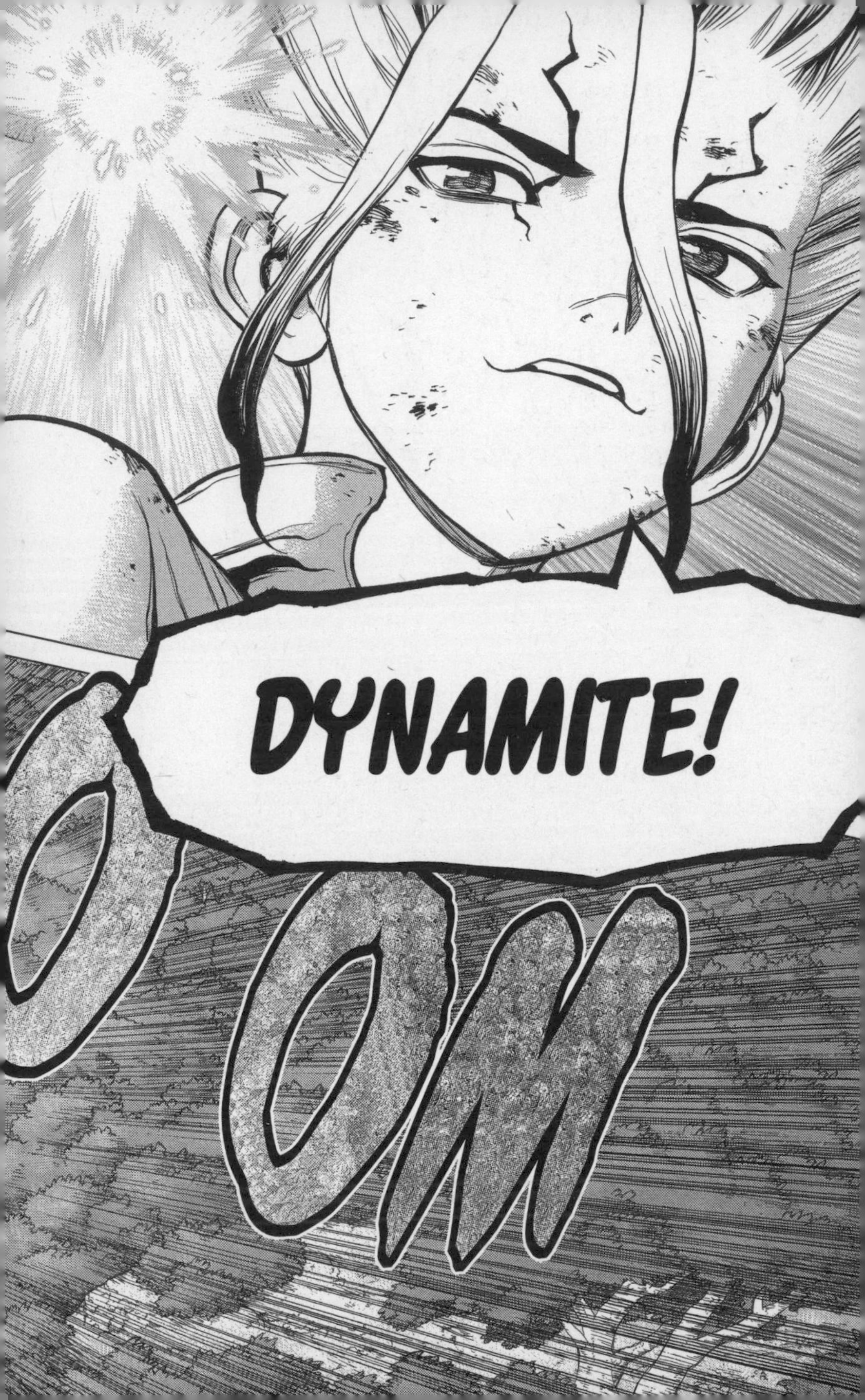
DYNAMITE!
OOM

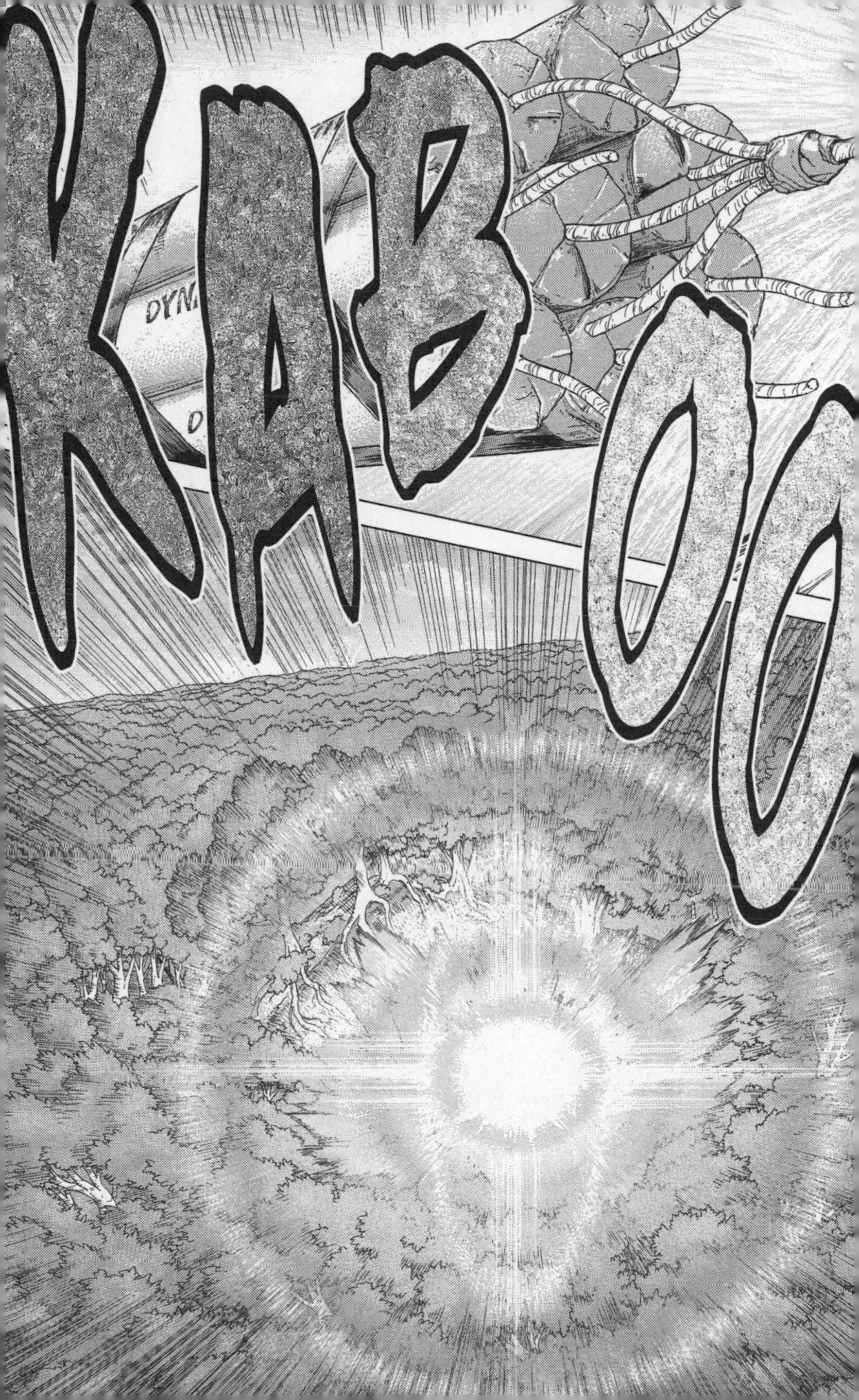
KABOO

MECHA SENKU Q&A

SEARCH
Question Corner

Is Taiju literally unable to use weapons? I know he took a shield into battle, but it's not like he could ever actually beat anyone with that!

M.G. from Osaka **SEARCH**

Taiju's ultimate mission was to use his unparalleled toughness and that shield to protect the science team at any cost!

If either Tsukasa or Hyoga had ignored the primary battle and made a beeline for the cave, the science team would have been slaughtered in an instant.

Taiju's dedication to being a human shield prevented that unfortunate outcome!

Each individual has a different role on the battlefield. Taiju's role may seem boring and thankless, but being a humble, unsung hero suits him quite well!!

Science Team

Taiju

Battle Team

Tsukasa & Hyoga

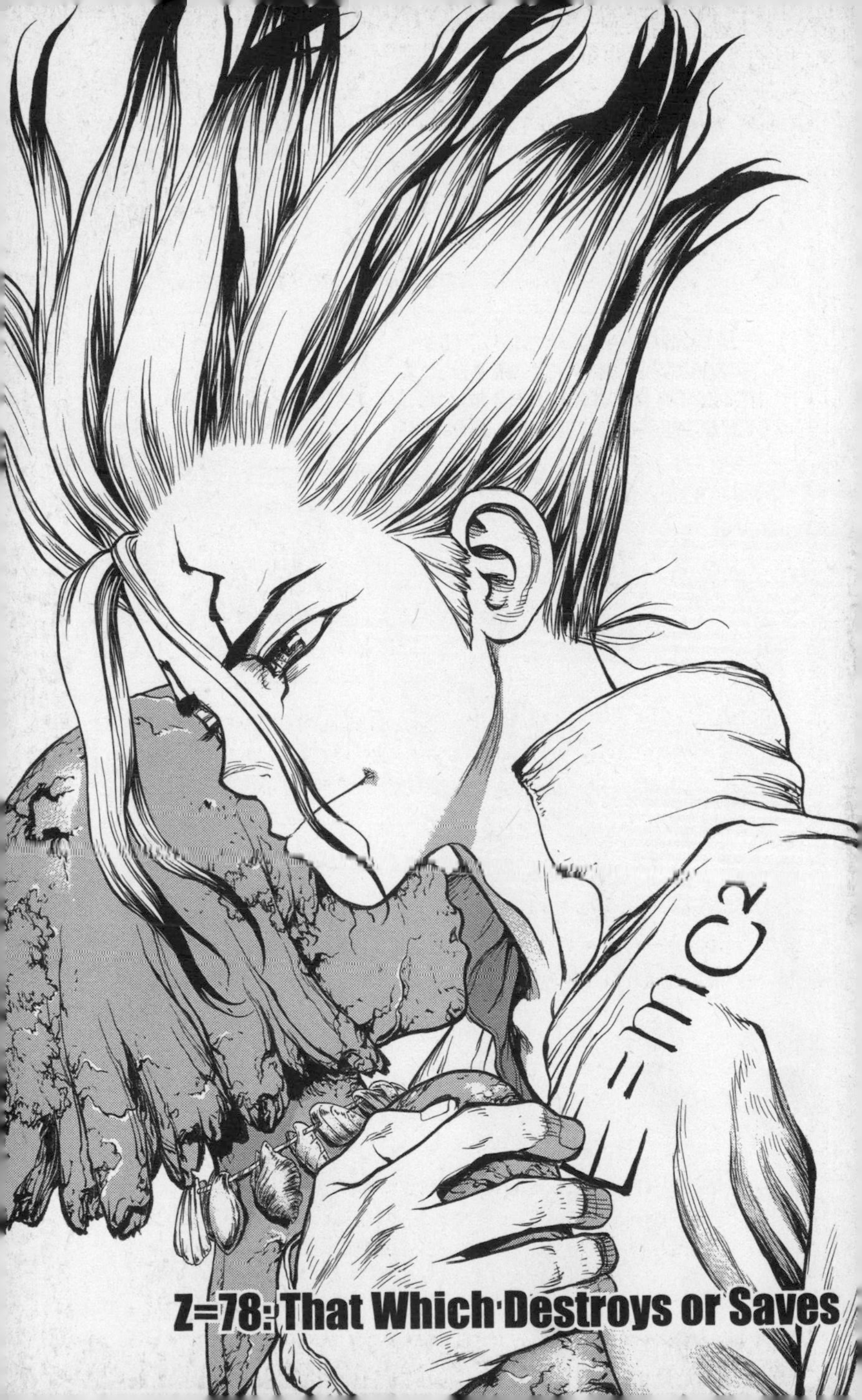
=mc²

Z=78: That Which Destroys or Saves

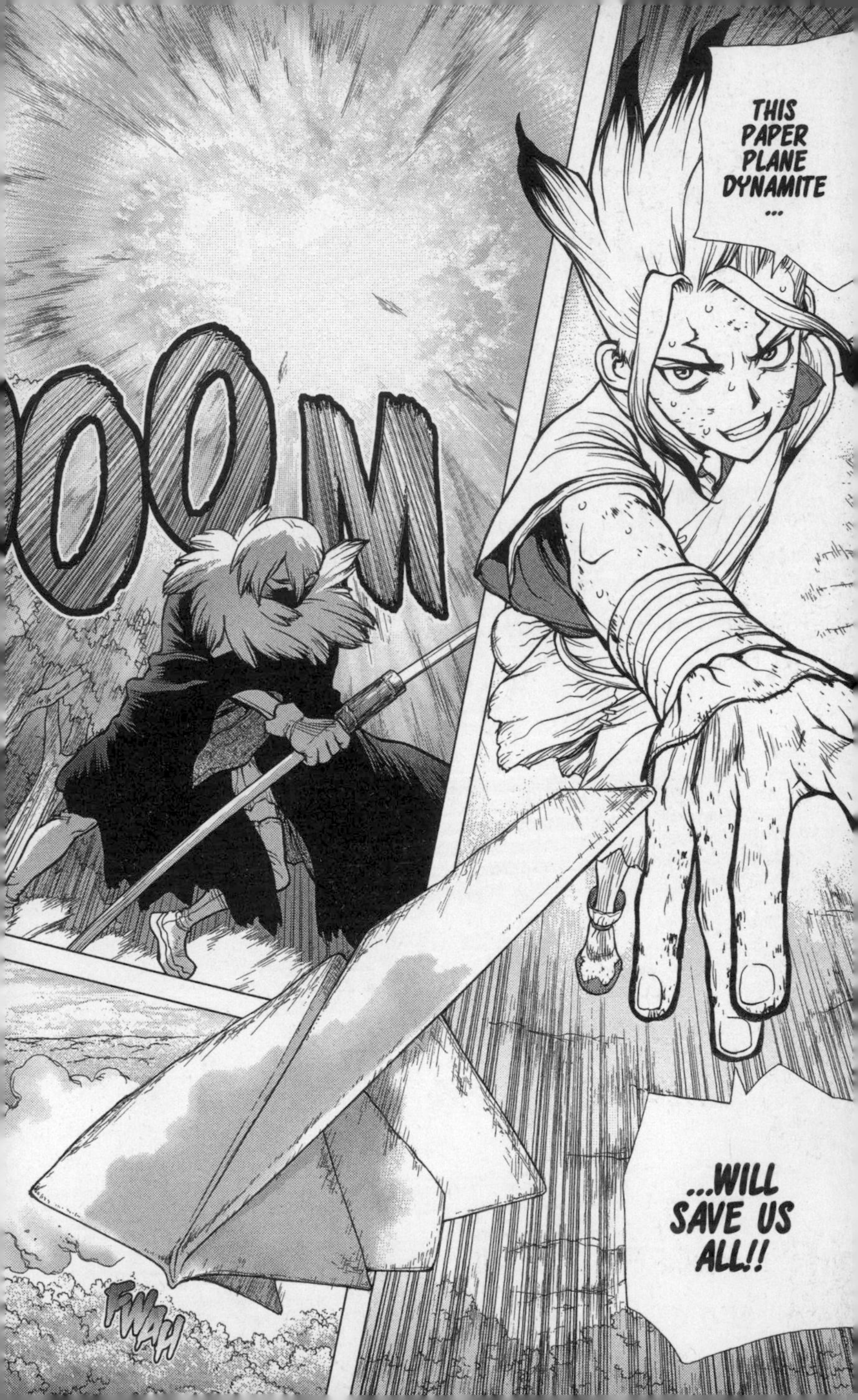
THIS PAPER PLANE DYNAMITE ...
...WILL SAVE US ALL!!
OOM
FWAH

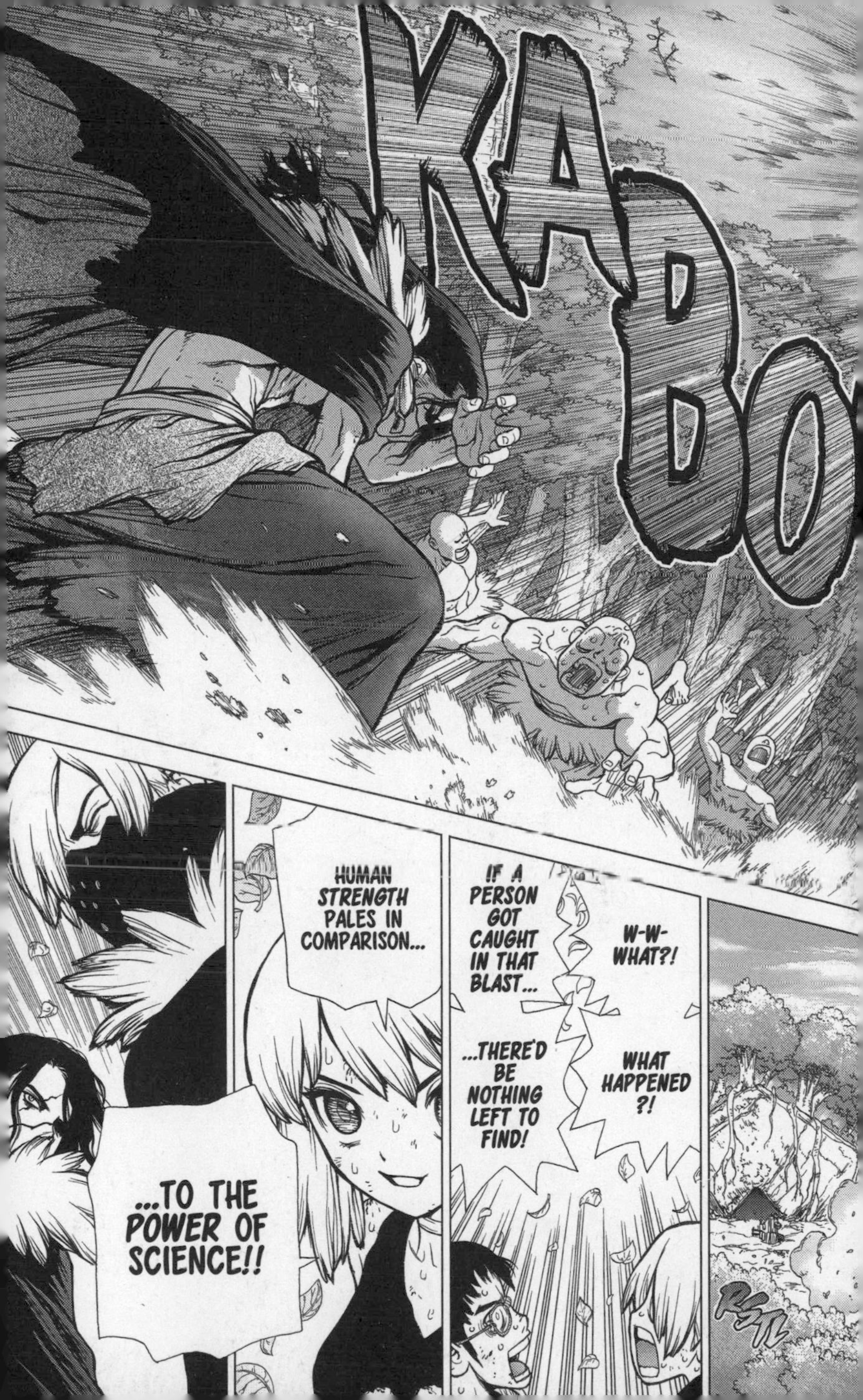
KABO
RSTL
W-W-WHAT?!
WHAT HAPPENED?!
IF A PERSON GOT CAUGHT IN THAT BLAST...
...THERE'D BE NOTHING LEFT TO FIND!
HUMAN STRENGTH PALES IN COMPARISON...
...TO THE POWER OF SCIENCE!!

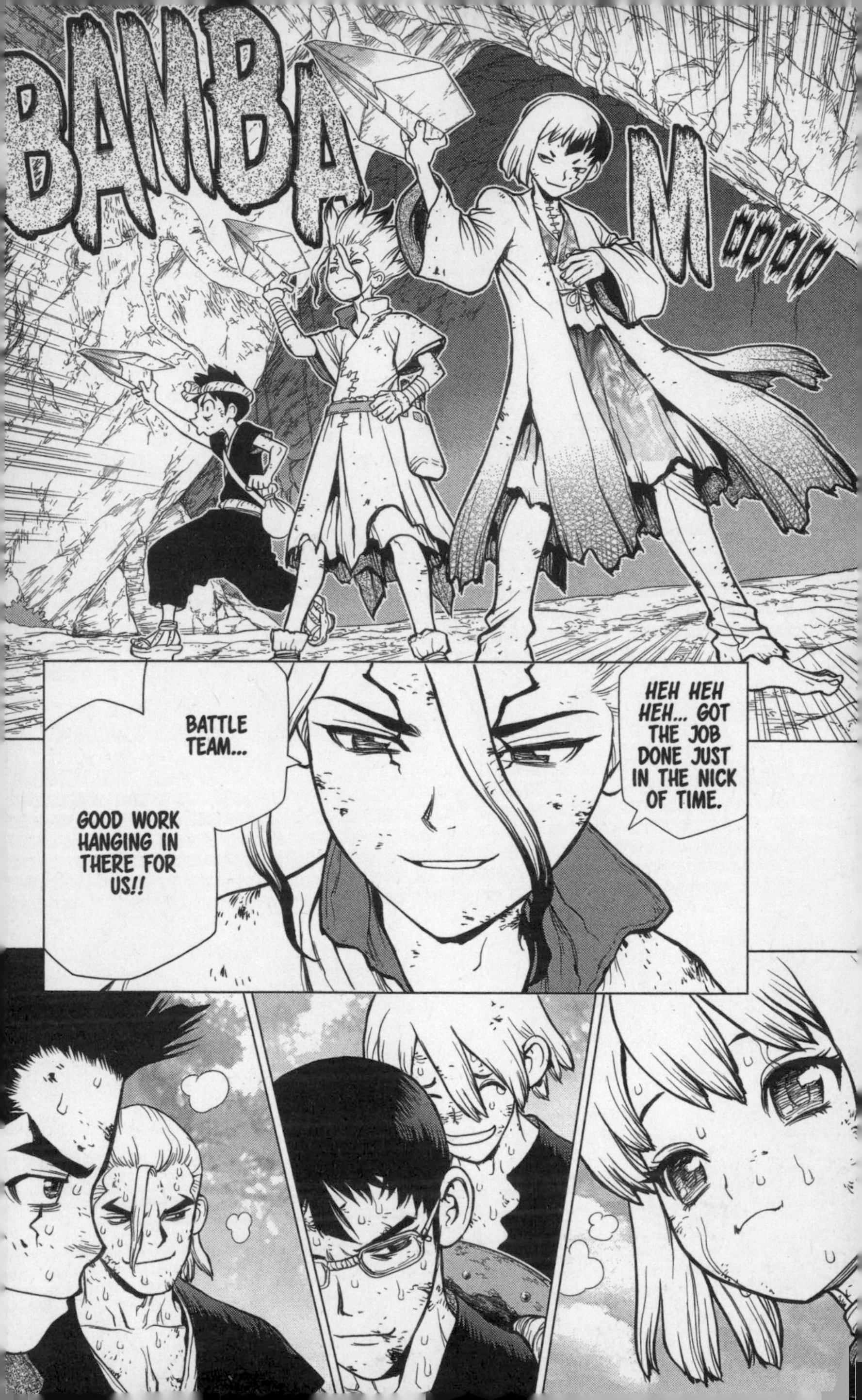
BAMBAM
HEH HEH HEH... GOT THE JOB DONE JUST IN THE NICK OF TIME.
BATTLE TEAM...
GOOD WORK HANGING IN THERE FOR US!!

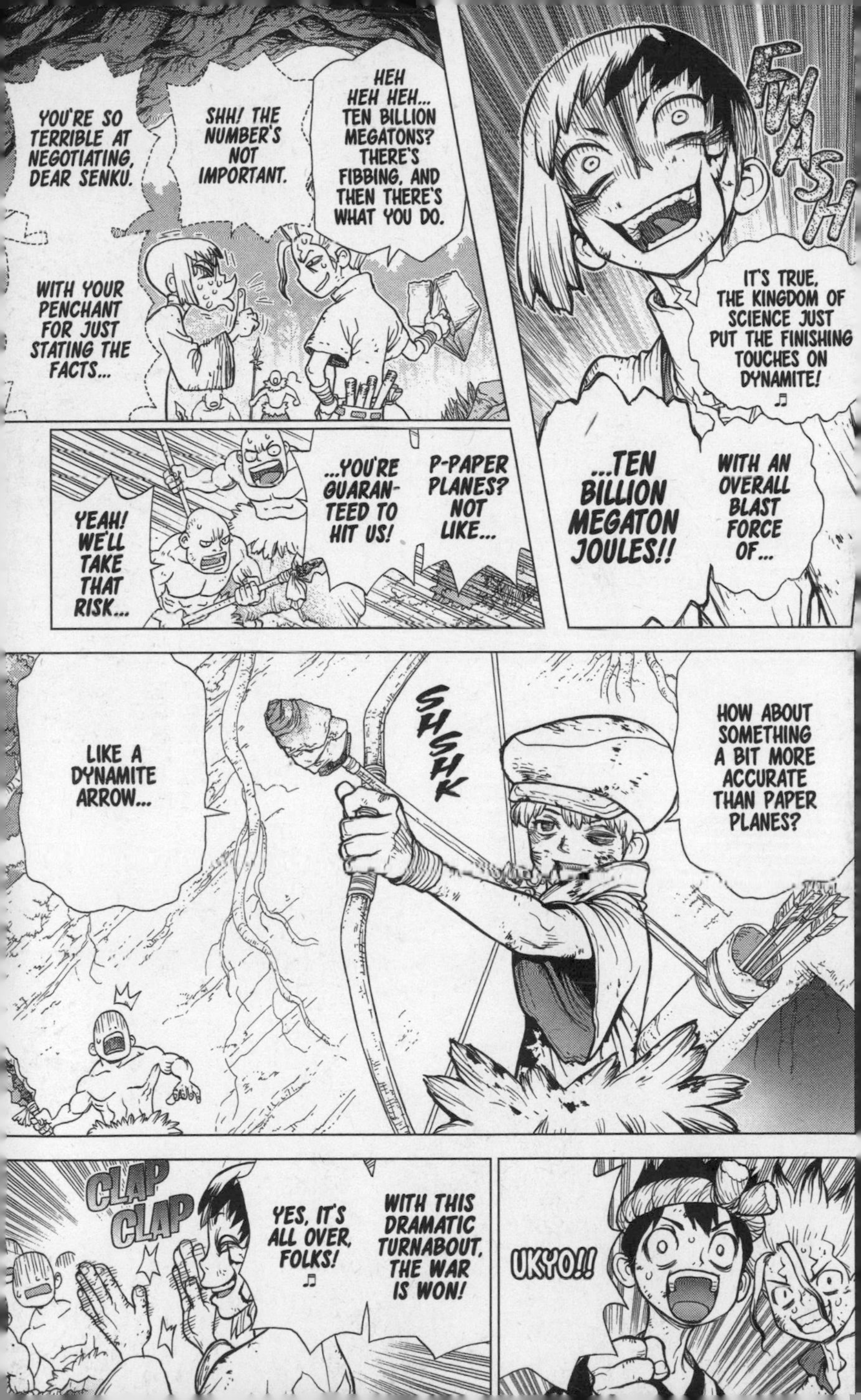
FWASH
IT'S TRUE, THE KINGDOM OF SCIENCE JUST PUT THE FINISHING TOUCHES ON DYNAMITE! ♪
WITH AN OVERALL BLAST FORCE OF...
...TEN BILLION MEGATON JOULES!!
HEH HEH HEH... TEN BILLION MEGATONS? THERE'S FIBBING, AND THEN THERE'S WHAT YOU DO.
SHH! THE NUMBER'S NOT IMPORTANT.
YOU'RE SO TERRIBLE AT NEGOTIATING, DEAR SENKU.
WITH YOUR PENCHANT FOR JUST STATING THE FACTS...
P-PAPER PLANES? NOT LIKE...
...YOU'RE GUARANTEED TO HIT US!
YEAH! WE'LL TAKE THAT RISK...
HOW ABOUT SOMETHING A BIT MORE ACCURATE THAN PAPER PLANES?
SHSHK
LIKE A DYNAMITE ARROW...
UKYO!!
WITH THIS DRAMATIC TURNABOUT, THE WAR IS WON!
YES, IT'S ALL OVER, FOLKS! ♪
CLAP CLAP

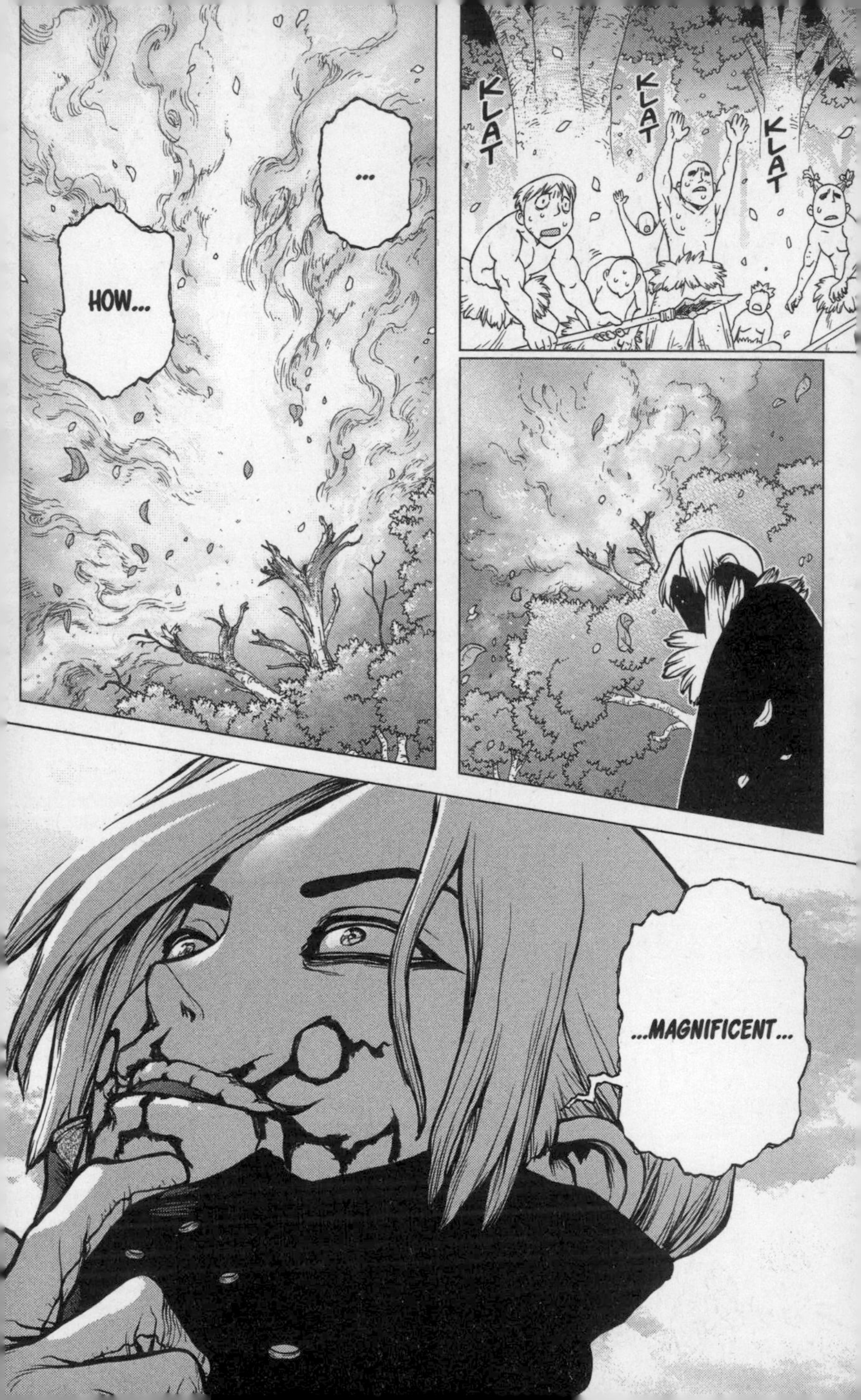
KLAT
KLAT
KLAT
...
HOW...
...MAGNIFICENT...

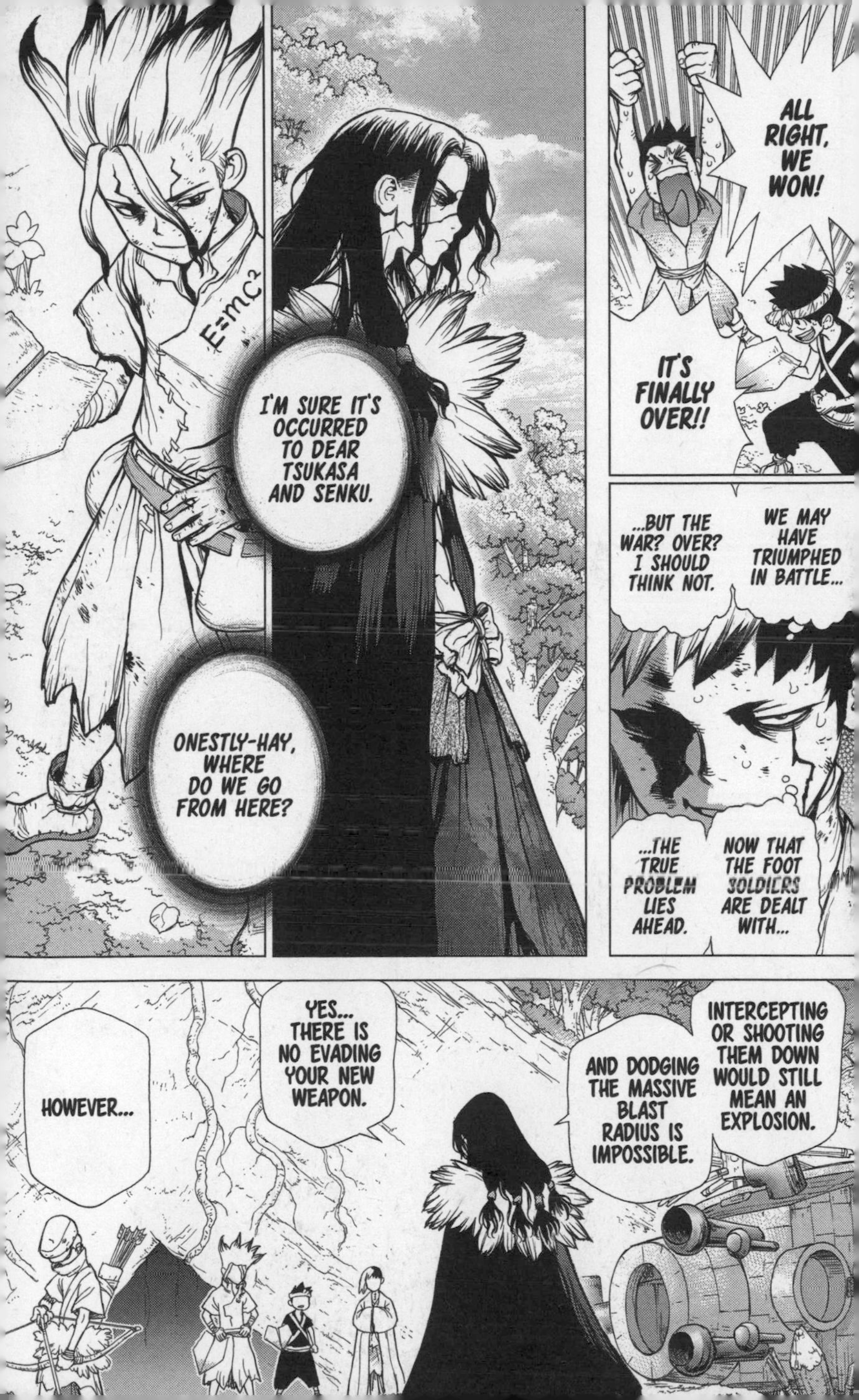
ALL RIGHT, WE WON!
IT'S FINALLY OVER!!
WE MAY HAVE TRIUMPHED IN BATTLE...
...BUT THE WAR? OVER? I SHOULD THINK NOT.
NOW THAT THE FOOT SOLDIERS ARE DEALT WITH...
...THE TRUE PROBLEM LIES AHEAD.
I'M SURE IT'S OCCURRED TO DEAR TSUKASA AND SENKU.
ONESTLY-HAY, WHERE DO WE GO FROM HERE?
$E=MC^2$
INTERCEPTING OR SHOOTING THEM DOWN WOULD STILL MEAN AN EXPLOSION.
AND DODGING THE MASSIVE BLAST RADIUS IS IMPOSSIBLE.
YES... THERE IS NO EVADING YOUR NEW WEAPON.
HOWEVER...

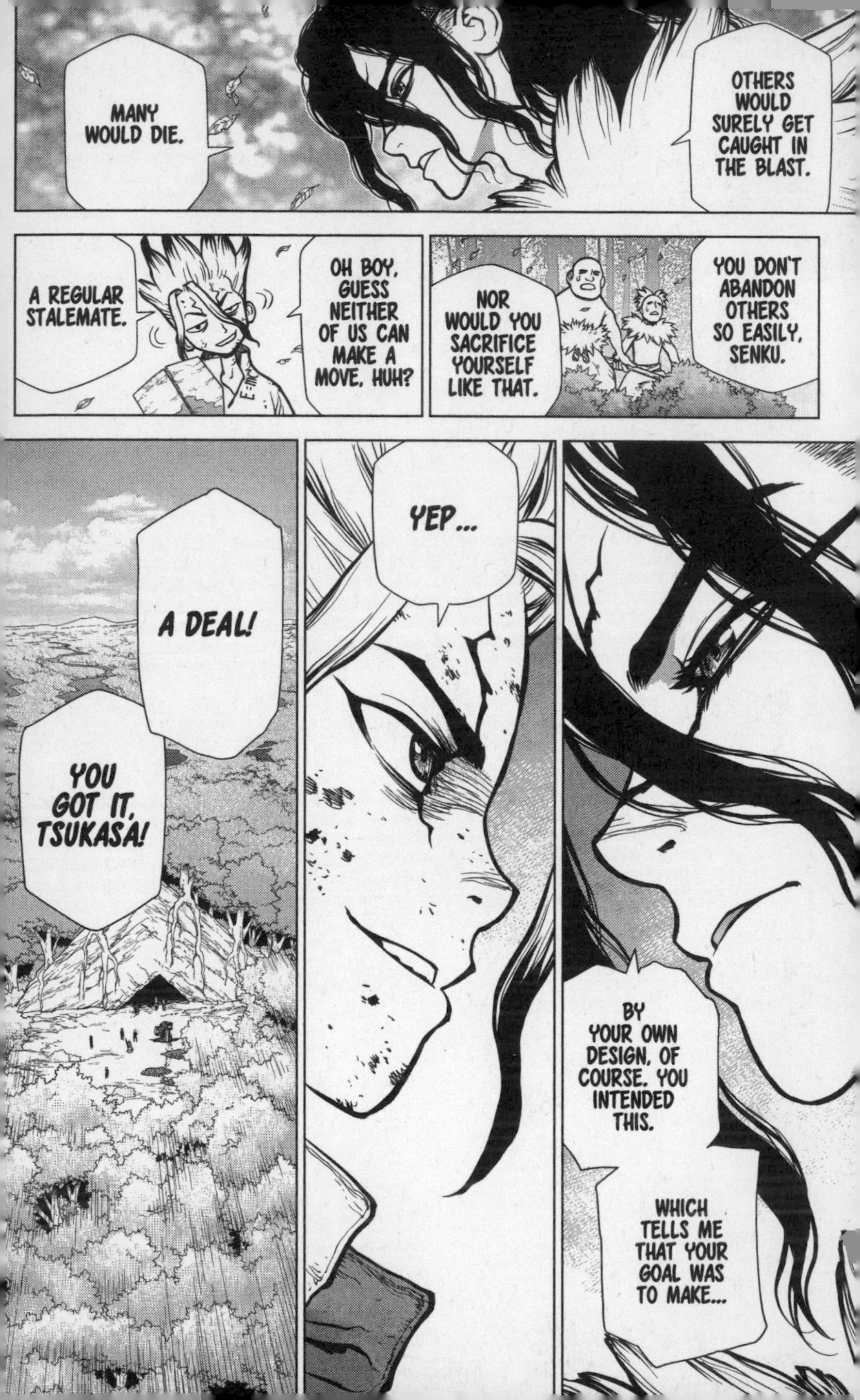
OTHERS WOULD SURELY GET CAUGHT IN THE BLAST.
MANY WOULD DIE.
YOU DON'T ABANDON OTHERS SO EASILY, SENKU.
NOR WOULD YOU SACRIFICE YOURSELF LIKE THAT.
OH BOY, GUESS NEITHER OF US CAN MAKE A MOVE, HUH?
A REGULAR STALEMATE.
BY YOUR OWN DESIGN, OF COURSE. YOU INTENDED THIS.
WHICH TELLS ME THAT YOUR GOAL WAS TO MAKE...
YEP...
A DEAL!
YOU GOT IT, TSUKASA!

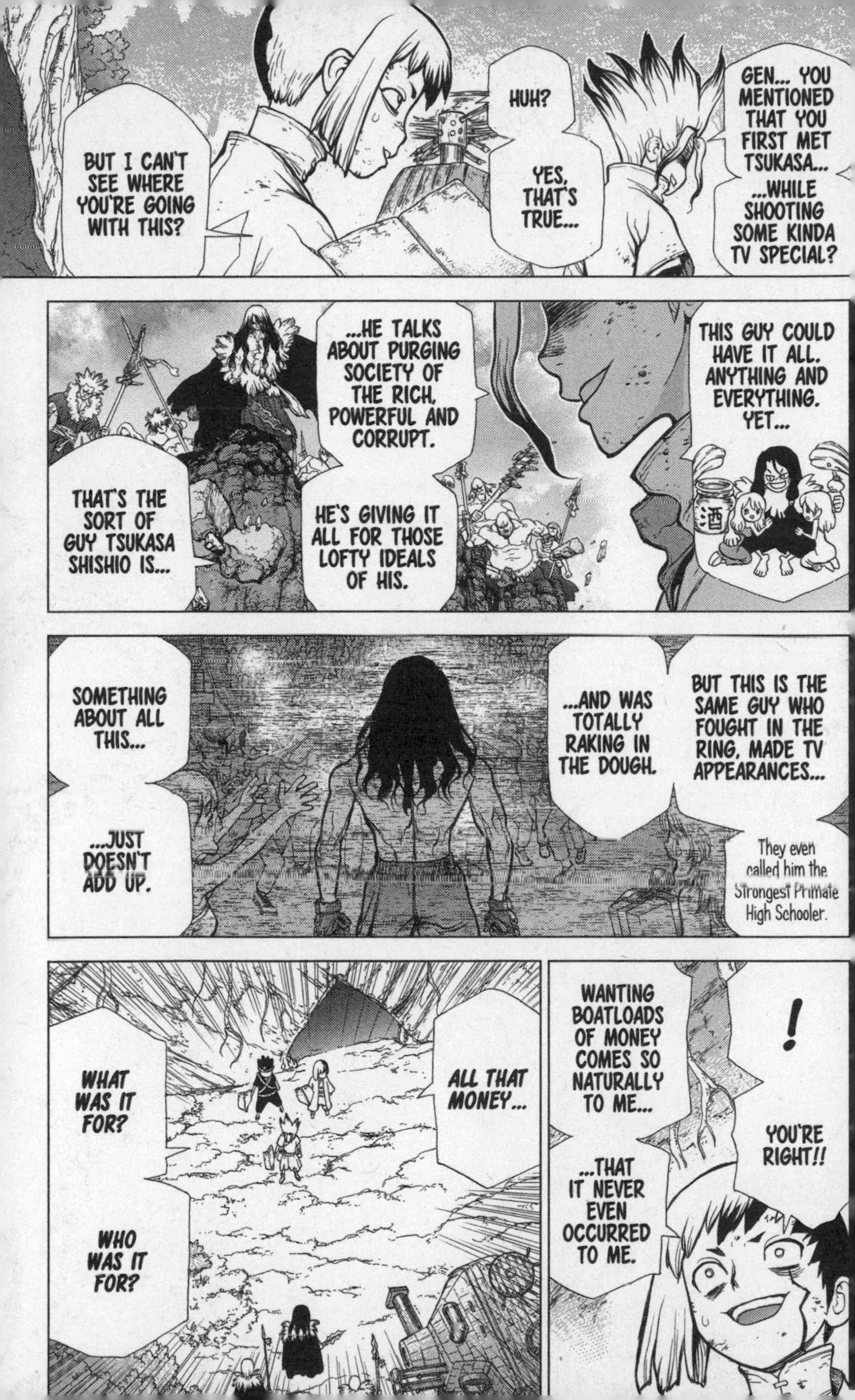
GEN... YOU MENTIONED THAT YOU FIRST MET TSUKASA...
...WHILE SHOOTING SOME KINDA TV SPECIAL?
HUH?
YES, THAT'S TRUE...
BUT I CAN'T SEE WHERE YOU'RE GOING WITH THIS?
THIS GUY COULD HAVE IT ALL. ANYTHING AND EVERYTHING. YET...
酒
...HE TALKS ABOUT PURGING SOCIETY OF THE RICH, POWERFUL AND CORRUPT.
HE'S GIVING IT ALL FOR THOSE LOFTY IDEALS OF HIS.
THAT'S THE SORT OF GUY TSUKASA SHISHIO IS...
BUT THIS IS THE SAME GUY WHO FOUGHT IN THE RING, MADE TV APPEARANCES...
They even called him the Strongest Primate High Schooler.
...AND WAS TOTALLY RAKING IN THE DOUGH.
SOMETHING ABOUT ALL THIS...
...JUST DOESN'T ADD UP.
!
YOU'RE RIGHT!!
WANTING BOATLOADS OF MONEY COMES SO NATURALLY TO ME...
...THAT IT NEVER EVEN OCCURRED TO ME.
ALL THAT MONEY...
WHAT WAS IT FOR?
WHO WAS IT FOR?

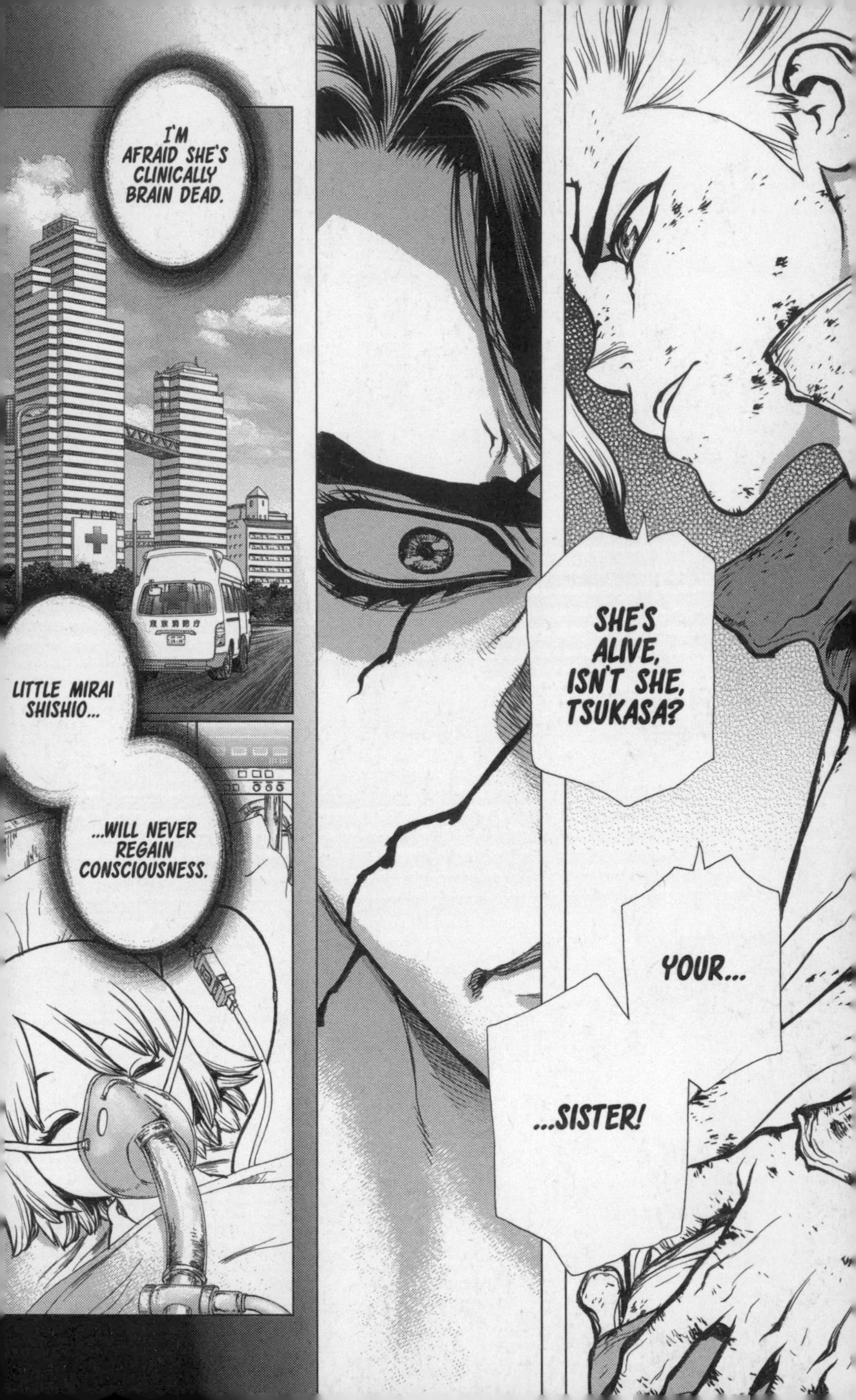
SHE'S ALIVE, ISN'T SHE, TSUKASA?
YOUR...
...SISTER!
I'M AFRAID SHE'S CLINICALLY BRAIN DEAD.
LITTLE MIRAI SHISHIO...
...WILL NEVER REGAIN CONSCIOUSNESS.

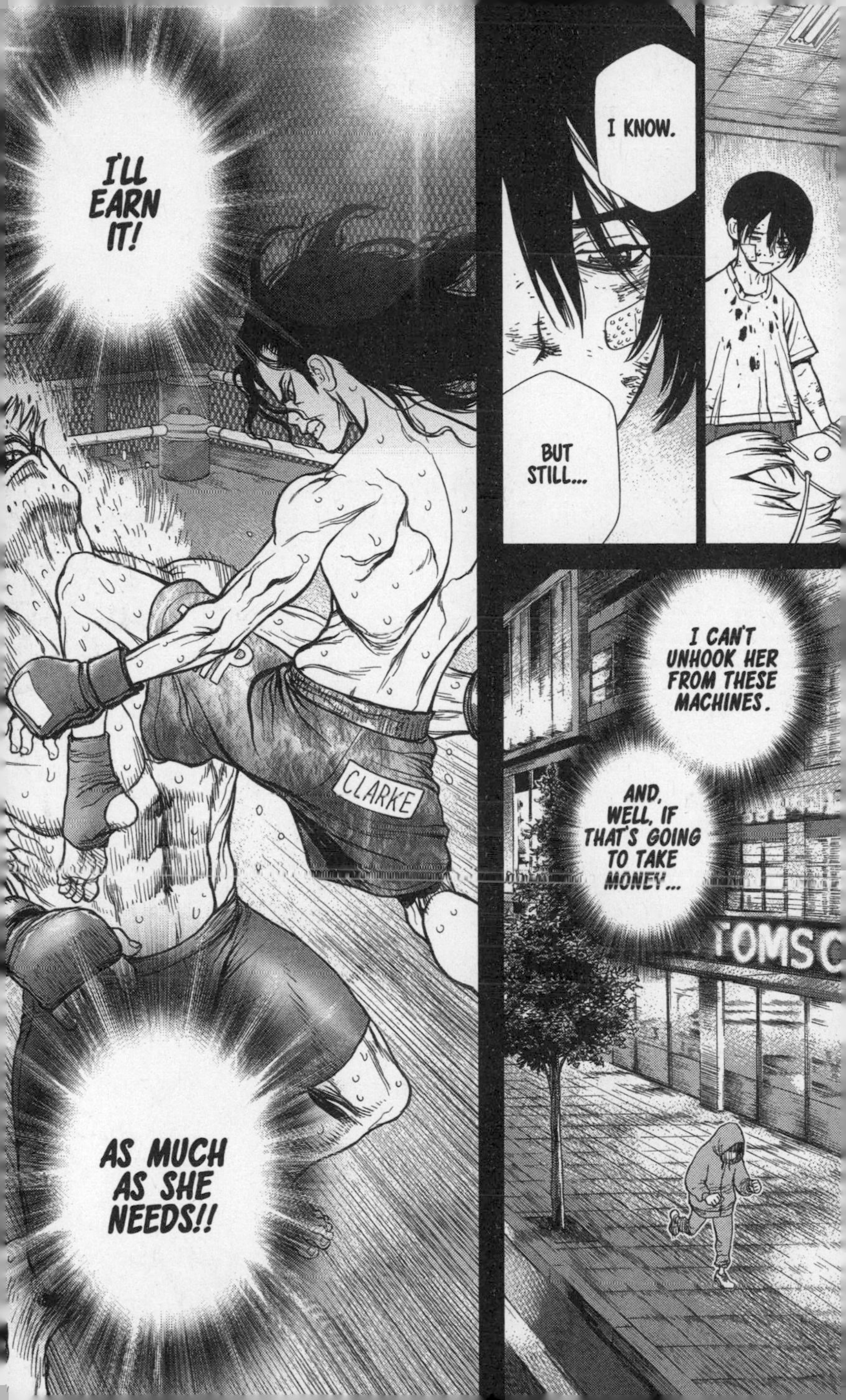
I KNOW.
BUT STILL...
I CAN'T UNHOOK HER FROM THESE MACHINES.
AND, WELL, IF THAT'S GOING TO TAKE MONEY...
I'LL EARN IT!
CLARKE
AS MUCH AS SHE NEEDS!!

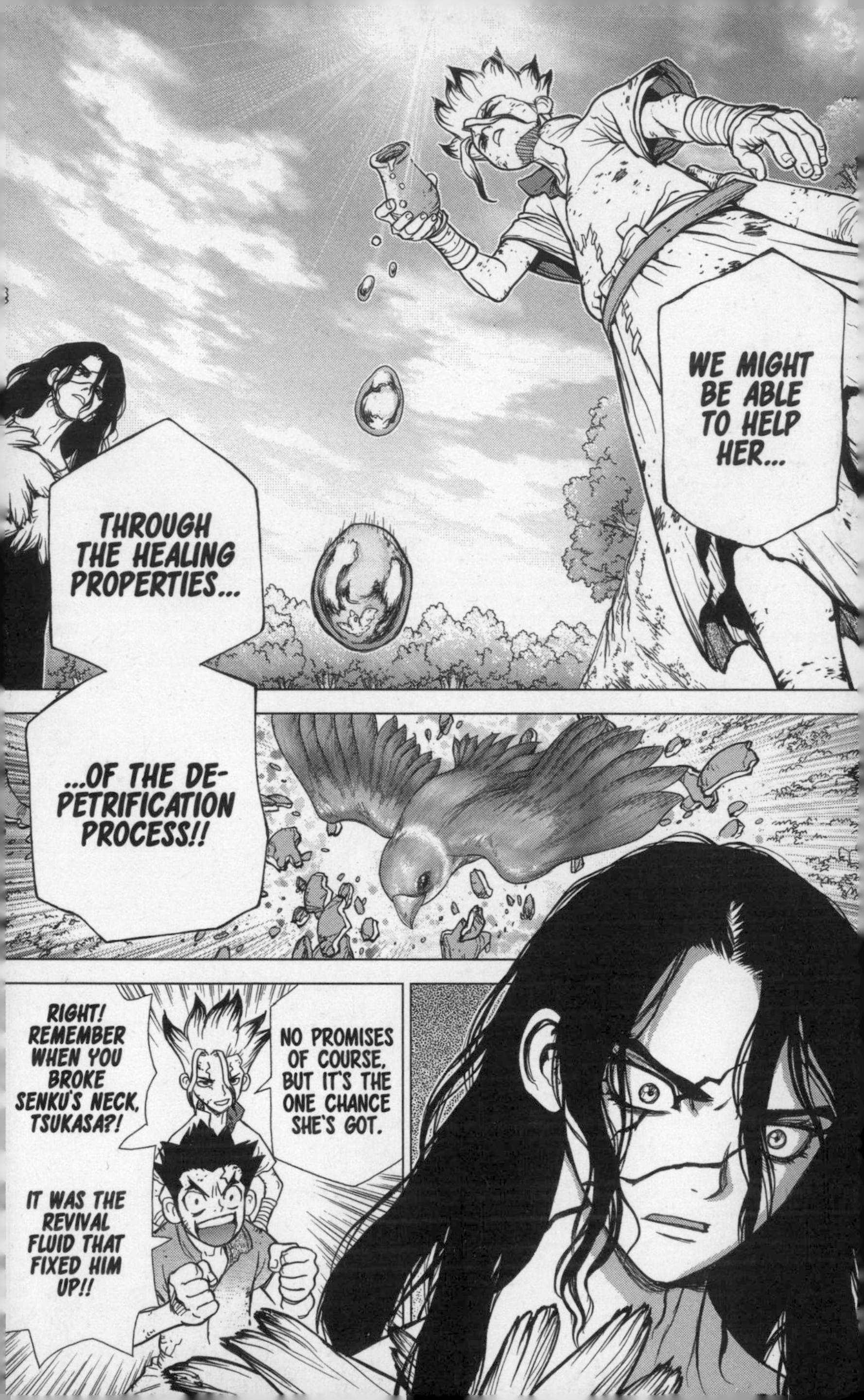
WE MIGHT BE ABLE TO HELP HER...
THROUGH THE HEALING PROPERTIES...
...OF THE DE-PETRIFICATION PROCESS!!
NO PROMISES OF COURSE, BUT IT'S THE ONE CHANCE SHE'S GOT.
RIGHT! REMEMBER WHEN YOU BROKE SENKU'S NECK, TSUKASA?!
IT WAS THE REVIVAL FLUID THAT FIXED HIM UP!!

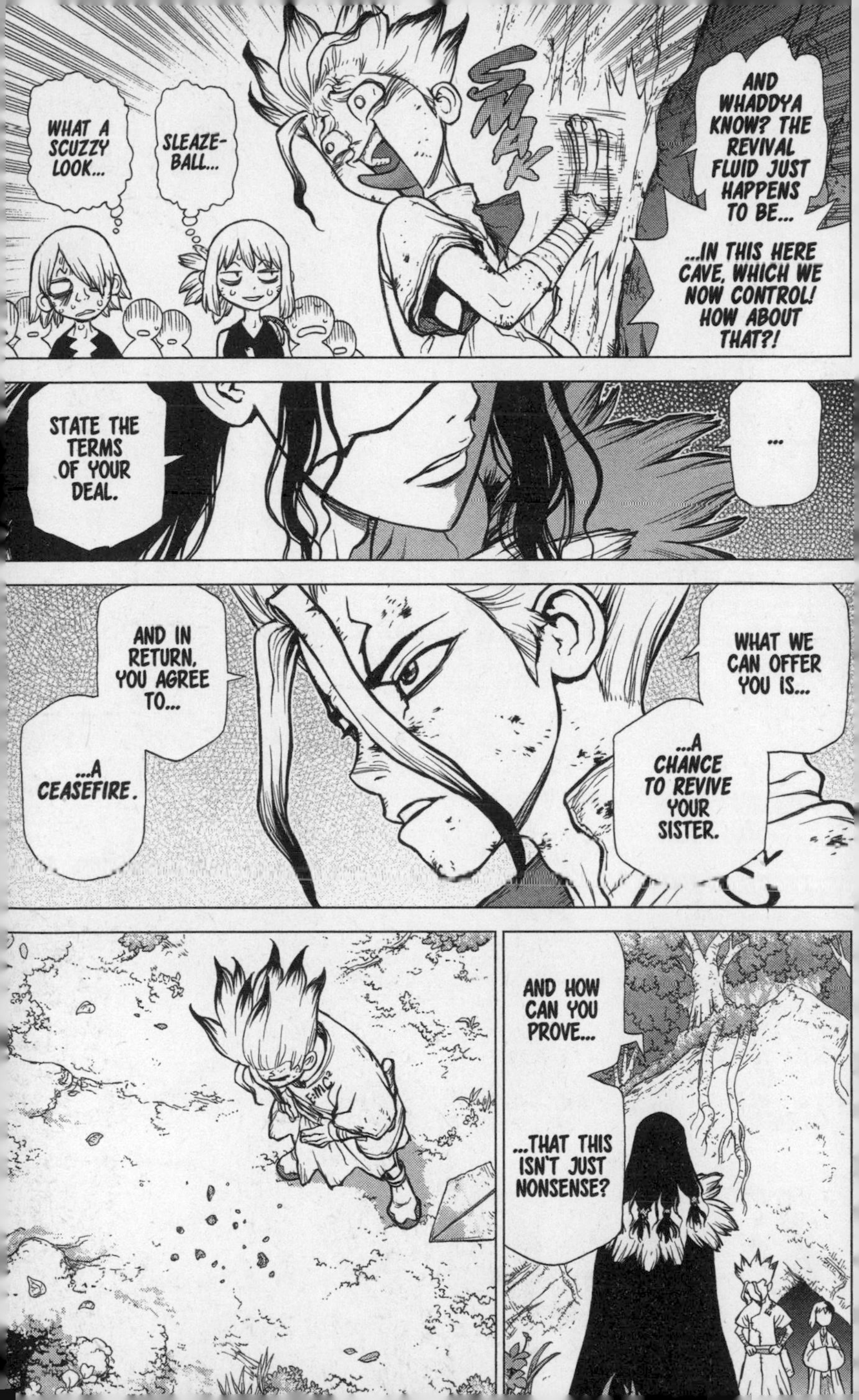
AND WHADDYA KNOW? THE REVIVAL FLUID JUST HAPPENS TO BE...
...IN THIS HERE CAVE, WHICH WE NOW CONTROL! HOW ABOUT THAT?!
SLEAZE-BALL...
WHAT A SCUZZY LOOK...
...
STATE THE TERMS OF YOUR DEAL.
WHAT WE CAN OFFER YOU IS...
...A CHANCE TO REVIVE YOUR SISTER.
AND IN RETURN, YOU AGREE TO...
...A CEASEFIRE.
AND HOW CAN YOU PROVE...
...THAT THIS ISN'T JUST NONSENSE?

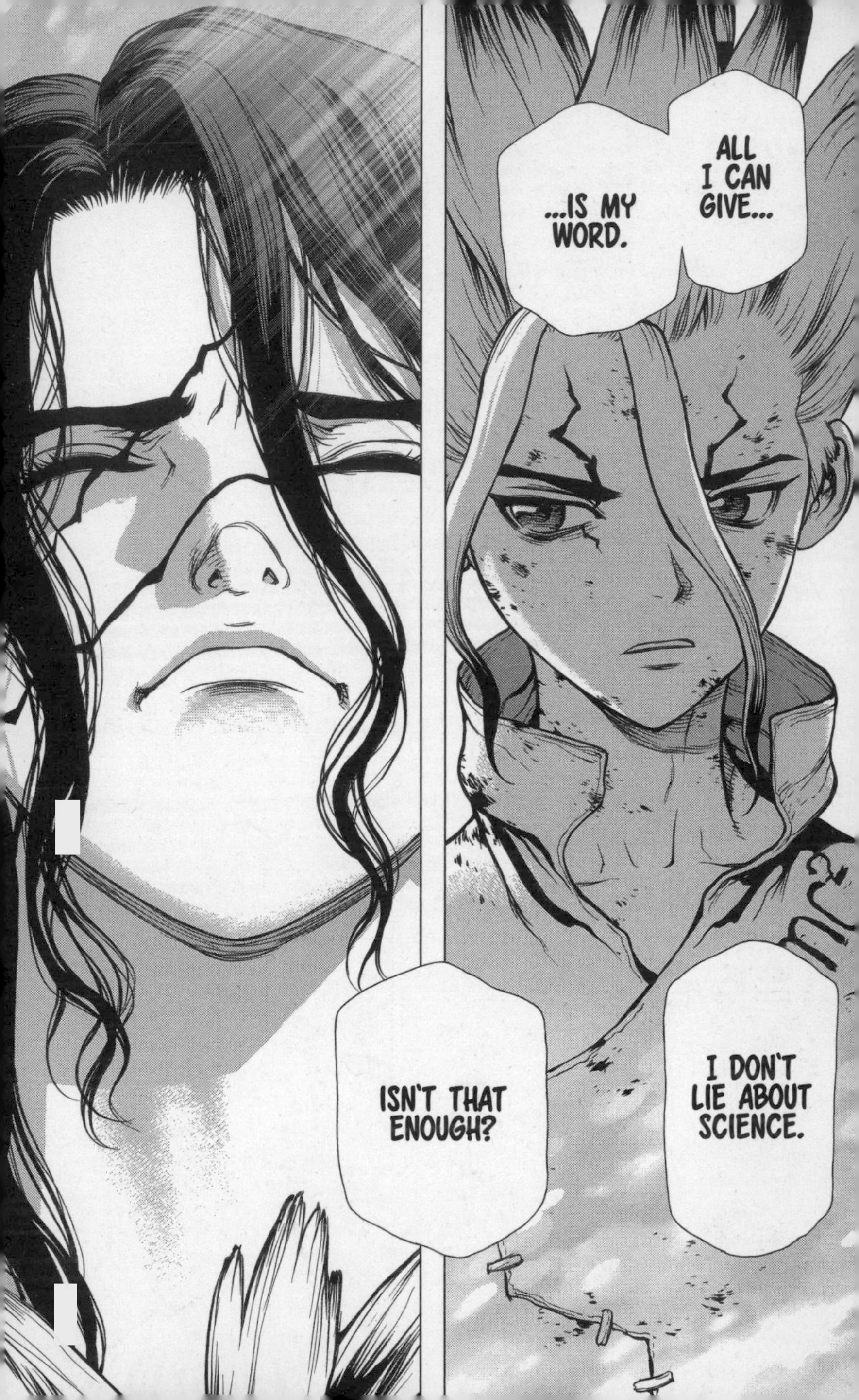
ALL I CAN GIVE...
...IS MY WORD.
I DON'T LIE ABOUT SCIENCE.
ISN'T THAT ENOUGH?

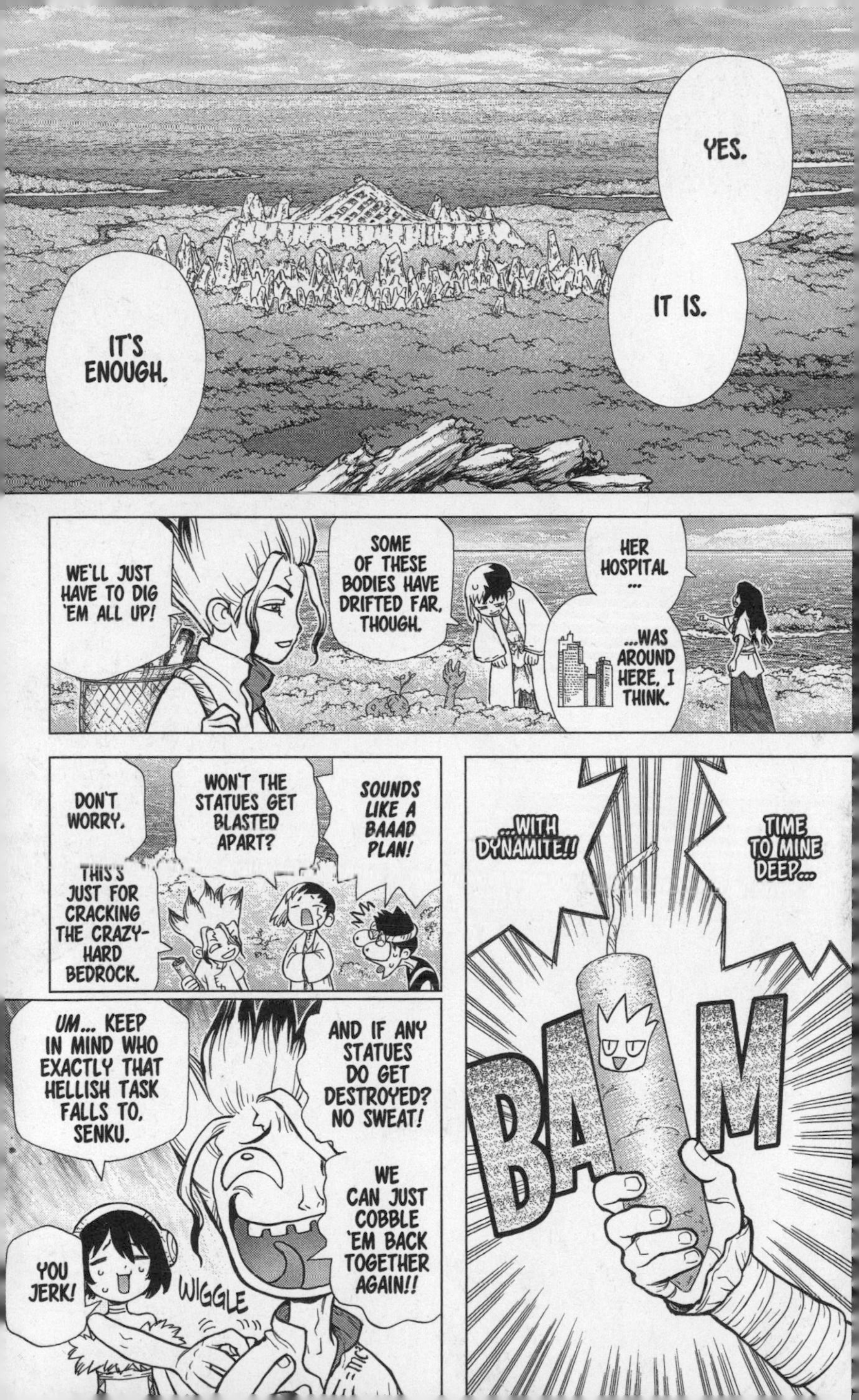
YES.
IT IS.
IT'S ENOUGH.
HER HOSPITAL...
...WAS AROUND HERE, I THINK.
SOME OF THESE BODIES HAVE DRIFTED FAR, THOUGH.
WE'LL JUST HAVE TO DIG 'EM ALL UP!
TIME TO MINE DEEP...
...WITH DYNAMITE!!
BAM
SOUNDS LIKE A BAAAD PLAN!
WON'T THE STATUES GET BLASTED APART?
DON'T WORRY.
THIS'S JUST FOR CRACKING THE CRAZY-HARD BEDROCK.
AND IF ANY STATUES DO GET DESTROYED? NO SWEAT!
WE CAN JUST COBBLE 'EM BACK TOGETHER AGAIN!!
UM... KEEP IN MIND WHO EXACTLY THAT HELLISH TASK FALLS TO, SENKU.
WIGGLE
YOU JERK!

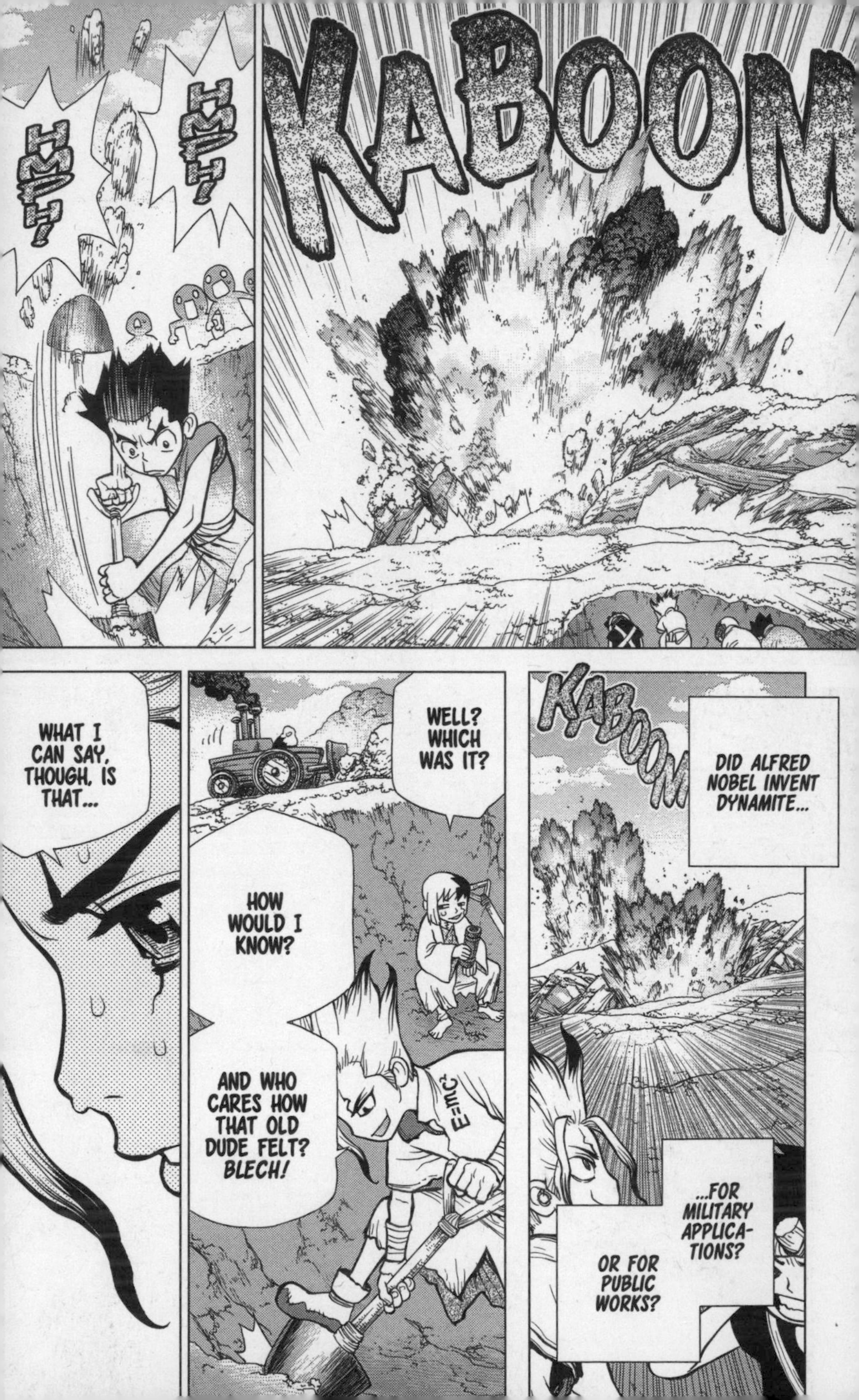
KABOOM
HMPH!
HMPH!
KABOOM
DID ALFRED NOBEL INVENT DYNAMITE...
...FOR MILITARY APPLICATIONS?
OR FOR PUBLIC WORKS?
WELL? WHICH WAS IT?
HOW WOULD I KNOW?
AND WHO CARES HOW THAT OLD DUDE FELT? BLECH!
$E=mc^2$
WHAT I CAN SAY, THOUGH, IS THAT...

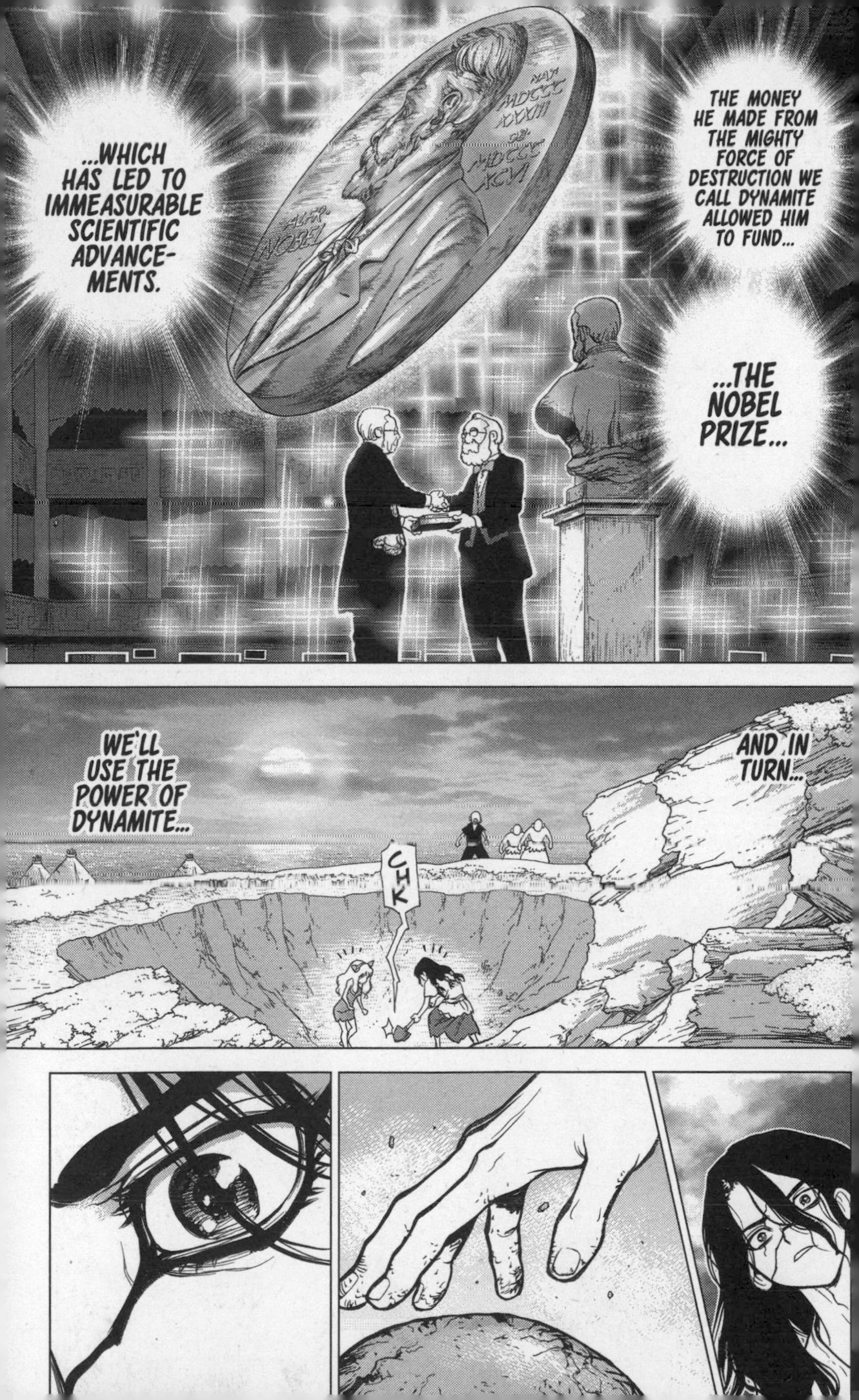
THE MONEY HE MADE FROM THE MIGHTY FORCE OF DESTRUCTION WE CALL DYNAMITE ALLOWED HIM TO FUND...
...THE NOBEL PRIZE...
...WHICH HAS LED TO IMMEASURABLE SCIENTIFIC ADVANCE-MENTS.
AND IN TURN...
WE'LL USE THE POWER OF DYNAMITE...
CHK

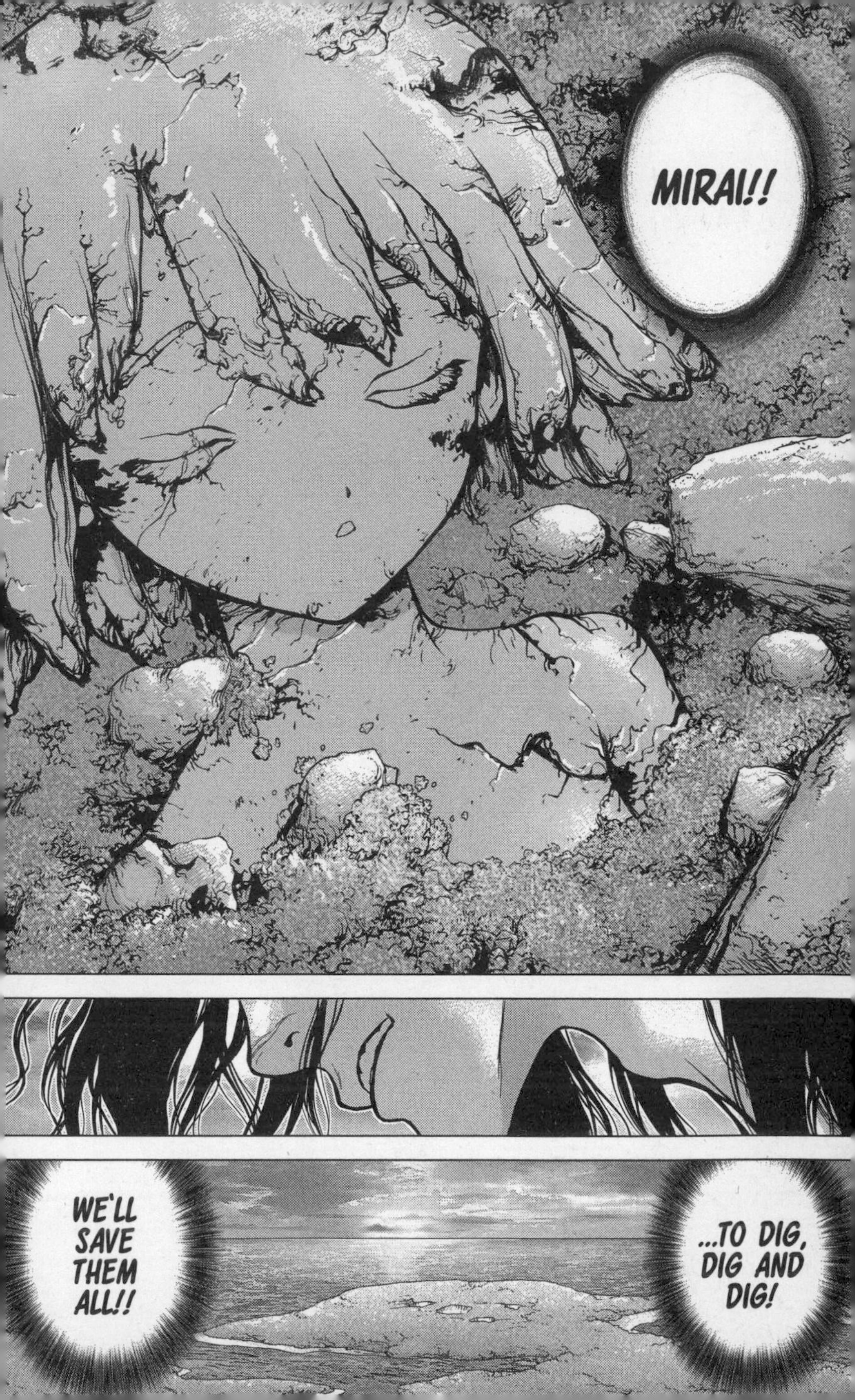
MIRAI!!
...TO DIG, DIG AND DIG!
WE'LL SAVE THEM ALL!!

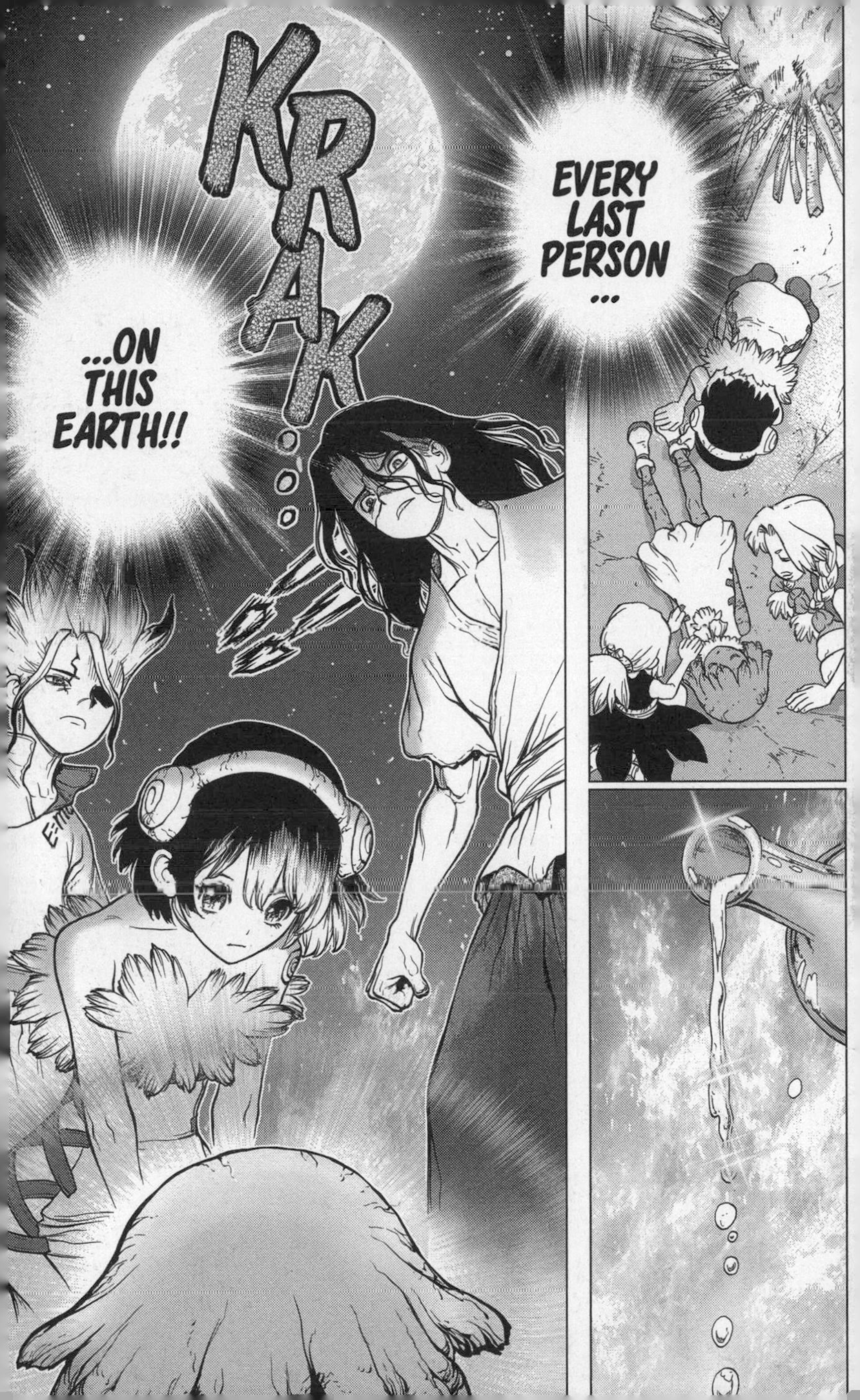
EVERY LAST PERSON ...
KRAK
...ON THIS EARTH!!

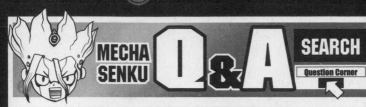

MECHA SENKU Q&A SEARCH

Question Corner

Gen and Tsukasa apparently met while doing an episode of a TV show. What kind of show was it, exactly?

D.I. from Kochi Prefecture SEARCH

Mental Battle!!

Brains clash against brawn in this showdown of the century! It's mentalist vs. top athlete!

It was a variety program where Gen utilized psychology to guess which card Tsukasa had drawn!

In truth, though, Gen had a vibrating transmitter hidden in his shoe to tell him the correct card. It was all a ruse!

A ruse? Please. I prefer the term "mental magic." ♪

Science Questions	How does one make gasoline out of plastic bottle caps?
Character Questions	If Taiju and Tsukasa really fought, who would win?
Questions That Aren't Really Questions	I wanna get petrified and challenge myself to count the seconds...

My name is MECHA SENKU!!

Now accepting any and all queries! Submit ten billion questions to me!

WHRRR KLANG

Dr.STONE

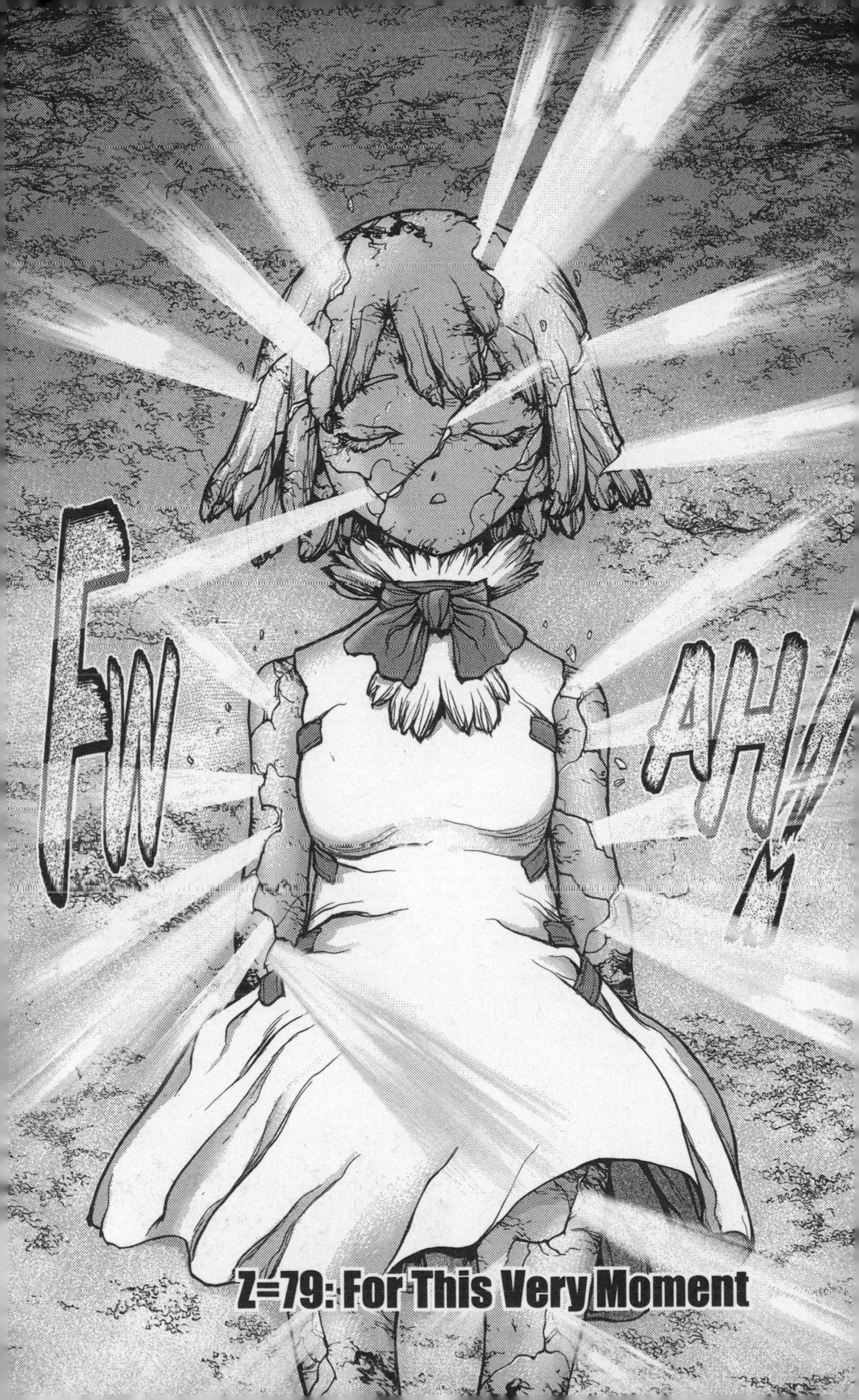
FWAHM
Z=79: For This Very Moment

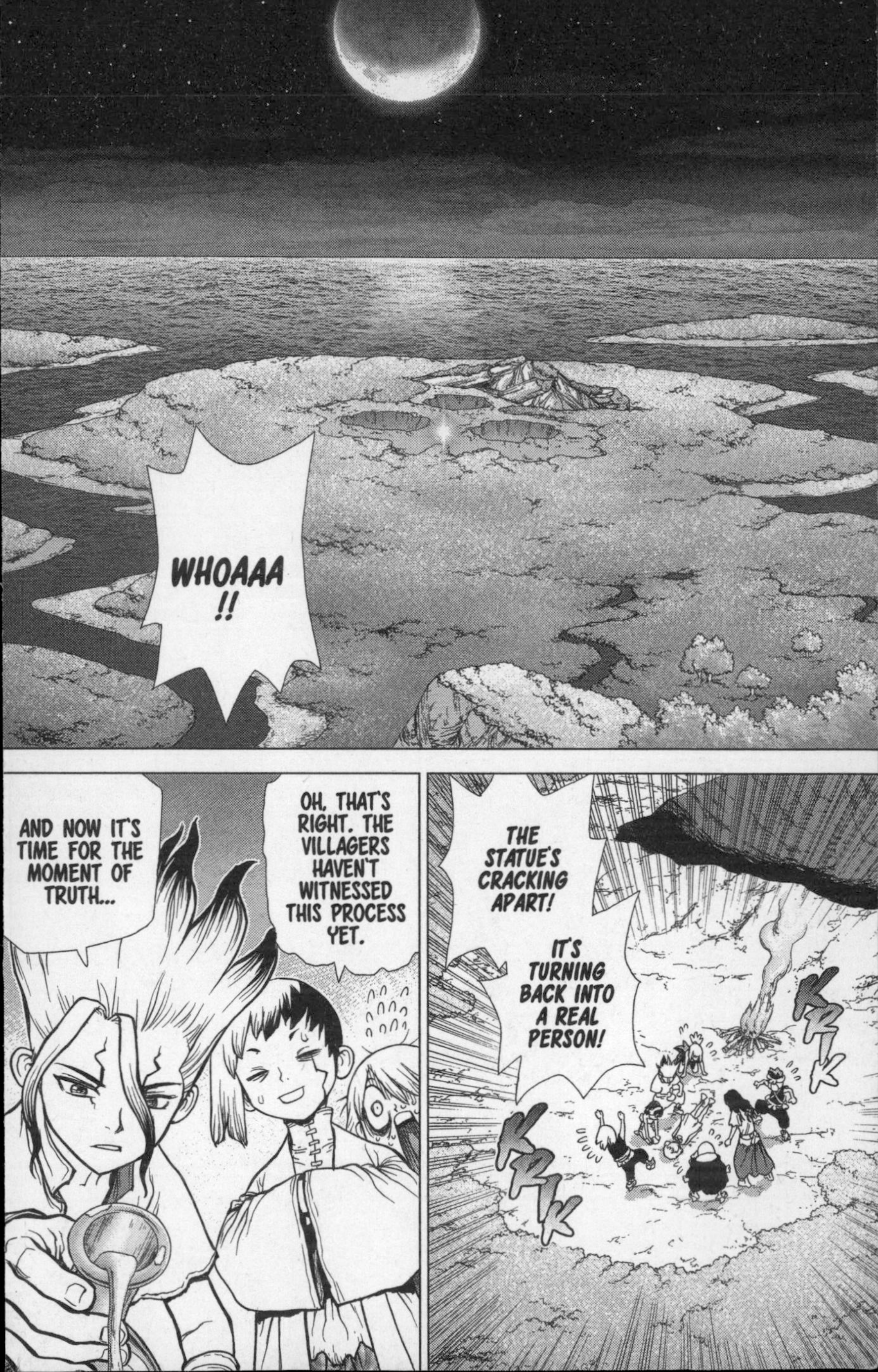
WHOAAA !!
THE STATUE'S CRACKING APART!
IT'S TURNING BACK INTO A REAL PERSON!
KRK
KRK
OH, THAT'S RIGHT. THE VILLAGERS HAVEN'T WITNESSED THIS PROCESS YET.
AND NOW IT'S TIME FOR THE MOMENT OF TRUTH...

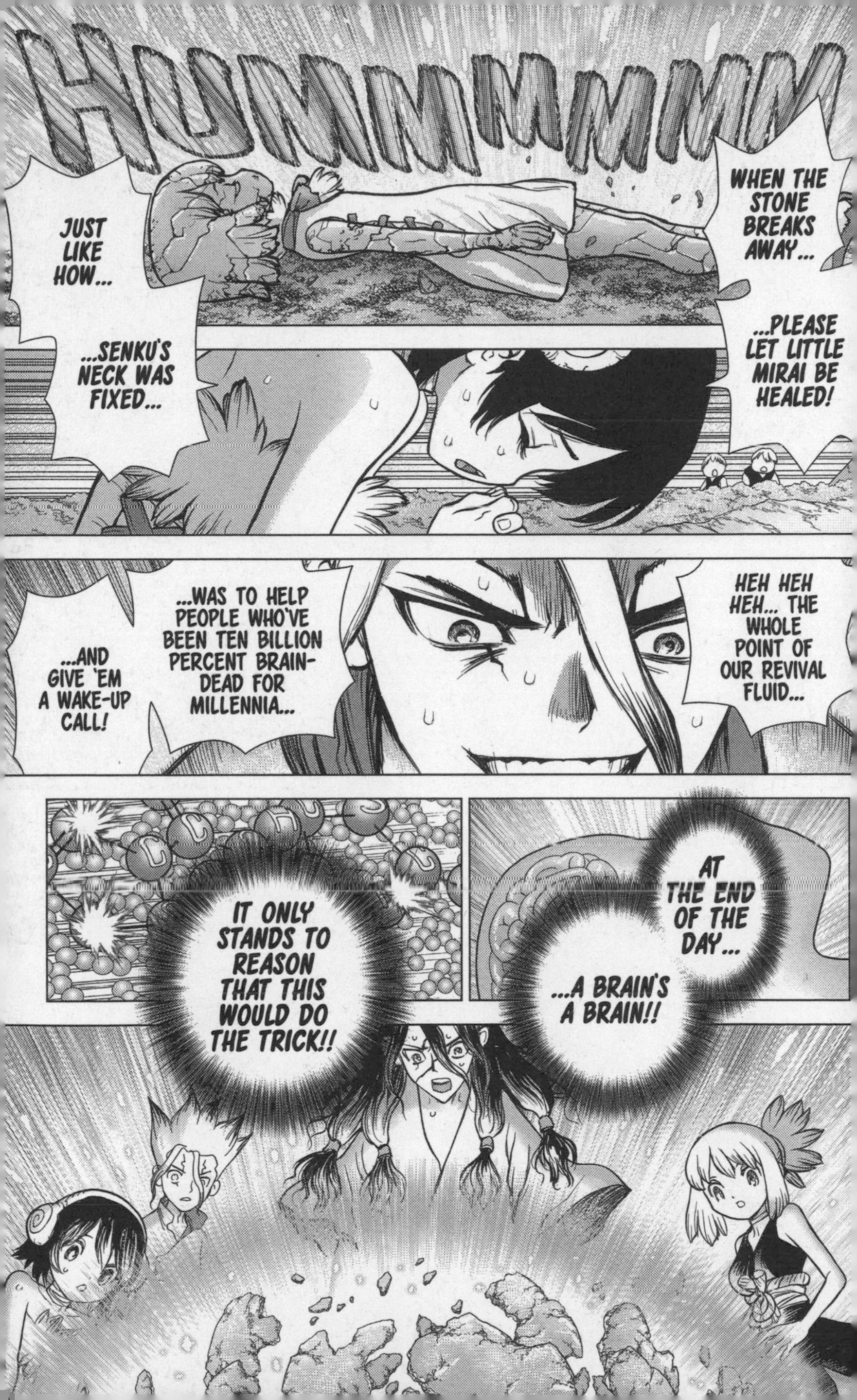
HUMMMMMM
WHEN THE STONE BREAKS AWAY...
...PLEASE LET LITTLE MIRAI BE HEALED!
JUST LIKE HOW...
...SENKU'S NECK WAS FIXED...
HEH HEH HEH... THE WHOLE POINT OF OUR REVIVAL FLUID...
...WAS TO HELP PEOPLE WHO'VE BEEN TEN BILLION PERCENT BRAIN-DEAD FOR MILLENNIA...
...AND GIVE 'EM A WAKE-UP CALL!
AT THE END OF THE DAY...
...A BRAIN'S A BRAIN!!
IT ONLY STANDS TO REASON THAT THIS WOULD DO THE TRICK!!

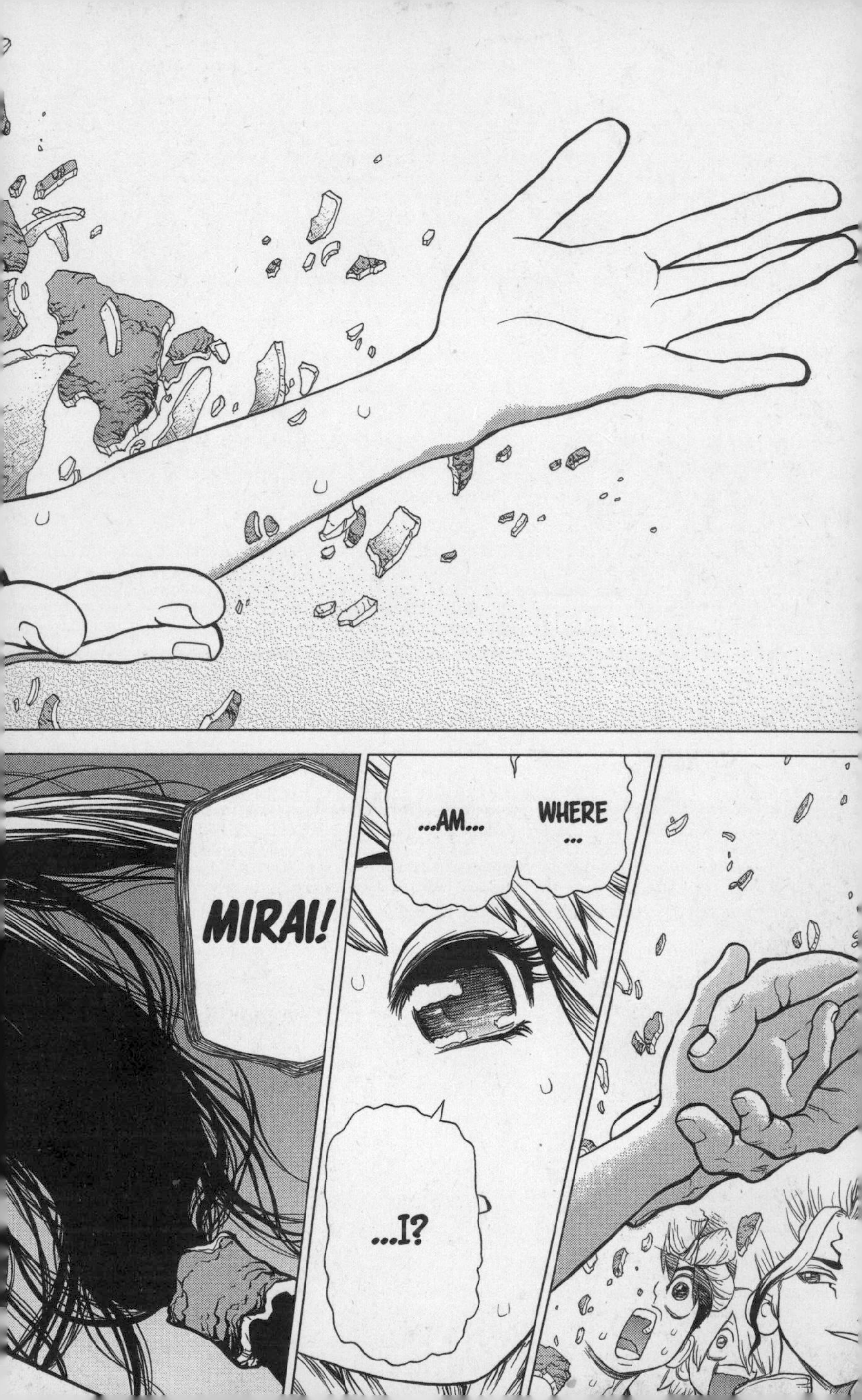
WHERE ...
...AM...
...I?
MIRAI!

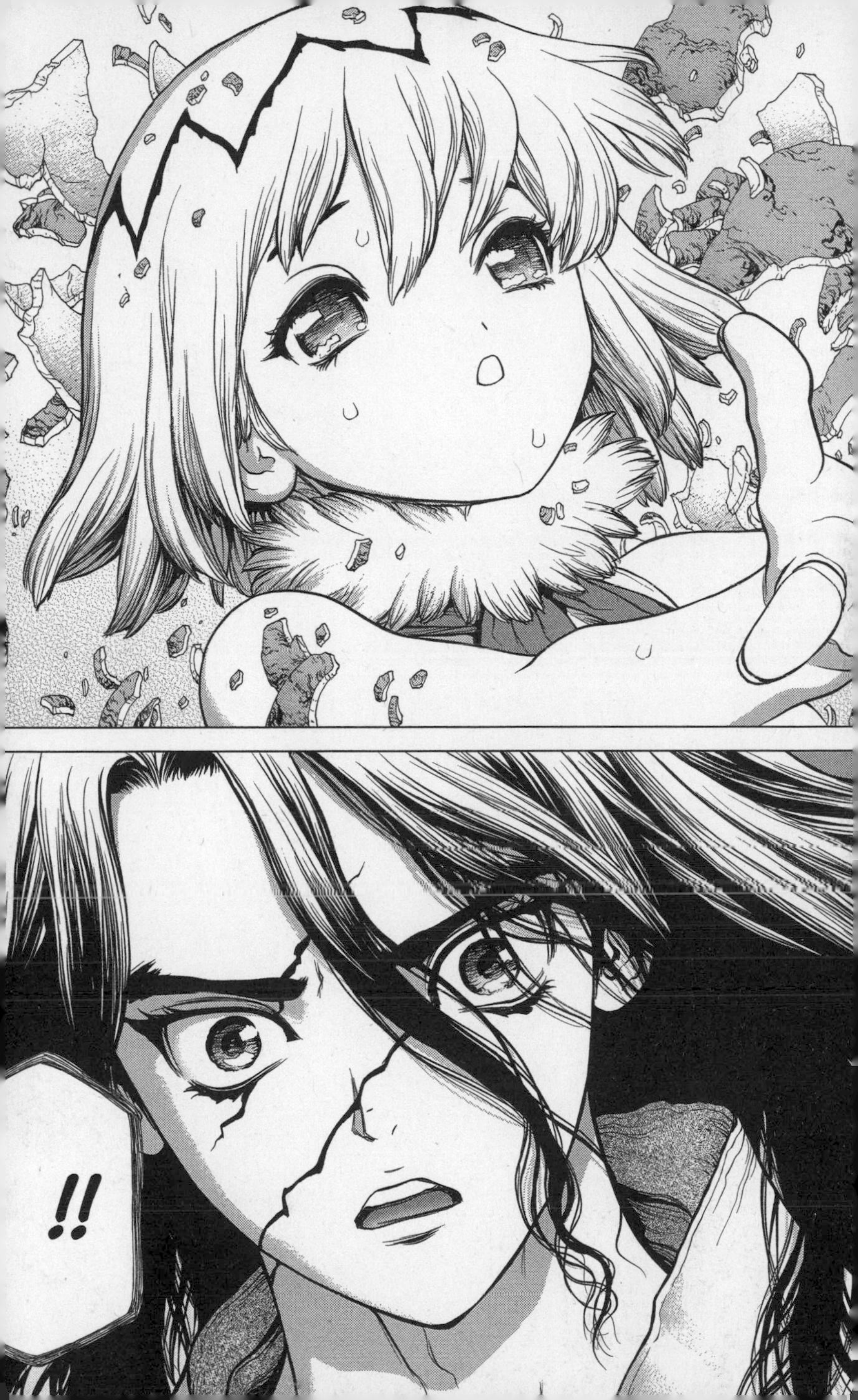
!!

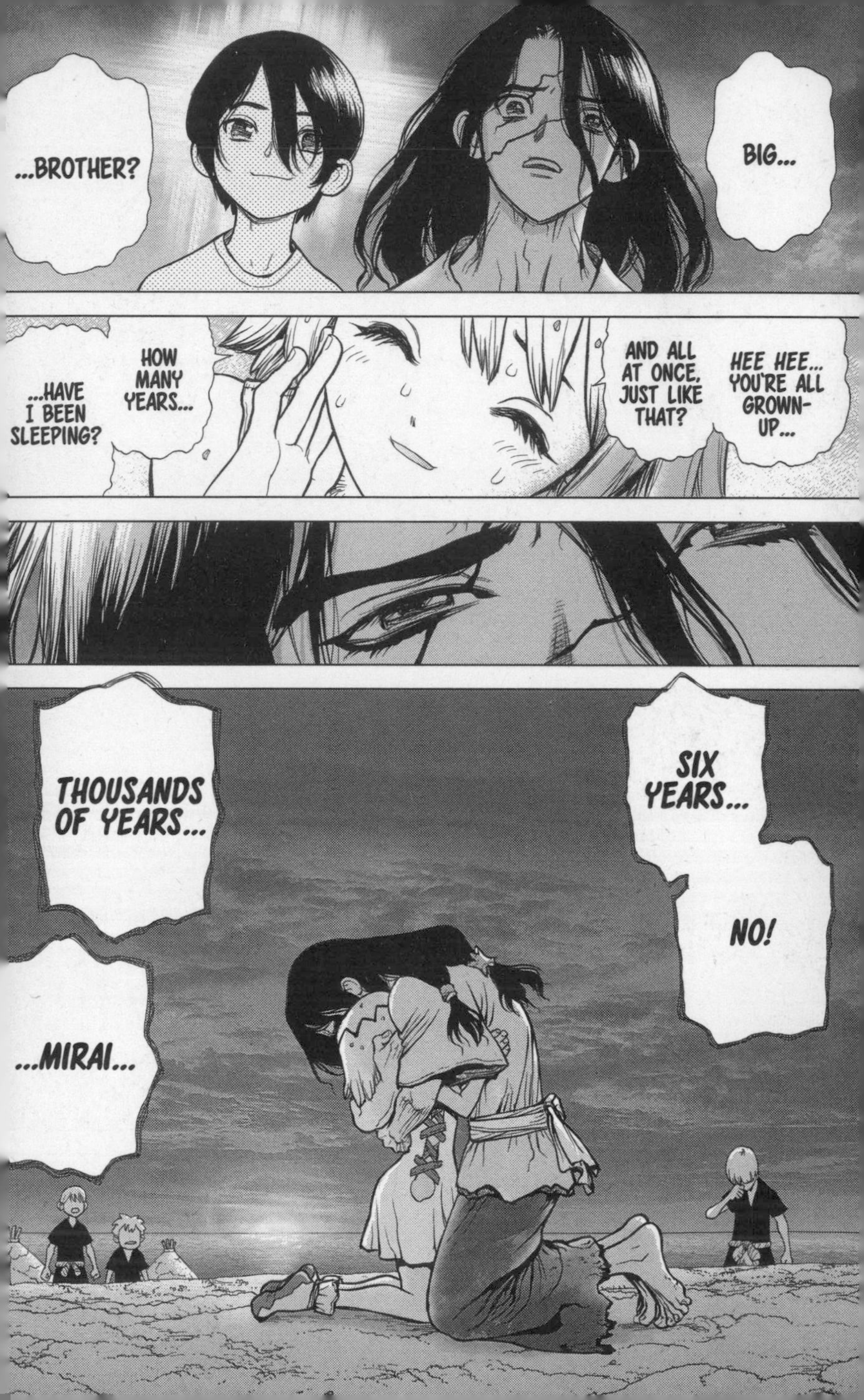
BIG...
...BROTHER?
HEE HEE... YOU'RE ALL GROWN-UP...
AND ALL AT ONCE, JUST LIKE THAT?
HOW MANY YEARS...
...HAVE I BEEN SLEEPING?
SIX YEARS...
NO!
THOUSANDS OF YEARS...
...MIRAI...

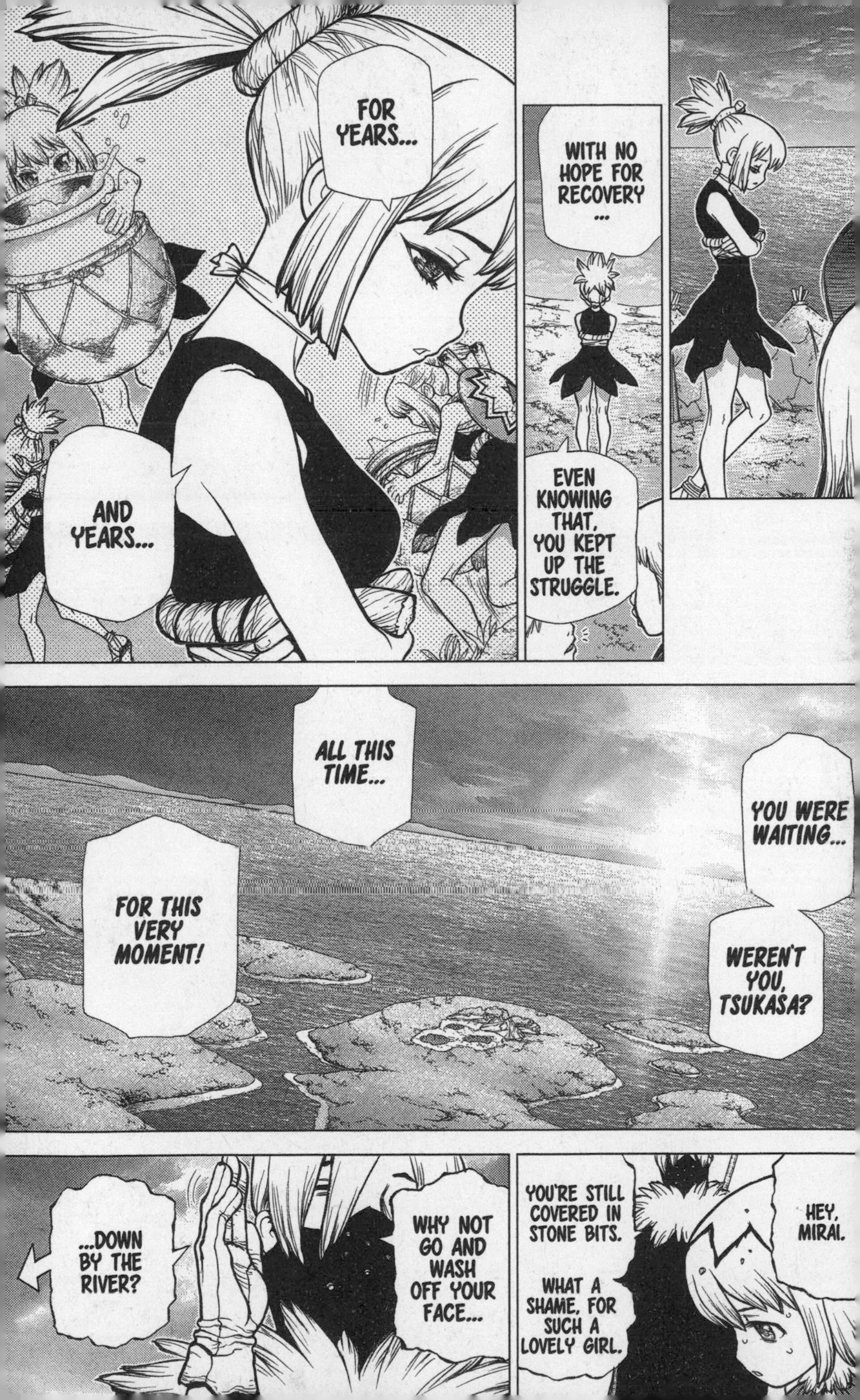
WITH NO HOPE FOR RECOVERY ...
EVEN KNOWING THAT, YOU KEPT UP THE STRUGGLE.
FOR YEARS...
AND YEARS...
ALL THIS TIME...
YOU WERE WAITING...
FOR THIS VERY MOMENT!
WEREN'T YOU, TSUKASA?
HEY, MIRAI.
YOU'RE STILL COVERED IN STONE BITS.
WHAT A SHAME, FOR SUCH A LOVELY GIRL.
WHY NOT GO AND WASH OFF YOUR FACE...
...DOWN BY THE RIVER?

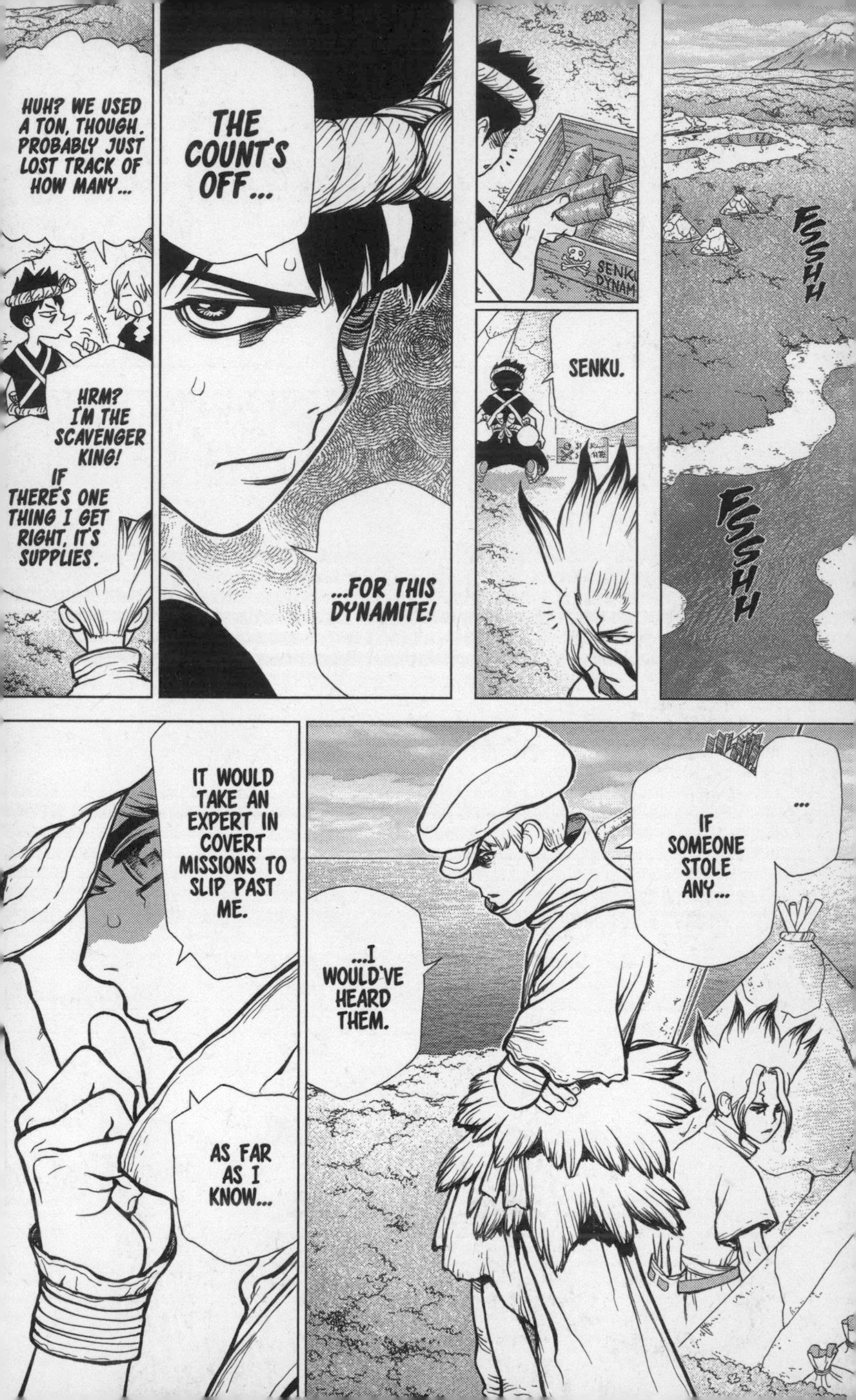
FSSHH
FSSHH
SENKU.
THE COUNT'S OFF...
...FOR THIS DYNAMITE!
HUH? WE USED A TON, THOUGH. PROBABLY JUST LOST TRACK OF HOW MANY...
HRM? I'M THE SCAVENGER KING! IF THERE'S ONE THING I GET RIGHT, IT'S SUPPLIES.
...
IF SOMEONE STOLE ANY...
...I WOULD'VE HEARD THEM.
IT WOULD TAKE AN EXPERT IN COVERT MISSIONS TO SLIP PAST ME.
AS FAR AS I KNOW...

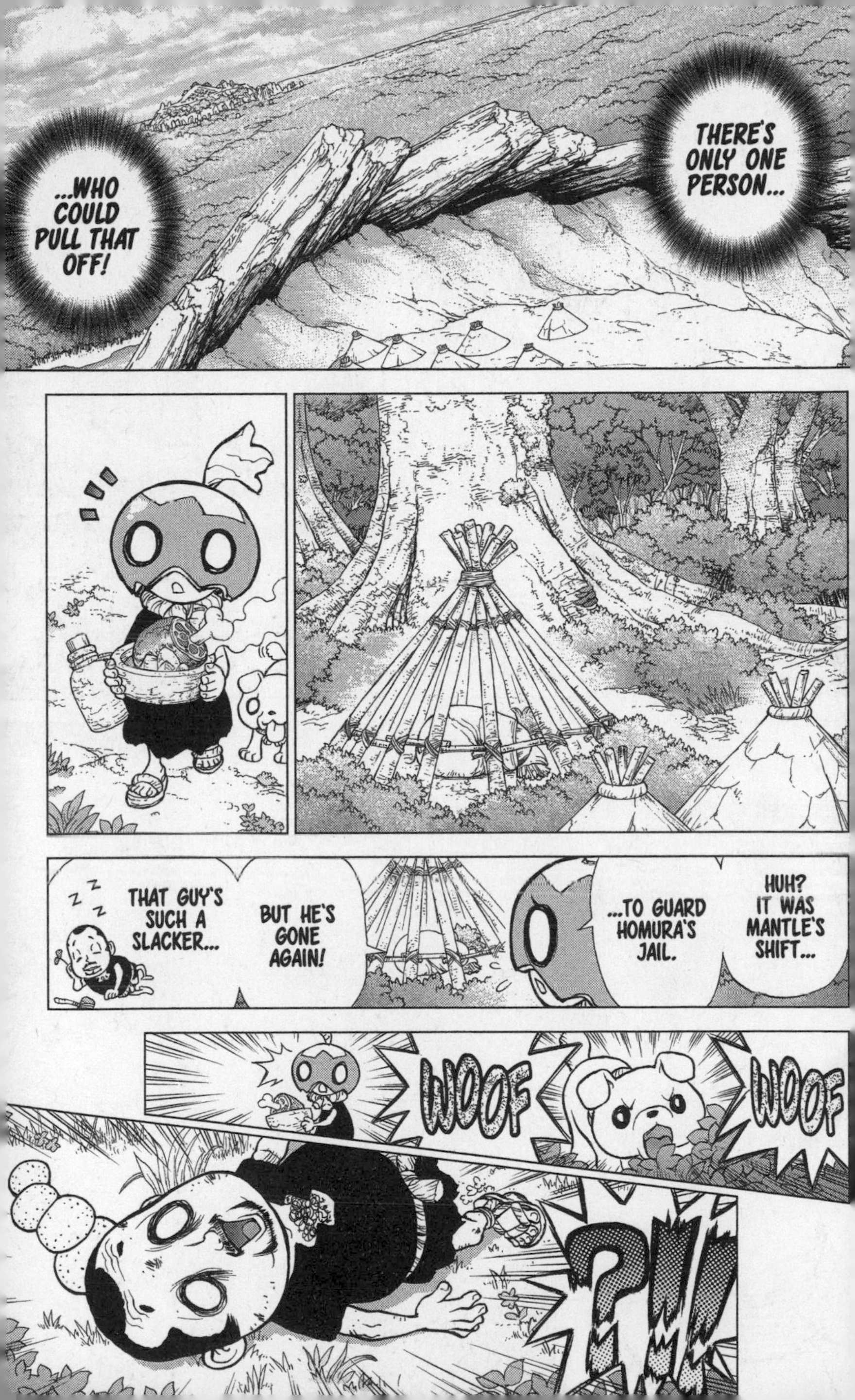
THERE'S ONLY ONE PERSON...
...WHO COULD PULL THAT OFF!
HUH? IT WAS MANTLE'S SHIFT...
...TO GUARD HOMURA'S JAIL.
BUT HE'S GONE AGAIN!
THAT GUY'S SUCH A SLACKER...
Z Z Z
WOOF
WOOF
?!!

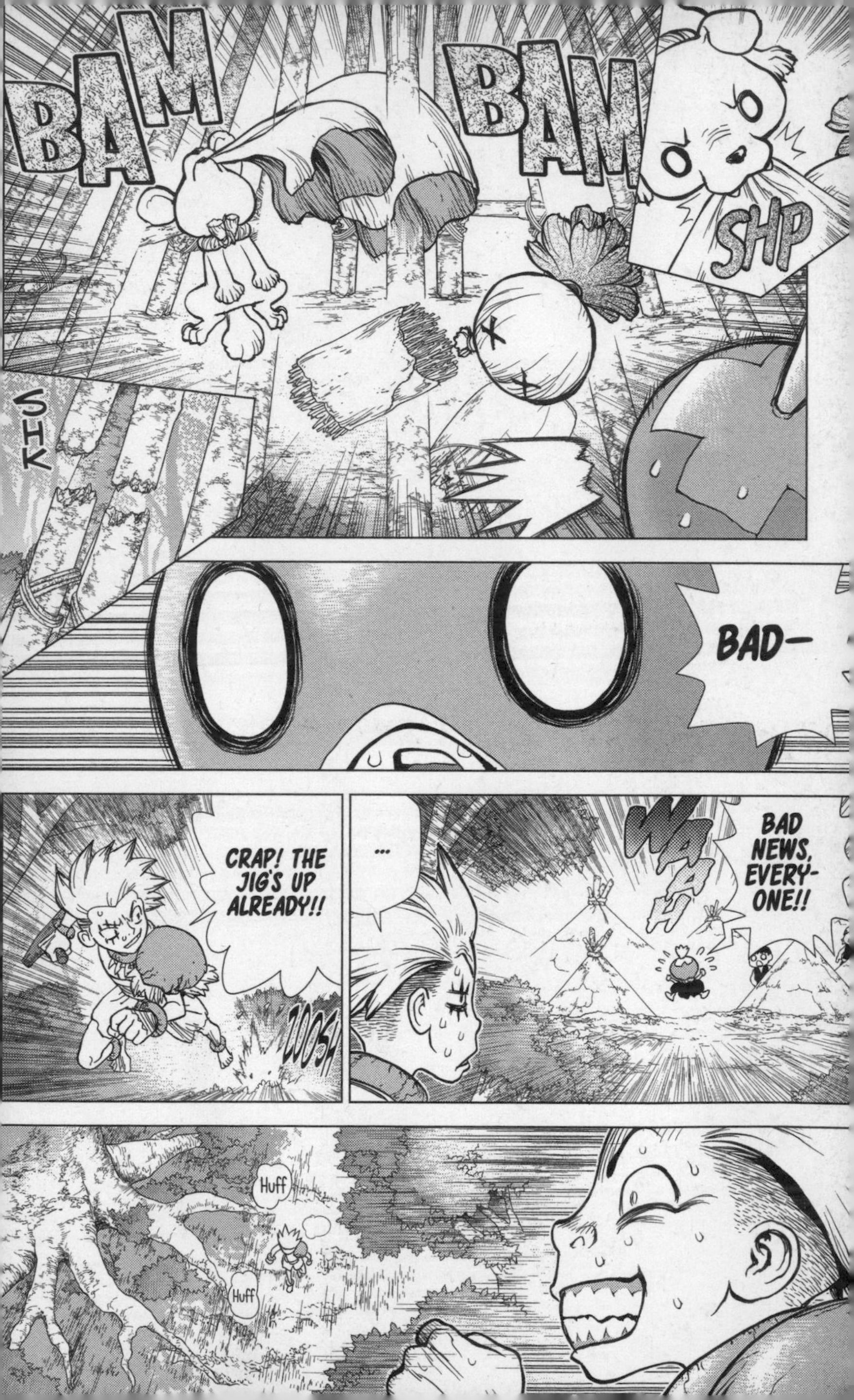
BAM
BAM
SHP
SHK
BAD-
BAD NEWS, EVERY-ONE!!
WAAAH
...
CRAP! THE JIG'S UP ALREADY!!
ZOOSH
Huff
Huff

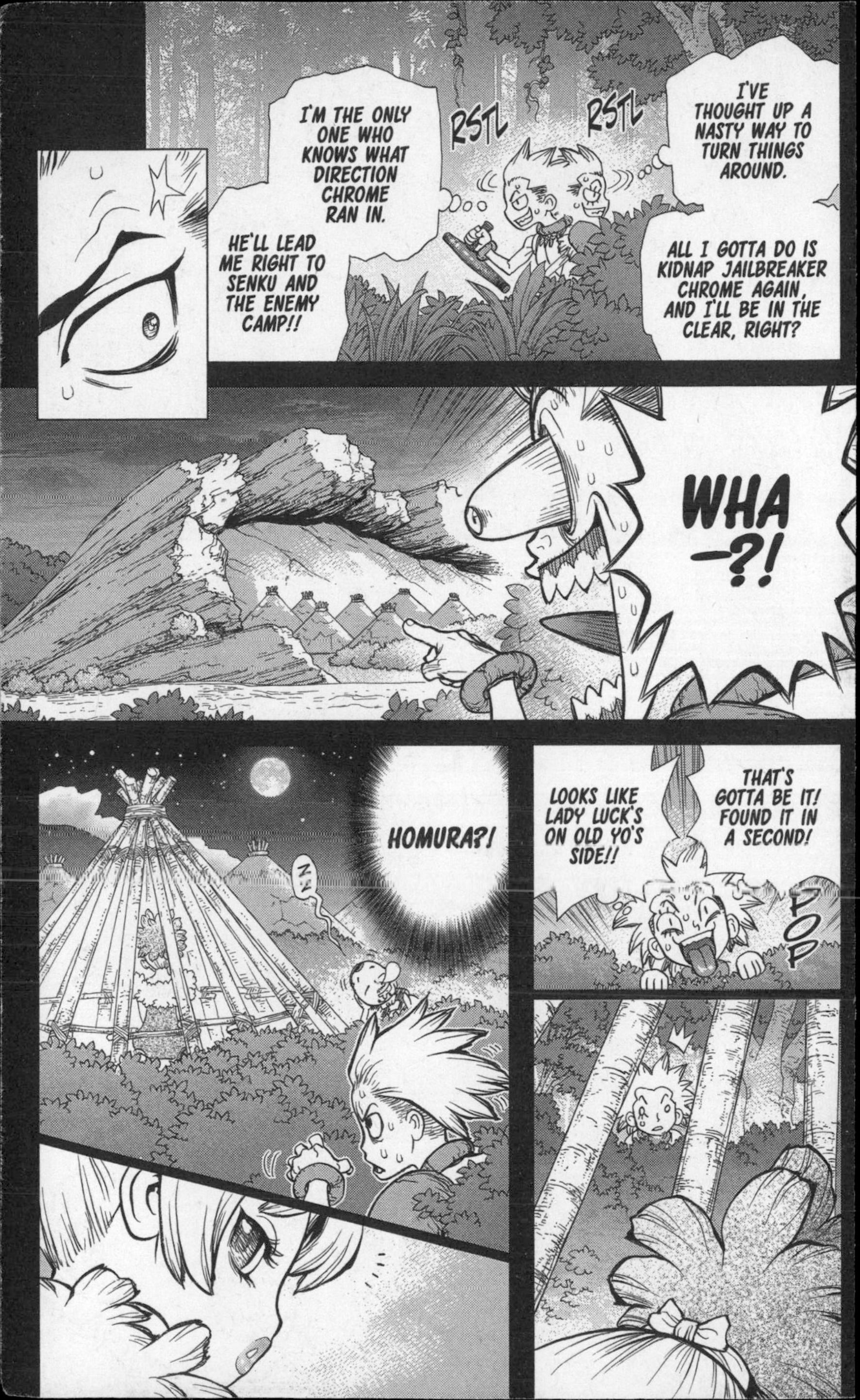
I'VE THOUGHT UP A NASTY WAY TO TURN THINGS AROUND.
ALL I GOTTA DO IS KIDNAP JAILBREAKER CHROME AGAIN, AND I'LL BE IN THE CLEAR, RIGHT?
RSTL
RSTL
I'M THE ONLY ONE WHO KNOWS WHAT DIRECTION CHROME RAN IN.
HE'LL LEAD ME RIGHT TO SENKU AND THE ENEMY CAMP!!
WHA-?!
THAT'S GOTTA BE IT! FOUND IT IN A SECOND!
LOOKS LIKE LADY LUCK'S ON OLD YO'S SIDE!!
POP
HOMURA?!

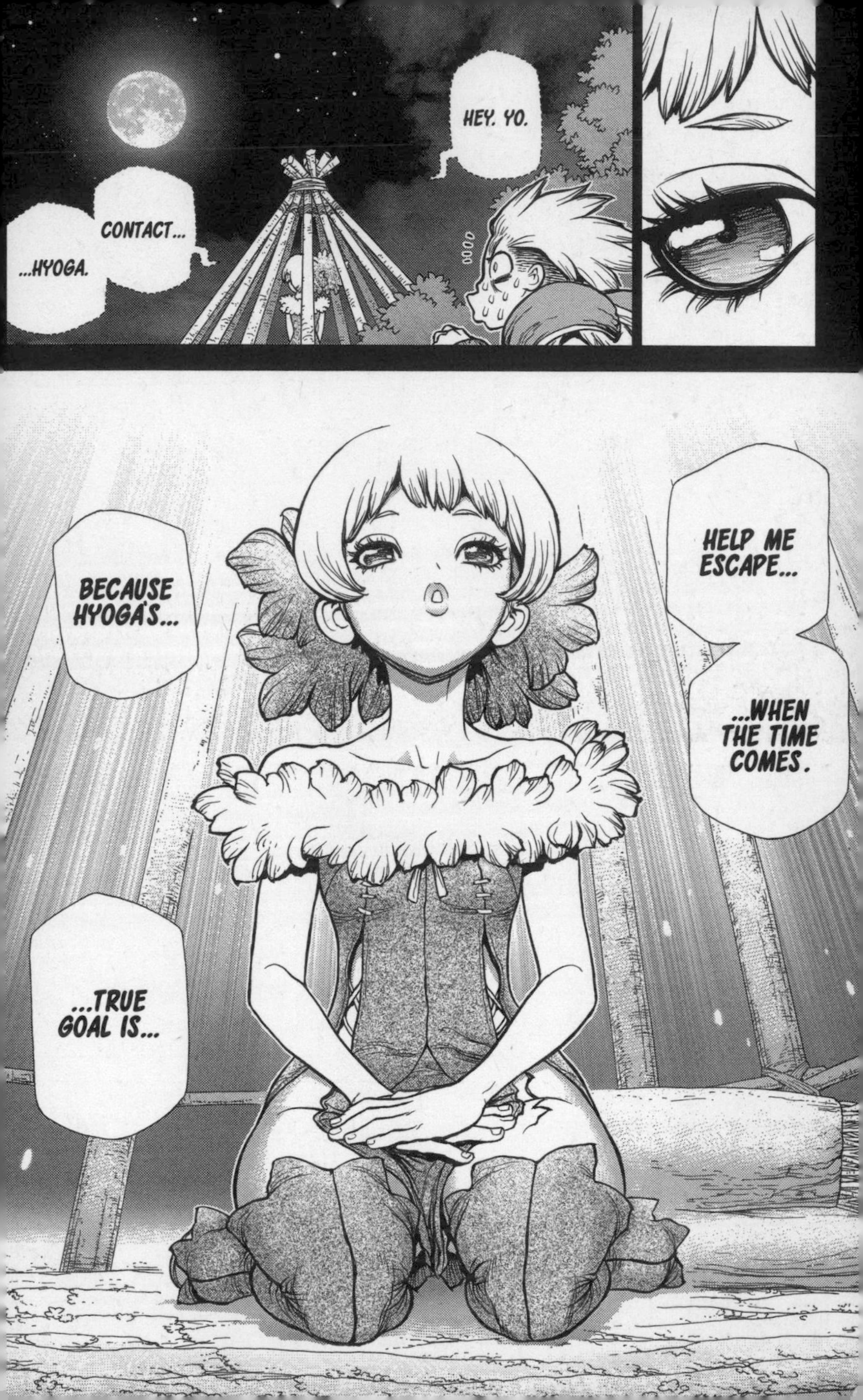
HEY. YO.
CONTACT...
...HYOGA.
HELP ME ESCAPE...
...WHEN THE TIME COMES.
BECAUSE HYOGA'S...
...TRUE GOAL IS...

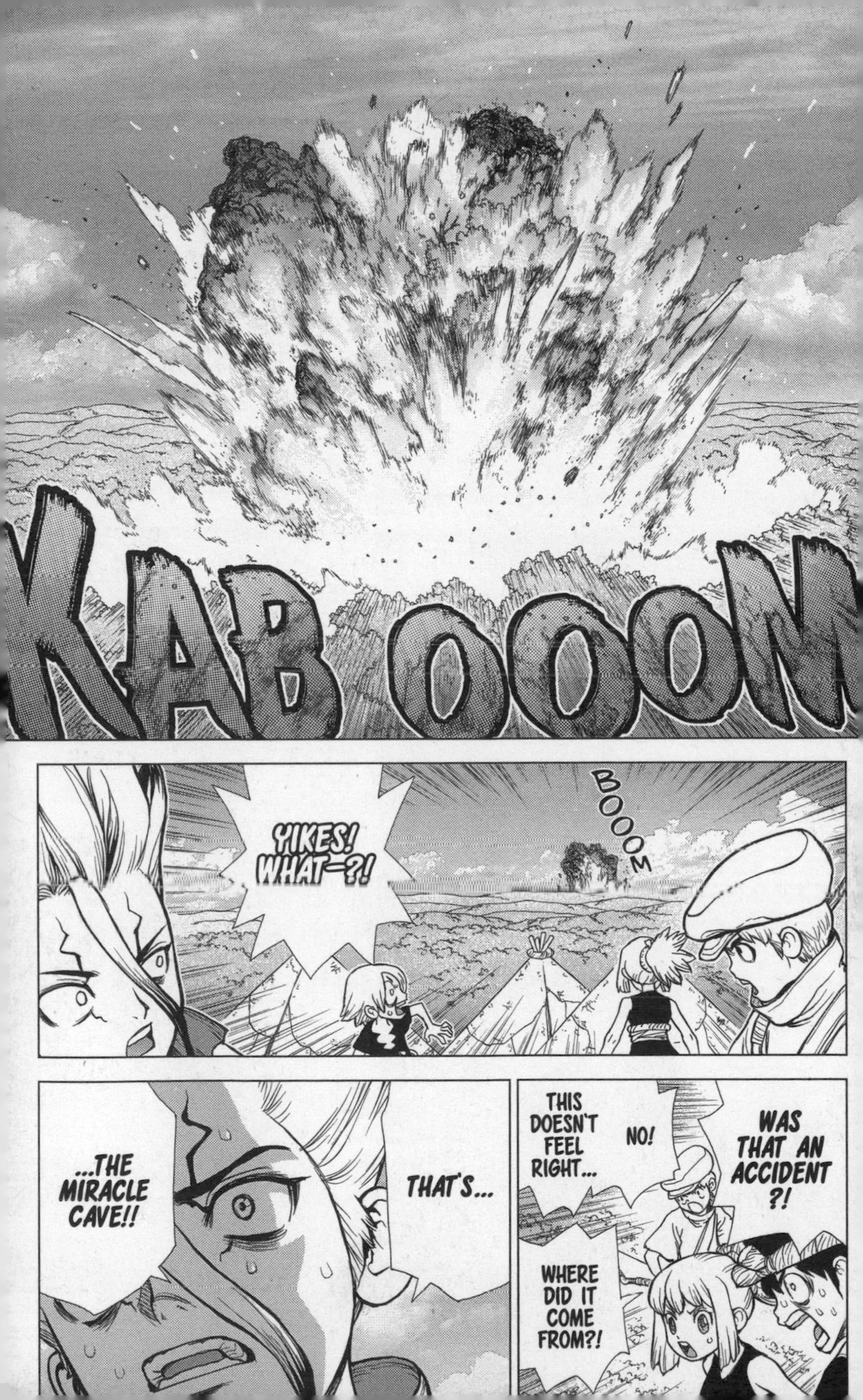
KABOOOM
BOOOOM
YIKES! WHAT—?!
WAS THAT AN ACCIDENT?!
NO!
THIS DOESN'T FEEL RIGHT...
WHERE DID IT COME FROM?!
THAT'S...
...THE MIRACLE CAVE!!

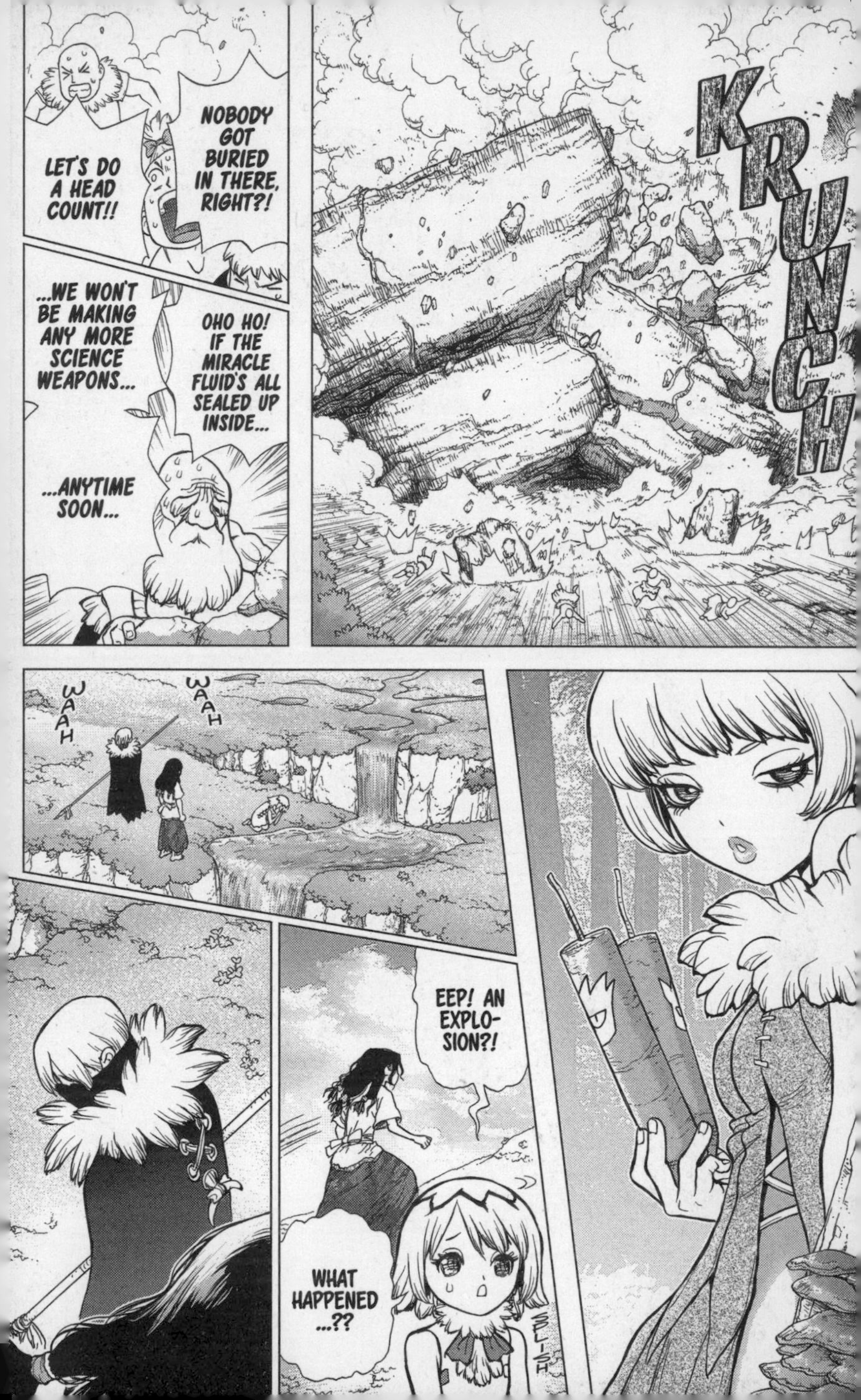
KRUNCH
NOBODY GOT BURIED IN THERE, RIGHT?!
LET'S DO A HEAD COUNT!!
OHO HO! IF THE MIRACLE FLUID'S ALL SEALED UP INSIDE...
...WE WON'T BE MAKING ANY MORE SCIENCE WEAPONS...
...ANYTIME SOON...
WAAH
WAAH
EEP! AN EXPLOSION?!
WHAT HAPPENED ...??
SPLISH

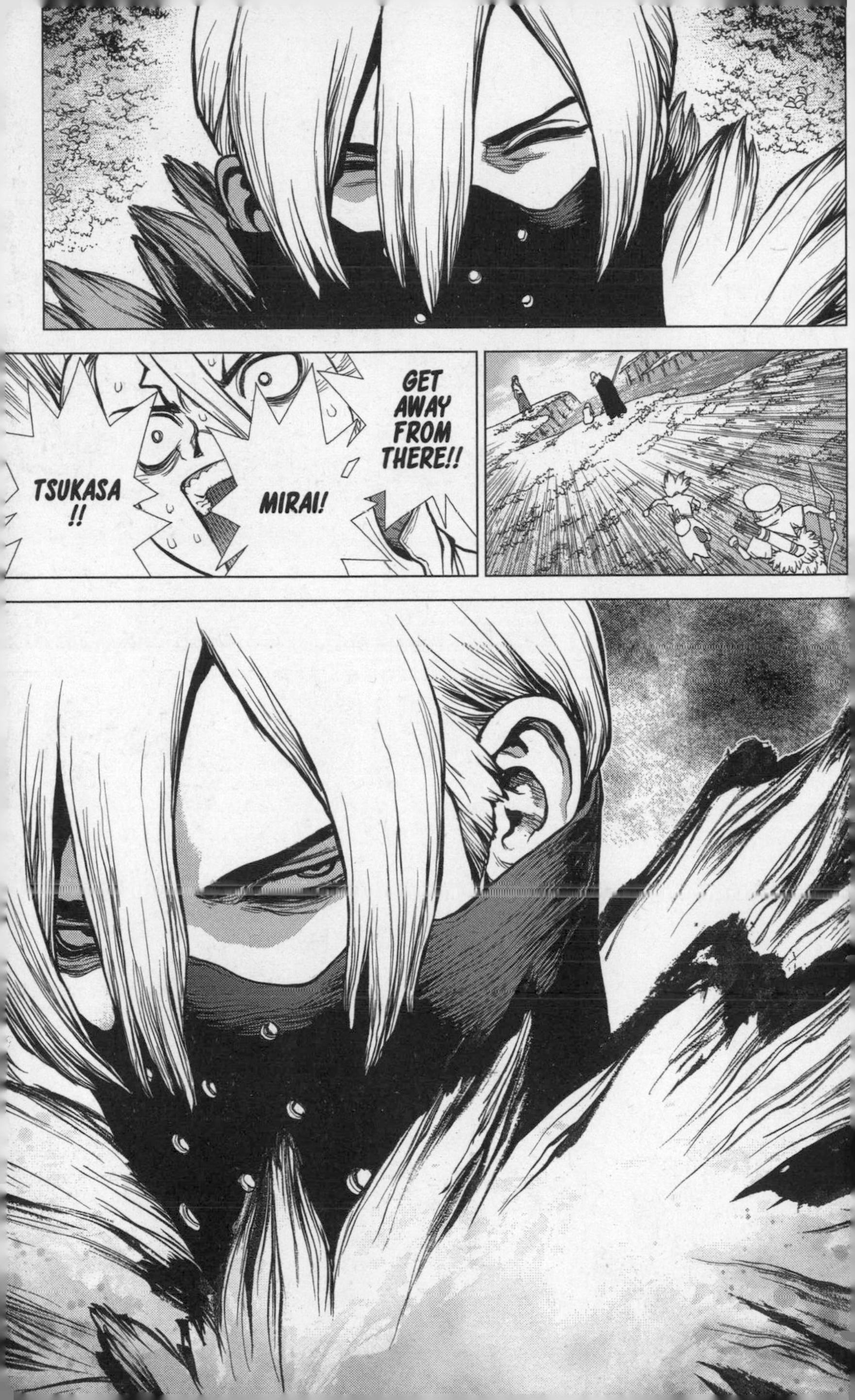
GET AWAY FROM THERE!!
MIRAI!
TSUKASA !!

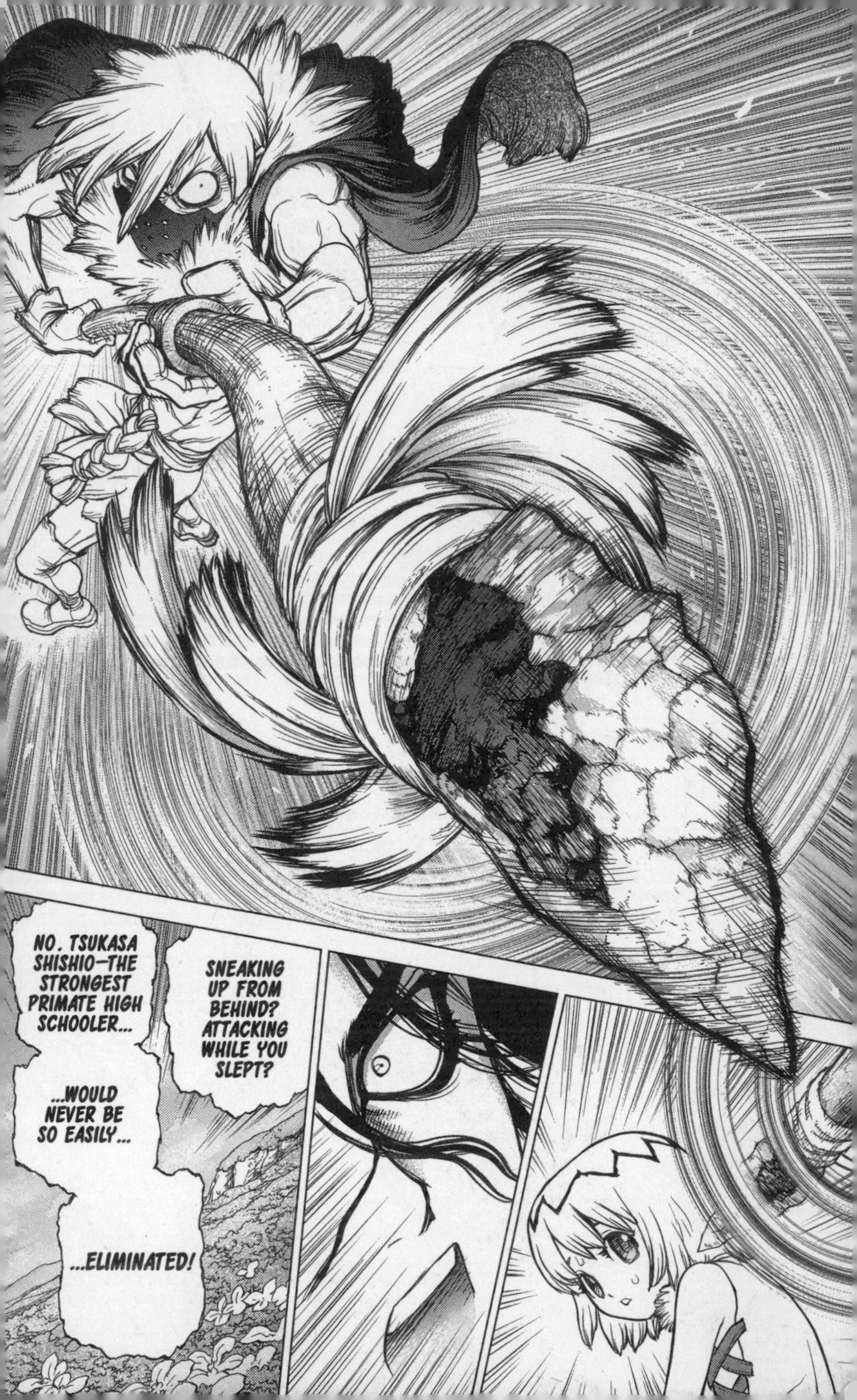
SNEAKING UP FROM BEHIND? ATTACKING WHILE YOU SLEPT?
NO. TSUKASA SHISHIO—THE STRONGEST PRIMATE HIGH SCHOOLER...
...WOULD NEVER BE SO EASILY...
...ELIMINATED!

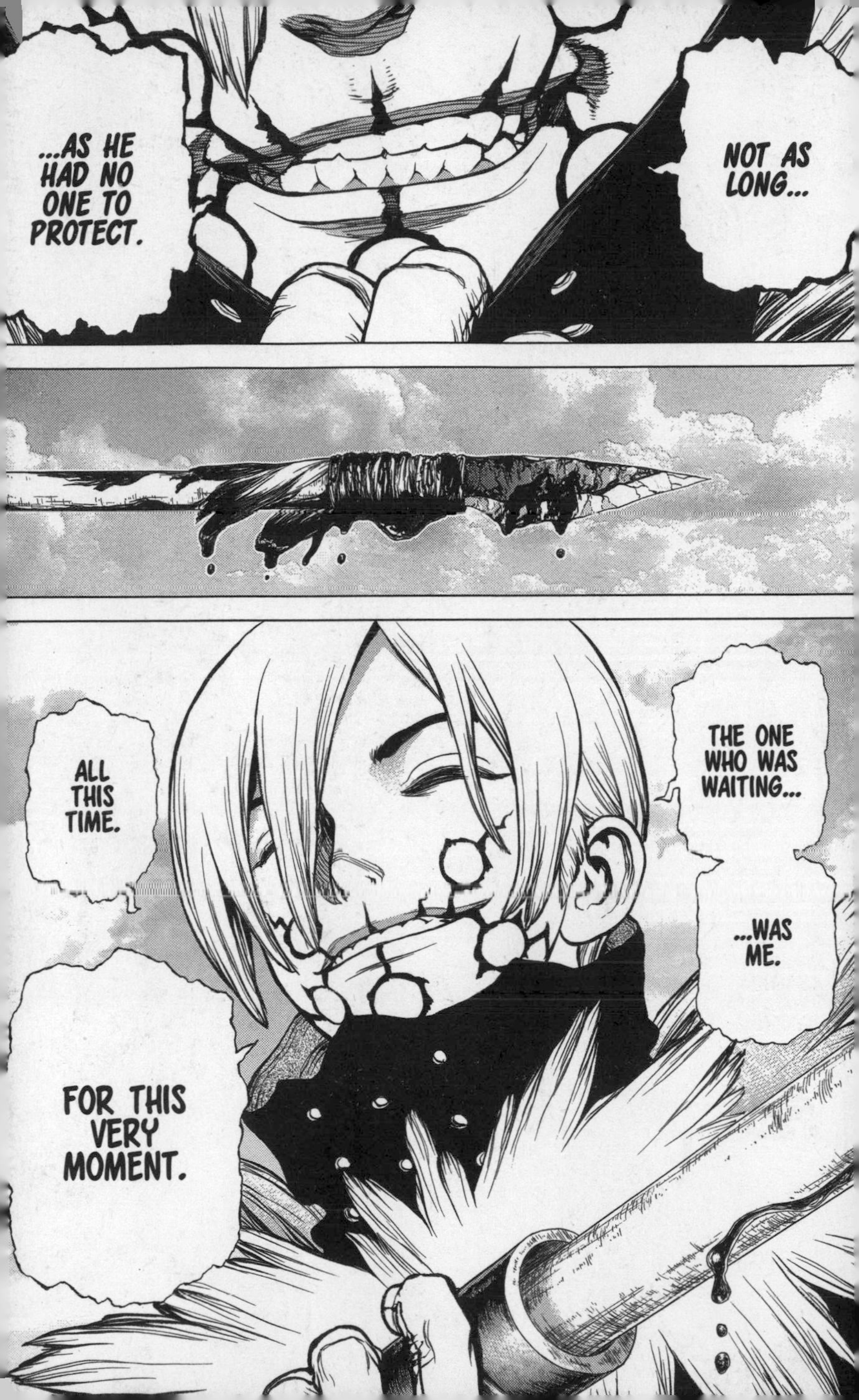
NOT AS LONG...
...AS HE HAD NO ONE TO PROTECT.
THE ONE WHO WAS WAITING...
ALL THIS TIME.
...WAS ME.
FOR THIS VERY MOMENT.

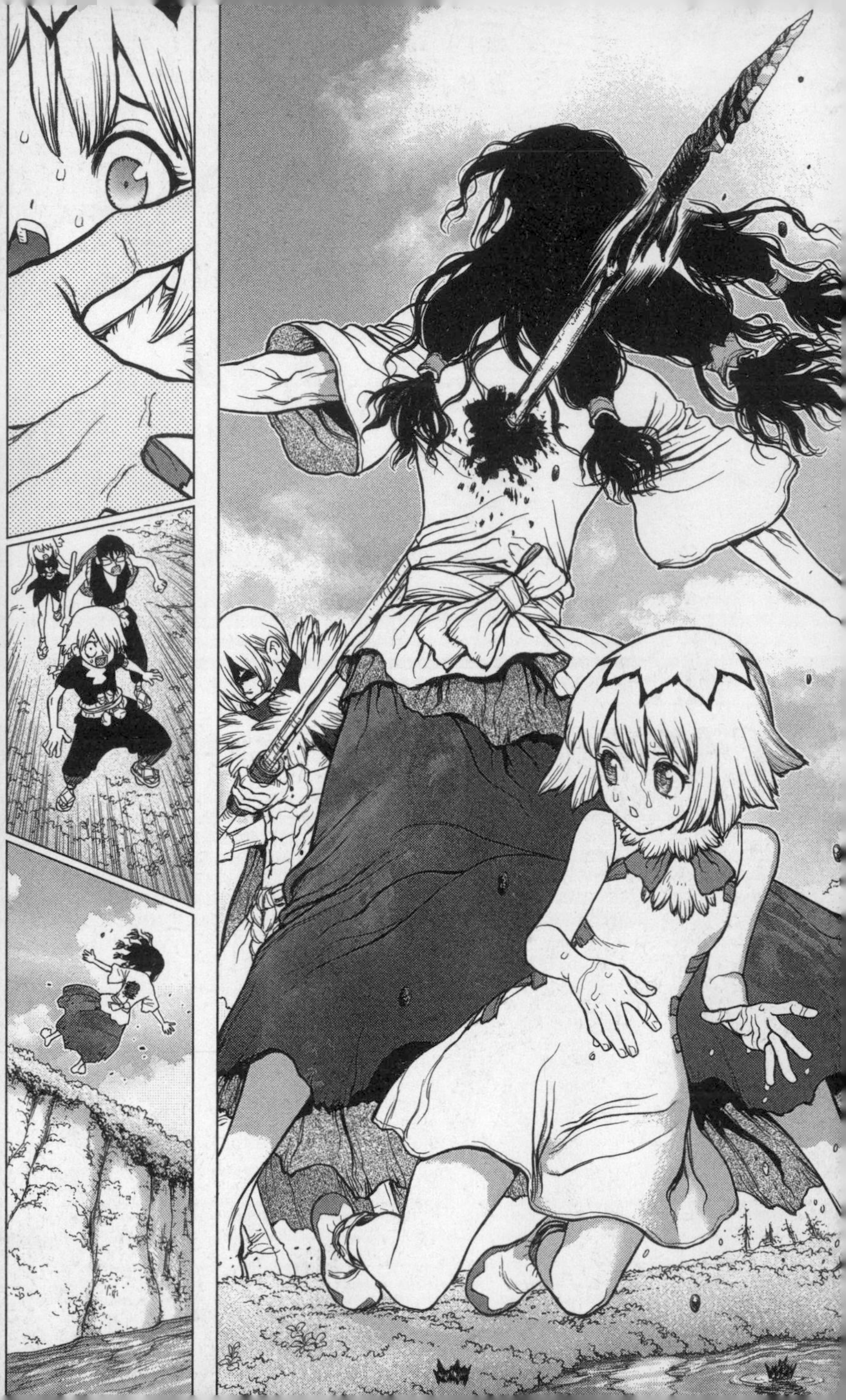

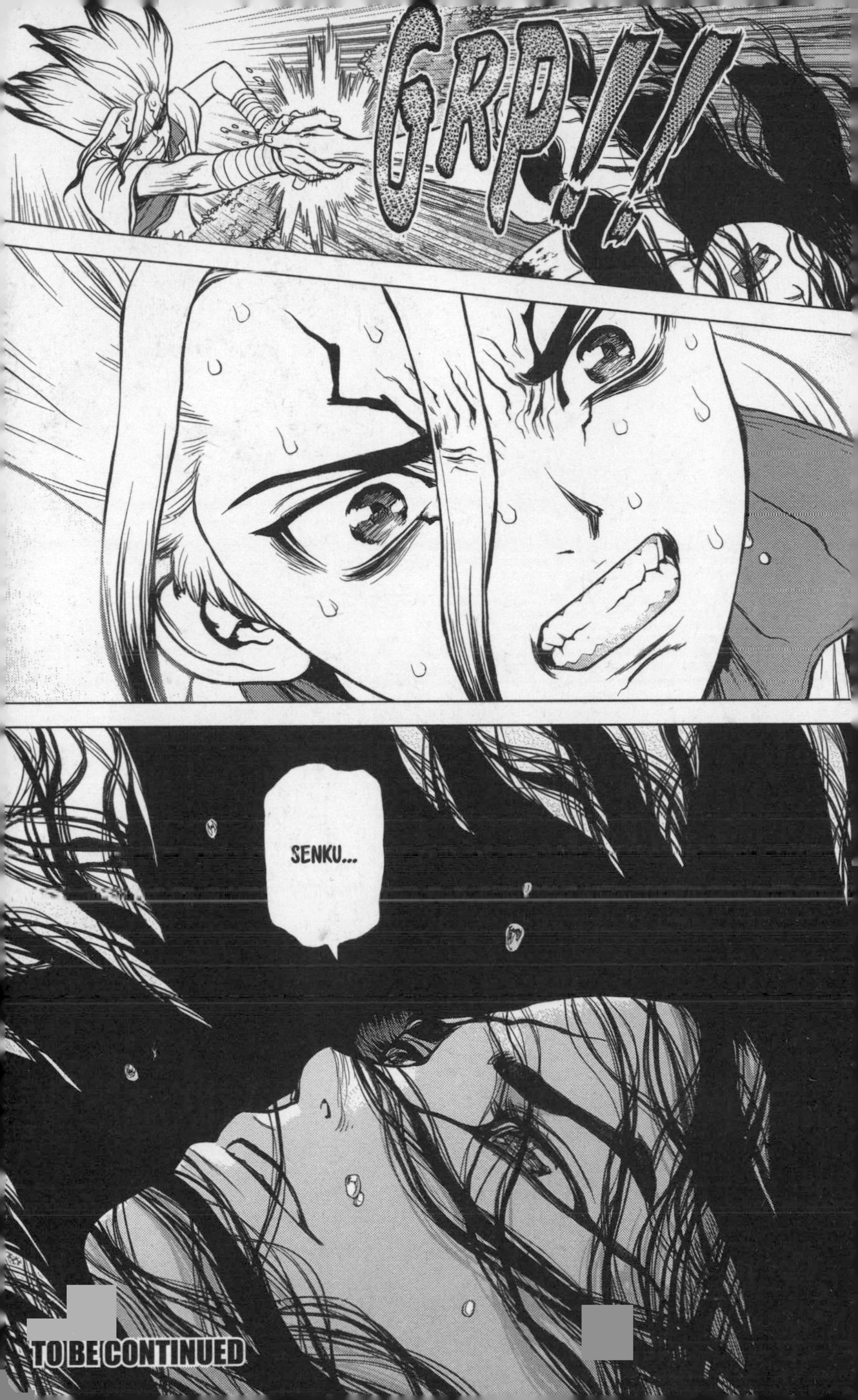
GRP!!
SENKU...
TO BE CONTINUED

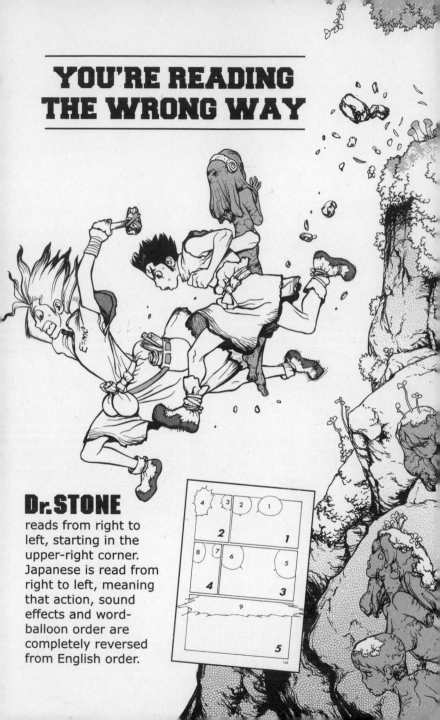

YOU'RE READING THE WRONG WAY

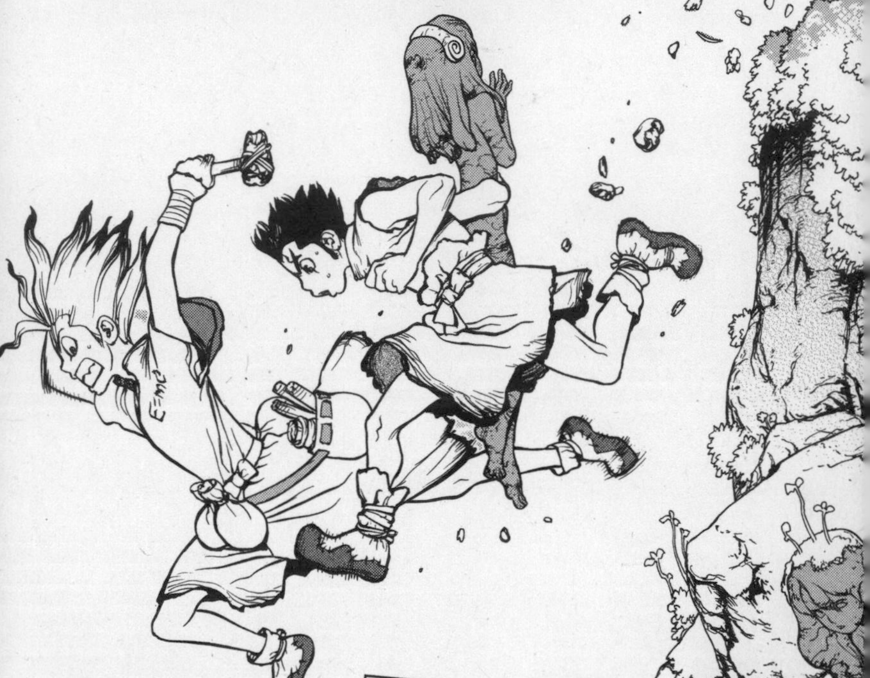

Dr.STONE

reads from right to left, starting in the upper-right corner. Japanese is read from right to left, meaning that action, sound effects and word-balloon order are completely reversed from English order.

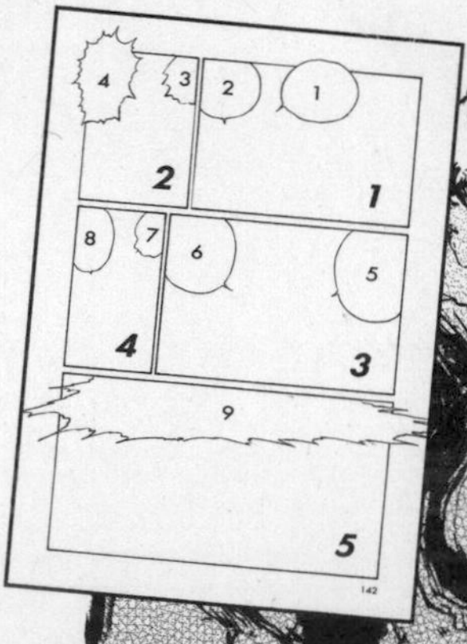

1
2
3
4
1
2
5
6
7
8
3
4
9
5
142